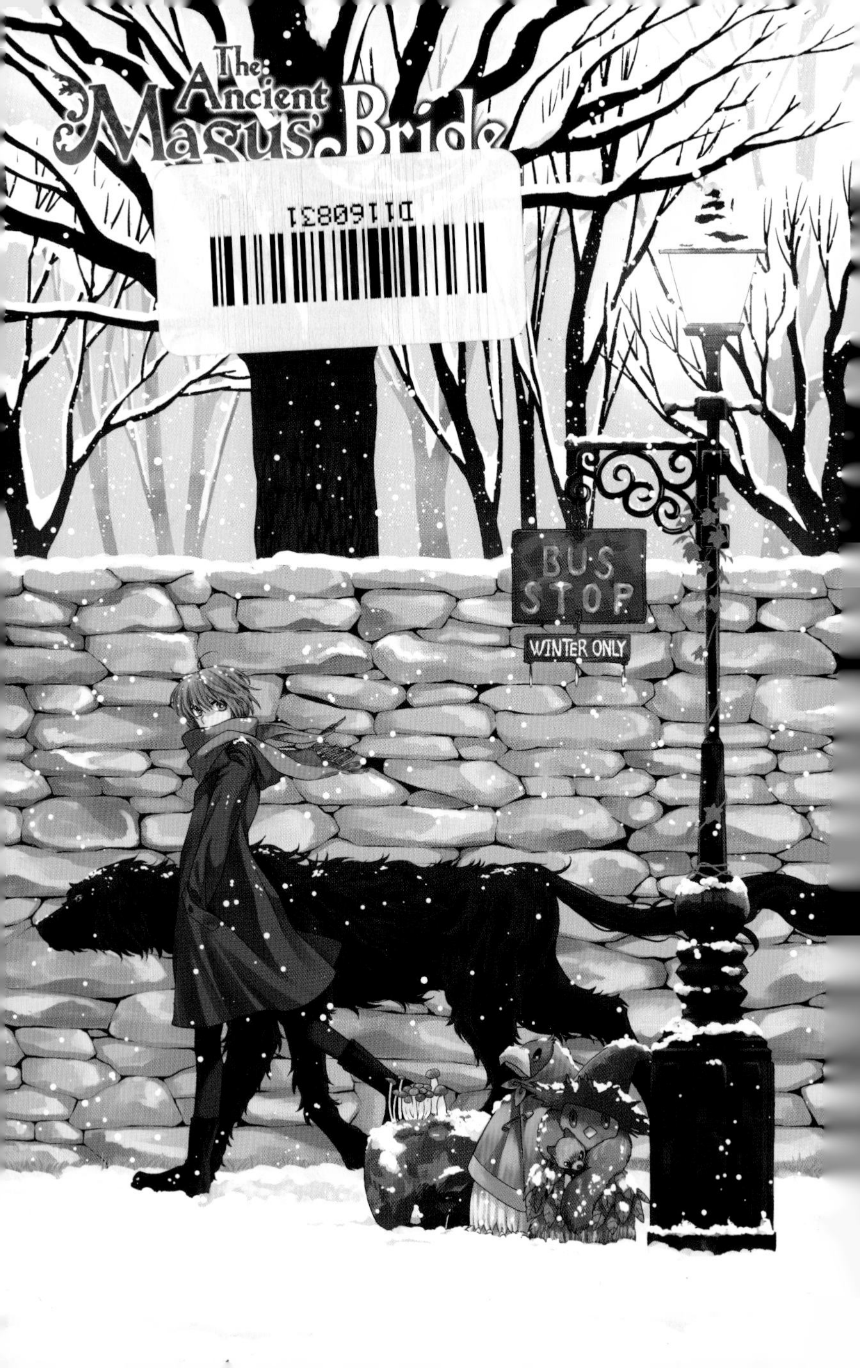
The Ancient Magus' Bride
BUS STOP
WINTER ONLY

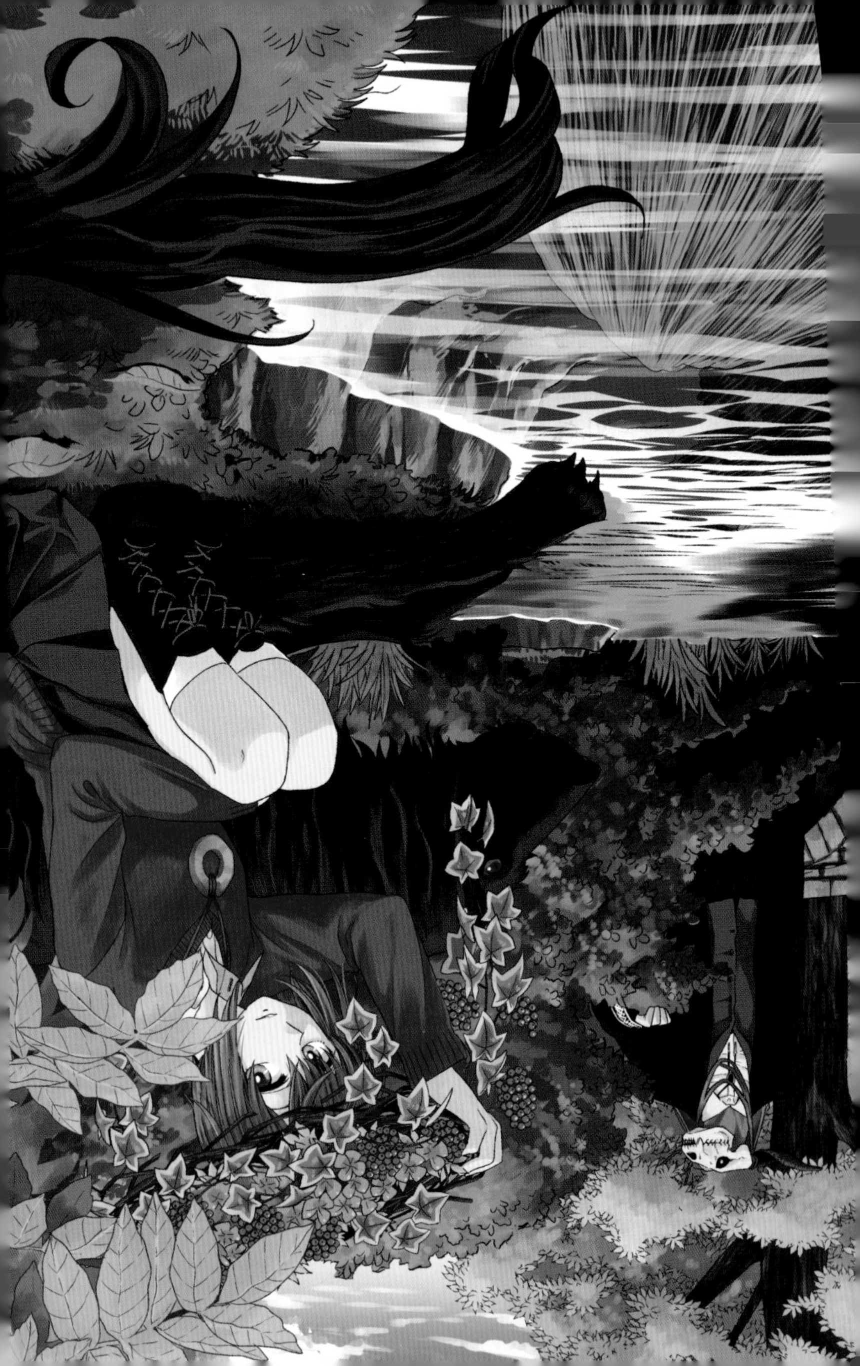

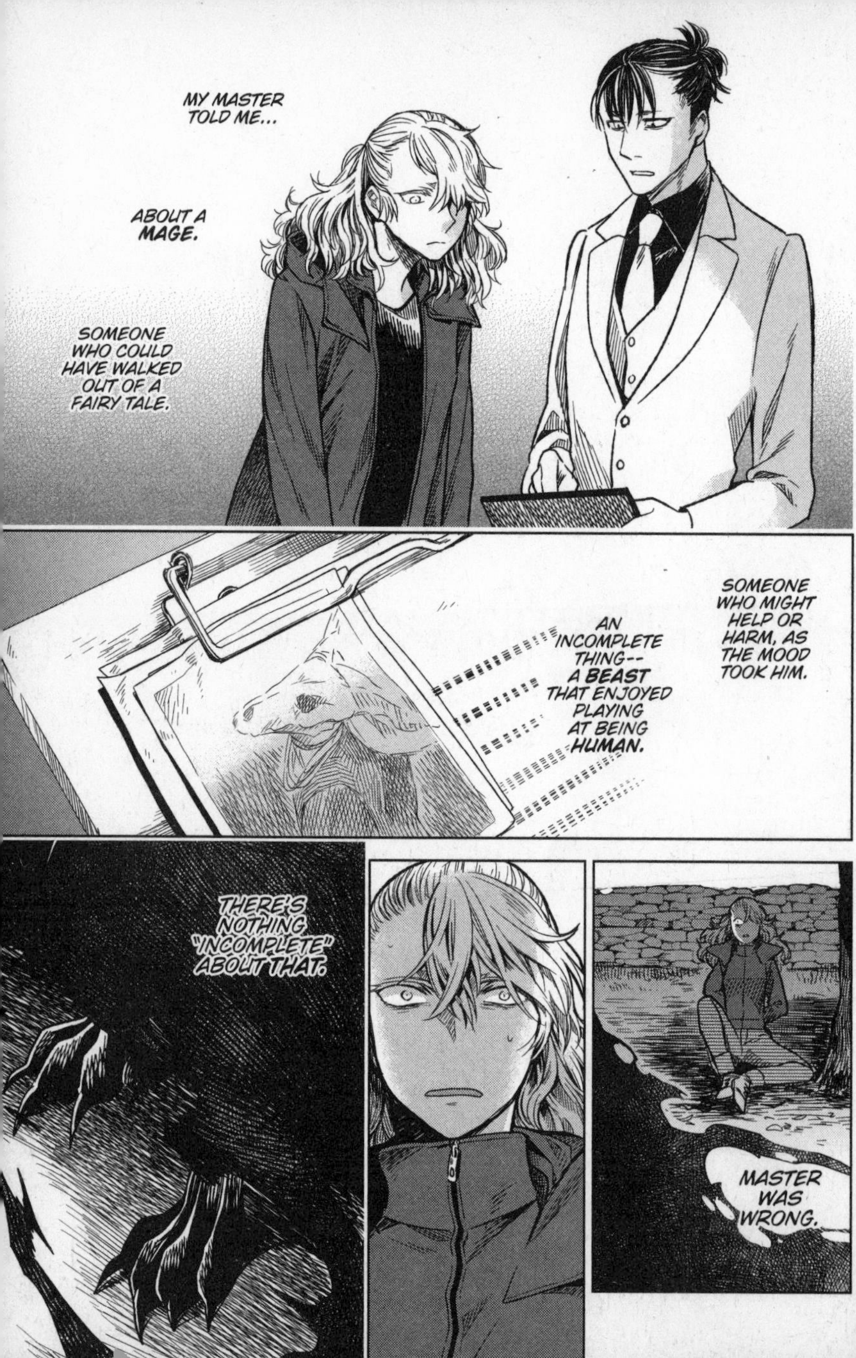
MY MASTER TOLD ME...
ABOUT A MAGE.
SOMEONE WHO COULD HAVE WALKED OUT OF A FAIRY TALE.
SOMEONE WHO MIGHT HELP OR HARM, AS THE MOOD TOOK HIM.
AN INCOMPLETE THING-- A BEAST THAT ENJOYED PLAYING AT BEING HUMAN.
MASTER WAS WRONG.
THERE'S NOTHING "INCOMPLETE" ABOUT THAT.

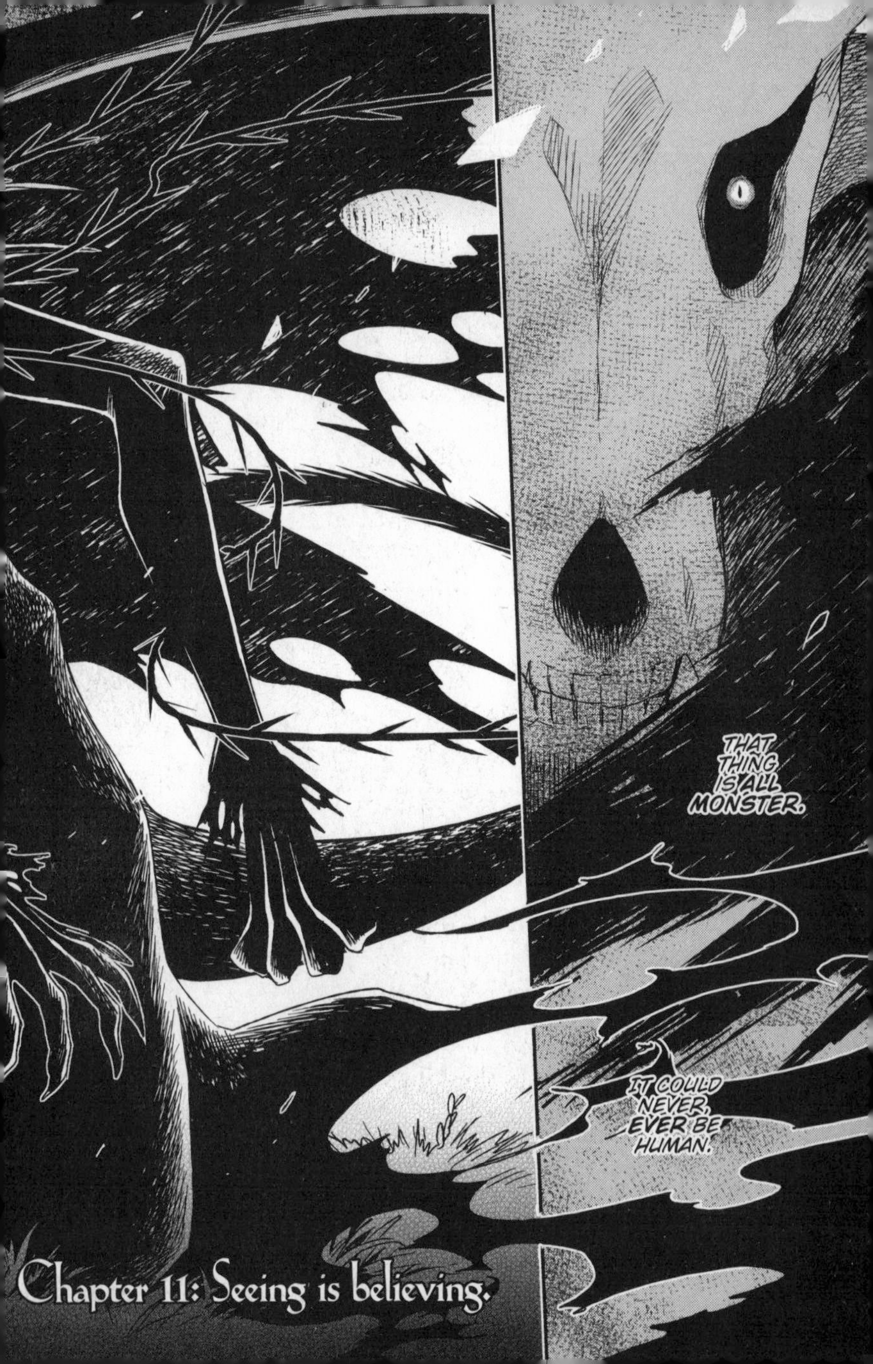
THAT THING IS ALL MONSTER.
IT COULD NEVER, EVER BE HUMAN.
Chapter 11: Seeing is believing.

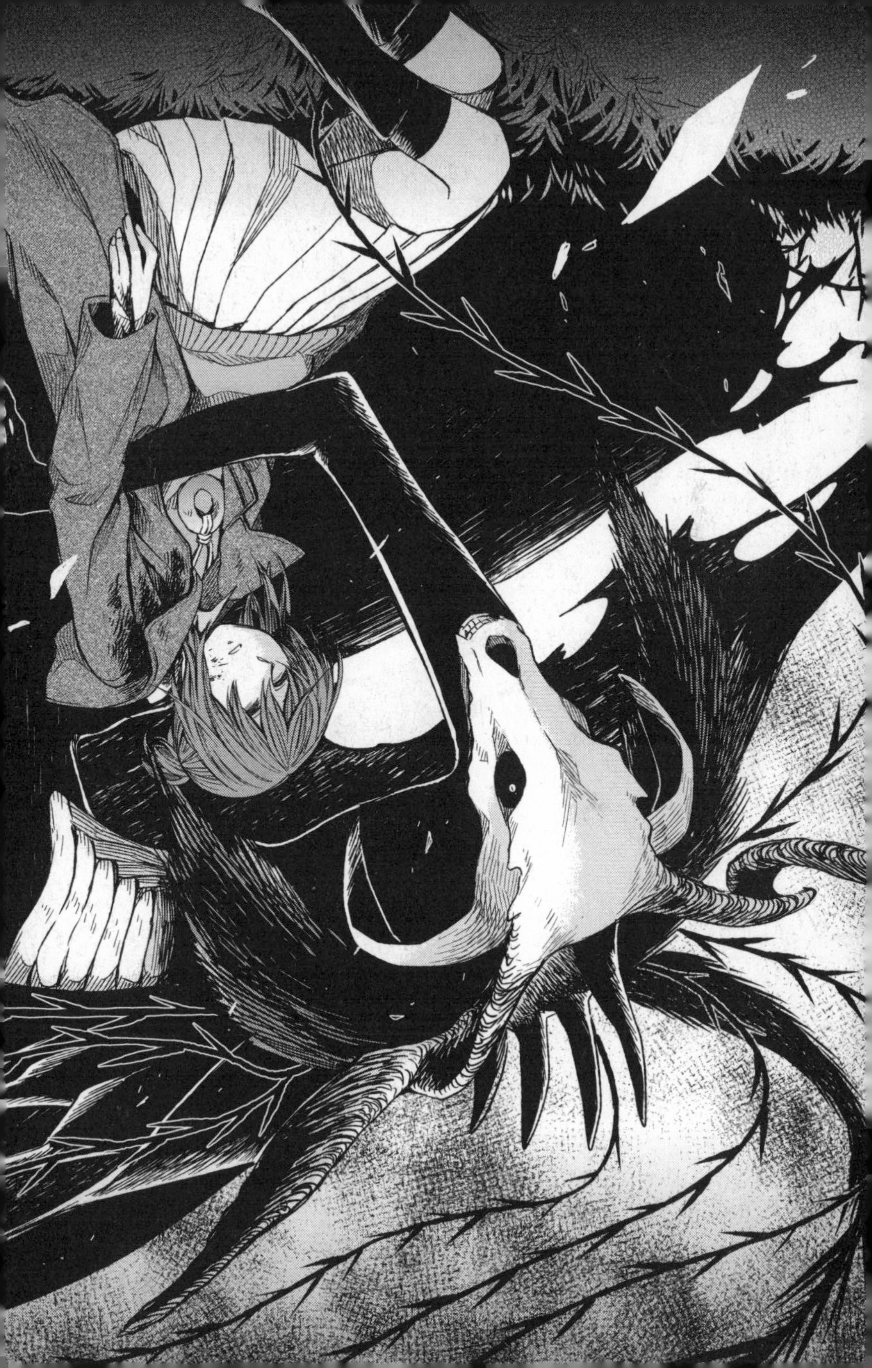

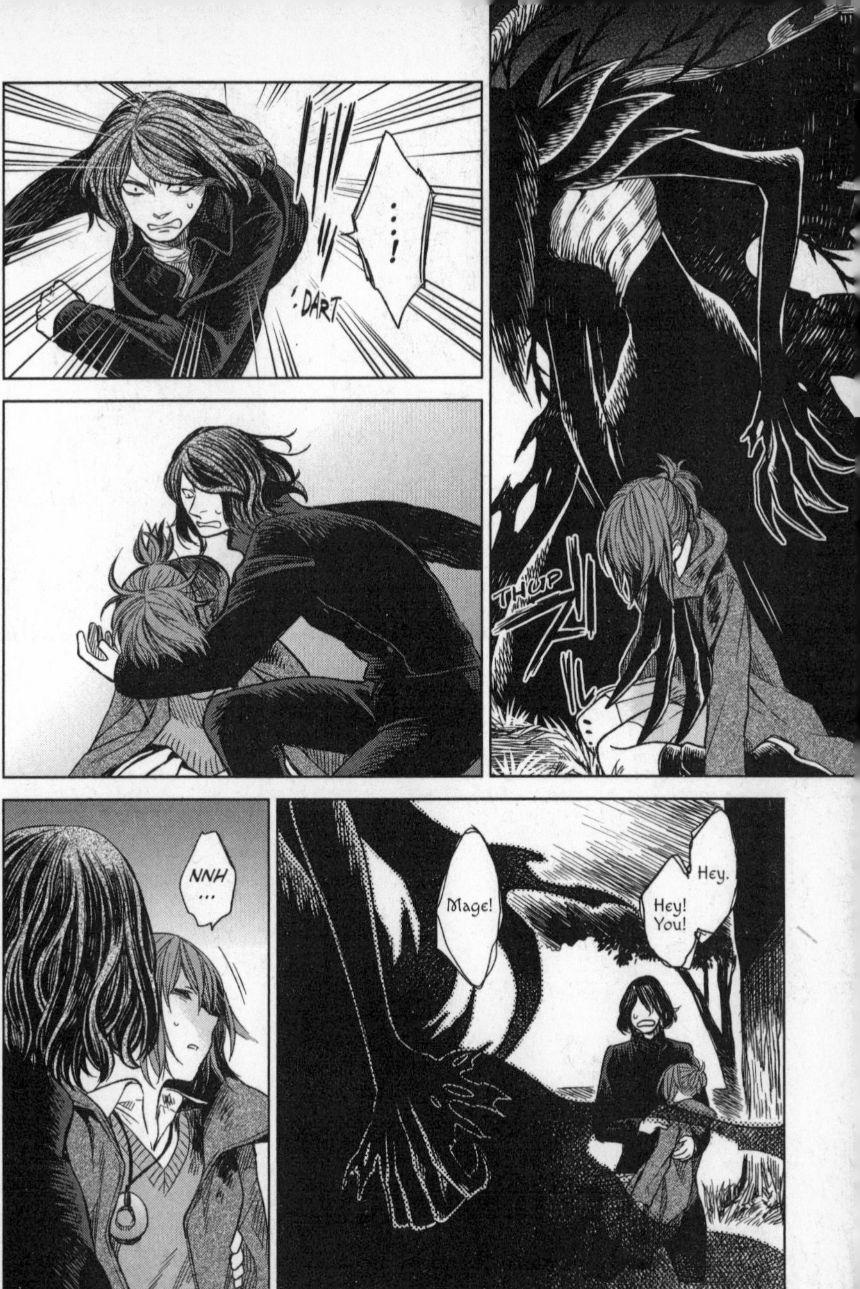
THUP
DART
...!
Hey.
Hey! You!
Mage!
NNH ...

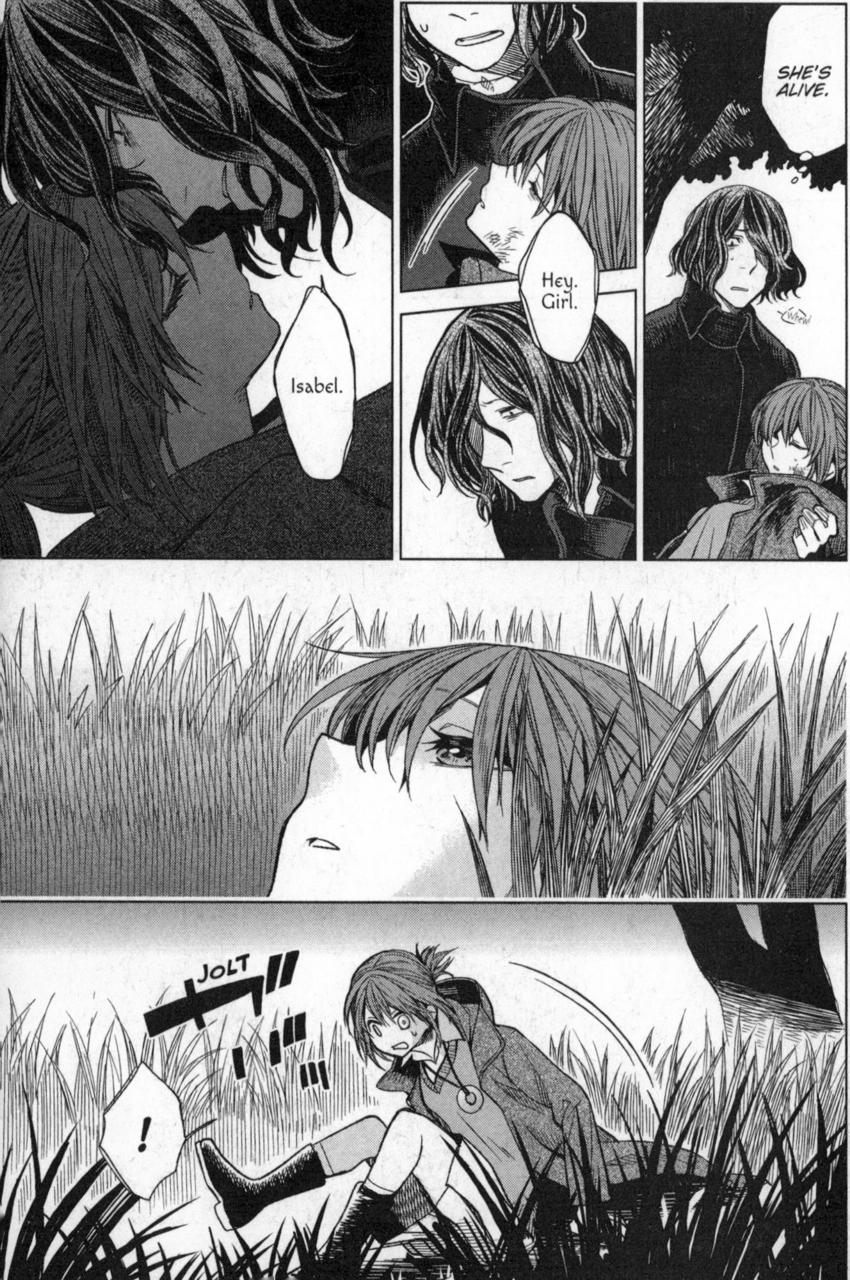
SHE'S ALIVE.
Whew!
Hey. Girl.
Isabel.
JOLT
!

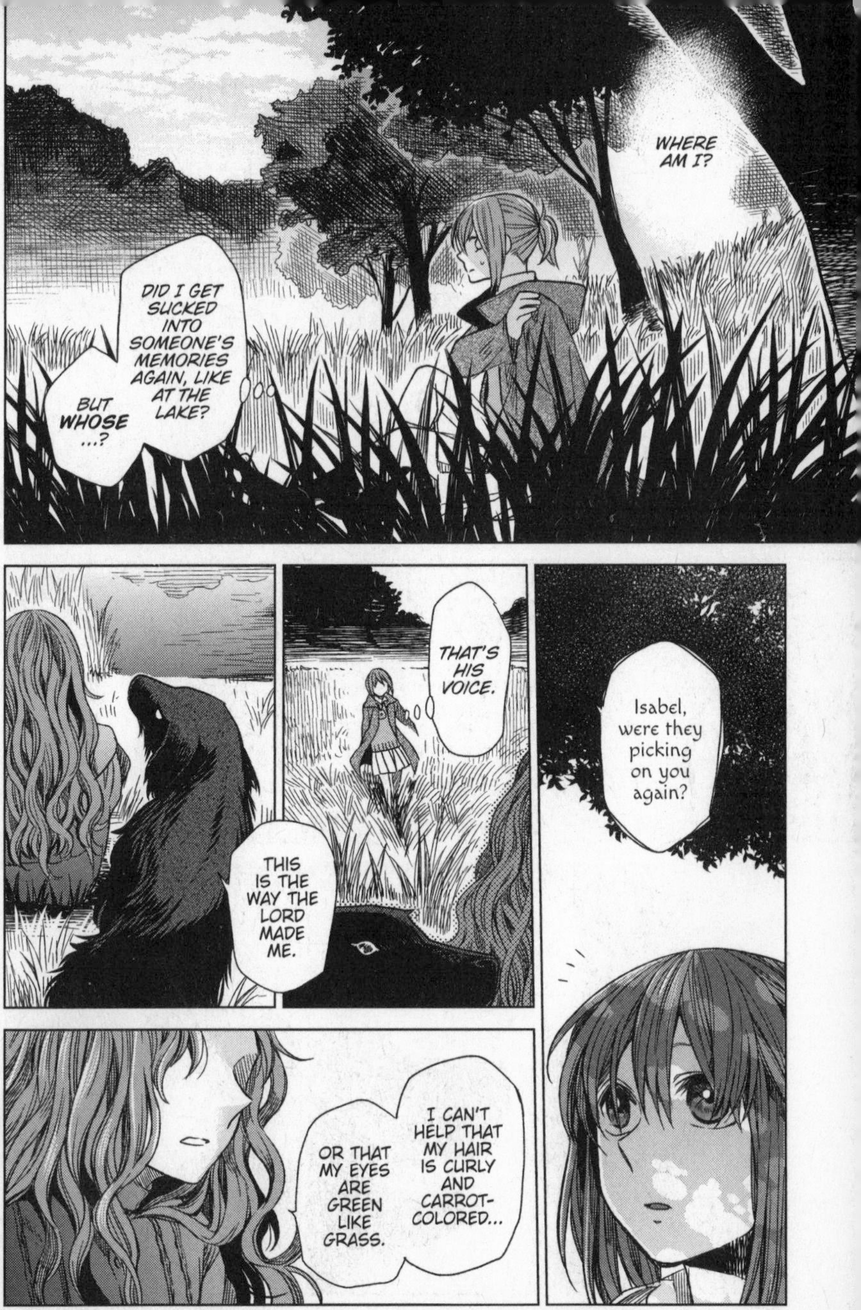
WHERE AM I?
DID I GET SUCKED INTO SOMEONE'S MEMORIES AGAIN, LIKE AT THE LAKE?
BUT WHOSE ...?
Isabel, were they picking on you again?
THAT'S HIS VOICE.
THIS IS THE WAY THE LORD MADE ME.
I CAN'T HELP THAT MY HAIR IS CURLY AND CARROT-COLORED...
OR THAT MY EYES ARE GREEN LIKE GRASS.

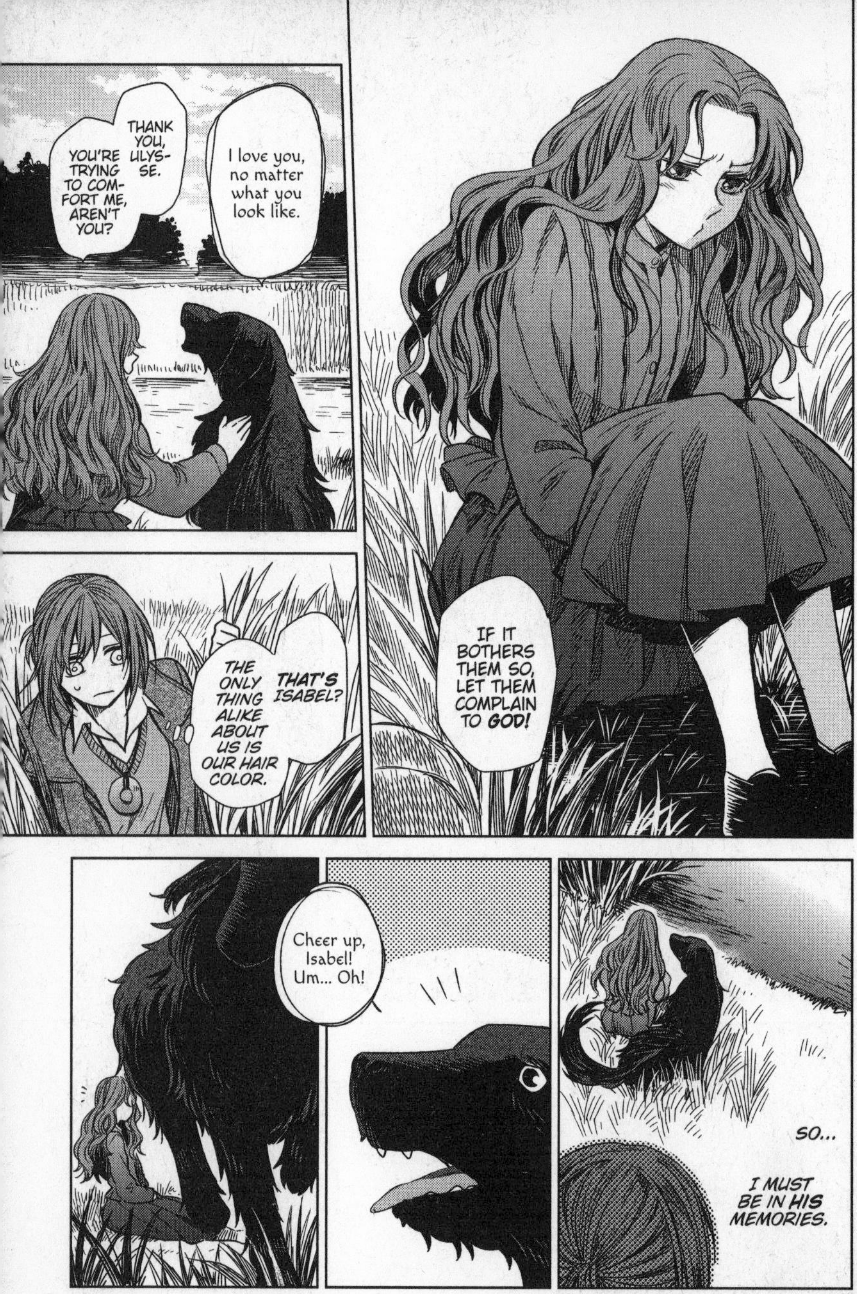
IF IT BOTHERS THEM SO, LET THEM COMPLAIN TO **GOD!**
I love you, no matter what you look like.
THANK YOU, ULYSSE.
YOU'RE TRYING TO COMFORT ME, AREN'T YOU?
THAT'S *ISABEL?*
THE ONLY THING ALIKE ABOUT US IS OUR HAIR COLOR.
SO...
I MUST BE IN **HIS** MEMORIES.
Cheer up, Isabel! Um... Oh!

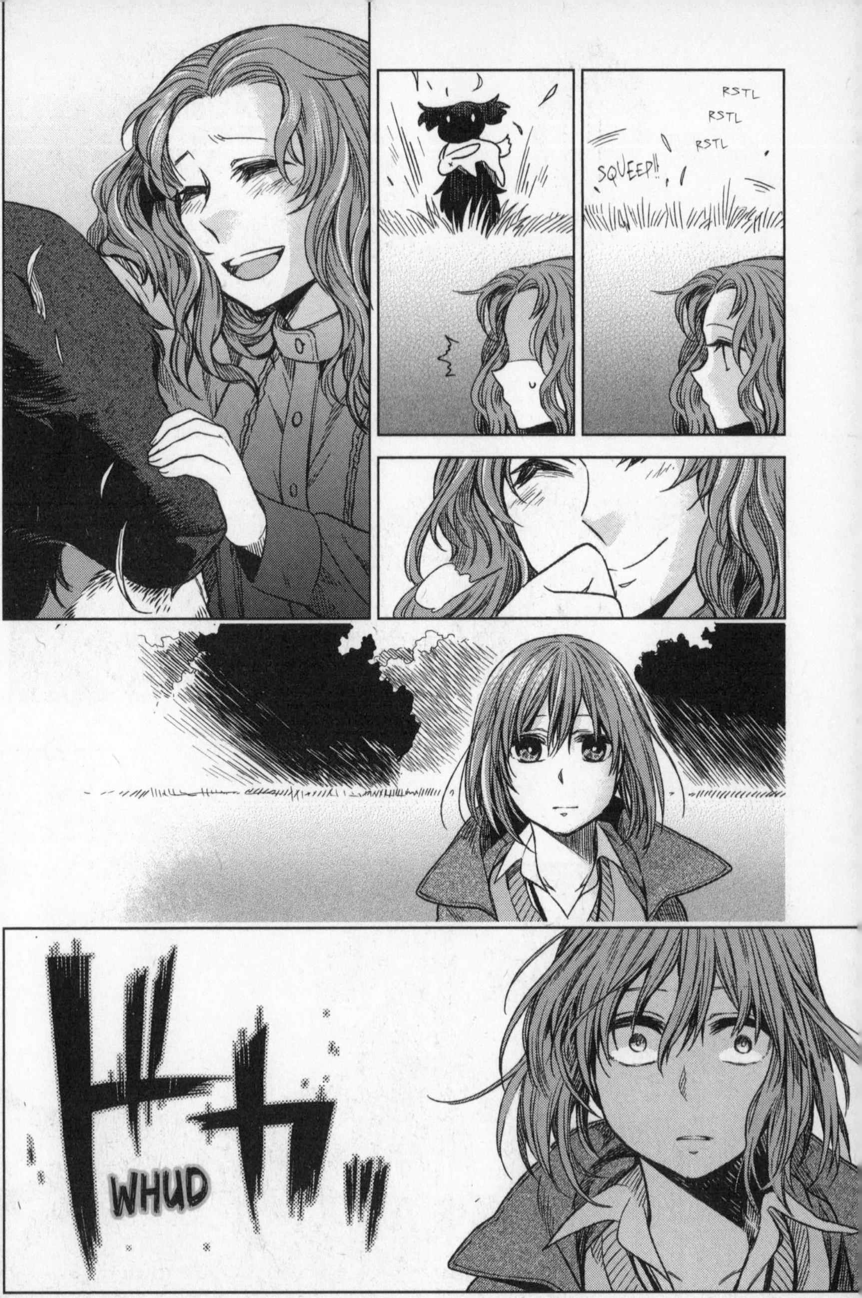
RSTL
RSTL
RSTL
SQUEEP!!
WHUD

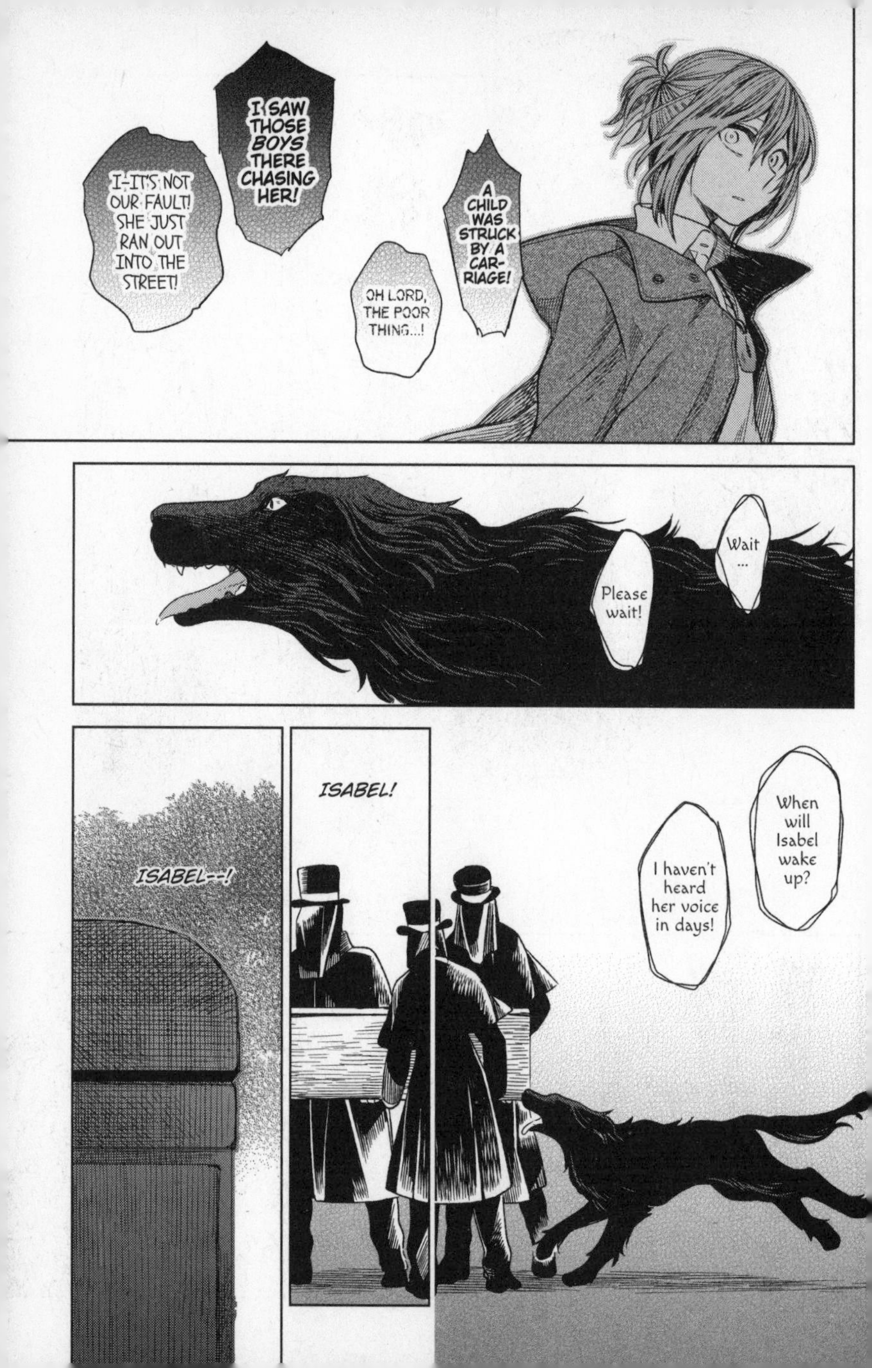
A CHILD WAS STRUCK BY A CAR-RIAGE!
OH LORD, THE POOR THING...!
I SAW THOSE BOYS THERE CHASING HER!
I-IT'S NOT OUR FAULT! SHE JUST RAN OUT INTO THE STREET!
Wait ...
Please wait!
When will Isabel wake up?
I haven't heard her voice in days!
ISABEL!
ISABEL--!

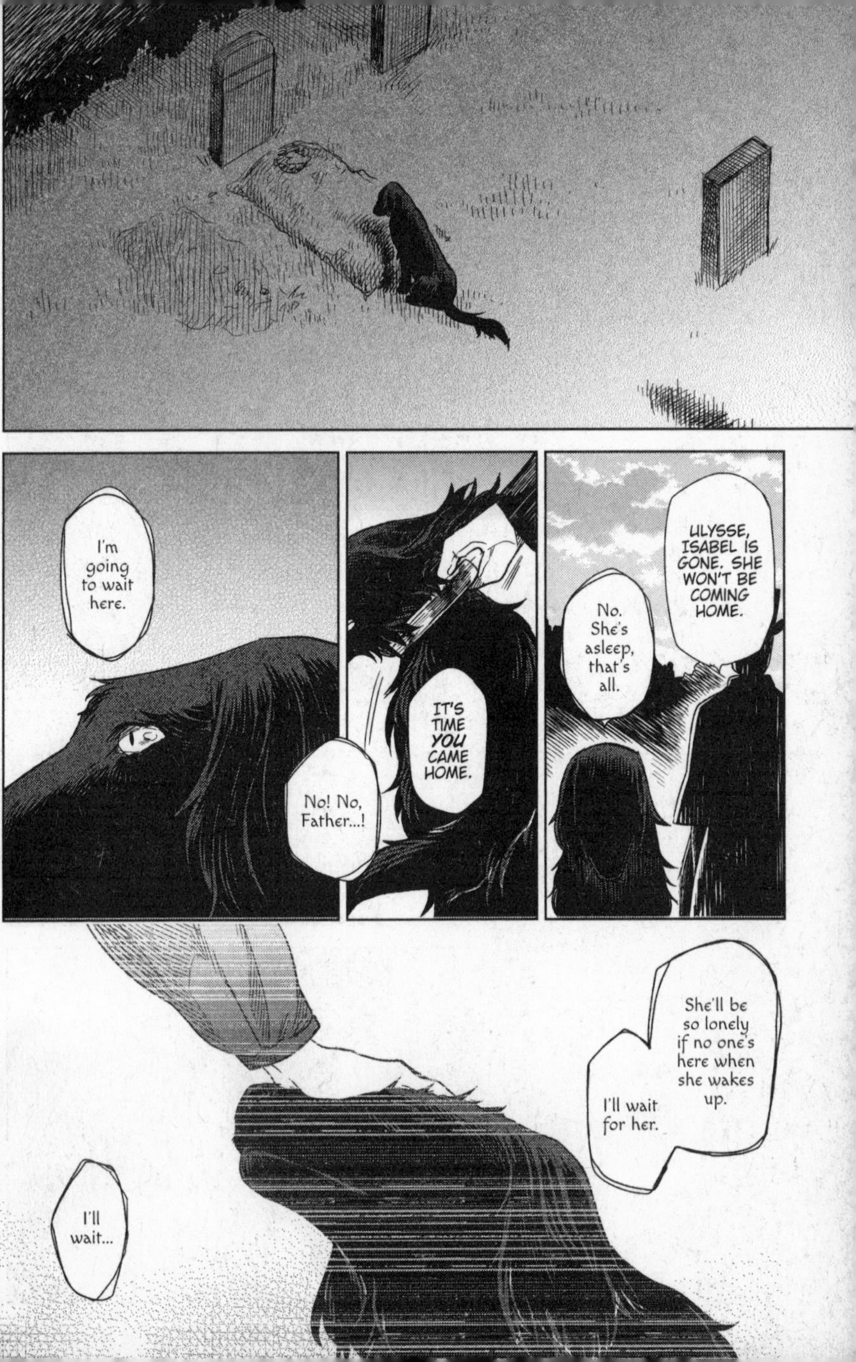
ULYSSE, ISABEL IS GONE. SHE WON'T BE COMING HOME.
No. She's asleep, that's all.
IT'S TIME YOU CAME HOME.
No! No, Father...!
I'm going to wait here.
She'll be so lonely if no one's here when she wakes up.
I'll wait for her.
I'll wait...

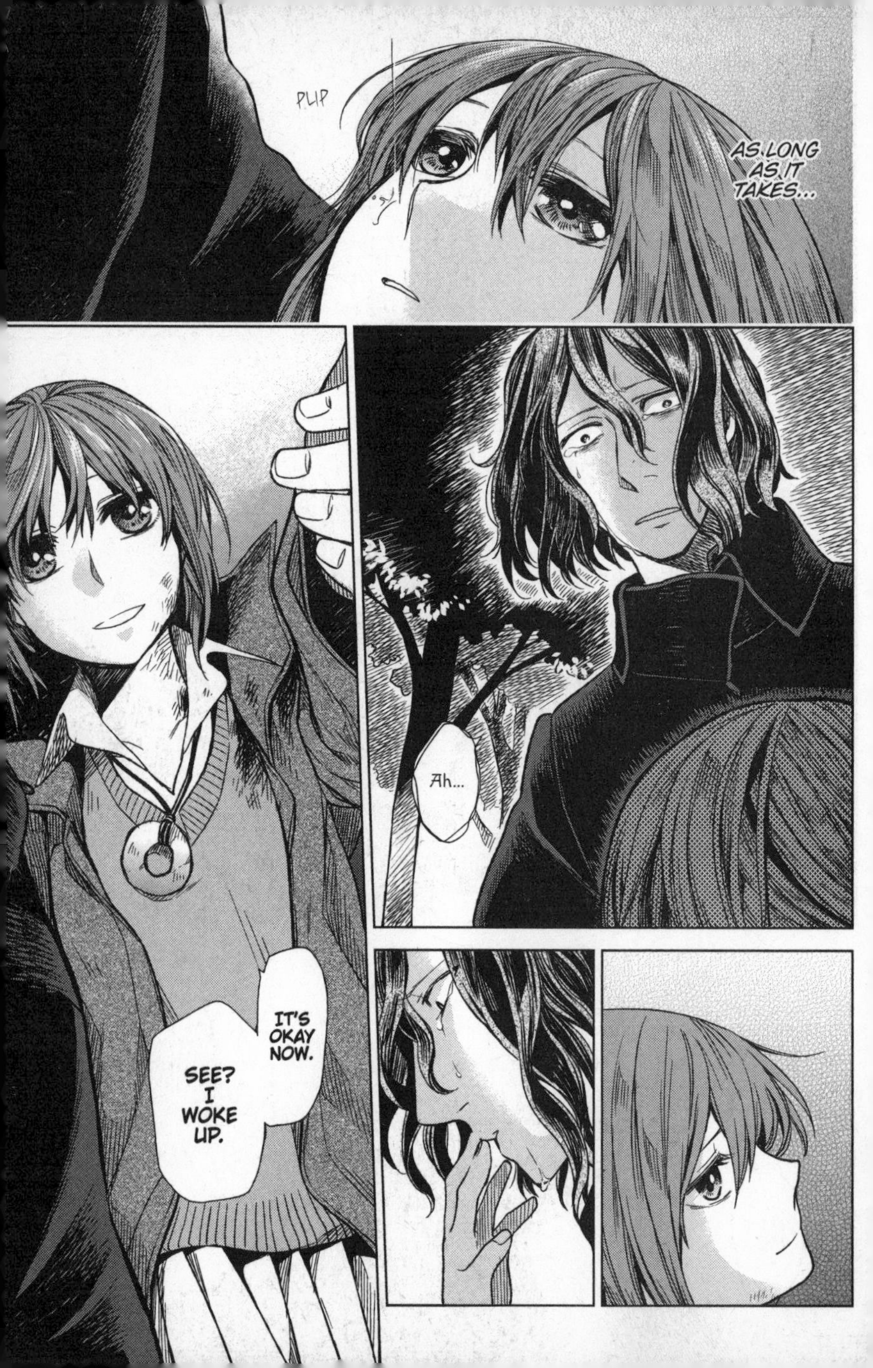
AS LONG AS IT TAKES...
PLIP
Ah...
IT'S OKAY NOW.
SEE? I WOKE UP.

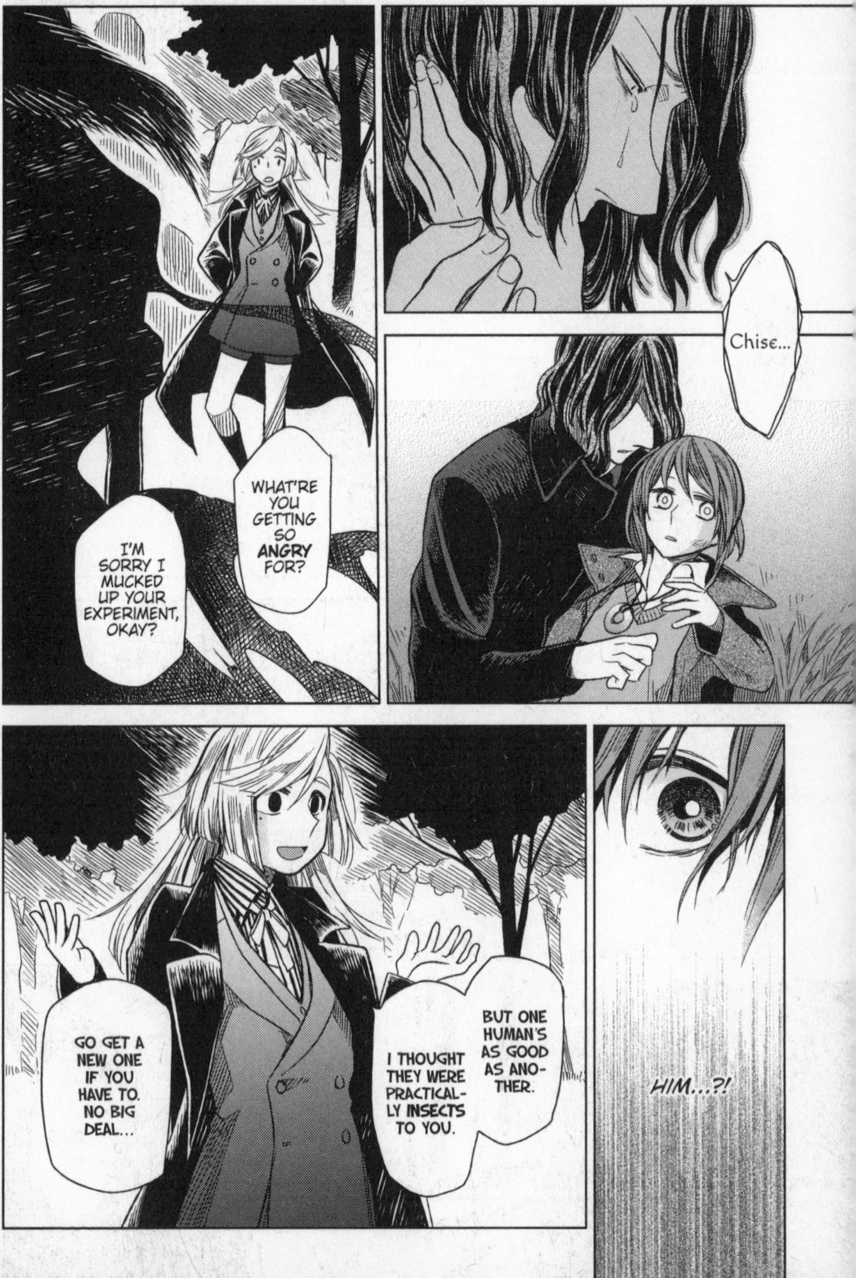
Chise...
WHAT'RE YOU GETTING SO ANGRY FOR?
I'M SORRY I MUCKED UP YOUR EXPERIMENT, OKAY?
HIM...?!
BUT ONE HUMAN'S AS GOOD AS ANO-THER.
I THOUGHT THEY WERE PRACTICAL-LY INSECTS TO YOU.
GO GET A NEW ONE IF YOU HAVE TO. NO BIG DEAL...

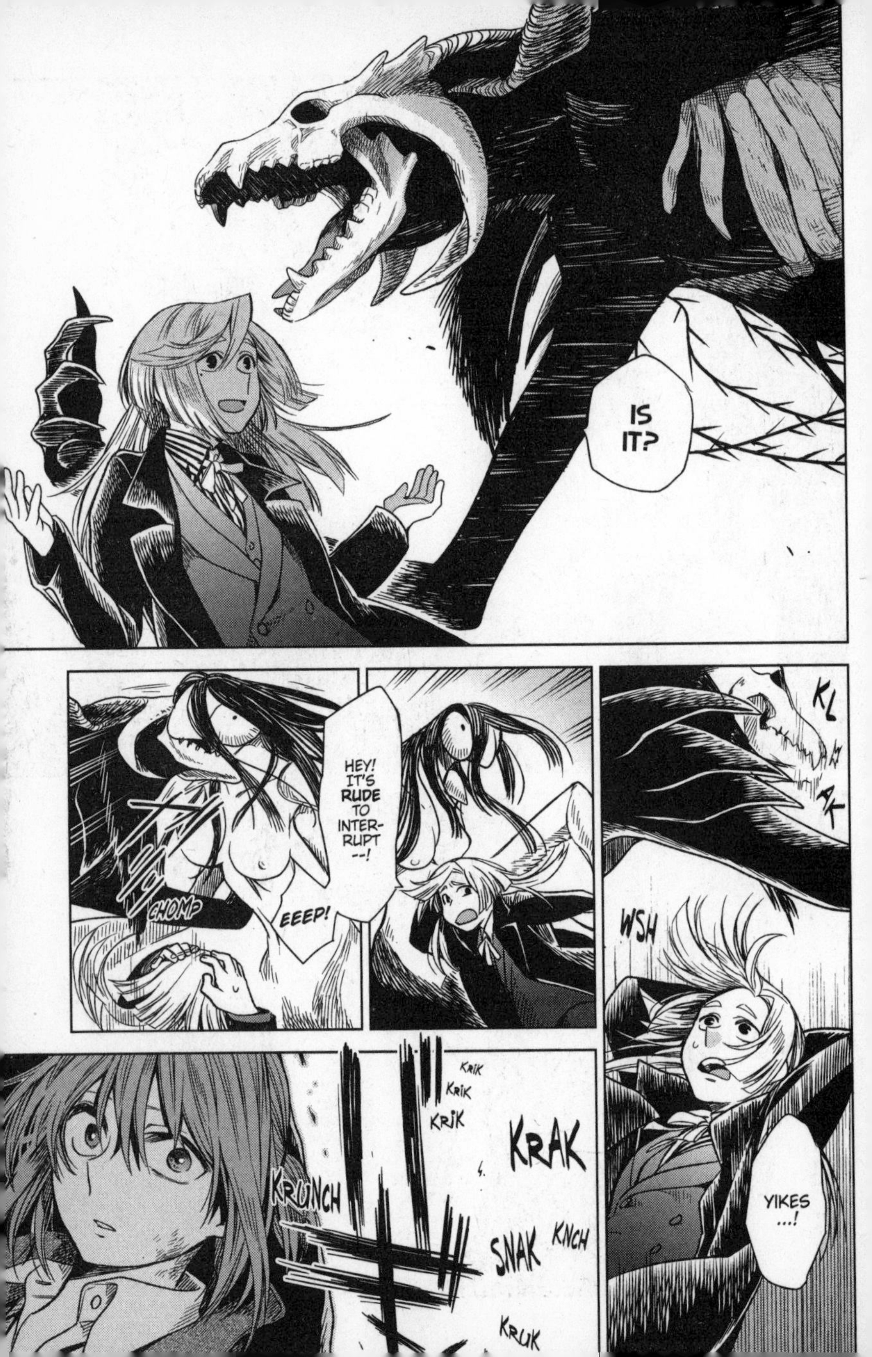
IS IT?
KL AK
WSH
YIKES ...!
HEY! IT'S RUDE TO INTER-RUPT --!
CHOMP
EEEP!
KRIK KRIK KRIK
KRAK
KRUNCH
SNAK
KNCH
KRUK

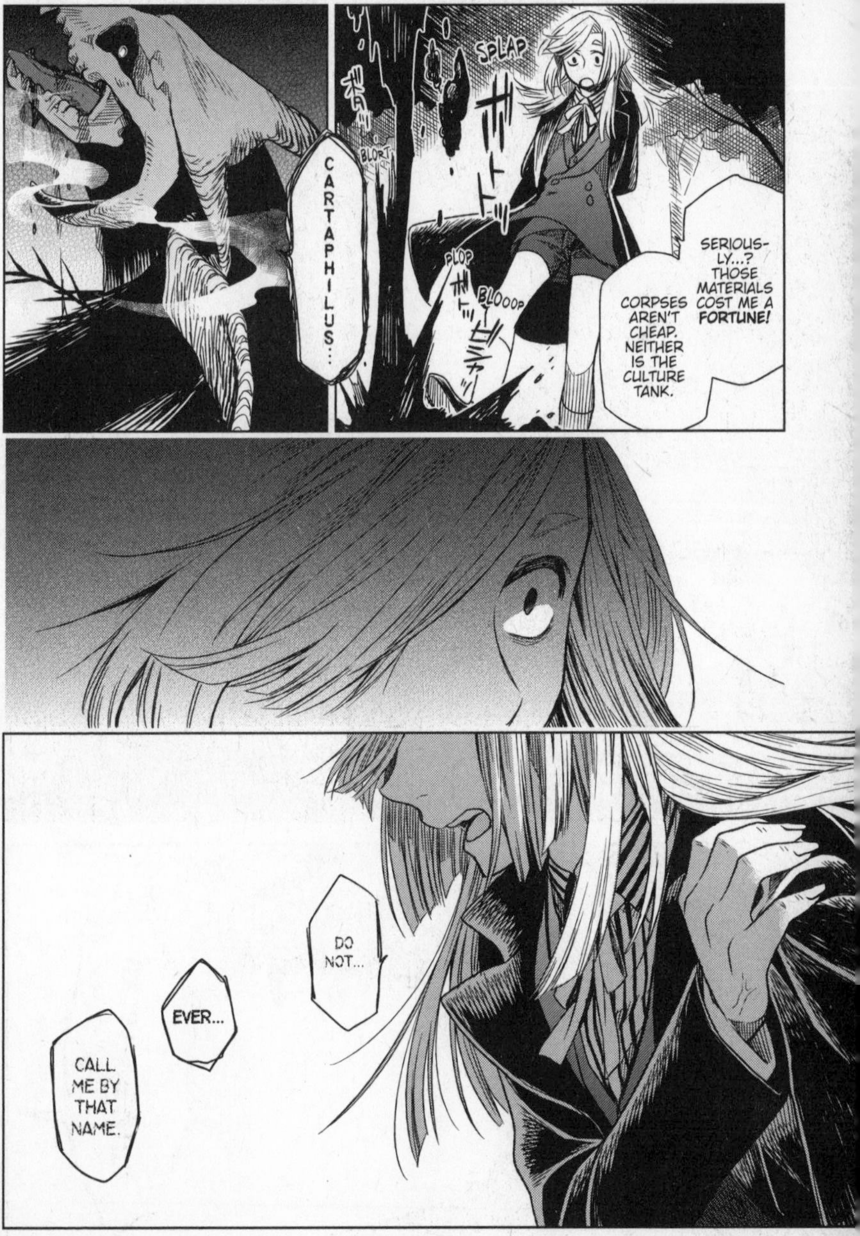
SPLAP
BLORT
PLOP
BLOOOP
SERIOUS-LY...? THOSE MATERIALS COST ME A **FORTUNE!**
CORPSES AREN'T CHEAP. NEITHER IS THE CULTURE TANK.
CARTAPHILUS...
DO NOT...
EVER...
CALL ME BY THAT NAME.

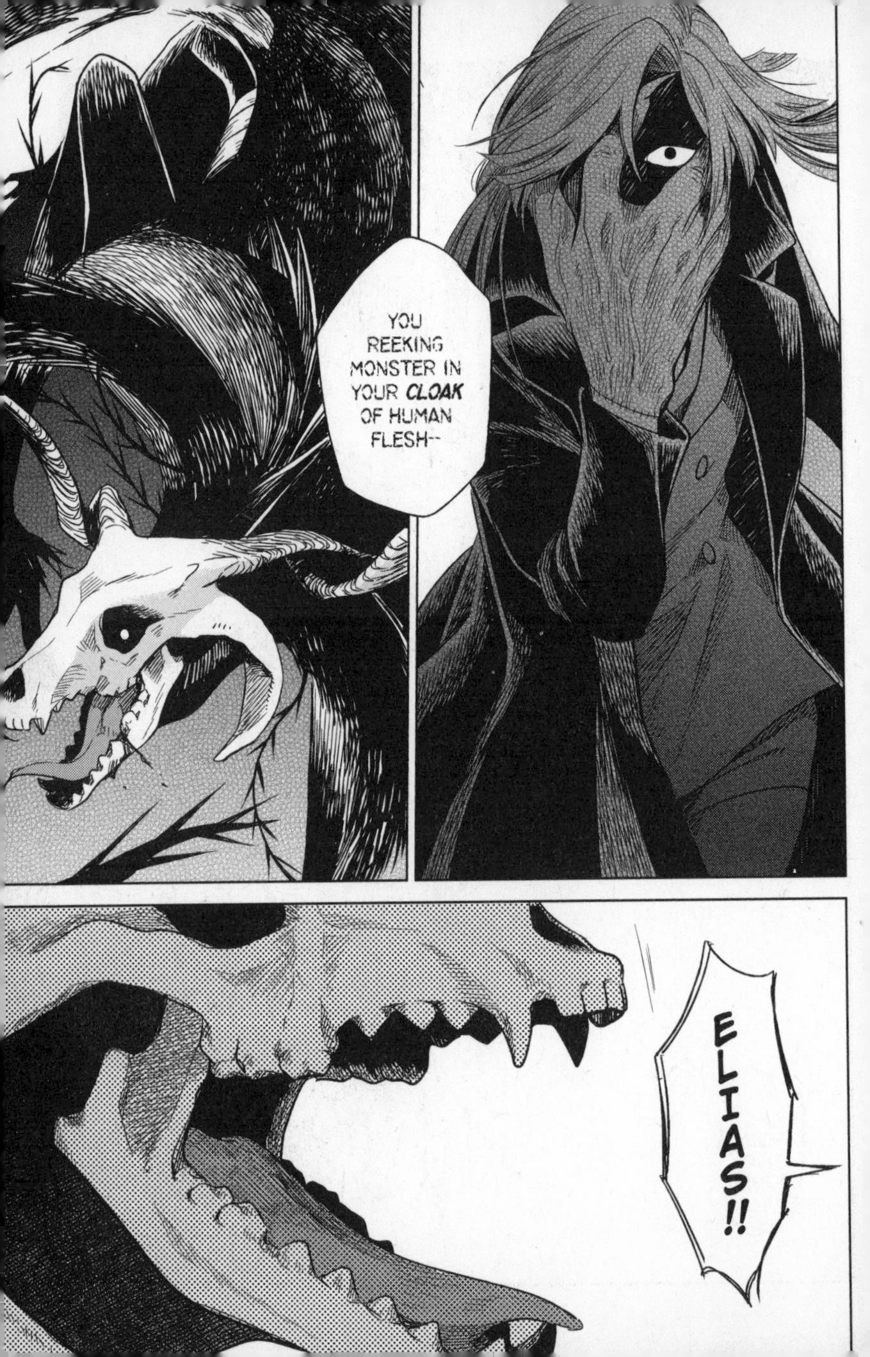
YOU REEKING MONSTER IN YOUR **CLOAK** OF HUMAN FLESH--
ELIAS!!

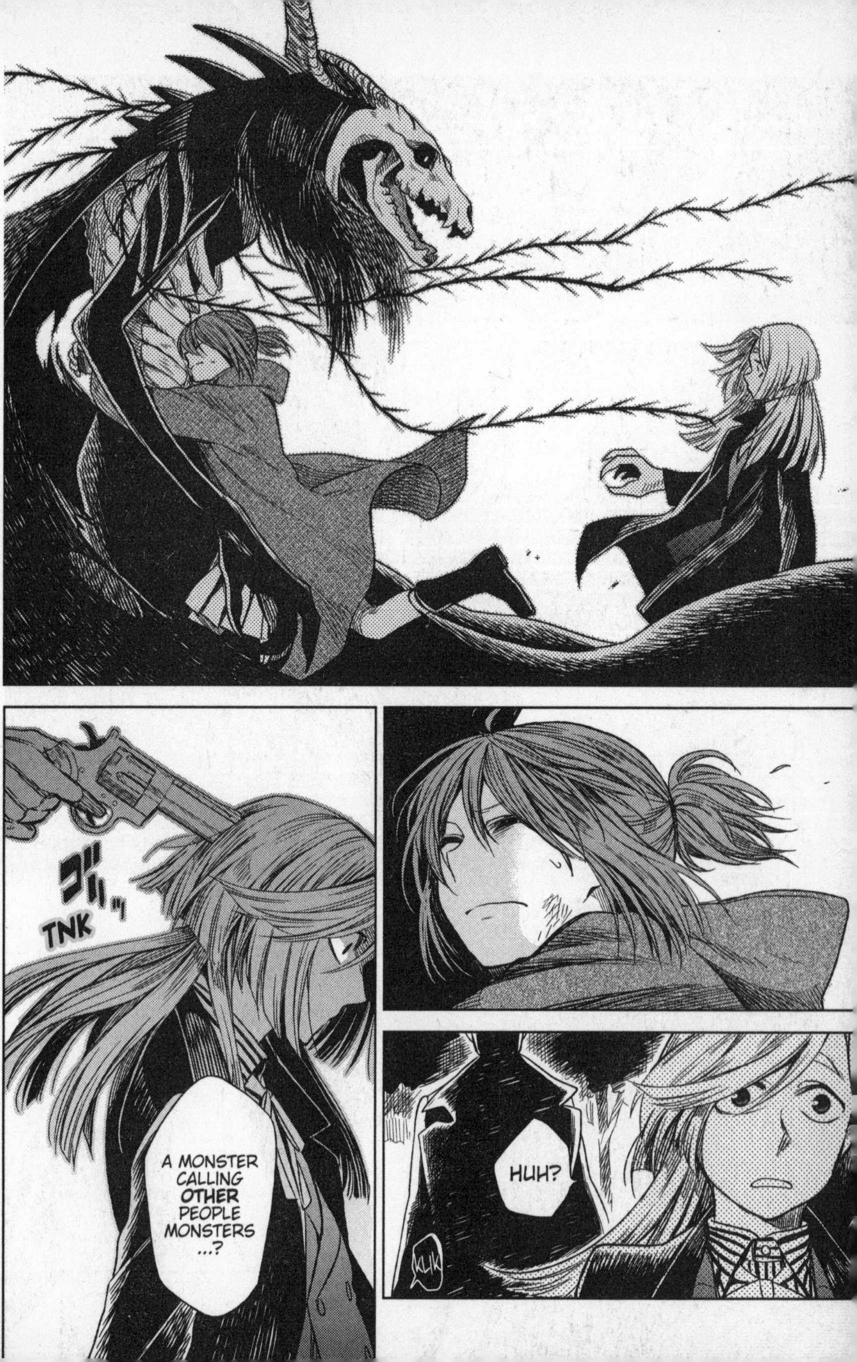
HUH?
KLIK
TNK
A MONSTER CALLING **OTHER** PEOPLE MONSTERS ...?

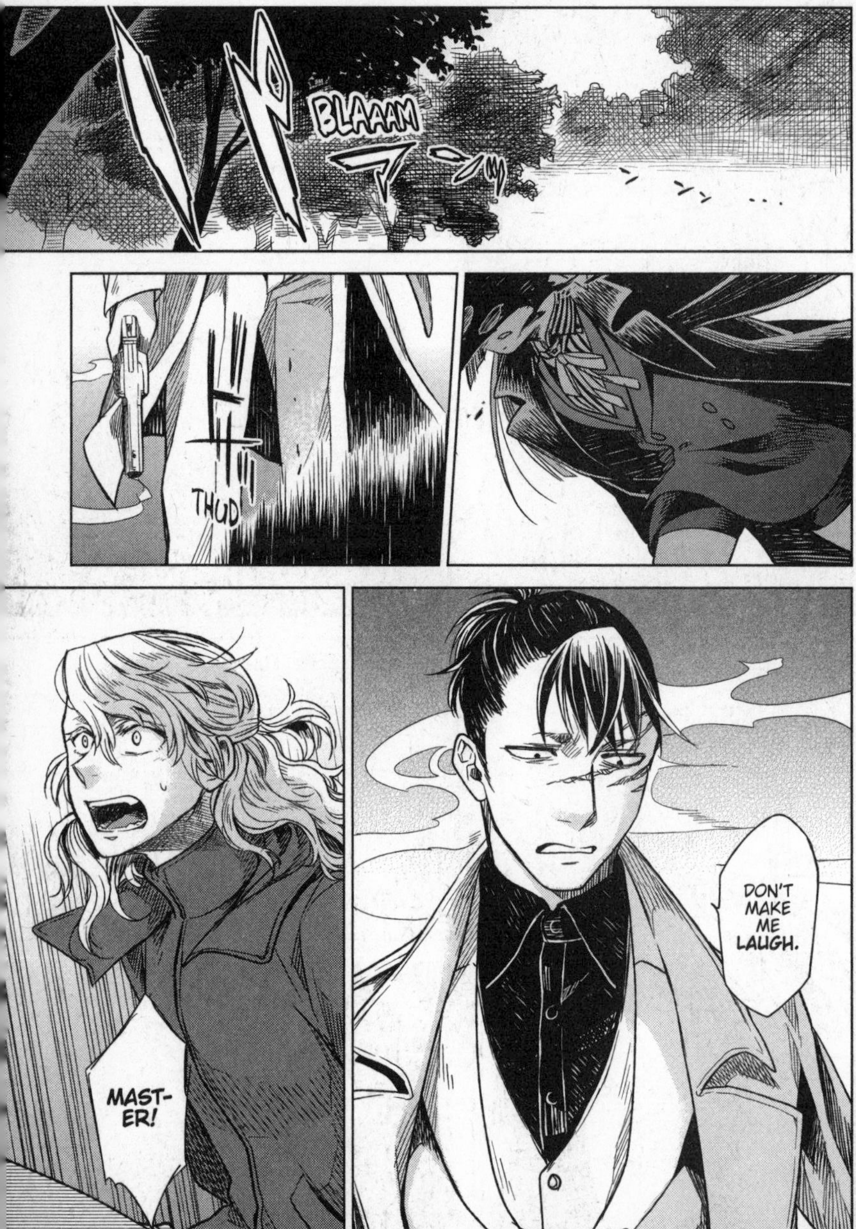
BLAAAM
THUD
DON'T MAKE ME LAUGH.
MAST-ER!

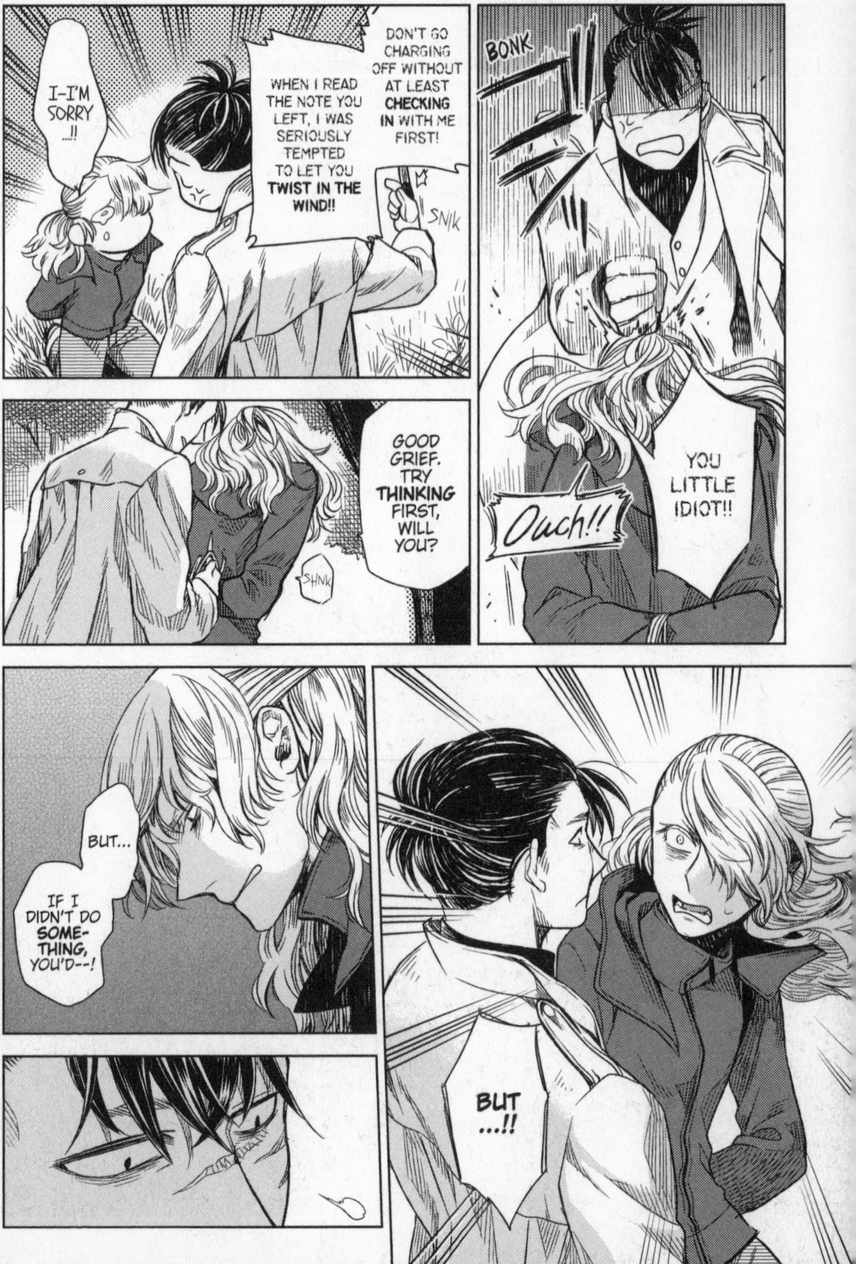
BONK
YOU LITTLE IDIOT!!
Ouch!!
DON'T GO CHARGING OFF WITHOUT AT LEAST CHECKING IN WITH ME FIRST!
WHEN I READ THE NOTE YOU LEFT, I WAS SERIOUSLY TEMPTED TO LET YOU TWIST IN THE WIND!!
SNIK
I-I'M SORRY ...!!
GOOD GRIEF. TRY THINKING FIRST, WILL YOU?
SHNK
BUT ...!!
BUT...
IF I DIDN'T DO SOME-THING, YOU'D--!

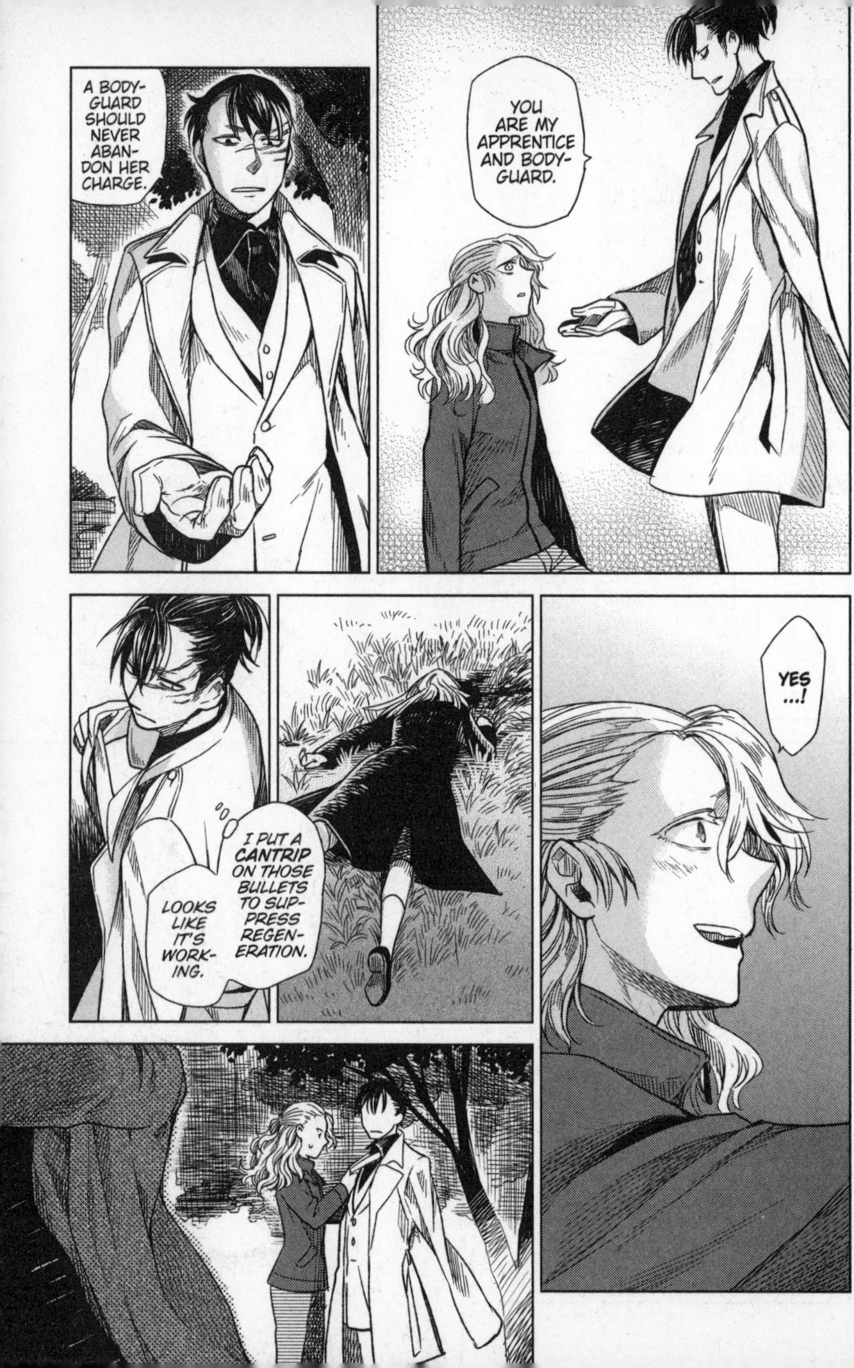
YOU ARE MY APPRENTICE AND BODY-GUARD.
A BODY-GUARD SHOULD NEVER ABAN-DON HER CHARGE.
YES ...!
I PUT A CANTRIP ON THOSE BULLETS TO SUP-PRESS REGEN-ERATION.
LOOKS LIKE IT'S WORK-ING.

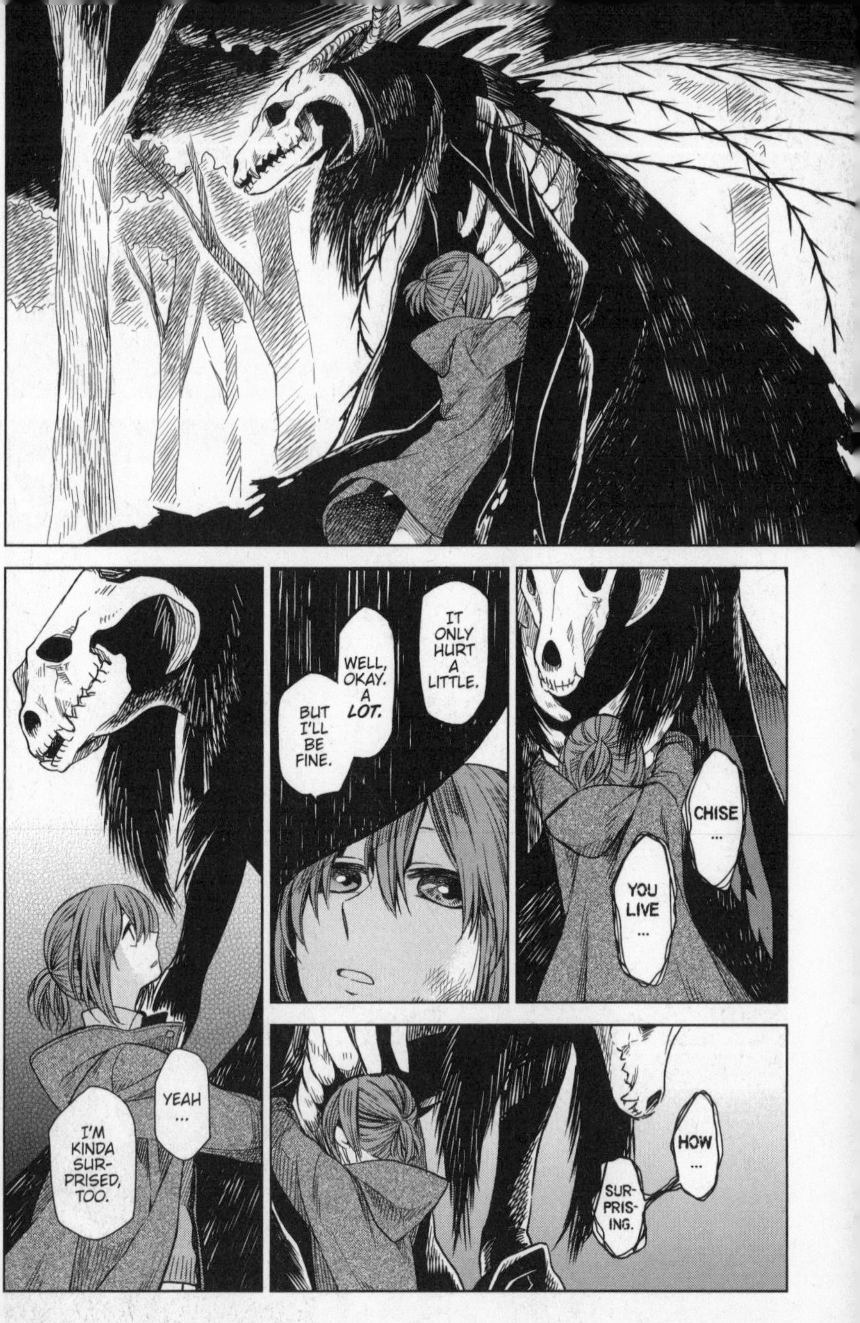
CHISE ...
YOU LIVE ...
IT ONLY HURT A LITTLE.
WELL, OKAY. A LOT.
BUT I'LL BE FINE.
HOW ...
SURPRISING.
YEAH ...
I'M KINDA SURPRISED, TOO.

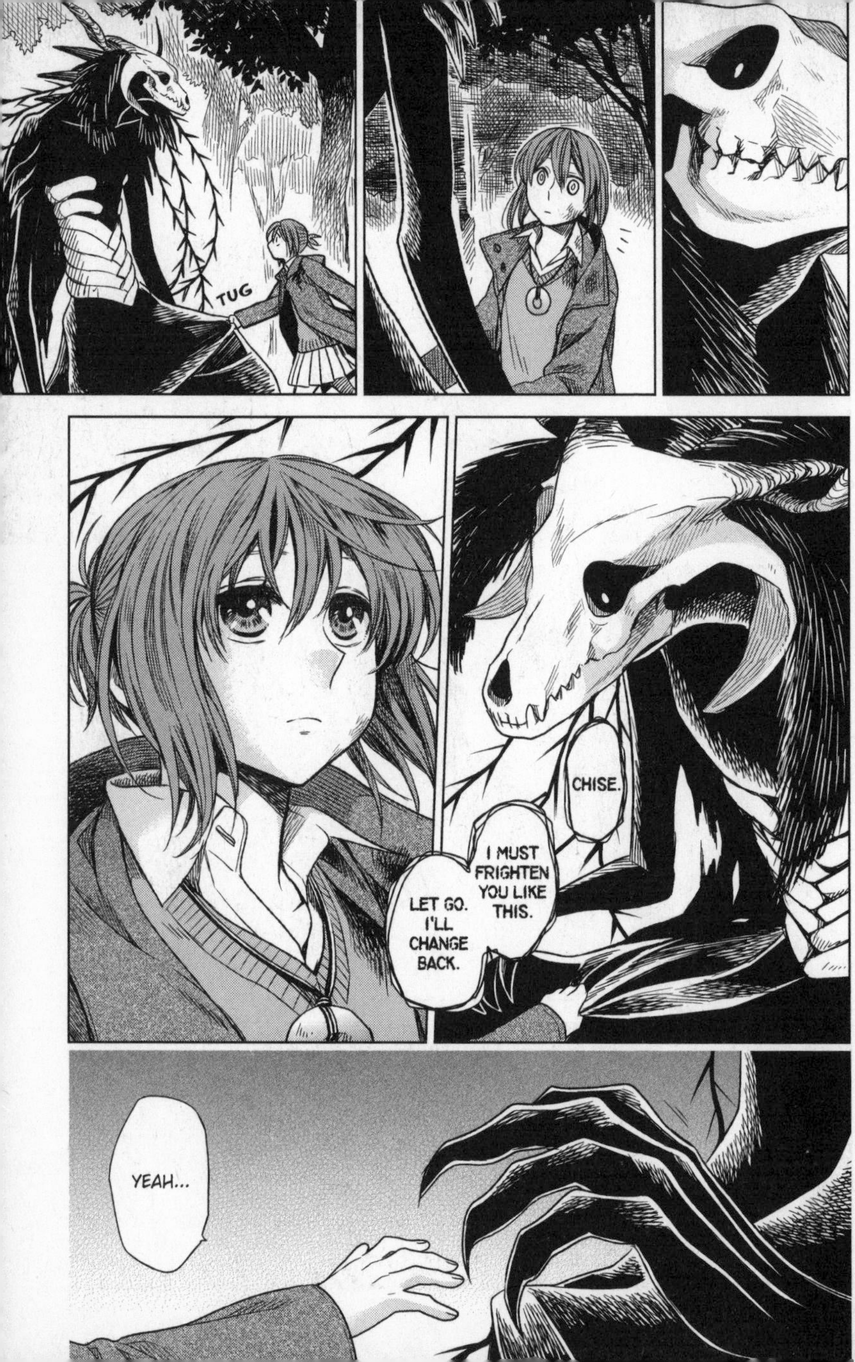
TUG
CHISE.
I MUST FRIGHTEN YOU LIKE THIS.
LET GO. I'LL CHANGE BACK.
YEAH...

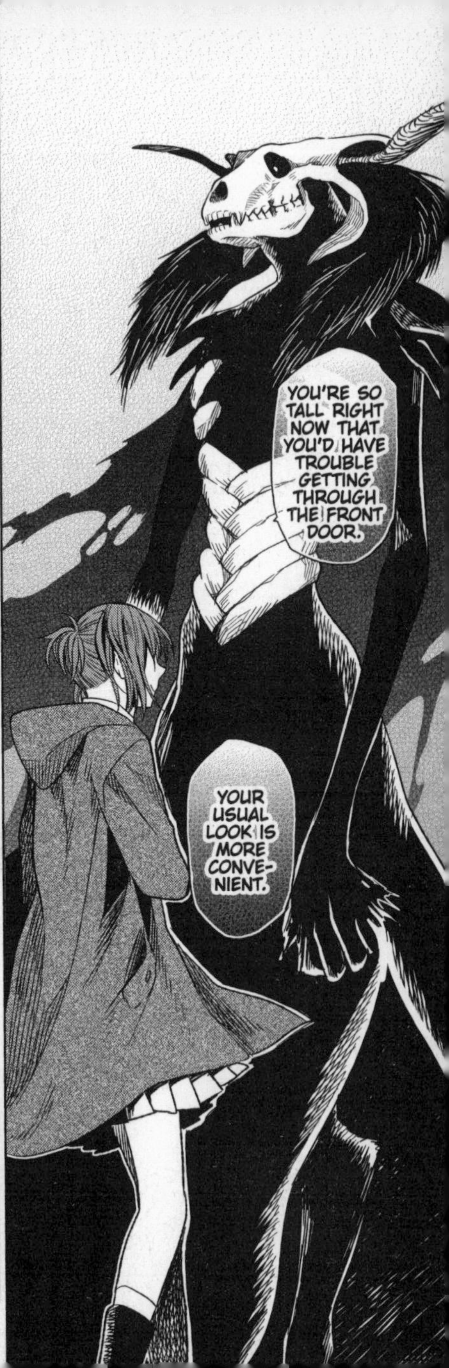
YOU'RE SO TALL RIGHT NOW THAT YOU'D HAVE TROUBLE GETTING THROUGH THE FRONT DOOR.
YOUR USUAL LOOK IS MORE CONVE-NIENT.

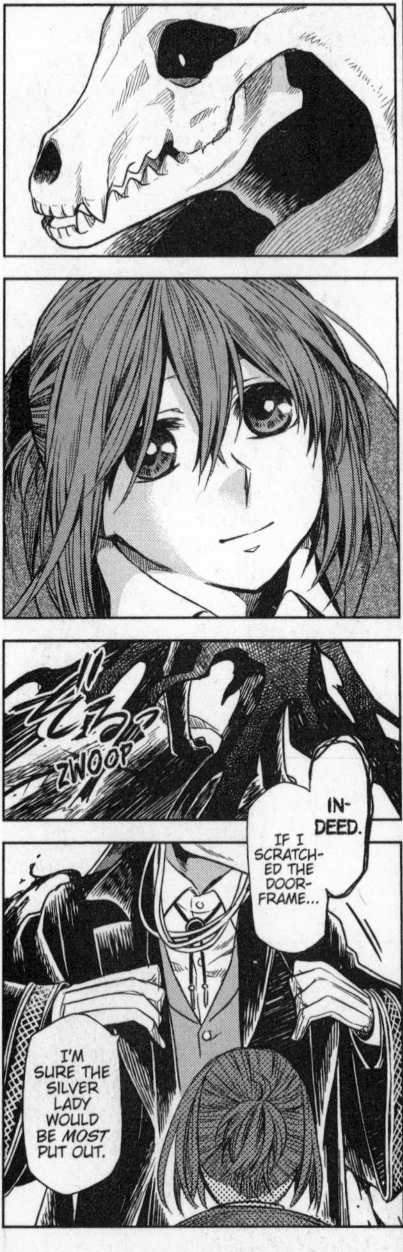
ZWOOP
IN-DEED.
IF I SCRATCH-ED THE DOOR-FRAME...
I'M SURE THE SILVER LADY WOULD BE MOST PUT OUT.

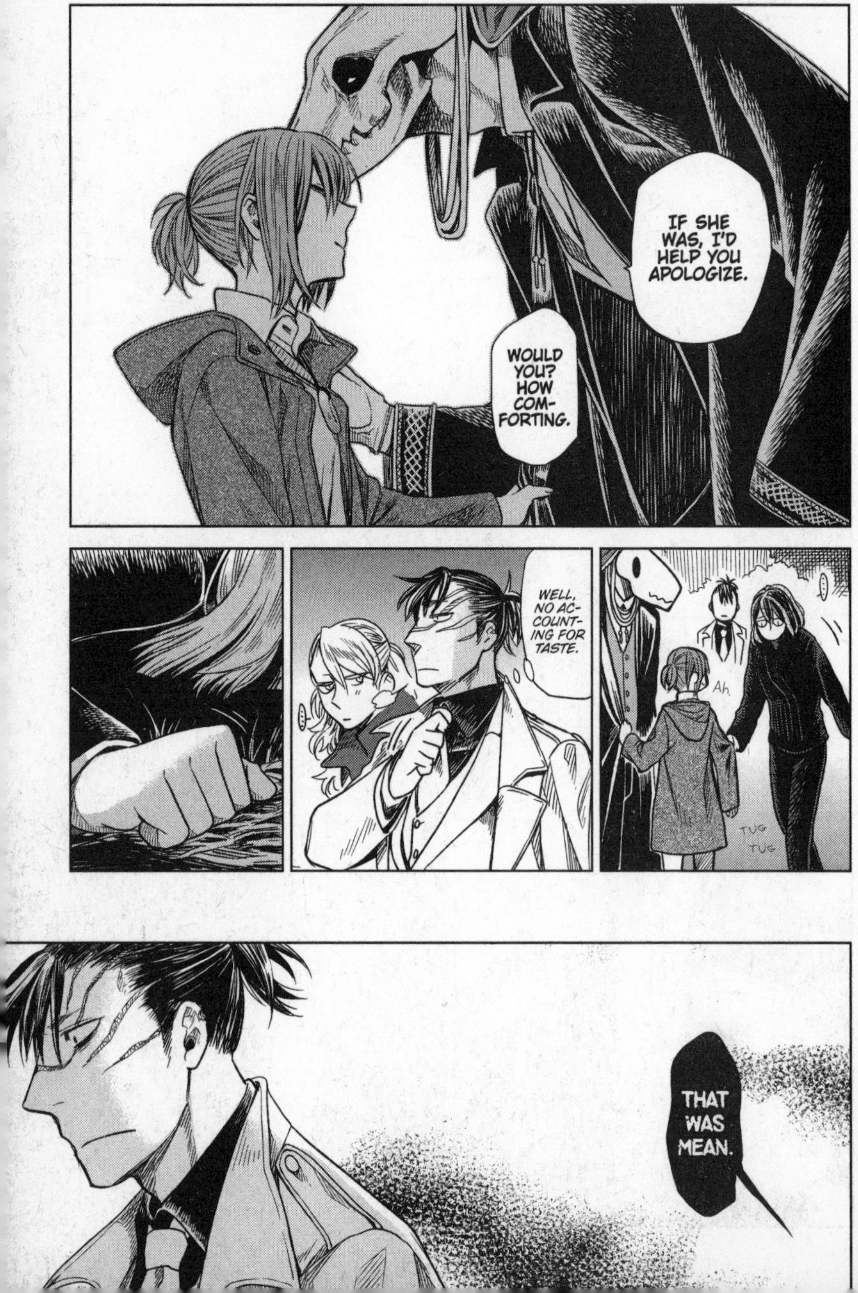
IF SHE WAS, I'D HELP YOU APOLOGIZE.
WOULD YOU? HOW COM-FORTING.
...
Ah.
TUG TUG
WELL, NO AC-COUNT-ING FOR TASTE.
...
THAT WAS MEAN.

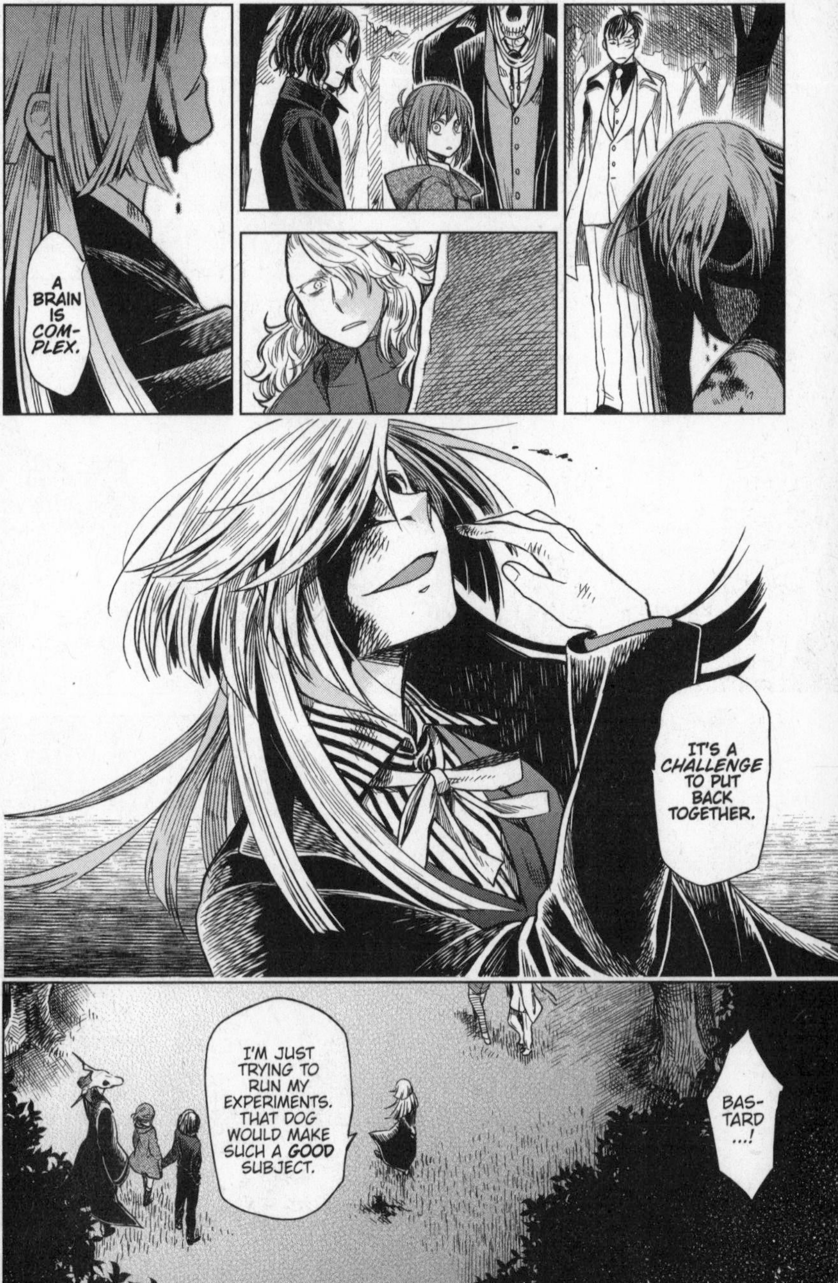
A BRAIN IS COMPLEX.
IT'S A CHALLENGE TO PUT BACK TOGETHER.
I'M JUST TRYING TO RUN MY EXPERIMENTS. THAT DOG WOULD MAKE SUCH A GOOD SUBJECT.
BASTARD...!

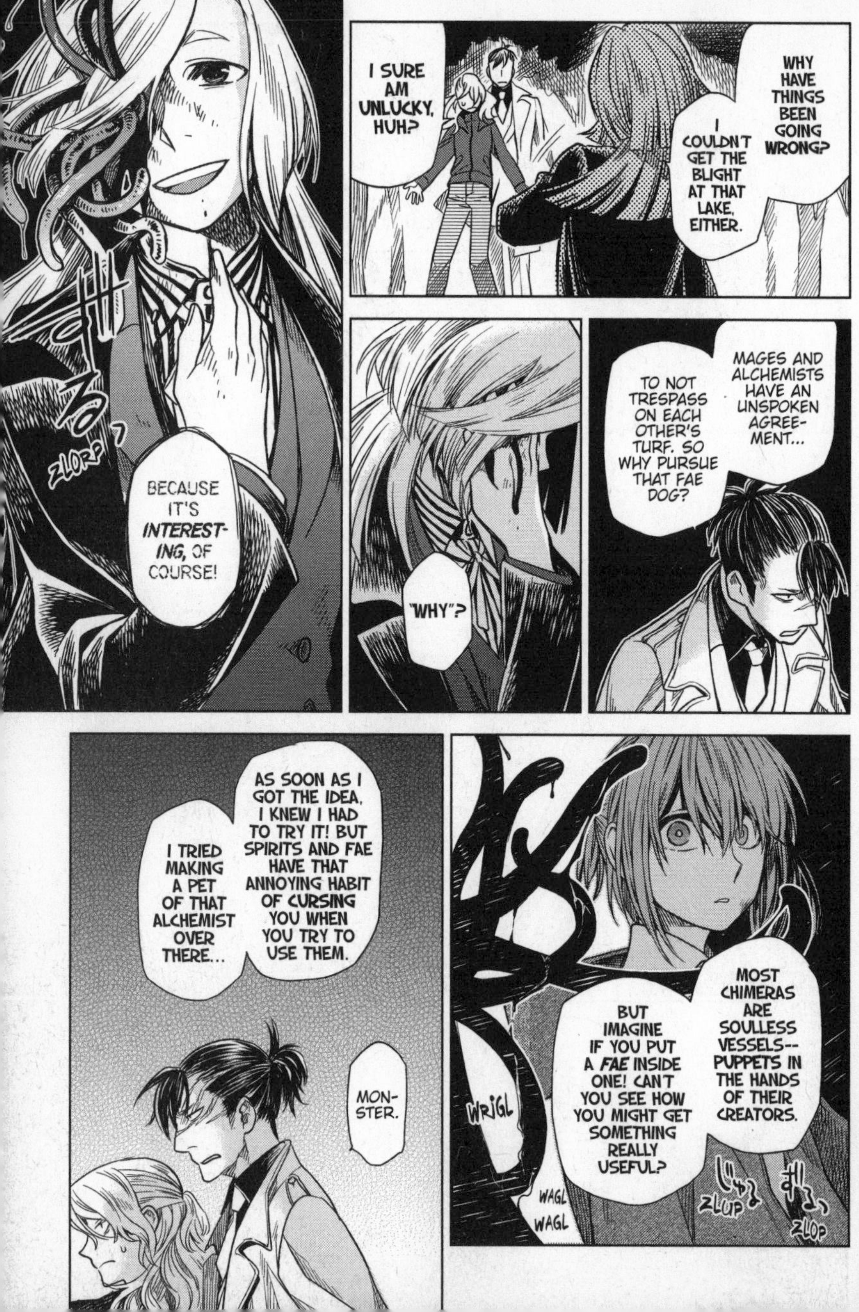
WHY HAVE THINGS BEEN GOING WRONG?
I COULDN'T GET THE BLIGHT AT THAT LAKE, EITHER.
I SURE AM UNLUCKY, HUH?
MAGES AND ALCHEMISTS HAVE AN UNSPOKEN AGREEMENT...
TO NOT TRESPASS ON EACH OTHER'S TURF. SO WHY PURSUE THAT FAE DOG?
"WHY"?
ZLORP
BECAUSE IT'S *INTERESTING*, OF COURSE!
MOST CHIMERAS ARE SOULLESS VESSELS-- PUPPETS IN THE HANDS OF THEIR CREATORS.
BUT IMAGINE IF YOU PUT A *FAE* INSIDE ONE! CAN'T YOU SEE HOW YOU MIGHT GET SOMETHING REALLY USEFUL?
WRIGL
WAGL WAGL
ZLUP
ZLOP
AS SOON AS I GOT THE IDEA, I KNEW I HAD TO TRY IT! BUT SPIRITS AND FAE HAVE THAT ANNOYING HABIT OF CURSING YOU WHEN YOU TRY TO USE THEM.
I TRIED MAKING A PET OF THAT ALCHEMIST OVER THERE...
MON-STER.

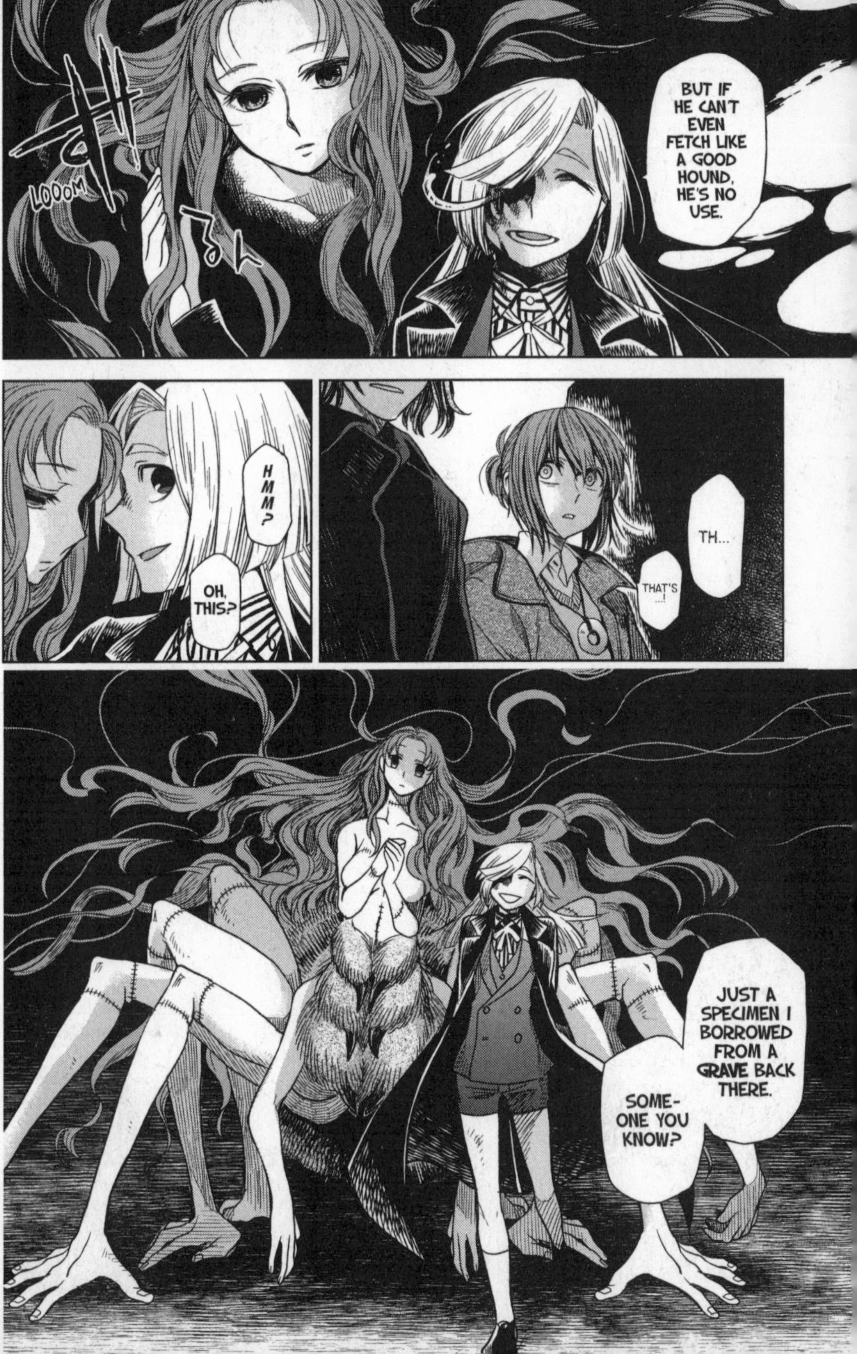
BUT IF HE CAN'T EVEN FETCH LIKE A GOOD HOUND, HE'S NO USE.
LOOOM
TH...
THAT'S ...!
HMM?
OH, THIS?
JUST A SPECIMEN I BORROWED FROM A GRAVE BACK THERE.
SOME-ONE YOU KNOW?

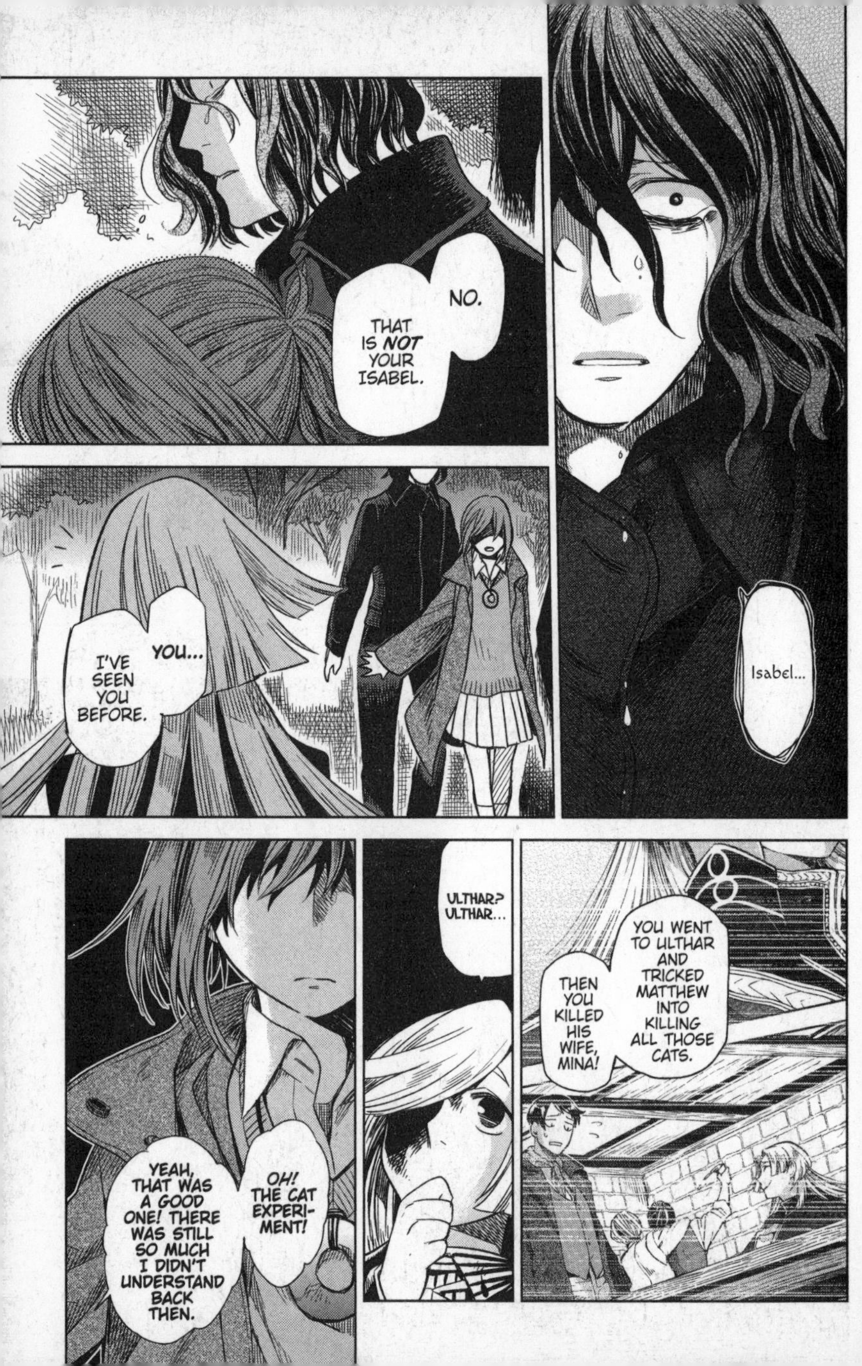
Isabel...
NO.
THAT IS *NOT* YOUR ISABEL.
YOU...
I'VE SEEN YOU BEFORE.
YOU WENT TO ULTHAR AND TRICKED MATTHEW INTO KILLING ALL THOSE CATS.
THEN YOU KILLED HIS WIFE, MINA!
ULTHAR? ULTHAR...
OH! THE CAT EXPERIMENT!
YEAH, THAT WAS A GOOD ONE! THERE WAS STILL SO MUCH I DIDN'T UNDERSTAND BACK THEN.

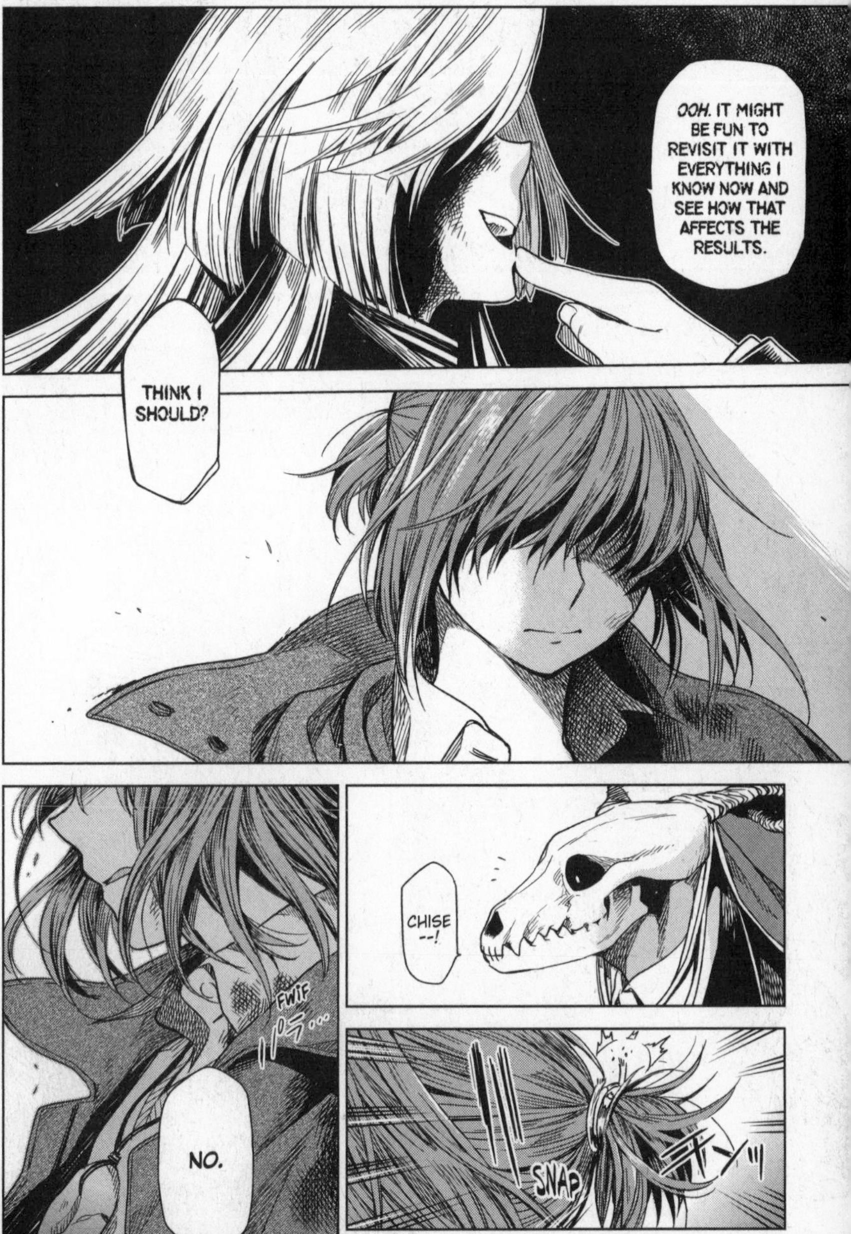
OOH. IT MIGHT BE FUN TO REVISIT IT WITH EVERYTHING I KNOW NOW AND SEE HOW THAT AFFECTS THE RESULTS.
THINK I SHOULD?
CHISE --!
SNAP
FWIF
NO.

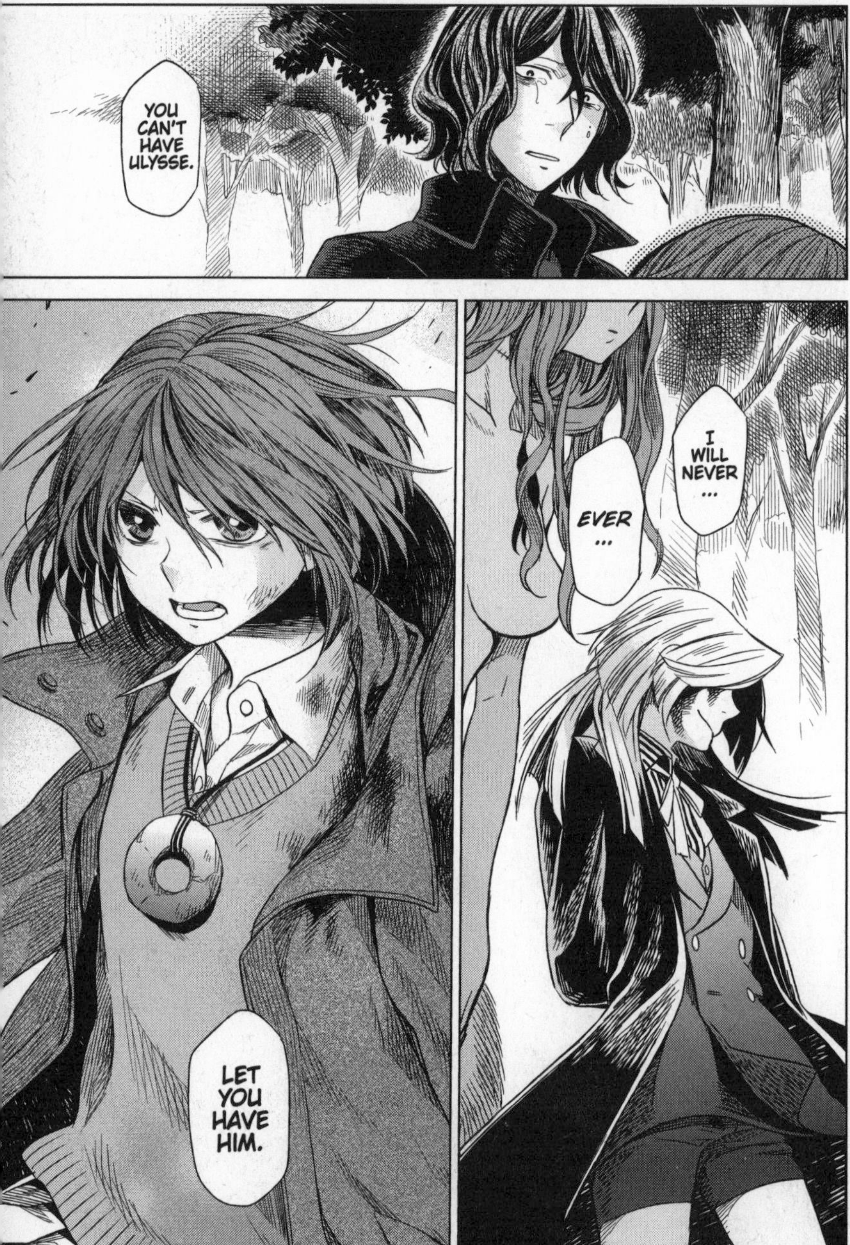
YOU CAN'T HAVE ULYSSE.
I WILL NEVER ...
EVER ...
LET YOU HAVE HIM.

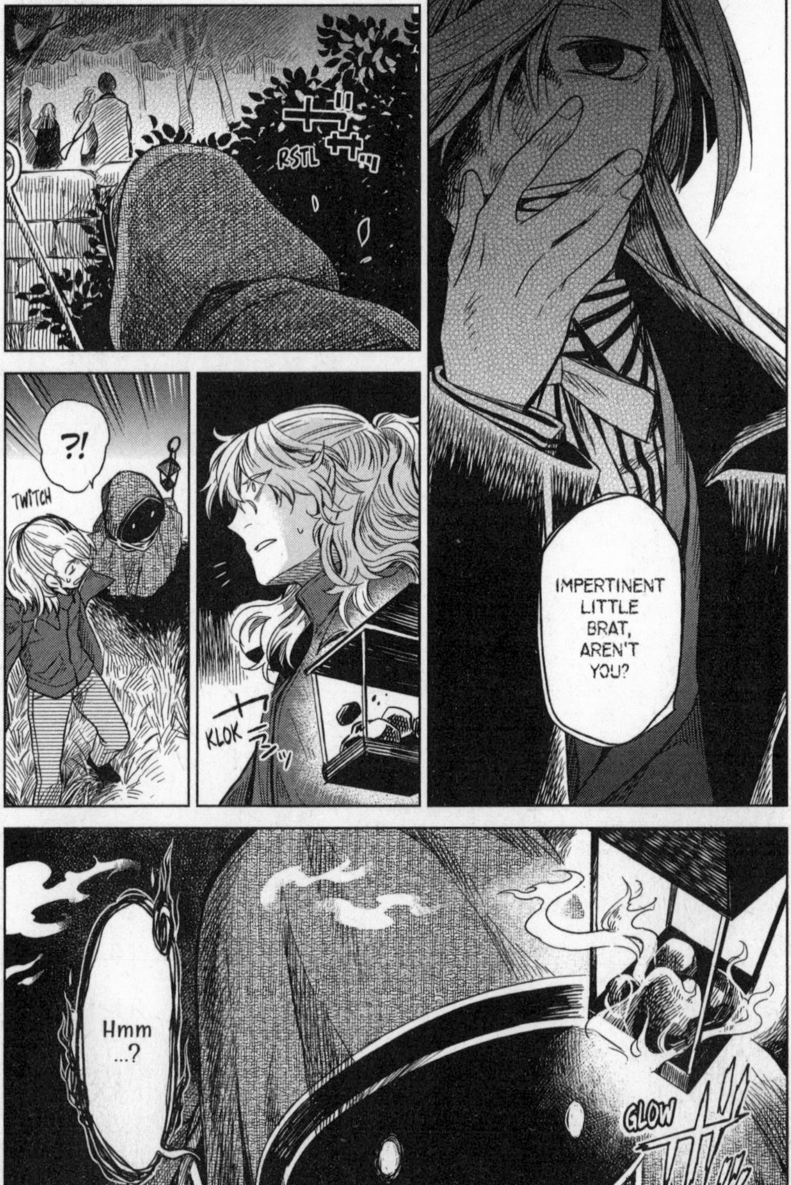
IMPERTINENT LITTLE BRAT, AREN'T YOU?
RSTL
KLOK
?!
TWITCH
GLOW
Hmm ...?

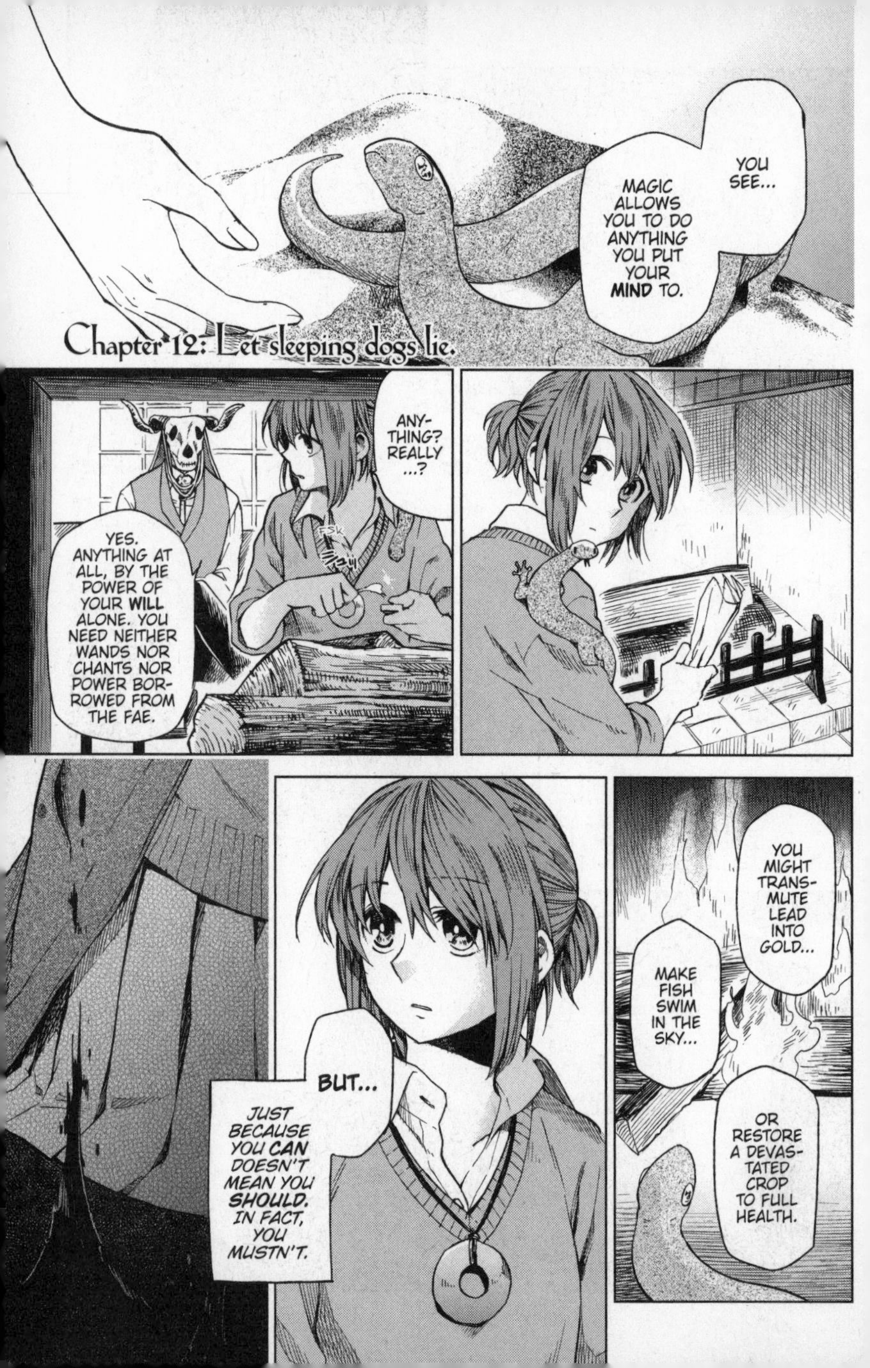
YOU SEE...
MAGIC ALLOWS YOU TO DO ANYTHING YOU PUT YOUR MIND TO.
Chapter 12: Let sleeping dogs lie.
ANY-THING? REALLY ...?
FSK
YES. ANYTHING AT ALL, BY THE POWER OF YOUR WILL ALONE. YOU NEED NEITHER WANDS NOR CHANTS NOR POWER BOR-ROWED FROM THE FAE.
YOU MIGHT TRANS-MUTE LEAD INTO GOLD...
MAKE FISH SWIM IN THE SKY...
OR RESTORE A DEVAS-TATED CROP TO FULL HEALTH.
BUT...
JUST BECAUSE YOU CAN DOESN'T MEAN YOU SHOULD. IN FACT, YOU MUSTN'T.

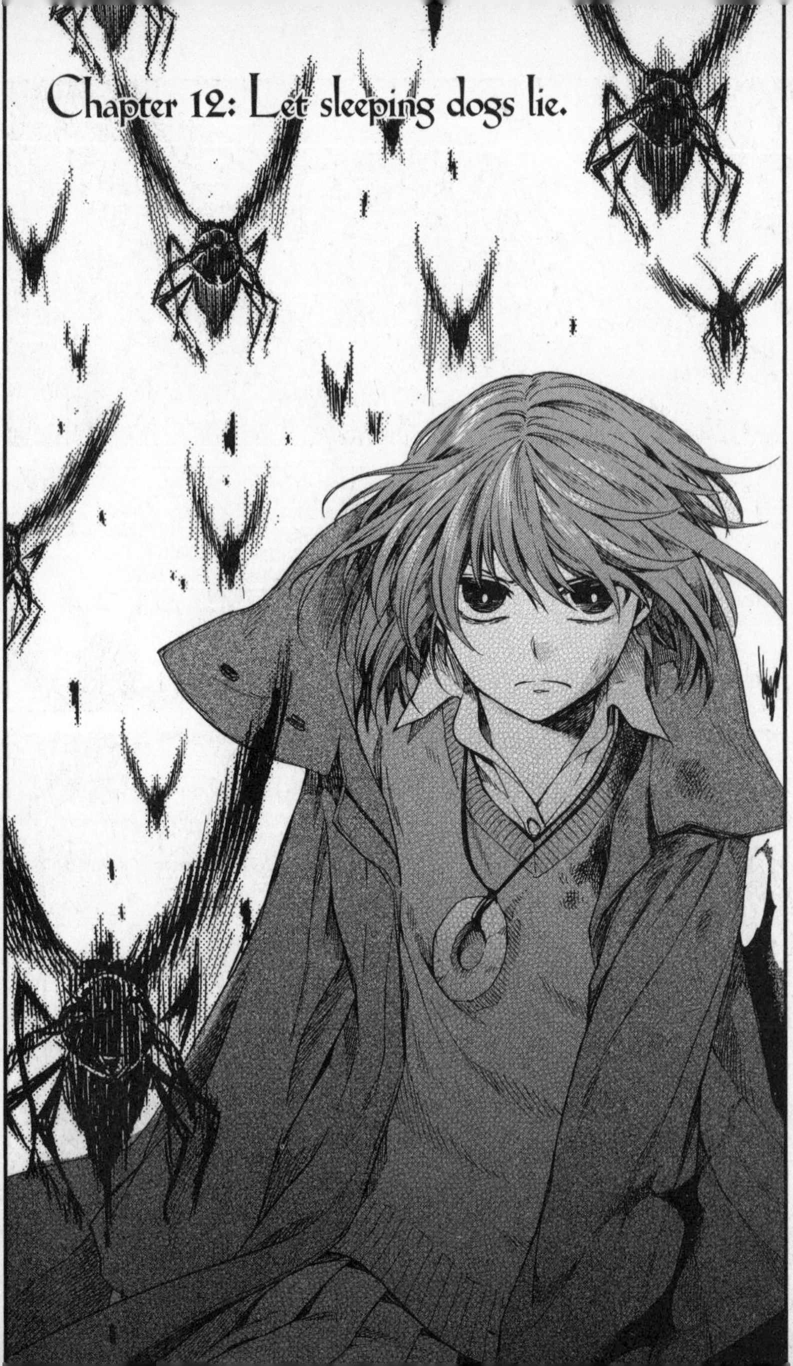
Chapter 12: Let sleeping dogs lie.

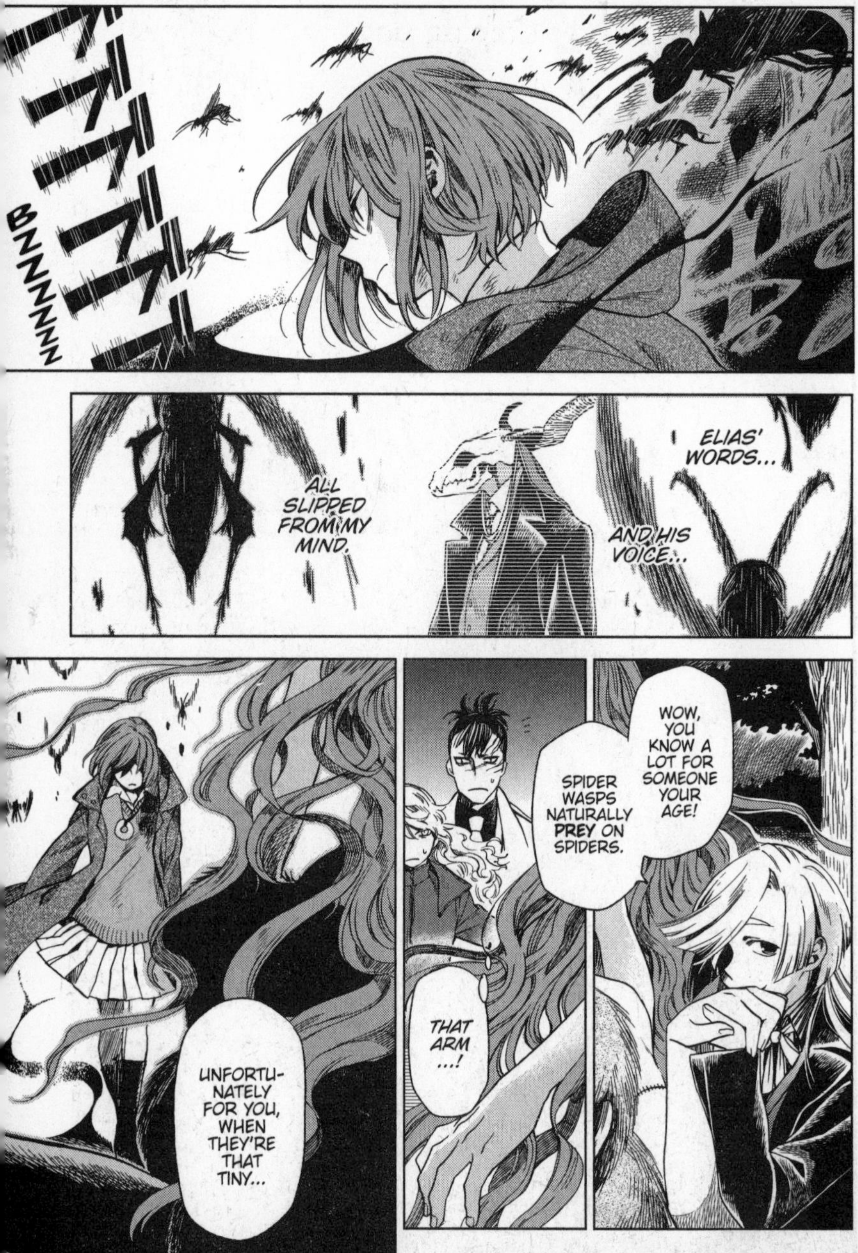
BZZZZZZ
ELIAS' WORDS...
AND HIS VOICE...
ALL SLIPPED FROM MY MIND.
WOW, YOU KNOW A LOT FOR SOMEONE YOUR AGE!
SPIDER WASPS NATURALLY PREY ON SPIDERS.
THAT ARM ...!
UNFORTUNATELY FOR YOU, WHEN THEY'RE THAT TINY...

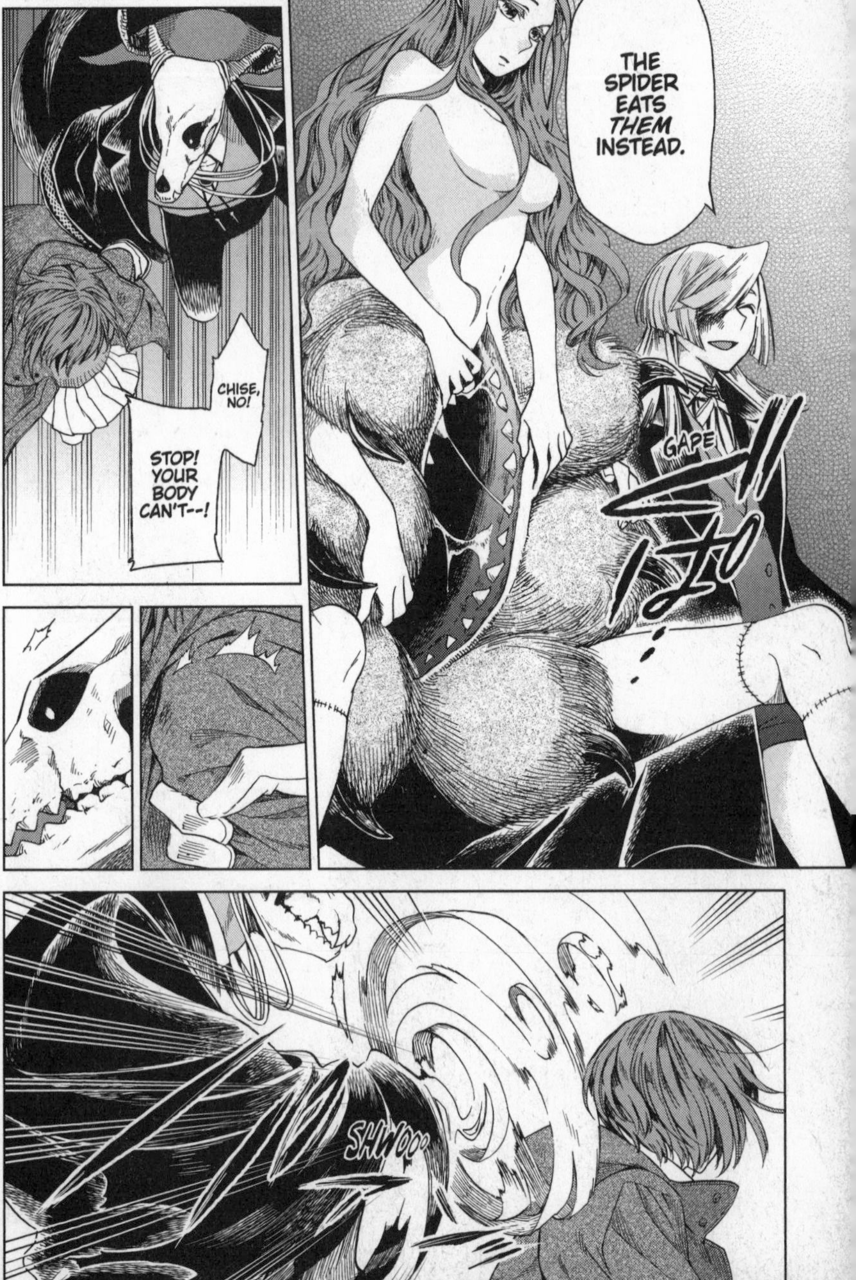
THE SPIDER EATS THEM INSTEAD.
GAPE
CHISE, NO!
STOP! YOUR BODY CAN'T--!
SHWOO

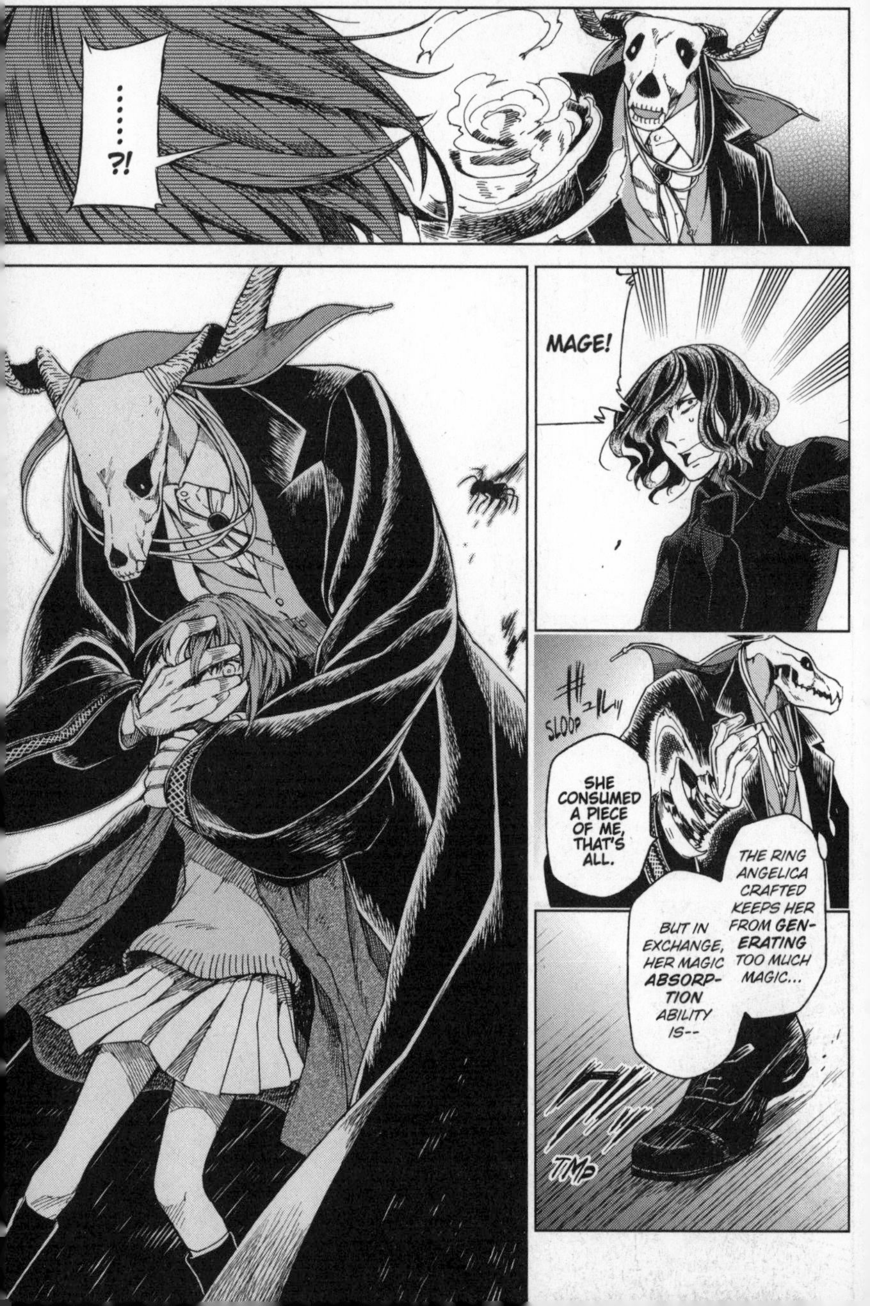
......?!
MAGE!
SLOOP
SHE CONSUMED A PIECE OF ME, THAT'S ALL.
THE RING ANGELICA CRAFTED KEEPS HER FROM GENERATING TOO MUCH MAGIC...
BUT IN EXCHANGE, HER MAGIC ABSORPTION ABILITY IS--
TMP

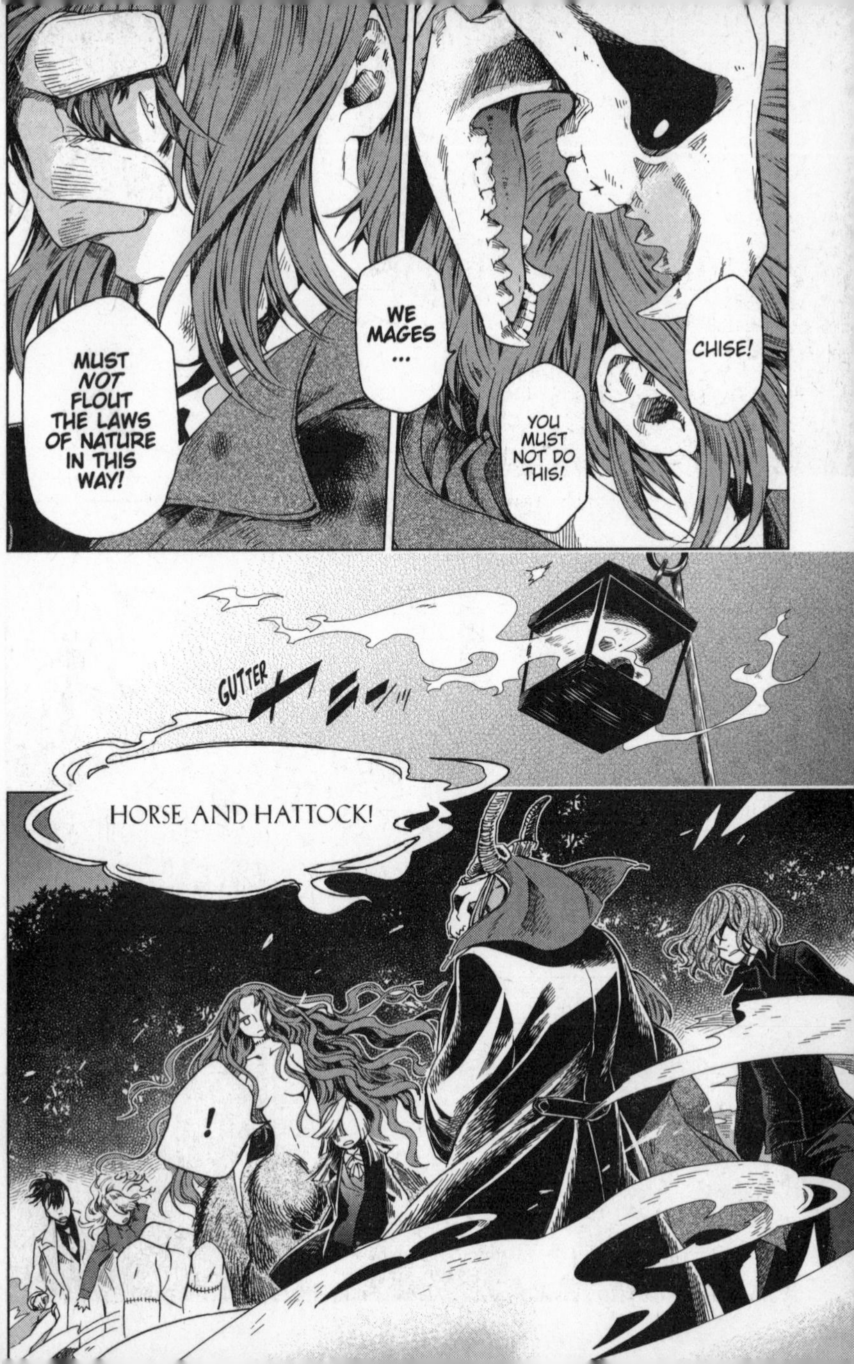
CHISE!
YOU MUST NOT DO THIS!
WE MAGES...
MUST NOT FLOUT THE LAWS OF NATURE IN THIS WAY!
GUTTER
HORSE AND HATTOCK!
!

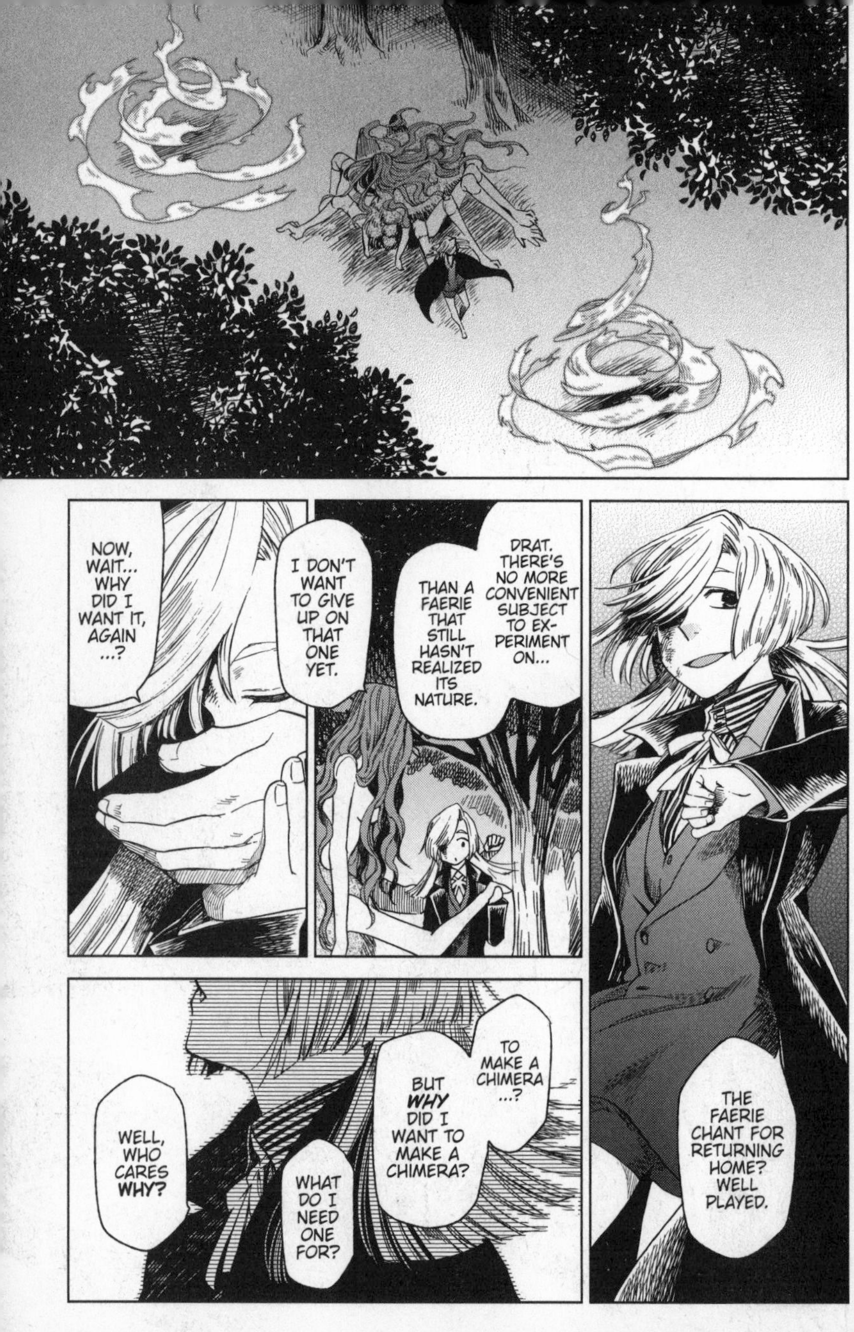
THE FAERIE CHANT FOR RETURNING HOME? WELL PLAYED.
DRAT. THERE'S NO MORE CONVENIENT SUBJECT TO EX-PERIMENT ON...
THAN A FAERIE THAT STILL HASN'T REALIZED ITS NATURE.
I DON'T WANT TO GIVE UP ON THAT ONE YET.
NOW, WAIT... WHY DID I WANT IT, AGAIN ...?
TO MAKE A CHIMERA ...?
BUT ***WHY*** DID I WANT TO MAKE A CHIMERA?
WHAT DO I NEED ONE FOR?
WELL, WHO CARES **WHY?**

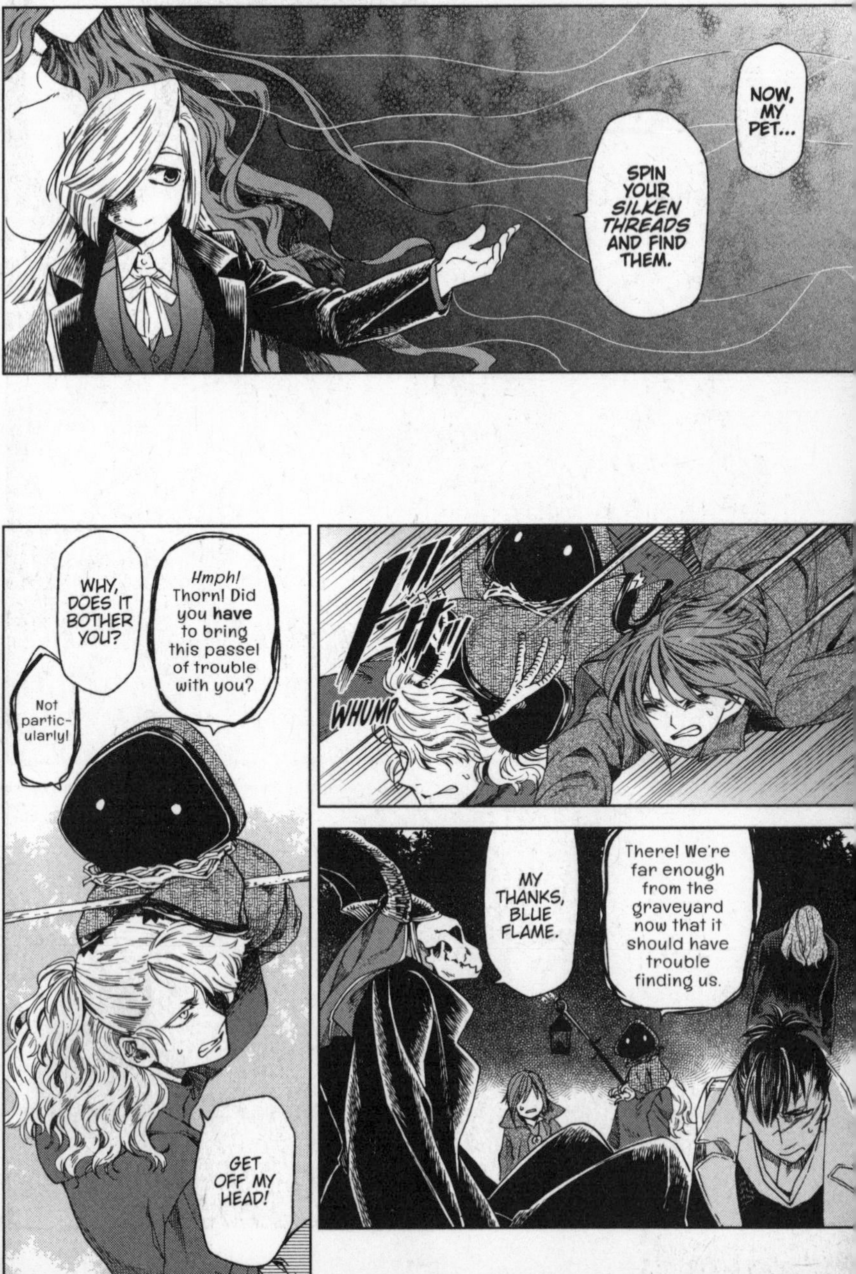
NOW, MY PET...
SPIN YOUR SILKEN THREADS AND FIND THEM.
WHUMP
There! We're far enough from the graveyard now that it should have trouble finding us.
MY THANKS, BLUE FLAME.
WHY, DOES IT BOTHER YOU?
Hmph! Thorn! Did you **have** to bring this passel of trouble with you?
Not partic-ularly!
GET OFF MY HEAD!

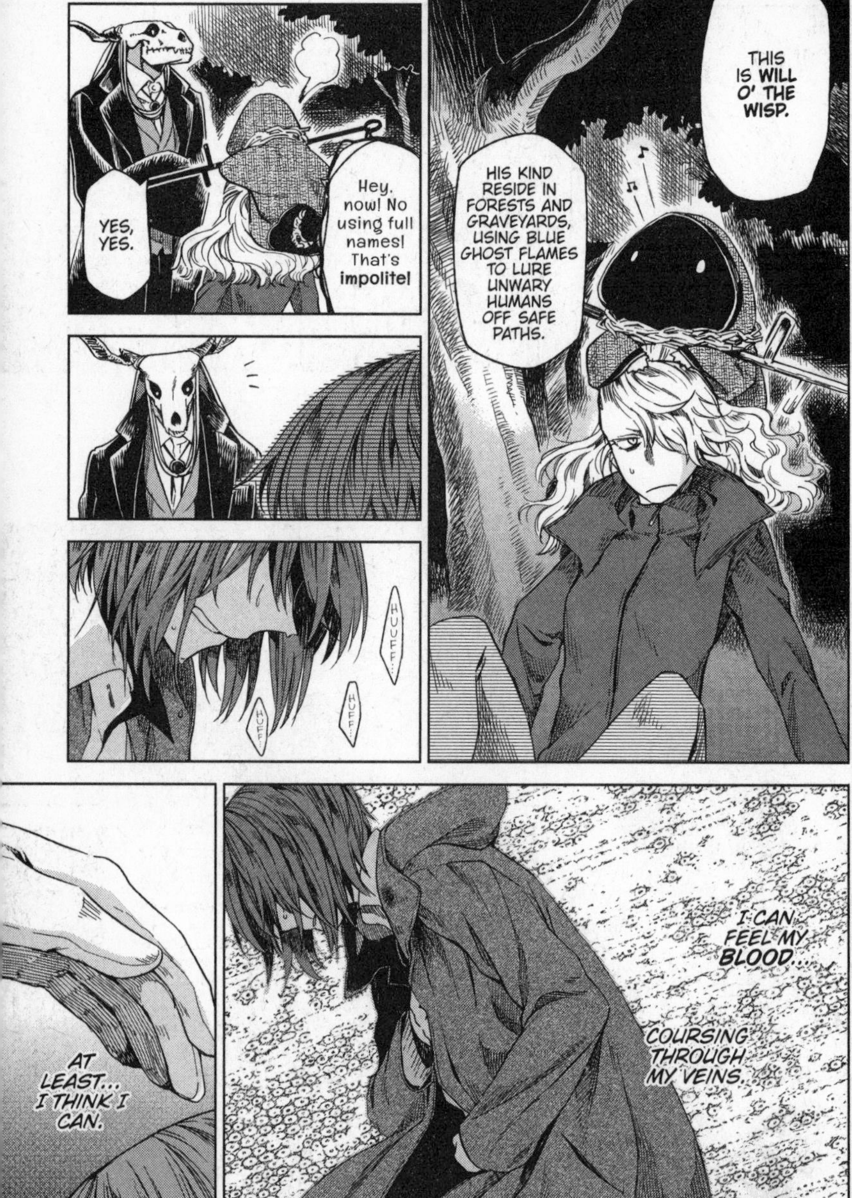
THIS IS WILL O' THE WISP.
HIS KIND RESIDE IN FORESTS AND GRAVEYARDS, USING BLUE GHOST FLAMES TO LURE UNWARY HUMANS OFF SAFE PATHS.
Hey, now! No using full names! That's impolite!
YES, YES.
HUUFF...
HUFF...
I CAN FEEL MY BLOOD...
COURSING THROUGH MY VEINS.
AT LEAST... I THINK I CAN.

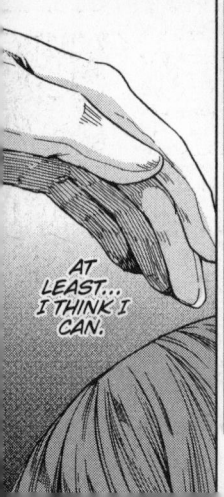

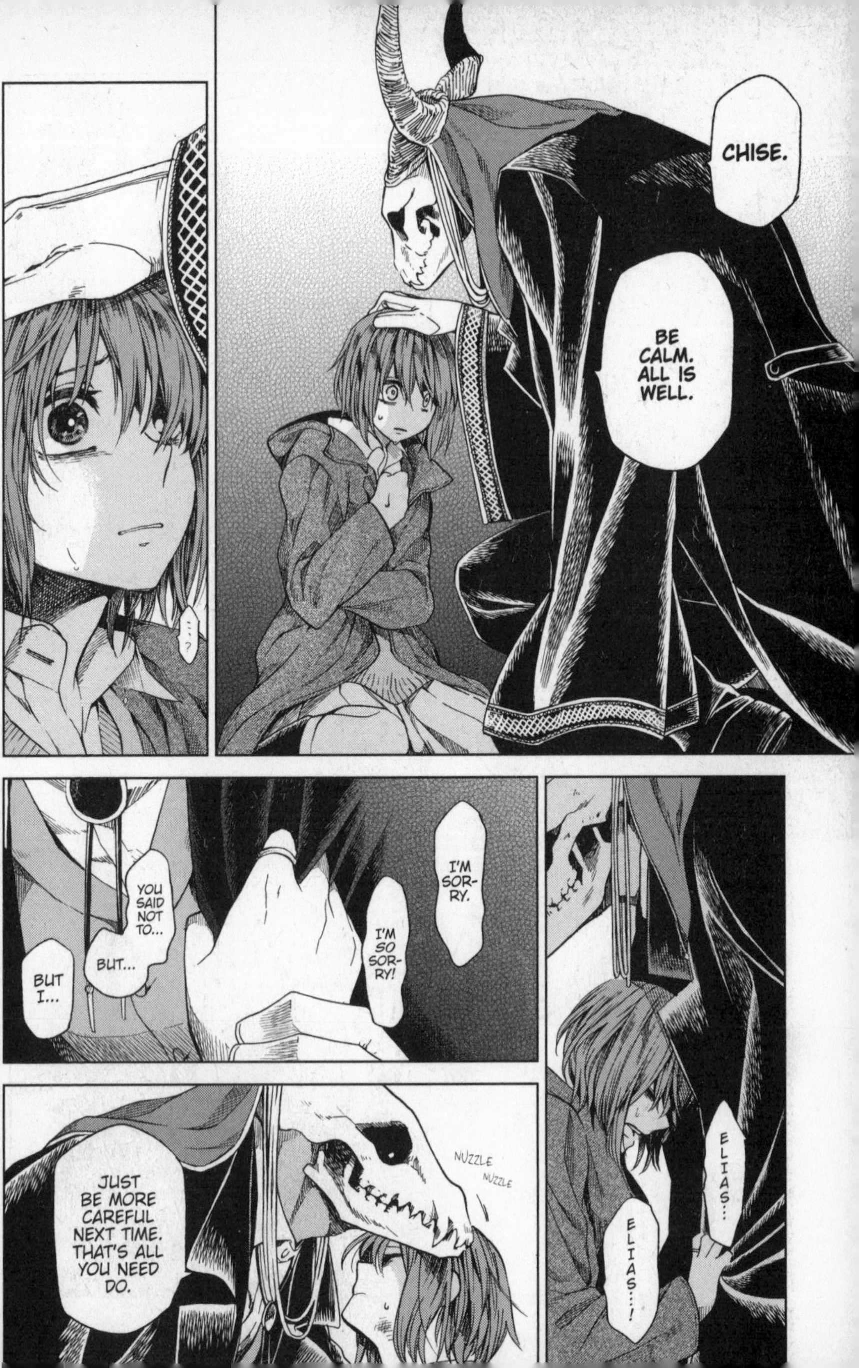
CHISE.
BE CALM. ALL IS WELL.
...?
ELIAS...
ELIAS...!
I'M SORRY.
I'M SO SORRY!
YOU SAID NOT TO...
BUT...
BUT I...
NUZZLE NUZZLE
JUST BE MORE CAREFUL NEXT TIME. THAT'S ALL YOU NEED DO.

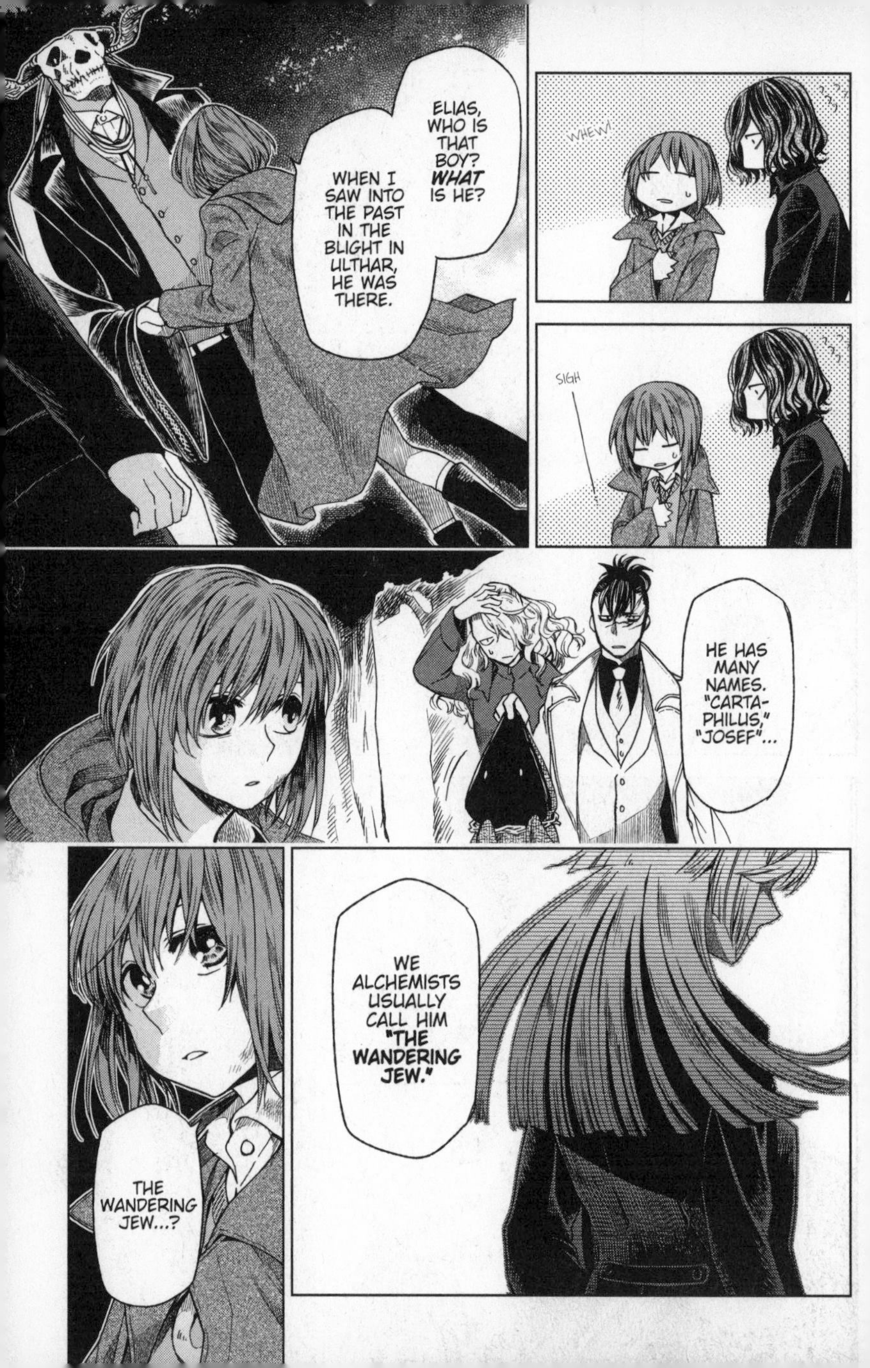
WHEW!
SIGH
ELIAS, WHO IS THAT BOY? *WHAT* IS HE?
WHEN I SAW INTO THE PAST IN THE BLIGHT IN ULTHAR, HE WAS THERE.
HE HAS MANY NAMES. "CARTA-PHILUS," "JOSEF"...
WE ALCHEMISTS USUALLY CALL HIM **"THE WANDERING JEW."**
THE WANDERING JEW...?

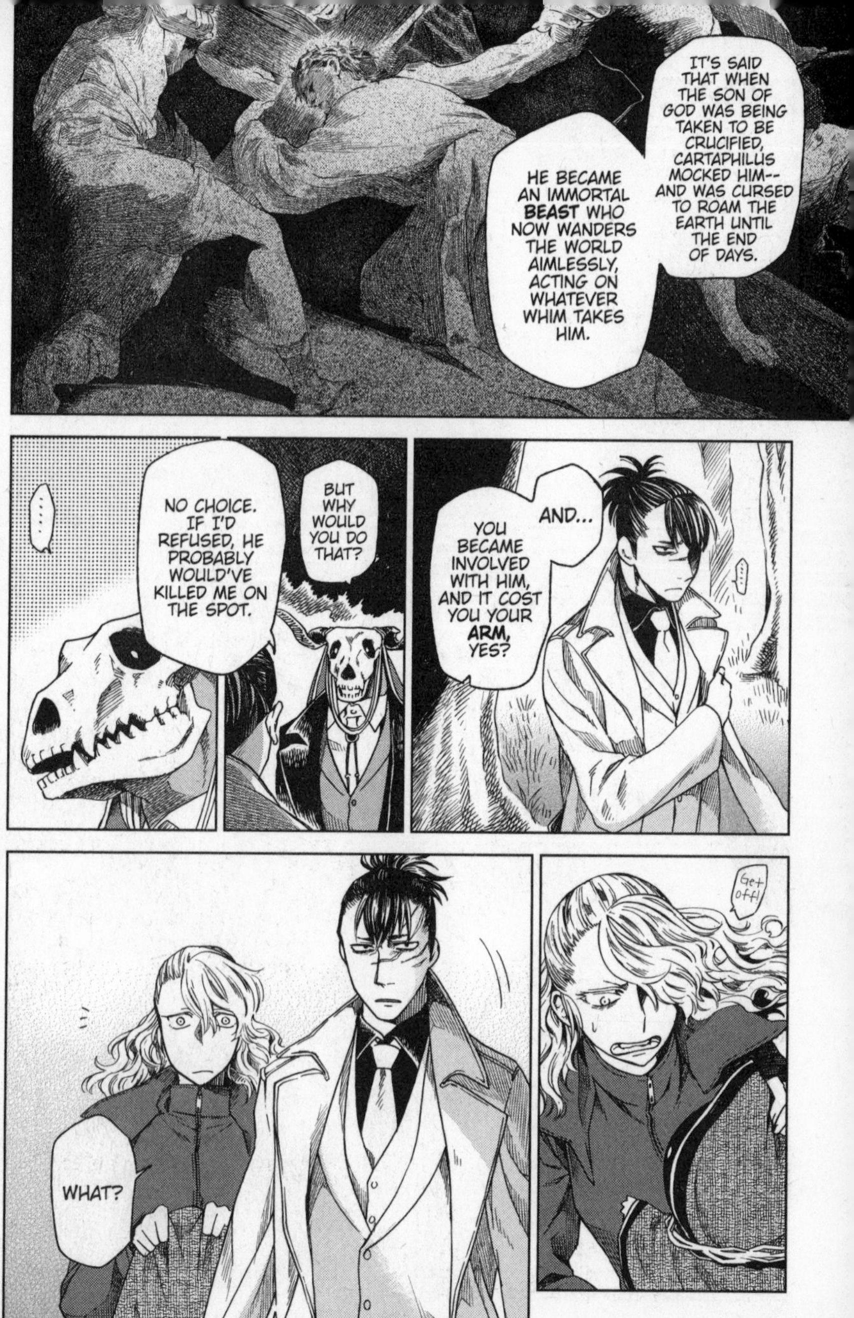
IT'S SAID THAT WHEN THE SON OF GOD WAS BEING TAKEN TO BE CRUCIFIED, CARTAPHILUS MOCKED HIM-- AND WAS CURSED TO ROAM THE EARTH UNTIL THE END OF DAYS.
HE BECAME AN IMMORTAL **BEAST** WHO NOW WANDERS THE WORLD AIMLESSLY, ACTING ON WHATEVER WHIM TAKES HIM.
AND...
...
YOU BECAME INVOLVED WITH HIM, AND IT COST YOU YOUR **ARM,** YES?
BUT WHY WOULD YOU DO THAT?
NO CHOICE. IF I'D REFUSED, HE PROBABLY WOULD'VE KILLED ME ON THE SPOT.
......
Get off!
WHAT?

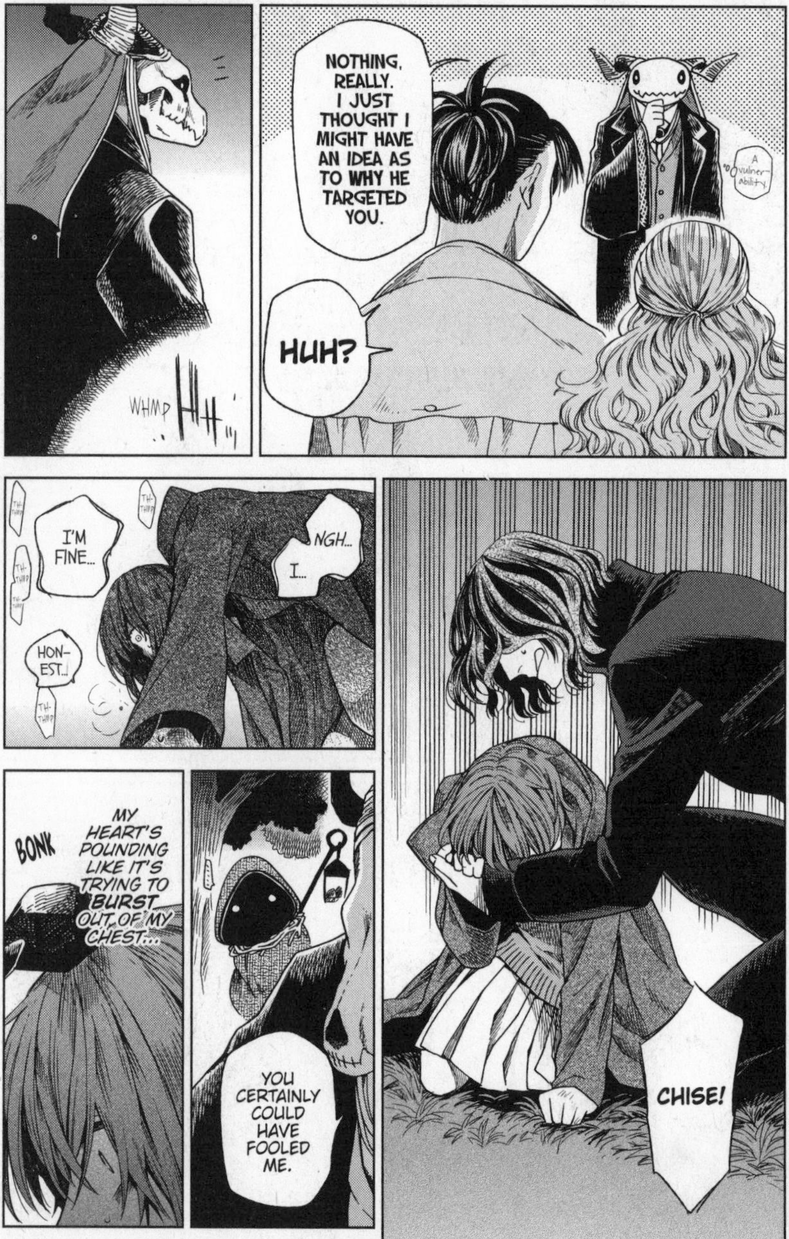
A vulner-ability.
NOTHING, REALLY. I JUST THOUGHT I MIGHT HAVE AN IDEA AS TO WHY HE TARGETED YOU.
HUH?
WHMP
CHISE!
NGH... I...
TH-THMP
I'M FINE...
TH-THMP
TH-THMP
HON-EST...
TH-THMP
YOU CERTAINLY COULD HAVE FOOLED ME.
BONK
MY HEART'S POUNDING LIKE IT'S TRYING TO BURST OUT OF MY CHEST...

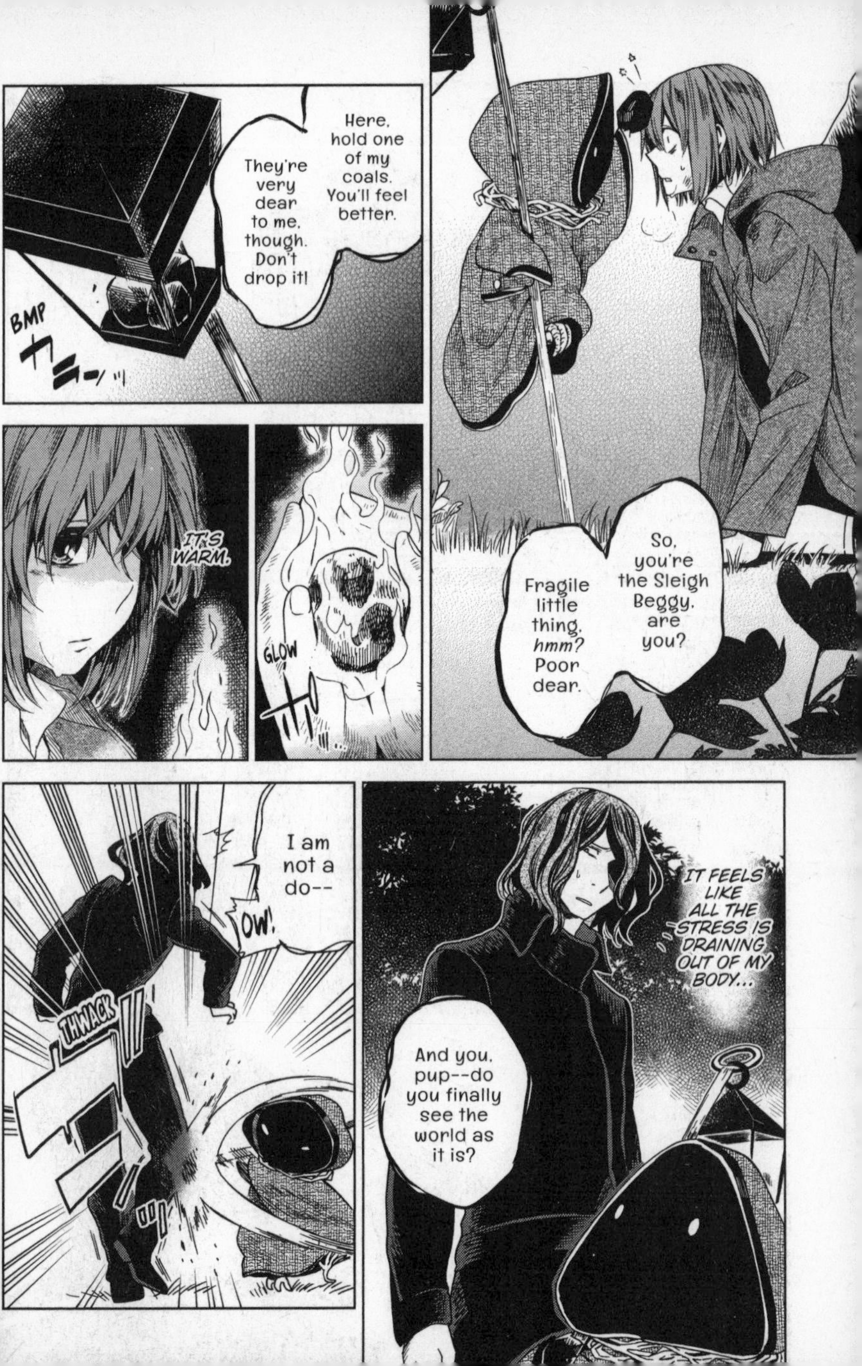
So, you're the Sleigh Beggy, are you?
Fragile little thing, *hmm?* Poor dear.
Here, hold one of my coals. You'll feel better.
They're very dear to me, though. Don't drop it!
BMP
GLOW
IT'S WARM.
IT FEELS LIKE ALL THE STRESS IS DRAINING OUT OF MY BODY...
And you, pup--do you finally see the world as it is?
I am not a do--
OW!
THWACK

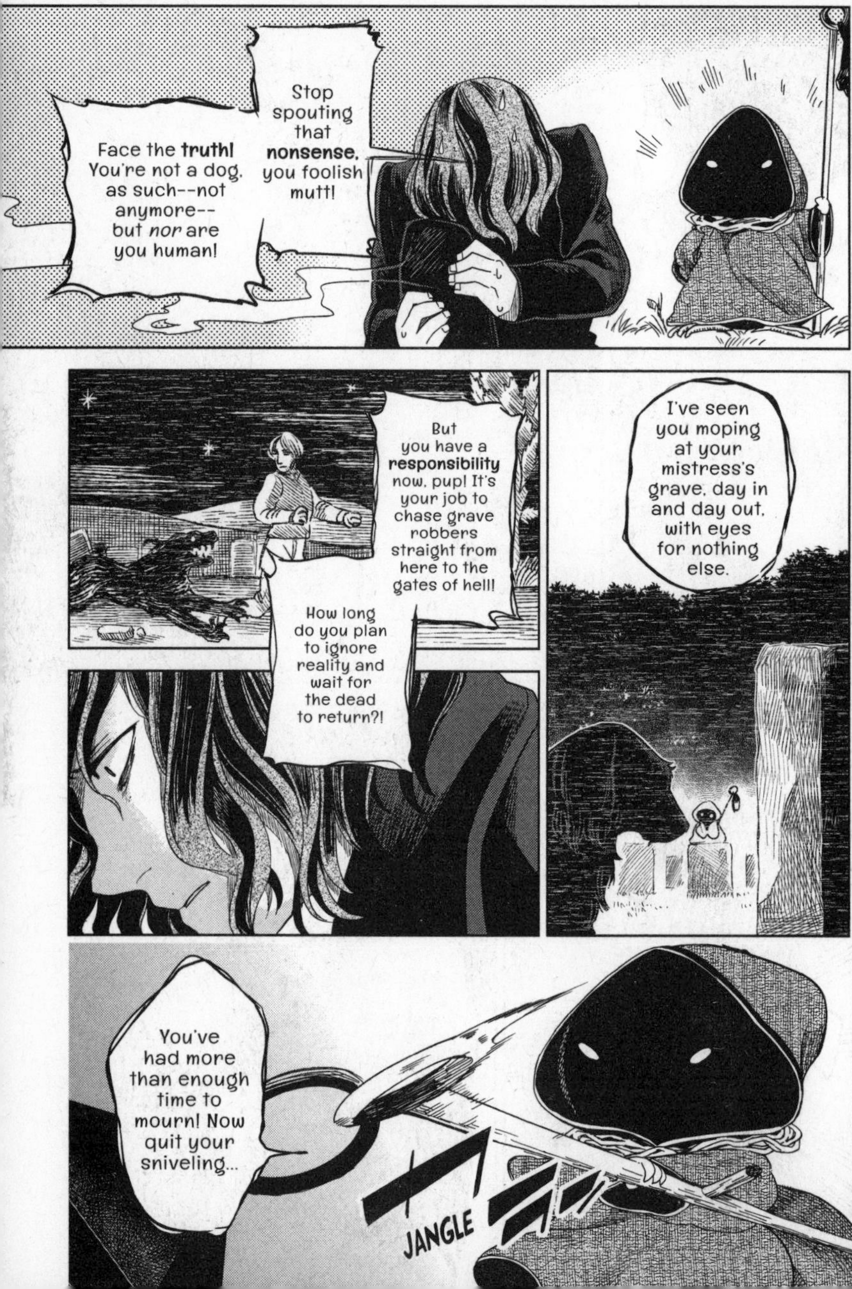
Stop spouting that **nonsense,** you foolish mutt!
Face the **truth!** You're not a dog, as such--not anymore--but *nor* are you human!
I've seen you moping at your mistress's grave, day in and day out, with eyes for nothing else.
But you have a **responsibility** now, pup! It's your job to chase grave robbers straight from here to the gates of hell!
How long do you plan to ignore reality and wait for the dead to return?!
You've had more than enough time to mourn! Now quit your sniveling...
JANGLE

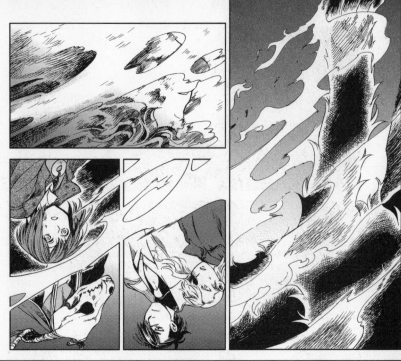

Church Grim!

And return to the form you were given to do your duty...

BWOOF

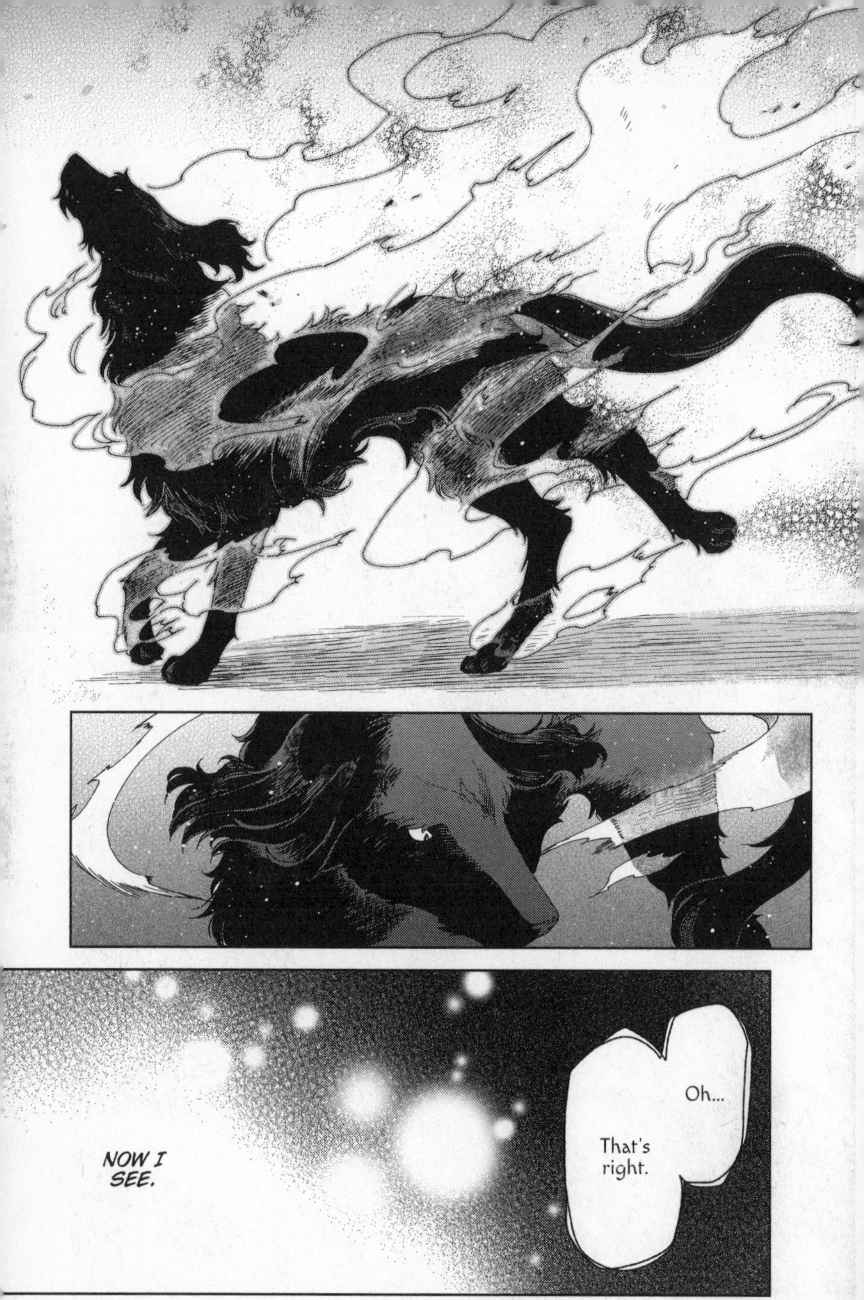
Oh...
That's right.
NOW I SEE.

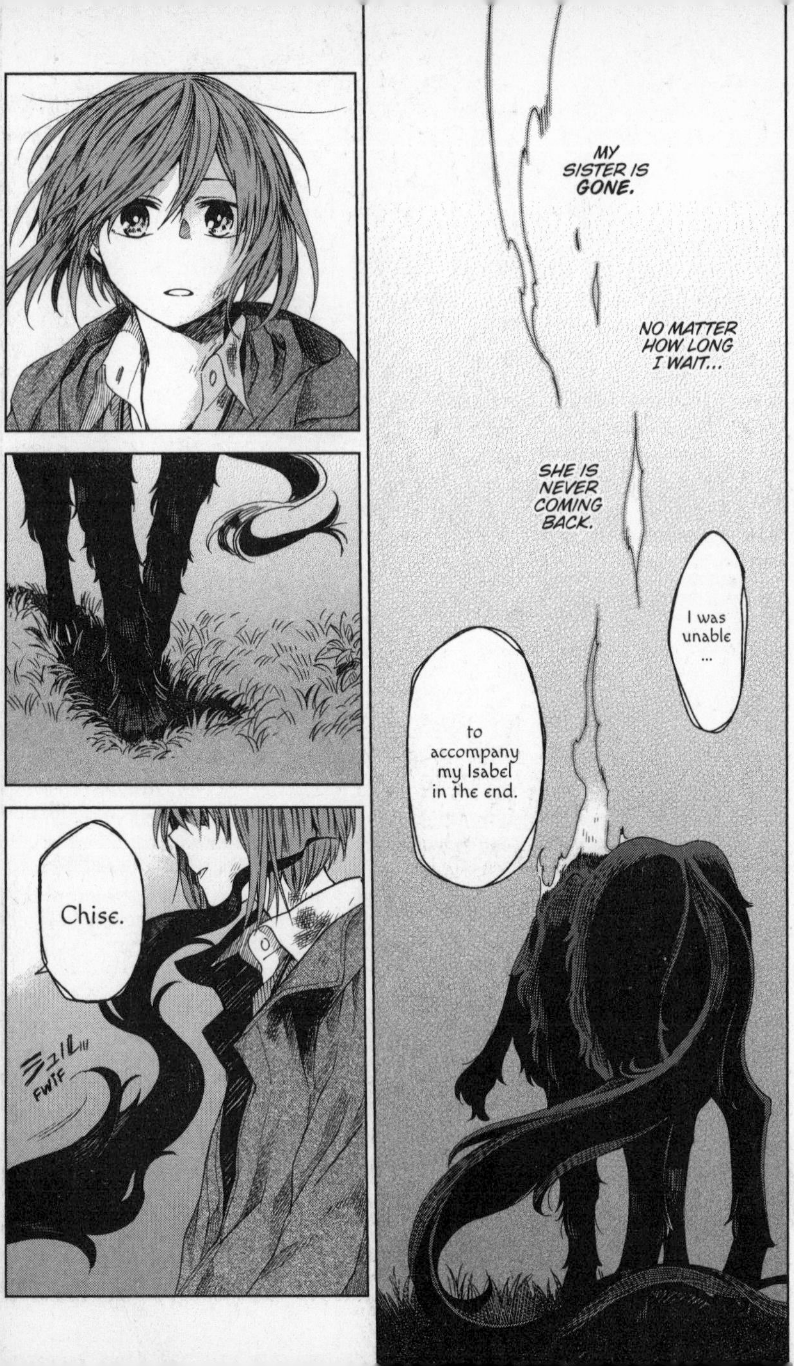
MY SISTER IS GONE.
NO MATTER HOW LONG I WAIT...
SHE IS NEVER COMING BACK.
I was unable ...
to accompany my Isabel in the end.
Chise.
ミュル FWIF

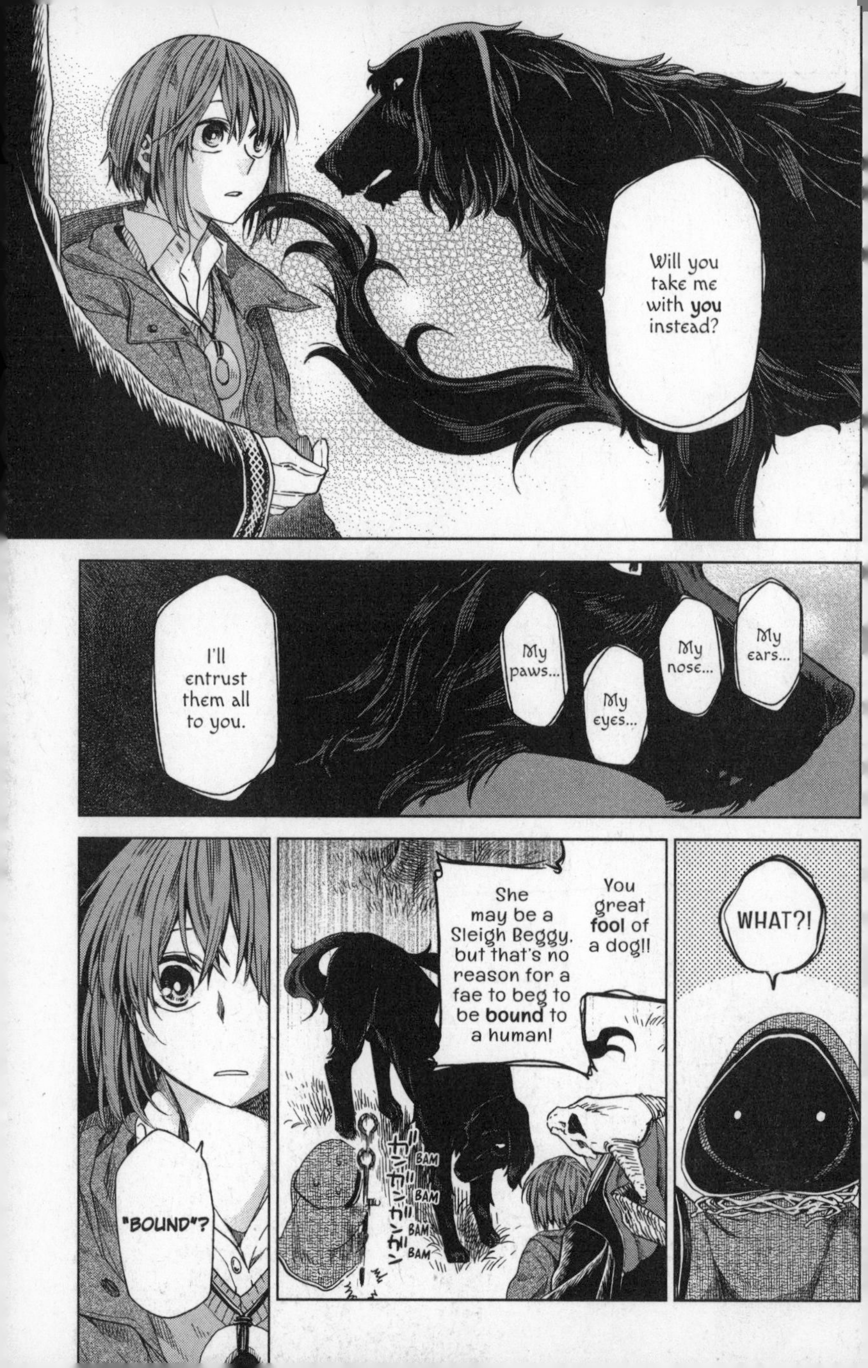
Will you take me with **you** instead?
My ears...
My nose...
My eyes...
My paws...
I'll entrust them all to you.
WHAT?!
You great **fool** of a dog!!
She may be a Sleigh Beggy, but that's no reason for a fae to beg to be **bound** to a human!
BAM BAM BAM BAM
"BOUND"?

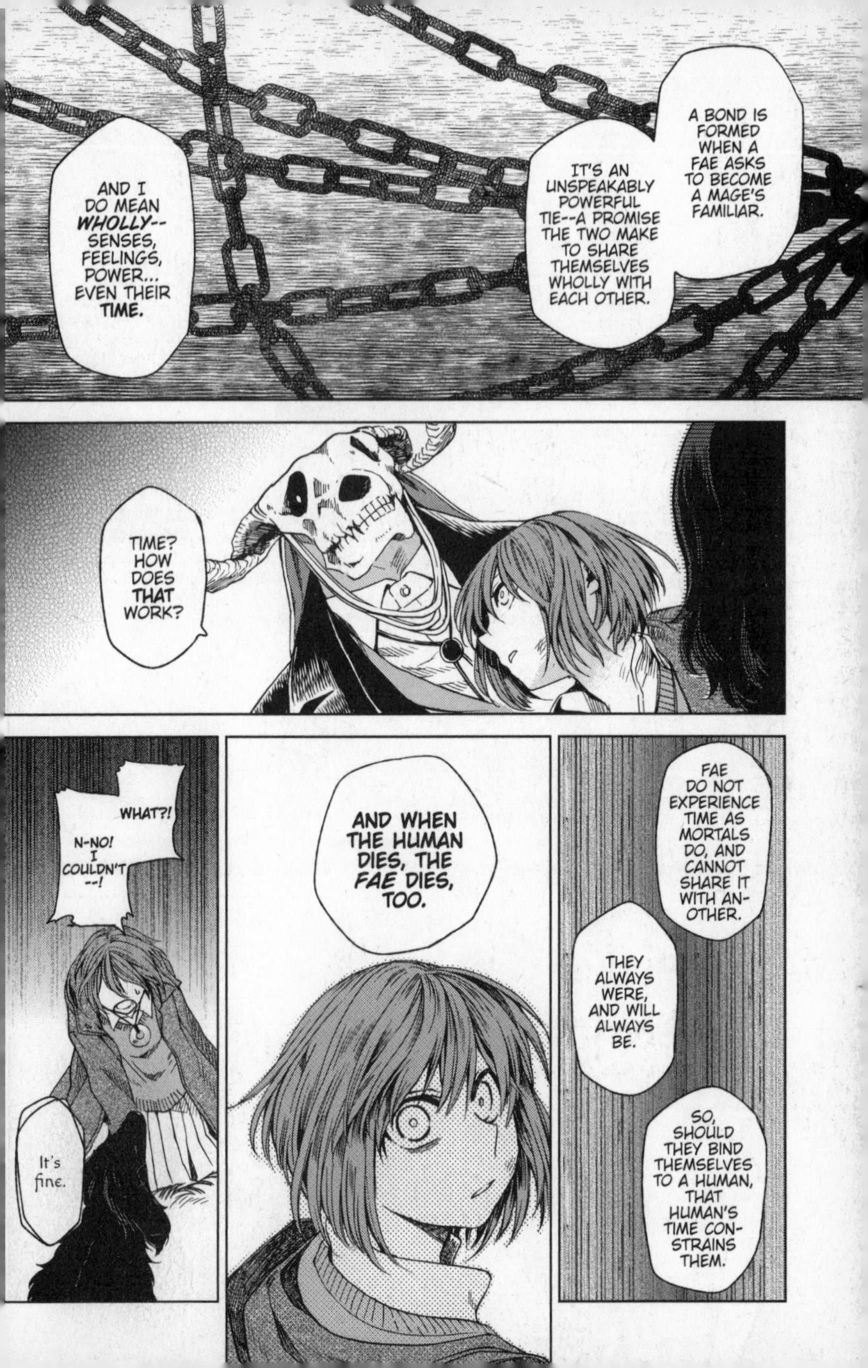
A BOND IS FORMED WHEN A FAE ASKS TO BECOME A MAGE'S FAMILIAR.
IT'S AN UNSPEAKABLY POWERFUL TIE--A PROMISE THE TWO MAKE TO SHARE THEMSELVES WHOLLY WITH EACH OTHER.
AND I DO MEAN *WHOLLY*--SENSES, FEELINGS, POWER... EVEN THEIR **TIME.**
TIME? HOW DOES **THAT** WORK?
FAE DO NOT EXPERIENCE TIME AS MORTALS DO, AND CANNOT SHARE IT WITH AN-OTHER.
THEY ALWAYS WERE, AND WILL ALWAYS BE.
SO, SHOULD THEY BIND THEMSELVES TO A HUMAN, THAT HUMAN'S TIME CON-STRAINS THEM.
AND WHEN THE HUMAN DIES, THE *FAE* DIES, TOO.
WHAT?!
N-NO! I COULDN'T --!
It's fine.

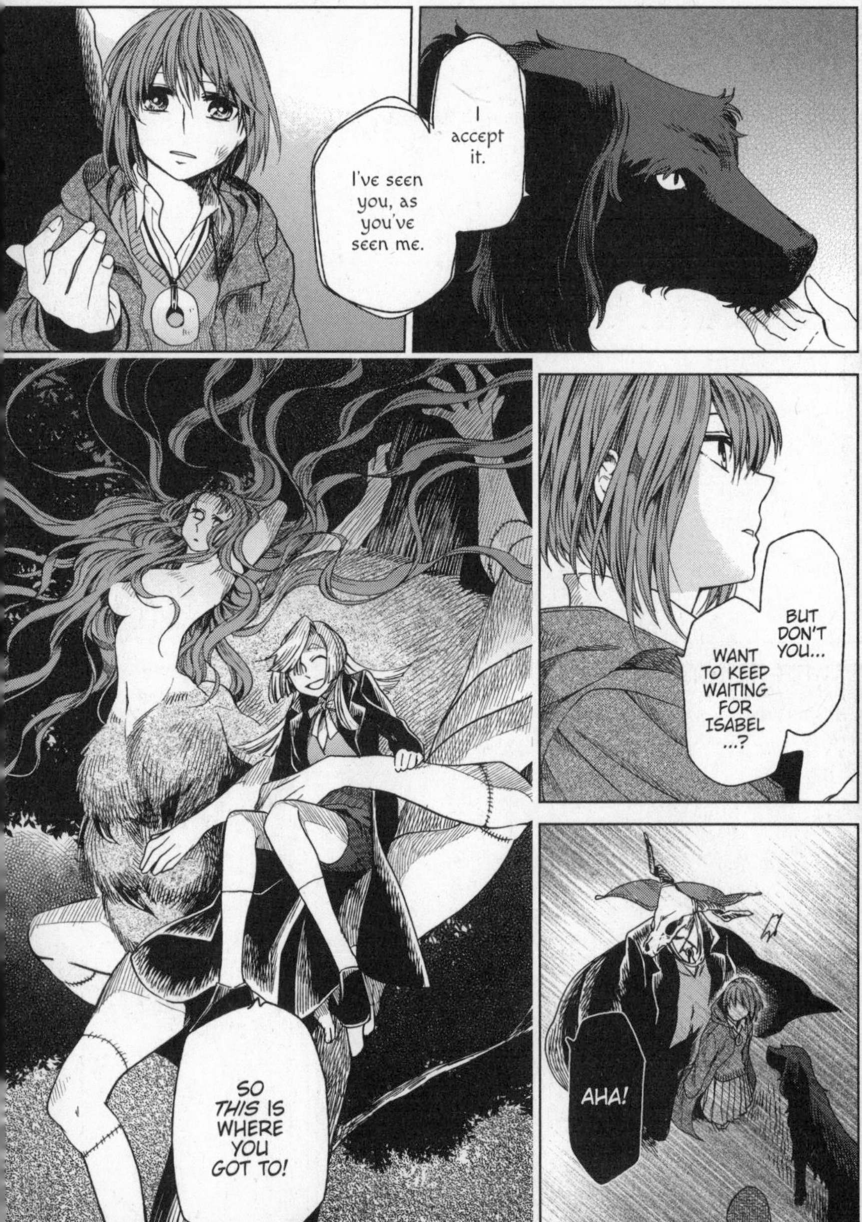
I accept it.
I've seen you, as you've seen me.
BUT DON'T YOU... WANT TO KEEP WAITING FOR ISABEL ...?
AHA!
SO THIS IS WHERE YOU GOT TO!

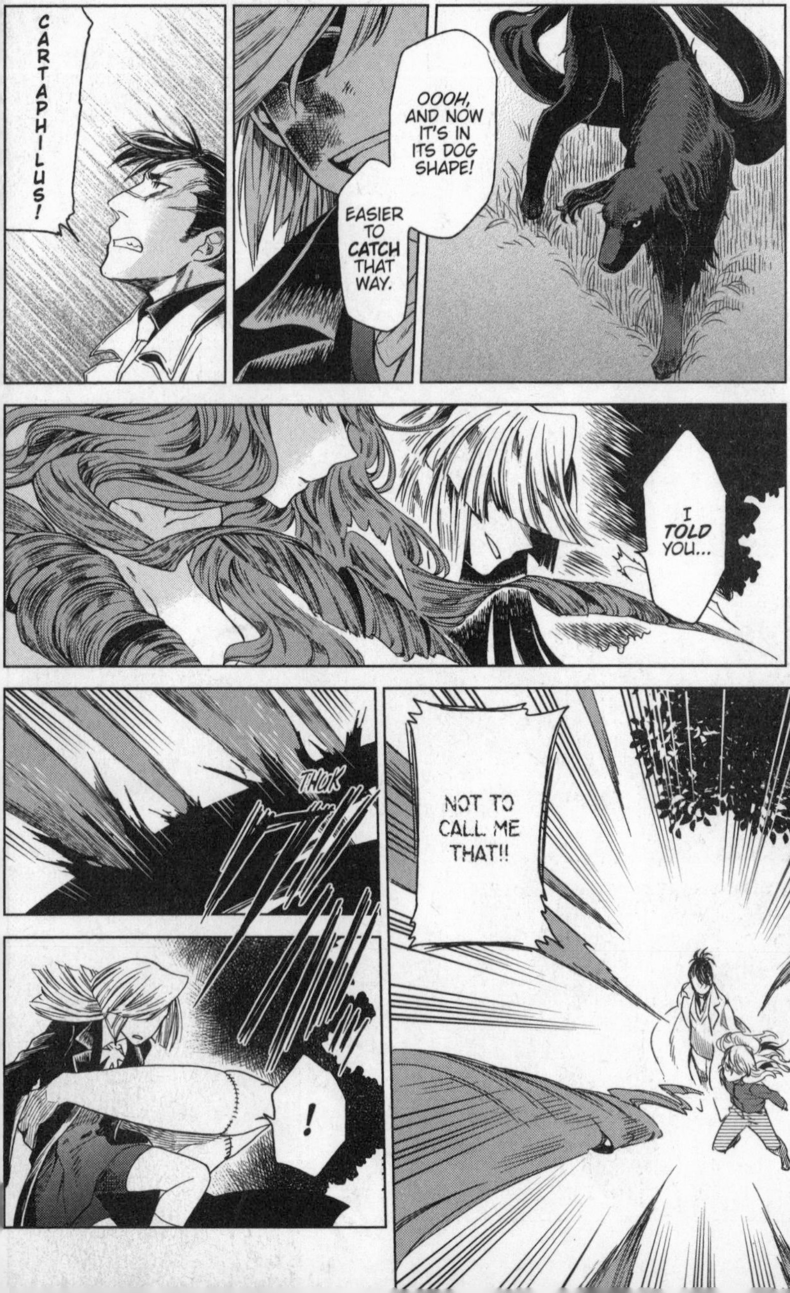
OOOH, AND NOW IT'S IN ITS DOG SHAPE!
EASIER TO CATCH THAT WAY.
CARTAPHILUS!
I TOLD YOU...
NOT TO CALL ME THAT!!
THUK
!

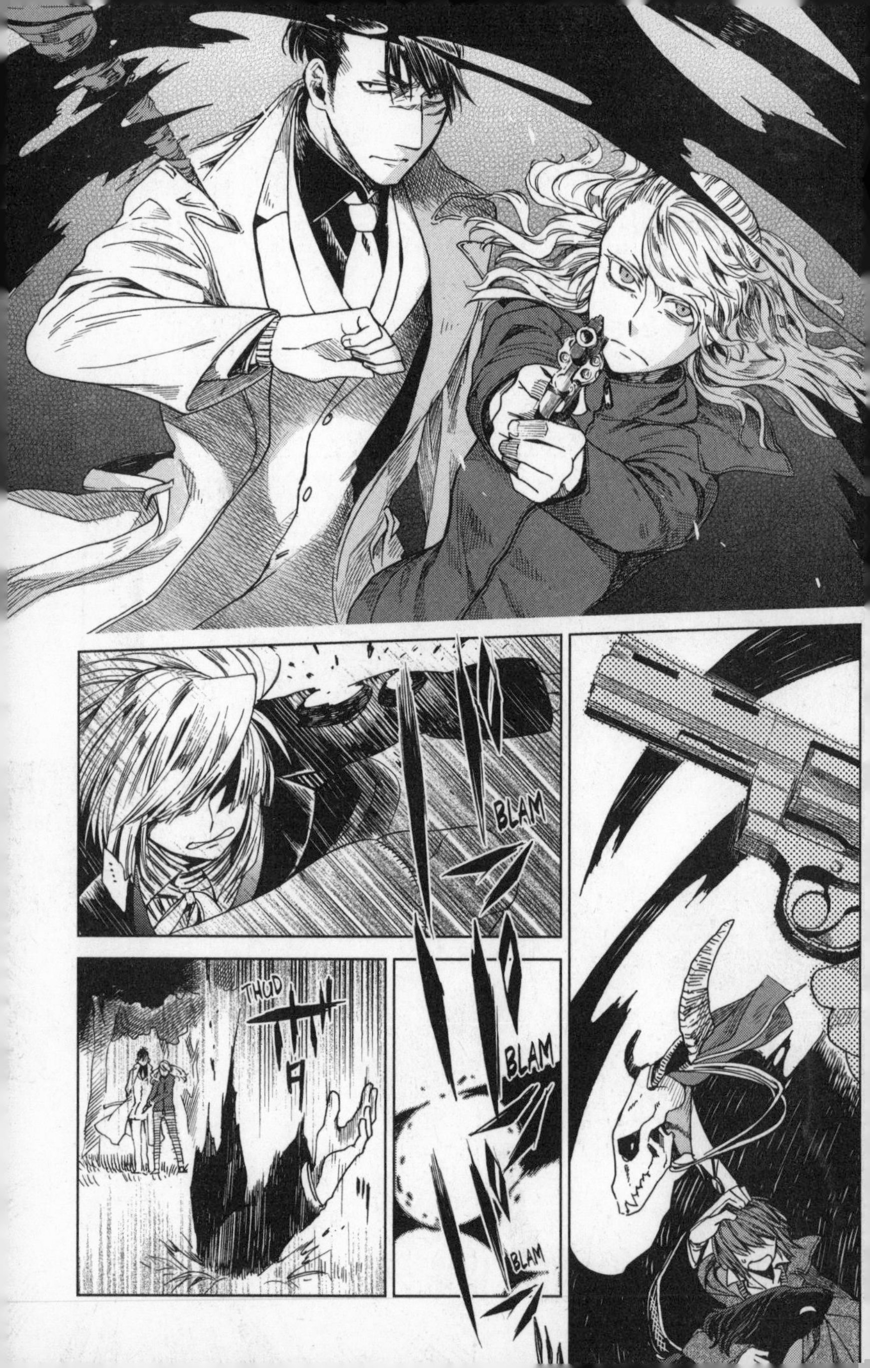
BLAM
BLAM
BLAM
THUD

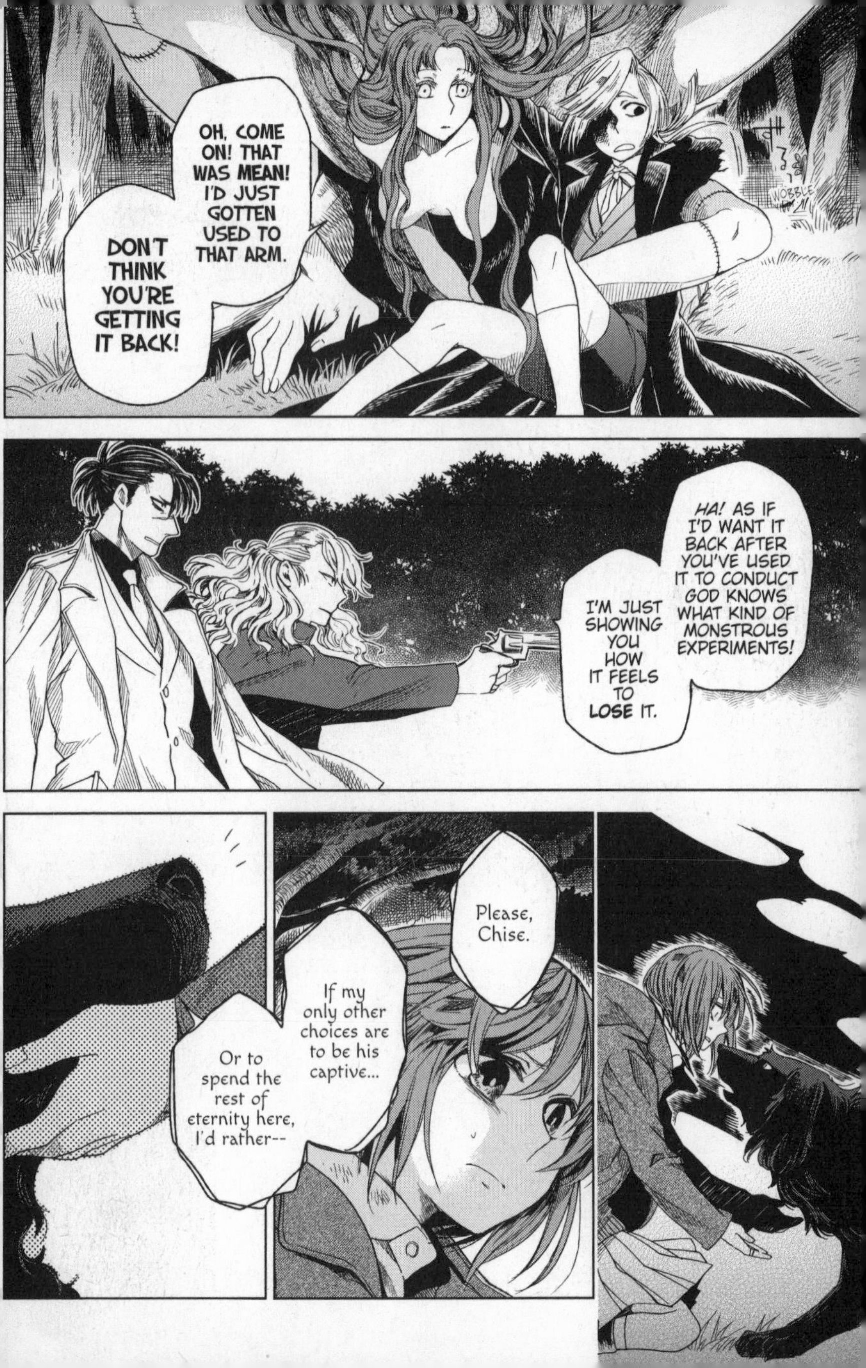
WOBBLE
OH, COME ON! THAT WAS MEAN! I'D JUST GOTTEN USED TO THAT ARM.
DON'T THINK YOU'RE GETTING IT BACK!
HA! AS IF I'D WANT IT BACK AFTER YOU'VE USED IT TO CONDUCT GOD KNOWS WHAT KIND OF MONSTROUS EXPERIMENTS!
I'M JUST SHOWING YOU HOW IT FEELS TO LOSE IT.
Please, Chise.
If my only other choices are to be his captive...
Or to spend the rest of eternity here, I'd rather--

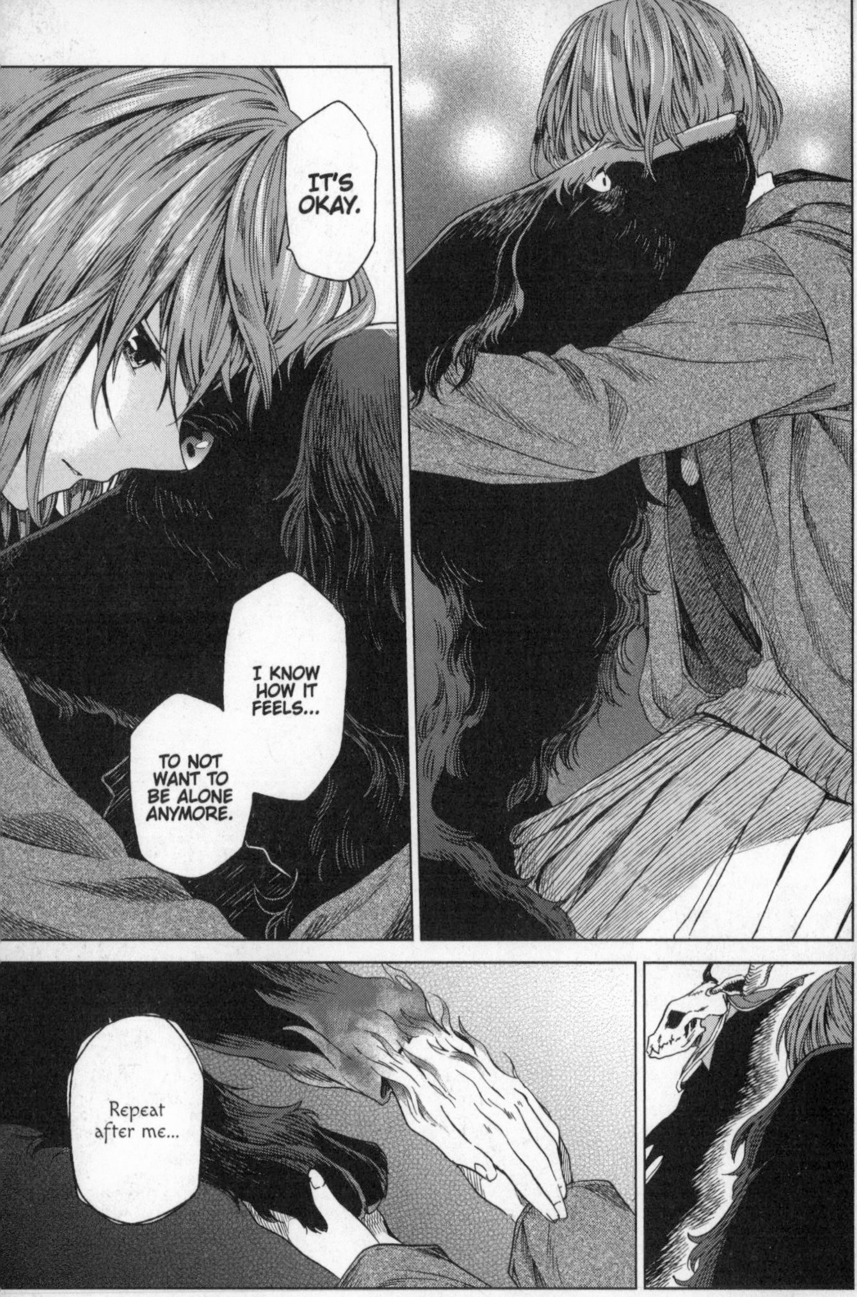
IT'S OKAY.
I KNOW HOW IT FEELS...
TO NOT WANT TO BE ALONE ANYMORE.
Repeat after me...

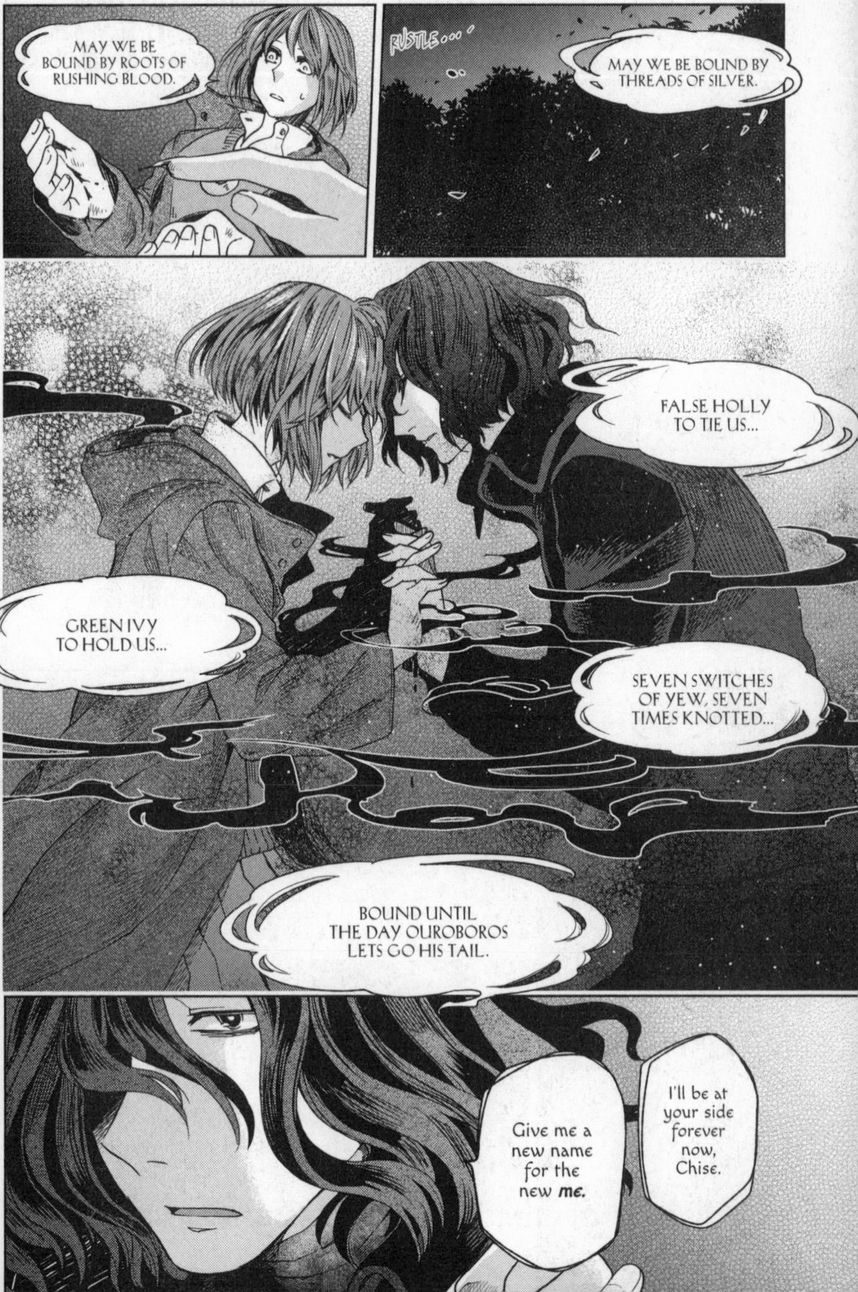
RUSTLE
MAY WE BE BOUND BY THREADS OF SILVER.
MAY WE BE BOUND BY ROOTS OF RUSHING BLOOD.
FALSE HOLLY TO TIE US...
GREEN IVY TO HOLD US...
SEVEN SWITCHES OF YEW, SEVEN TIMES KNOTTED...
BOUND UNTIL THE DAY OUROBOROS LETS GO HIS TAIL.
I'll be at your side forever now, Chise.
Give me a new name for the new *me.*

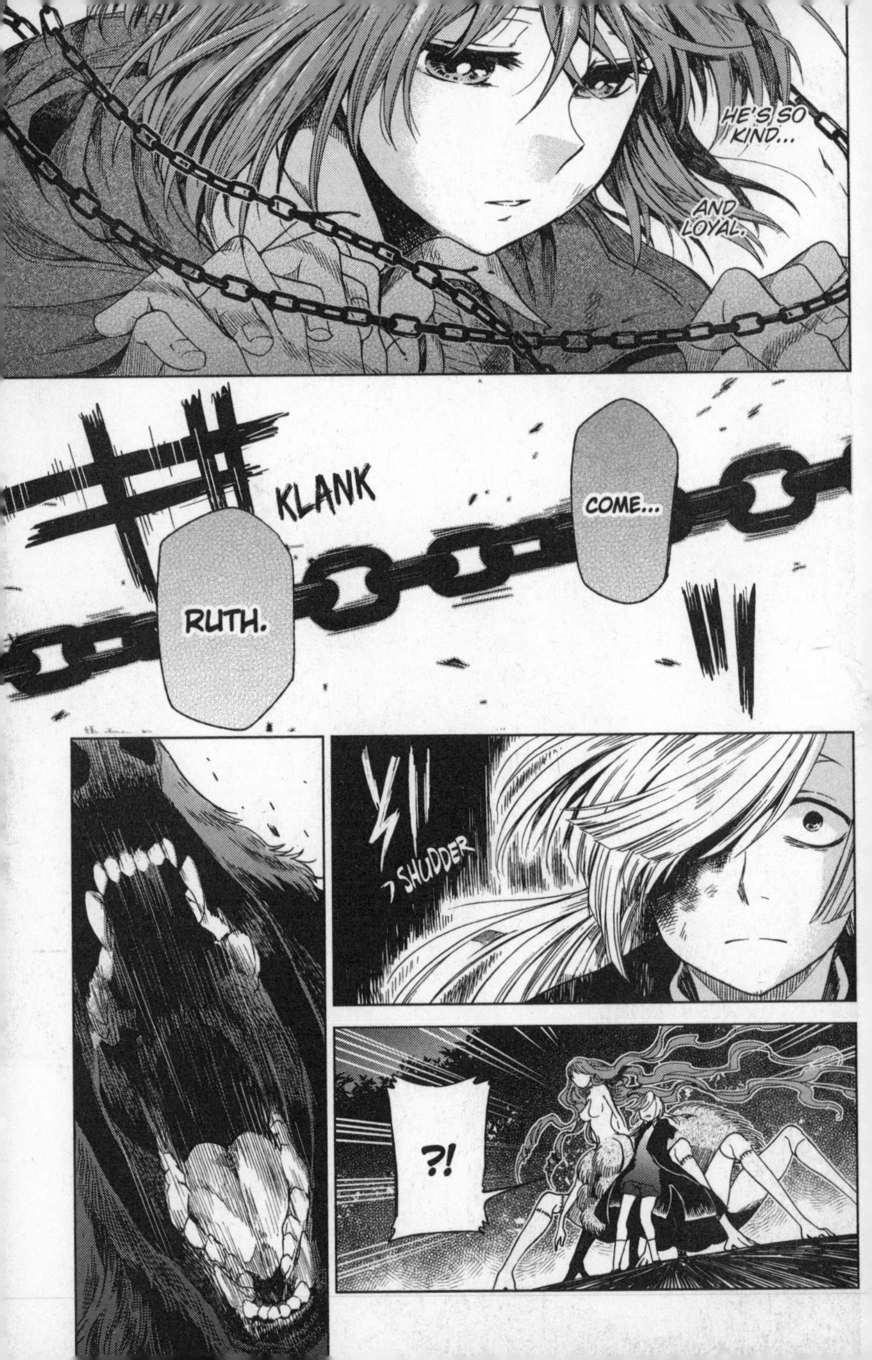
HE'S SO KIND...
AND LOYAL.
COME...
KLANK
RUTH.
SHUDDER
?!

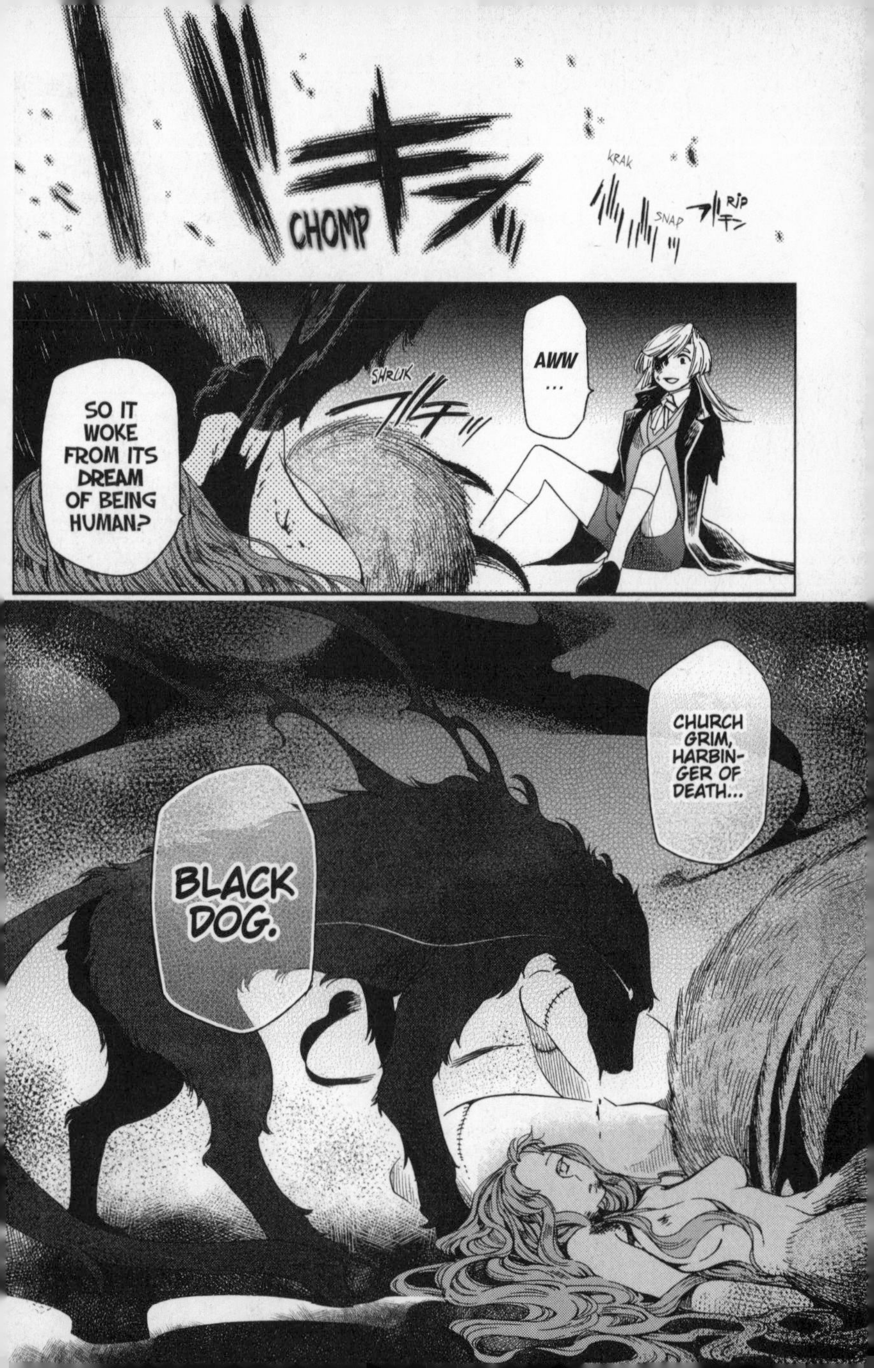
RIP
SNAP
KRAK
CHOMP
AWW ...
SHRUK
SO IT WOKE FROM ITS DREAM OF BEING HUMAN?
CHURCH GRIM, HARBIN-GER OF DEATH...
BLACK DOG.

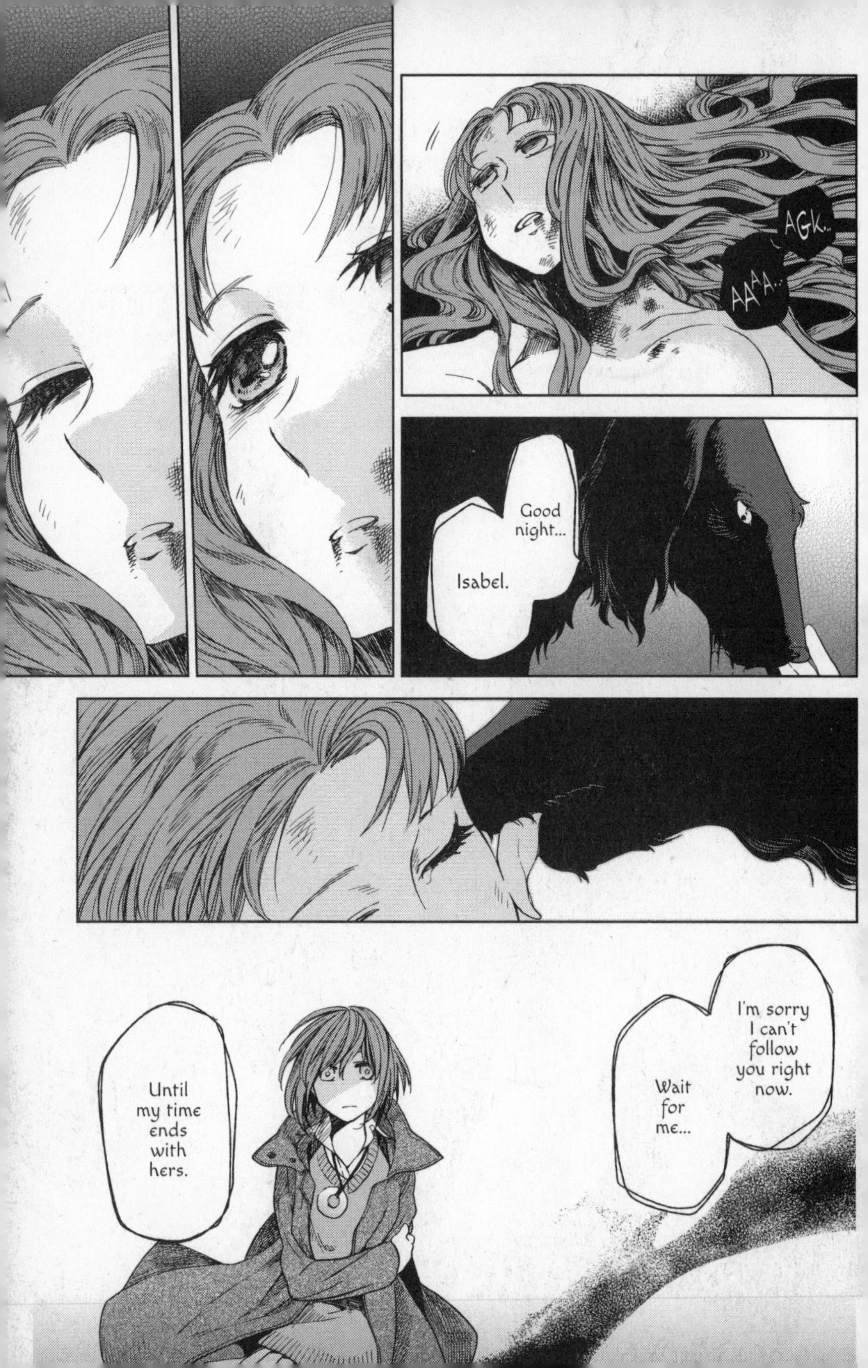
AGK..
AAAA..
Good night...
Isabel.
I'm sorry I can't follow you right now.
Wait for me...
Until my time ends with hers.

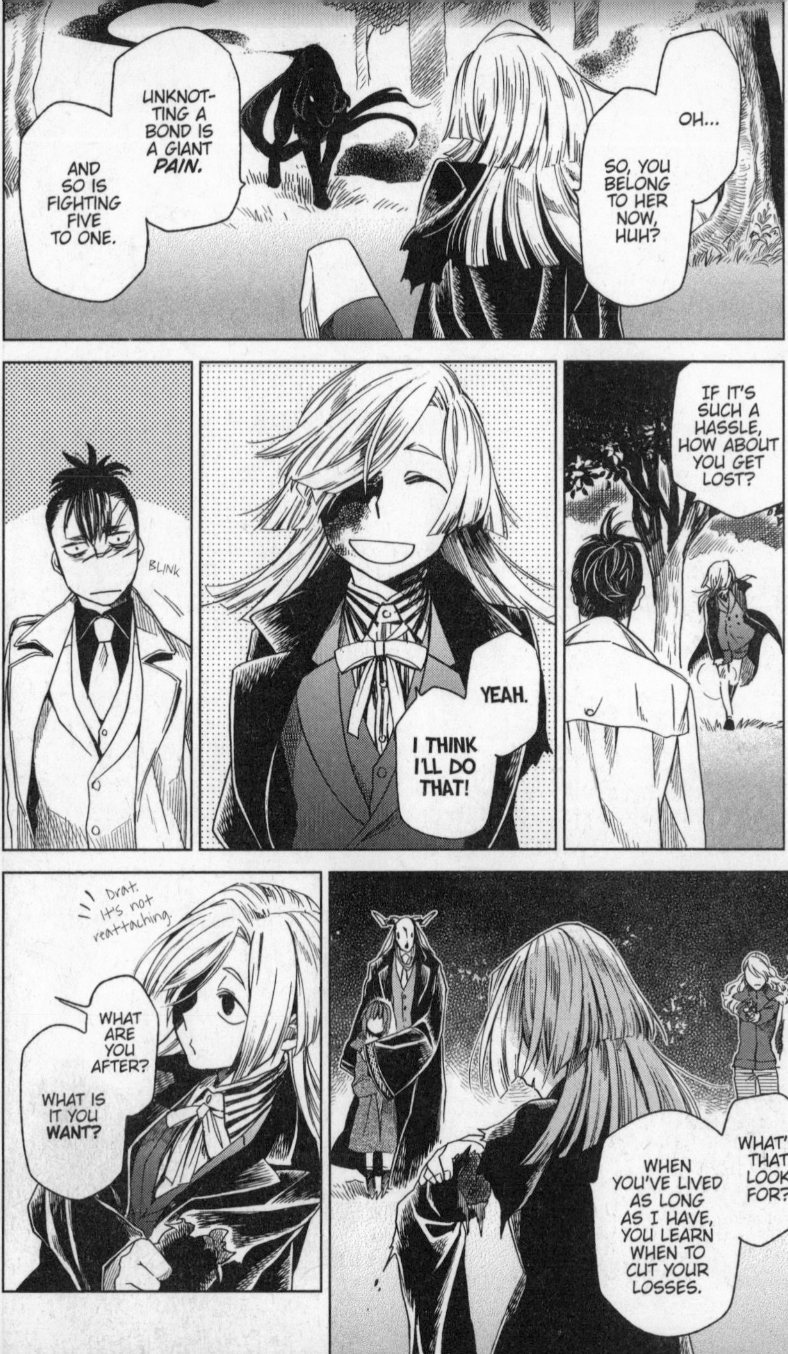
OH...
SO, YOU BELONG TO HER NOW, HUH?
UNKNOTTING A BOND IS A GIANT *PAIN.*
AND SO IS FIGHTING FIVE TO ONE.
IF IT'S SUCH A HASSLE, HOW ABOUT YOU GET LOST?
YEAH.
I THINK I'LL DO THAT!
BLINK
WHAT'S THAT LOOK FOR?
WHEN YOU'VE LIVED AS LONG AS I HAVE, YOU LEARN WHEN TO CUT YOUR LOSSES.
Drat. It's not reattaching.
WHAT ARE YOU AFTER?
WHAT IS IT YOU WANT?

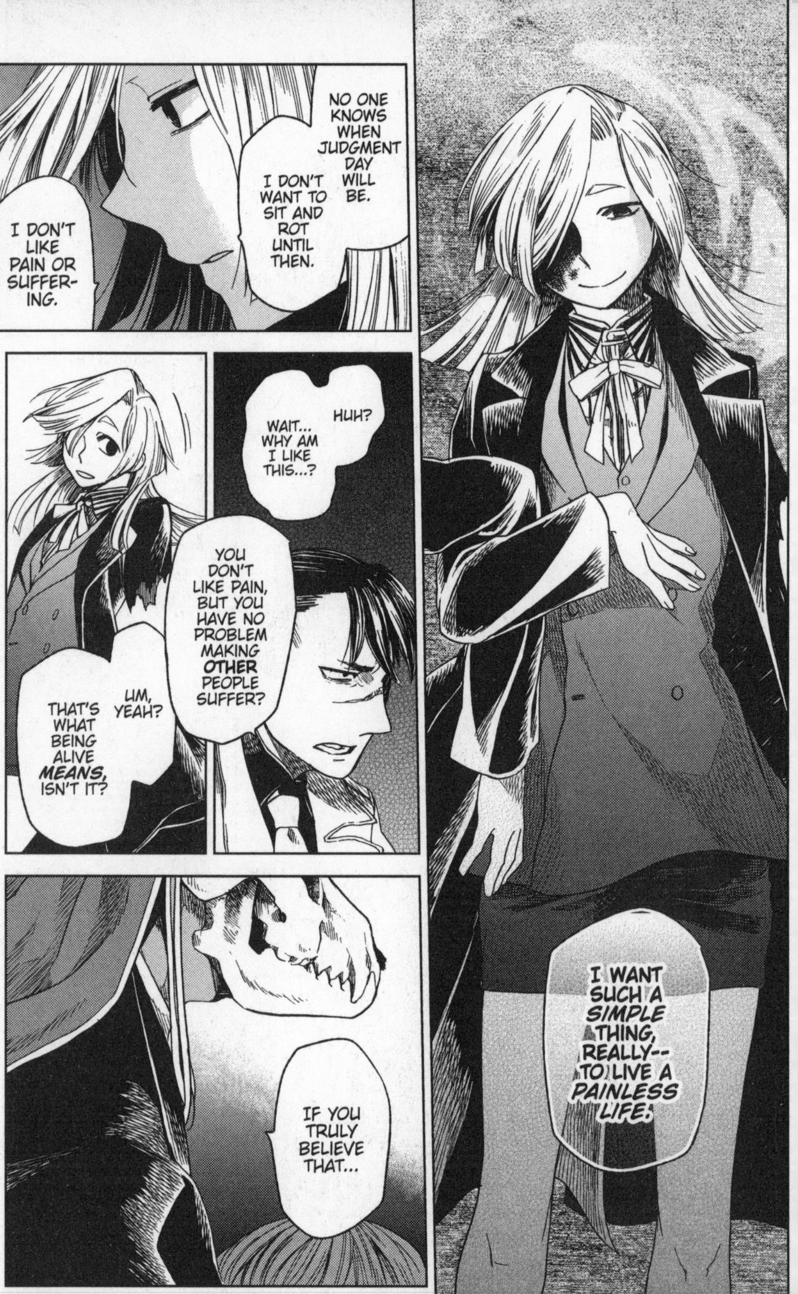
I WANT SUCH A SIMPLE THING, REALLY-- TO LIVE A PAINLESS LIFE.
NO ONE KNOWS WHEN JUDGMENT DAY WILL BE.
I DON'T WANT TO SIT AND ROT UNTIL THEN.
I DON'T LIKE PAIN OR SUFFER-ING.
HUH?
WAIT... WHY AM I LIKE THIS...?
YOU DON'T LIKE PAIN, BUT YOU HAVE NO PROBLEM MAKING OTHER PEOPLE SUFFER?
UM, YEAH?
THAT'S WHAT BEING ALIVE MEANS, ISN'T IT?
IF YOU TRULY BELIEVE THAT...

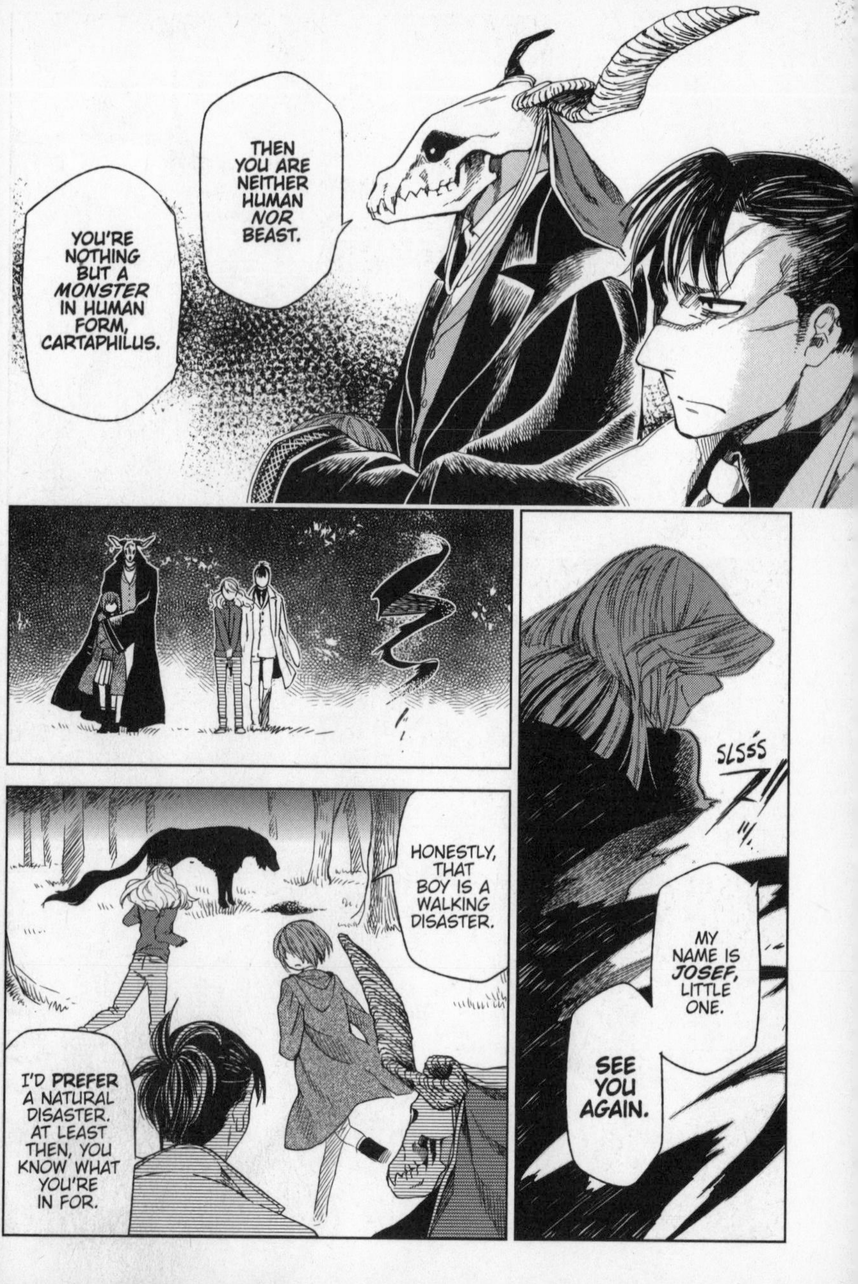
THEN YOU ARE NEITHER HUMAN *NOR* BEAST.
YOU'RE NOTHING BUT A *MONSTER* IN HUMAN FORM, CARTAPHILUS.
SLSSS
MY NAME IS *JOSEF*, LITTLE ONE.
SEE YOU AGAIN.
HONESTLY, THAT BOY IS A WALKING DISASTER.
I'D PREFER A NATURAL DISASTER. AT LEAST THEN, YOU KNOW WHAT YOU'RE IN FOR.

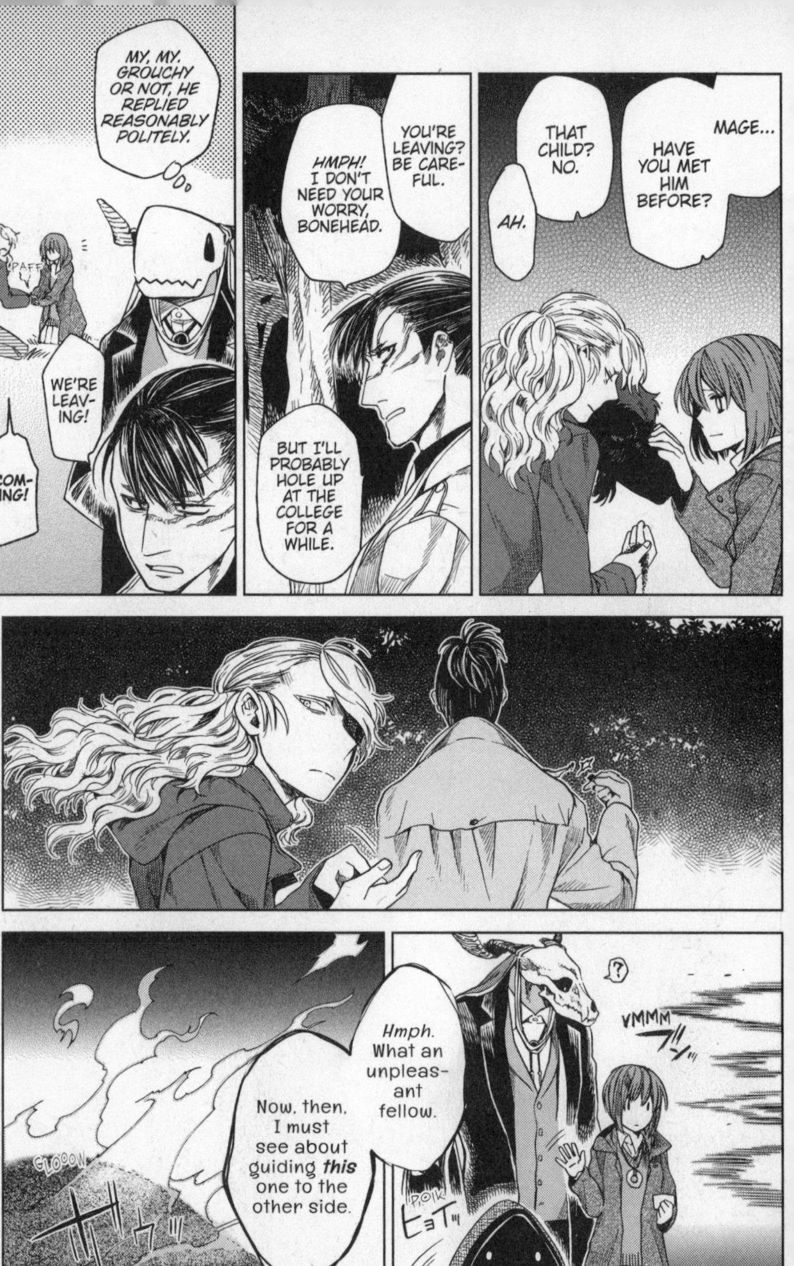
MAGE...
HAVE YOU MET HIM BEFORE?
THAT CHILD? NO.
AH.
YOU'RE LEAVING? BE CAREFUL.
HMPH! I DON'T NEED YOUR WORRY, BONEHEAD.
BUT I'LL PROBABLY HOLE UP AT THE COLLEGE FOR A WHILE.
MY, MY. GROUCHY OR NOT, HE REPLIED REASONABLY POLITELY.
PAFF
WE'RE LEAVING!
COMING!
?
VMMM
Hmph. What an unpleasant fellow.
POIK
ヒョT
Now, then, I must see about guiding *this* one to the other side.
GLOOON
ガサッ

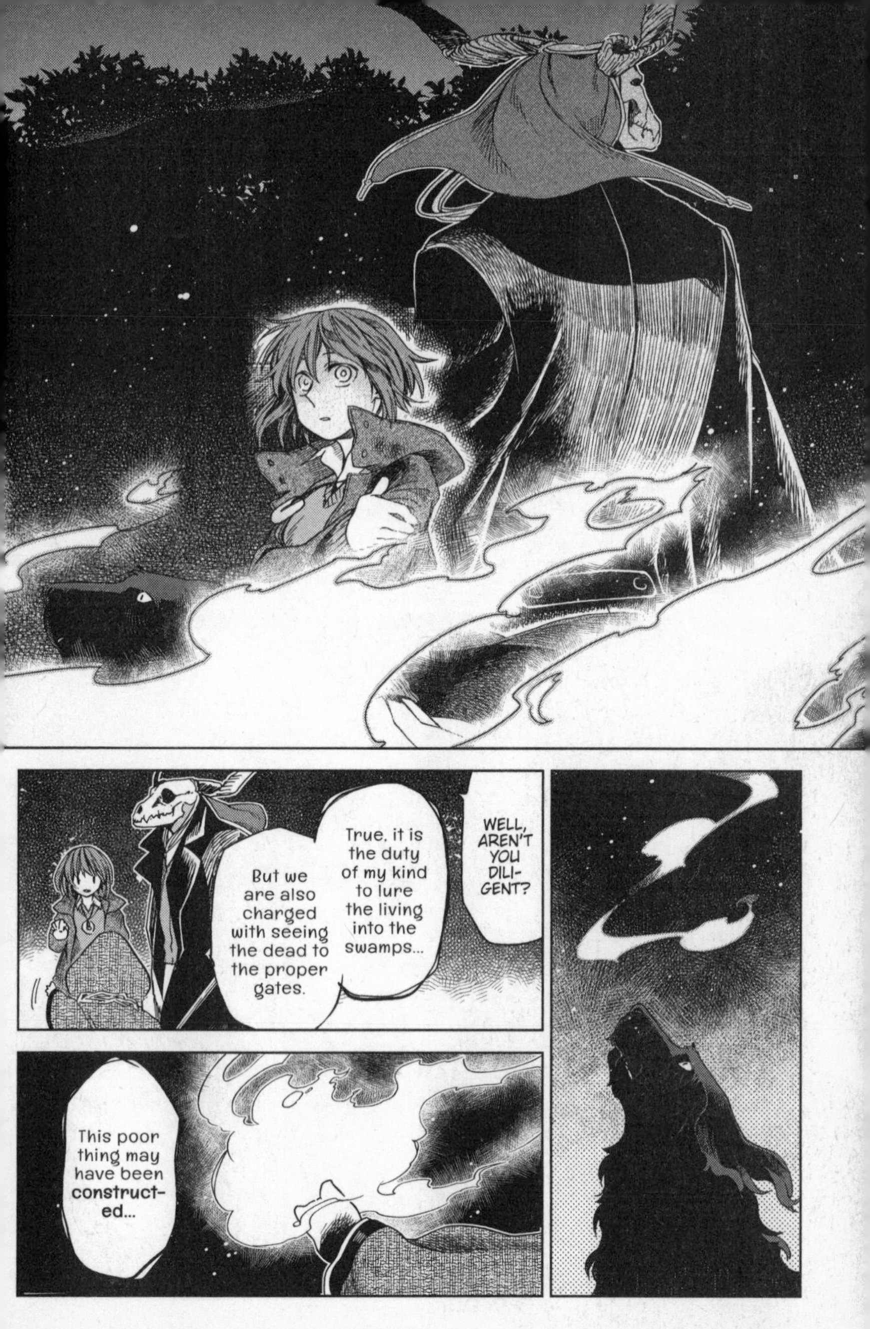
WELL, AREN'T YOU DILI-GENT?
True, it is the duty of my kind to lure the living into the swamps...
But we are also charged with seeing the dead to the proper gates.
This poor thing may have been constructed-ed...

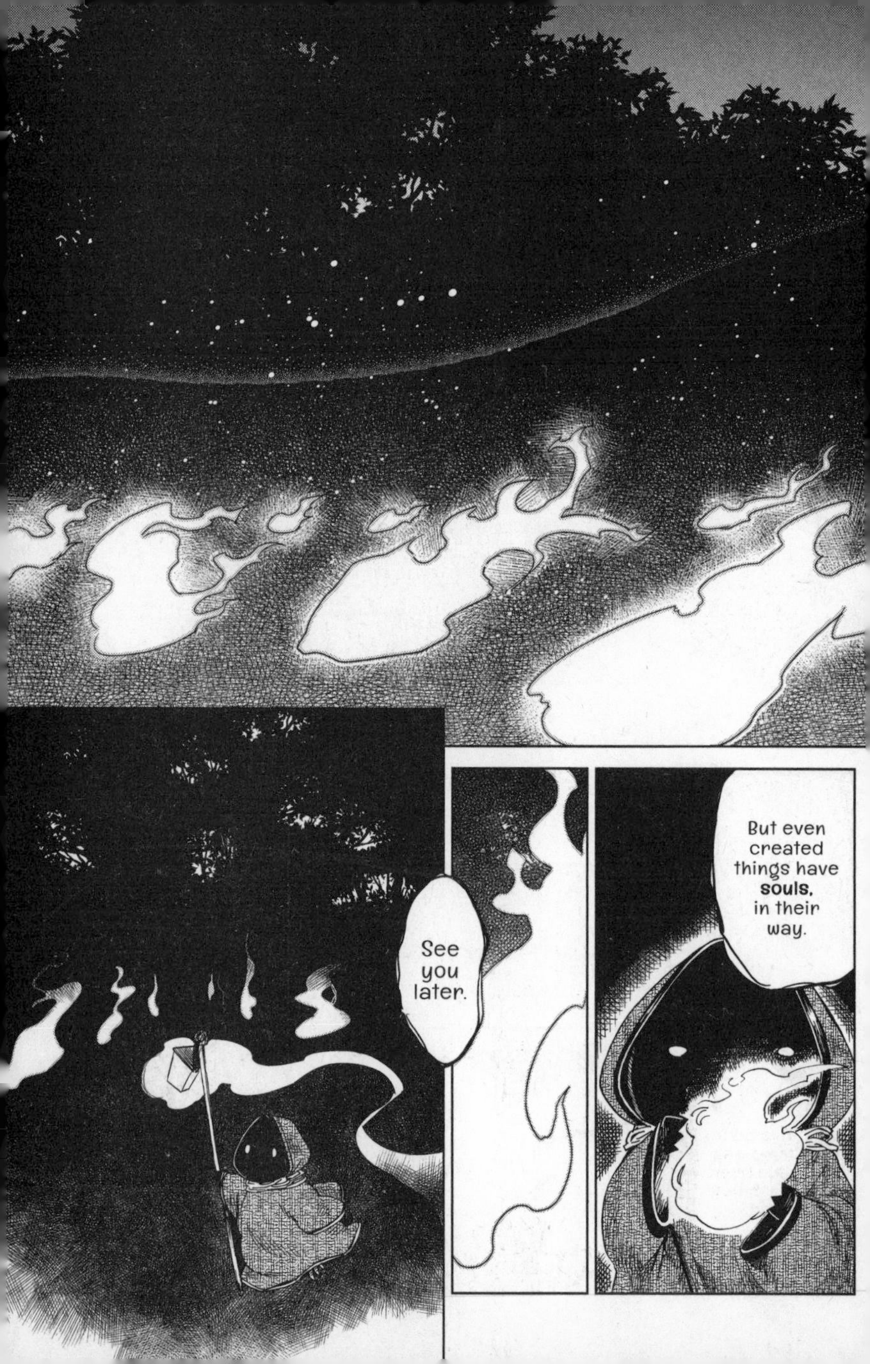
But even created things have **souls,** in their way.
See you later.

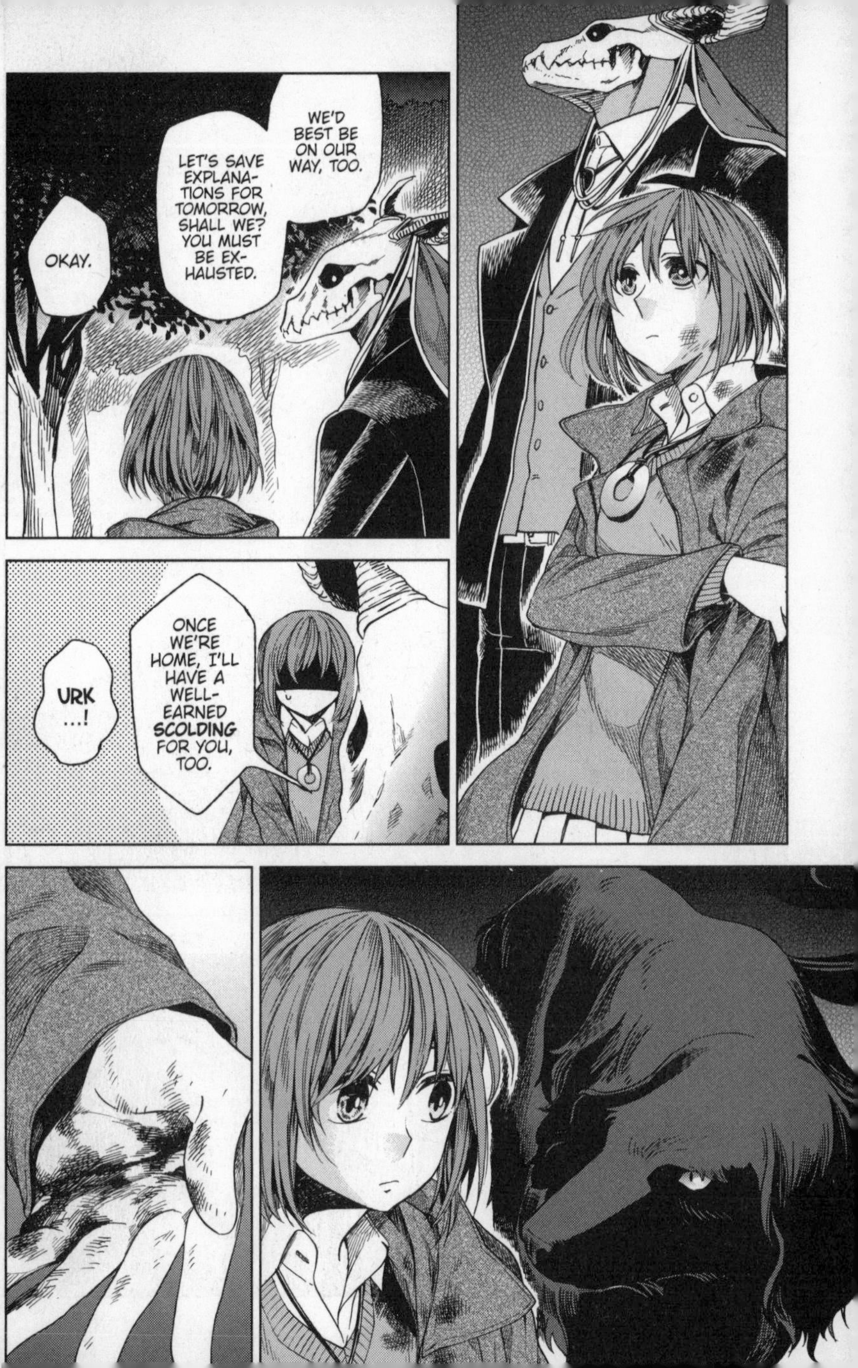
WE'D BEST BE ON OUR WAY, TOO.
LET'S SAVE EXPLANATIONS FOR TOMORROW, SHALL WE? YOU MUST BE EXHAUSTED.
OKAY.
ONCE WE'RE HOME, I'LL HAVE A WELL-EARNED **SCOLDING** FOR YOU, TOO.
URK ...!

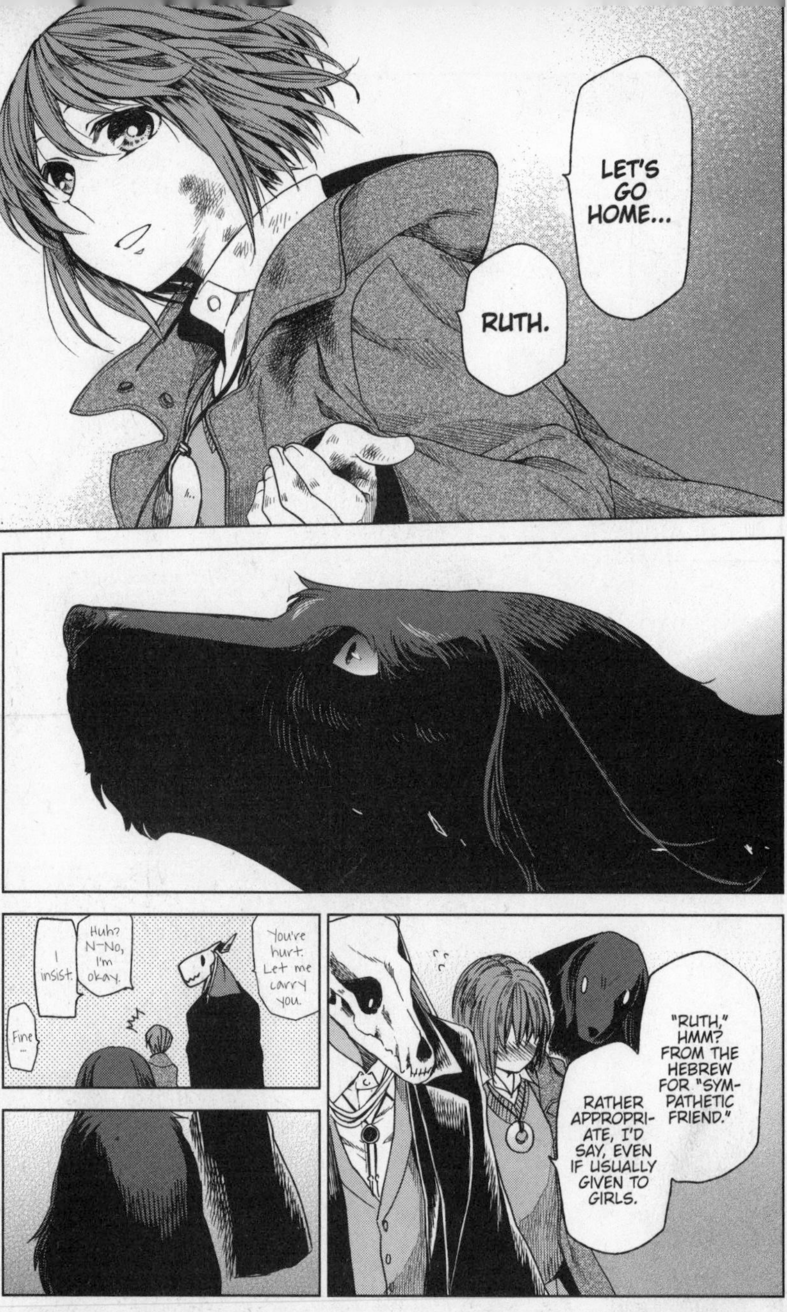
LET'S GO HOME...
RUTH.
"RUTH," HMM? FROM THE HEBREW FOR "SYMPATHETIC FRIEND."
RATHER APPROPRIATE, I'D SAY, EVEN IF USUALLY GIVEN TO GIRLS.
You're hurt. Let me carry you.
Huh? N-No, I'm okay.
I insist.
Fine...

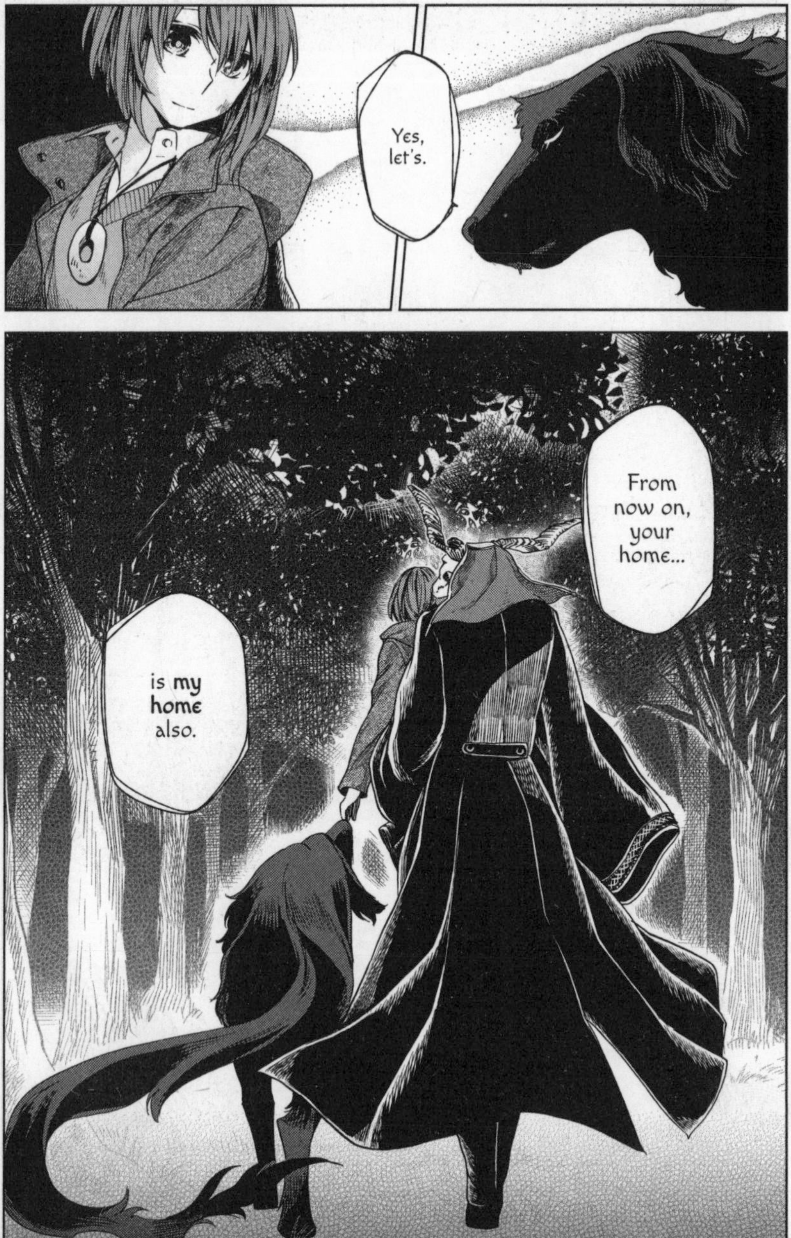
Yes, let's.
From now on, your home...
is my home also.

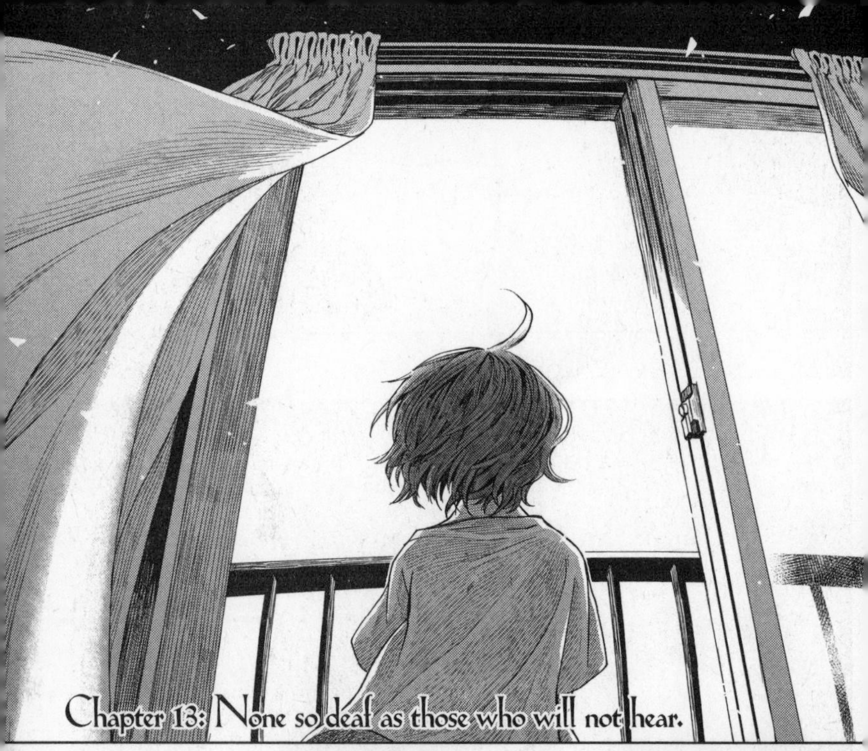

Chapter 13: None so deaf as those who will not hear.

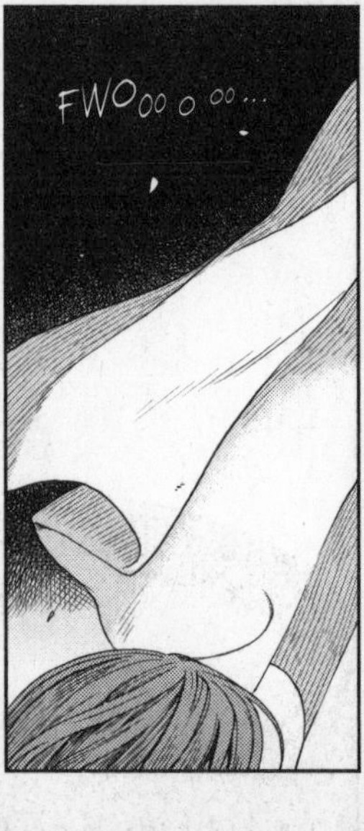
FWOoo o oo...

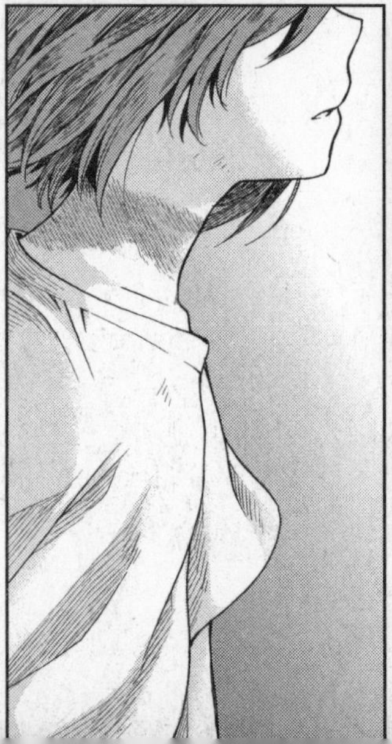

THAT DAY...

AN UNBREAKABLE CURSE WAS CAST ON ME.

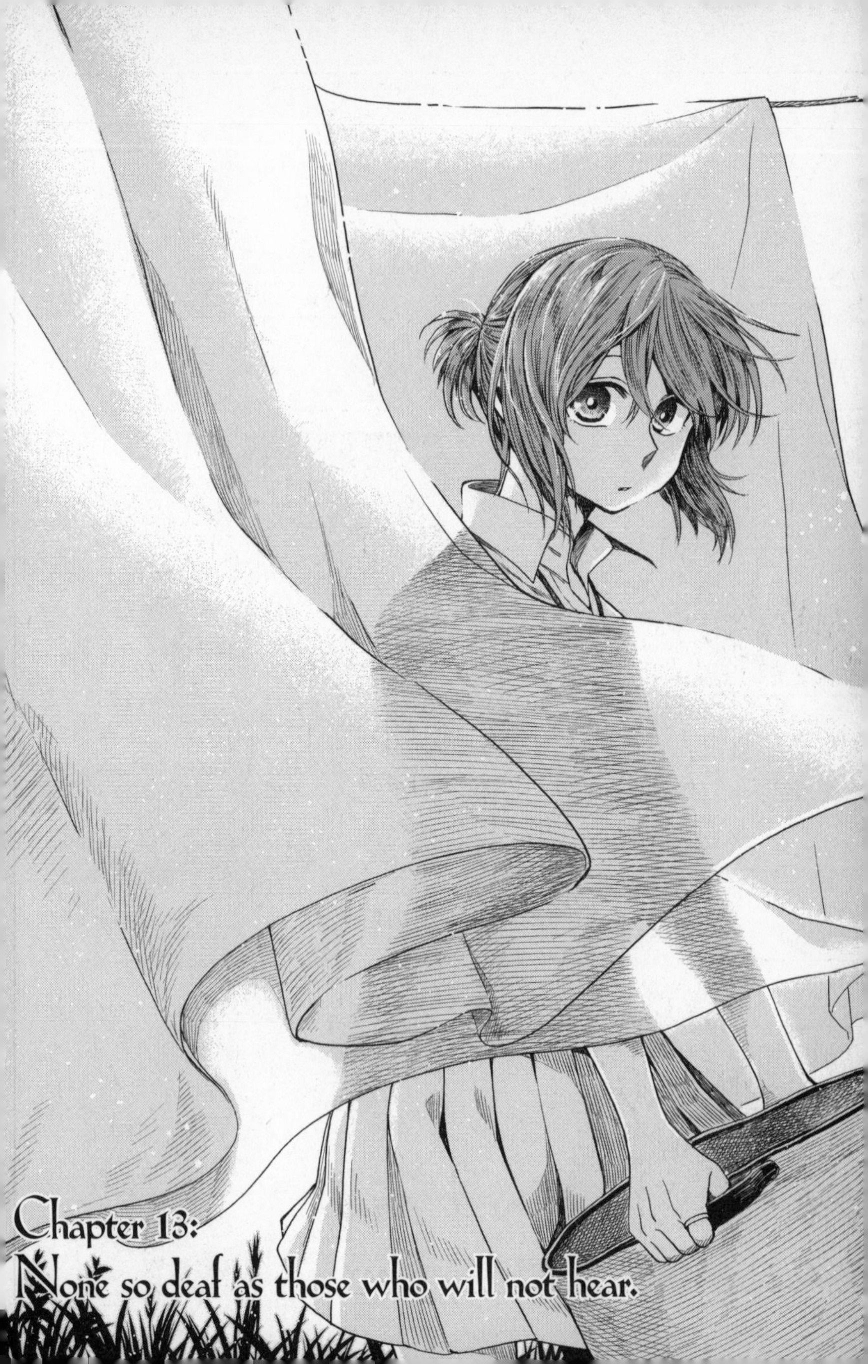
Chapter 13:
None so deaf as those who will not hear.

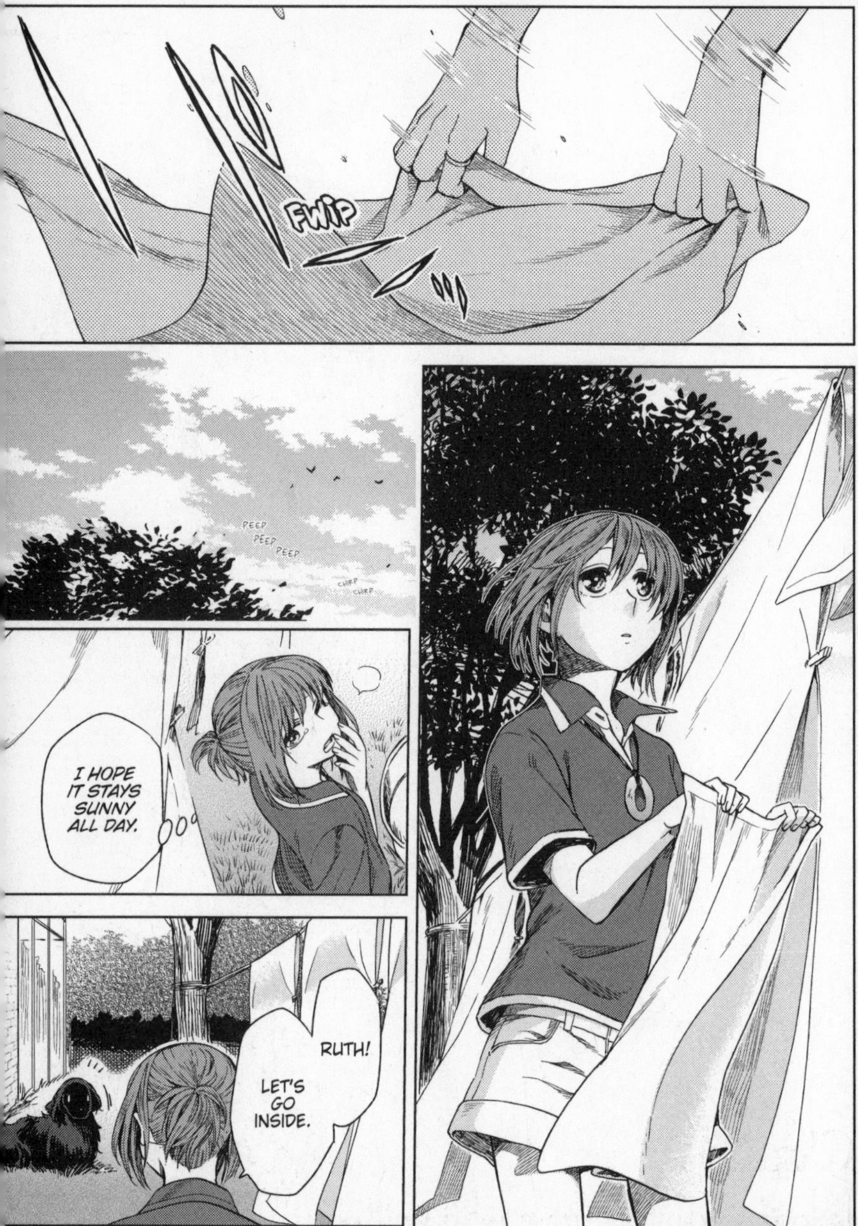
FWIP
PEEP
PEEP
PEEP
CHIRP
CHIRP
I HOPE IT STAYS SUNNY ALL DAY.
RUTH!
LET'S GO INSIDE.

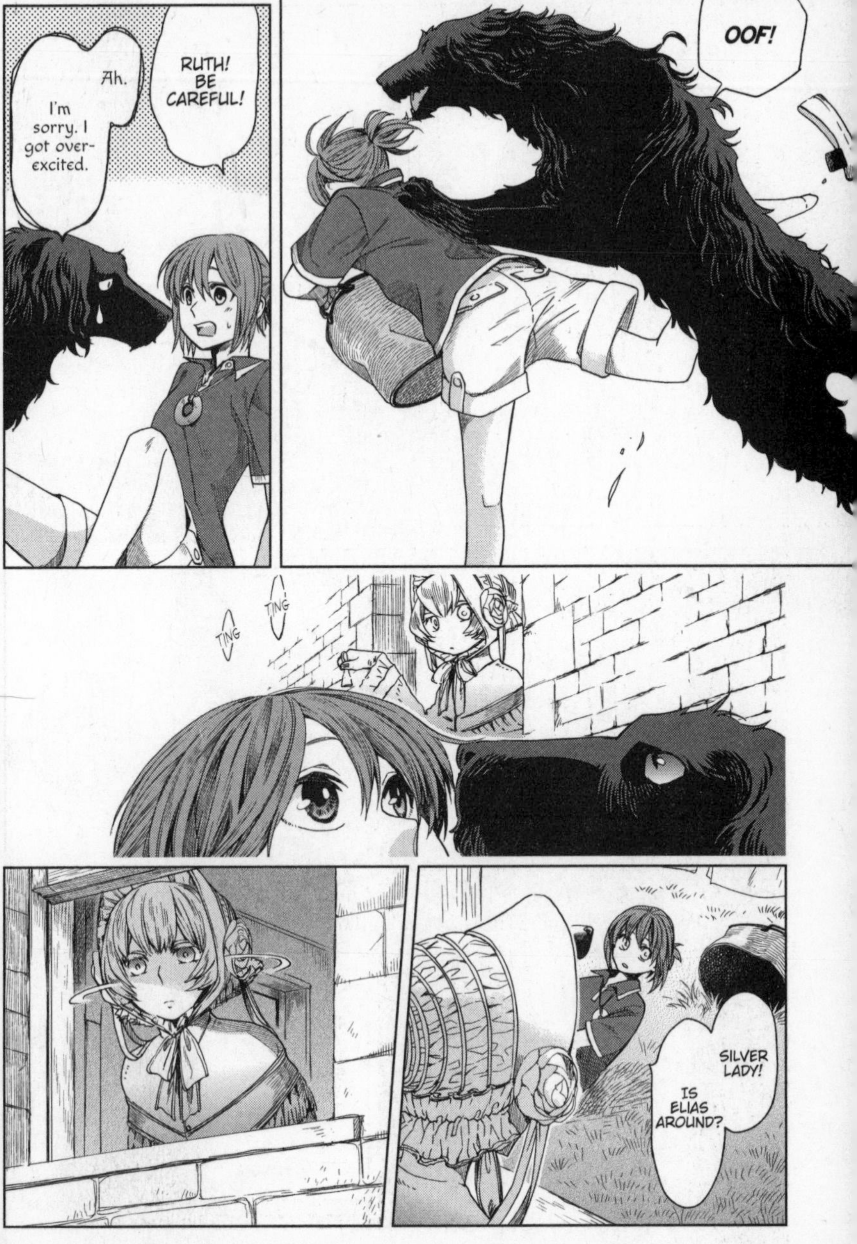
OOF!
RUTH! BE CAREFUL!
Ah.
I'm sorry. I got over-excited.
TING
TING
SILVER LADY!
IS ELIAS AROUND?

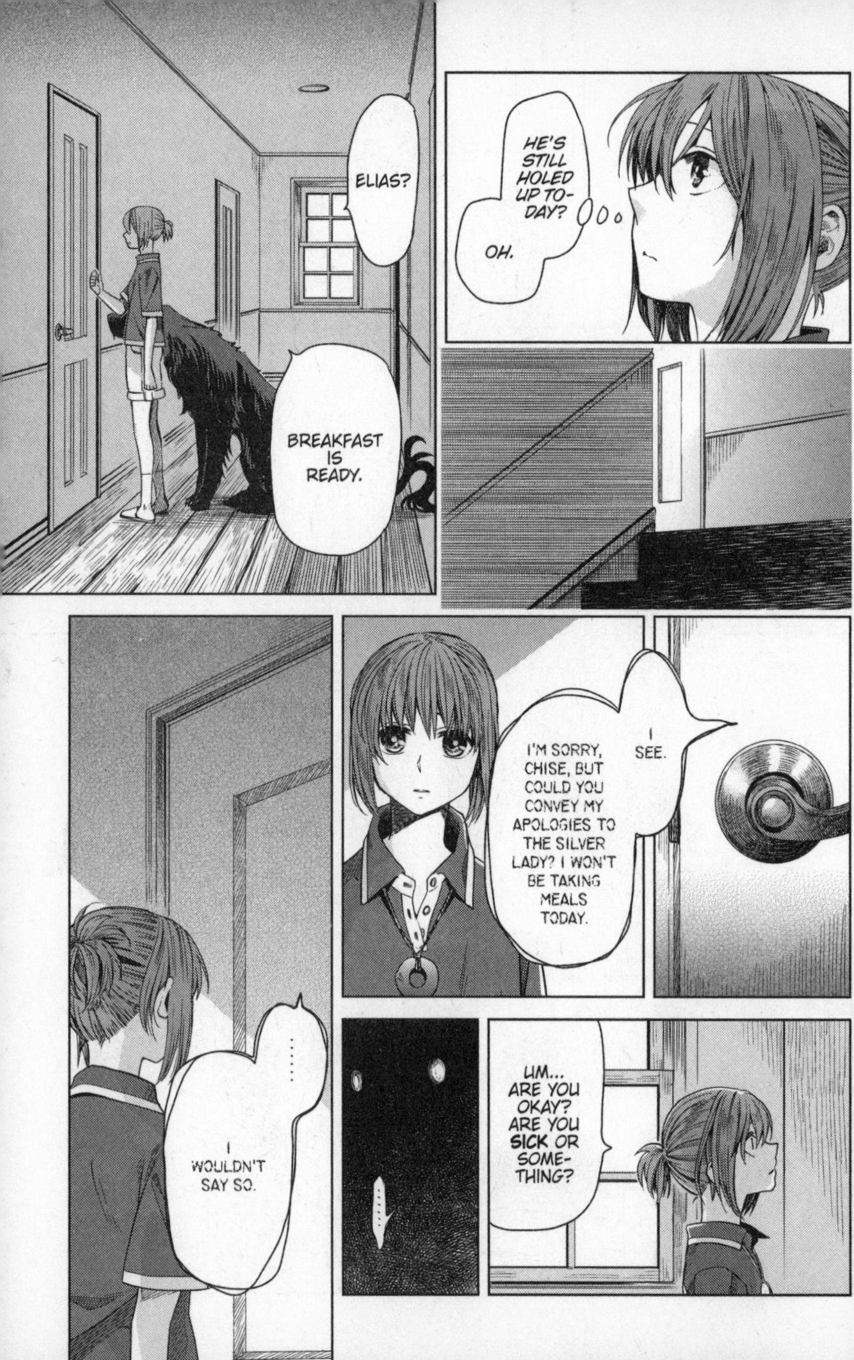
HE'S STILL HOLED UP TO-DAY?
OH.
ELIAS?
BREAKFAST IS READY.
I SEE.
I'M SORRY, CHISE, BUT COULD YOU CONVEY MY APOLOGIES TO THE SILVER LADY? I WON'T BE TAKING MEALS TODAY.
UM... ARE YOU OKAY? ARE YOU **SICK** OR SOME-THING?
......
......
I WOULDN'T SAY SO.

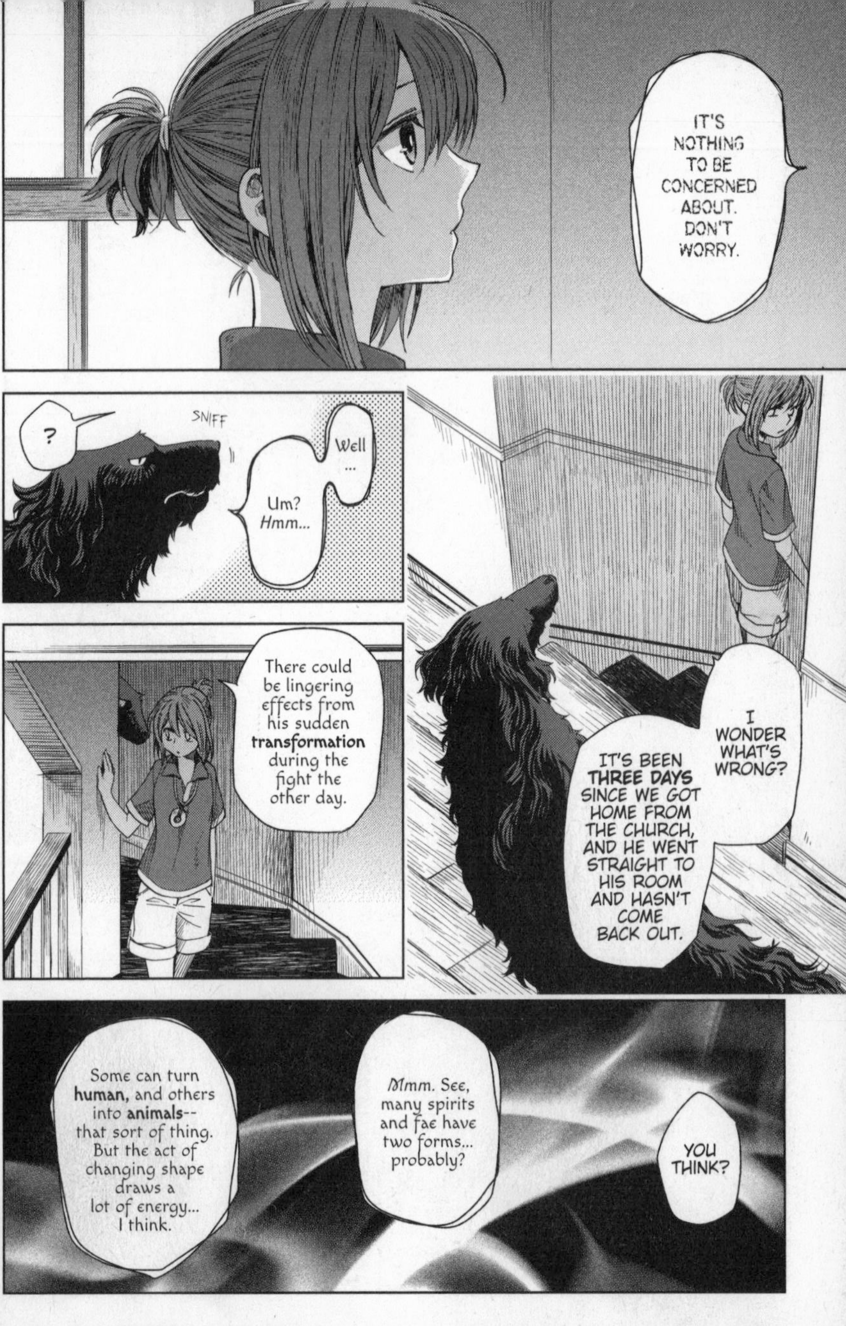
IT'S NOTHING TO BE CONCERNED ABOUT. DON'T WORRY.
I WONDER WHAT'S WRONG?
IT'S BEEN **THREE DAYS** SINCE WE GOT HOME FROM THE CHURCH, AND HE WENT STRAIGHT TO HIS ROOM AND HASN'T COME BACK OUT.
Well ...
Um? *Hmm...*
SNIFF
?
There could be lingering effects from his sudden **transformation** during the fight the other day.
YOU THINK?
Mmm. See, many spirits and fae have two forms... probably?
Some can turn **human,** and others into **animals**-- that sort of thing. But the act of changing shape draws a lot of energy... I think.

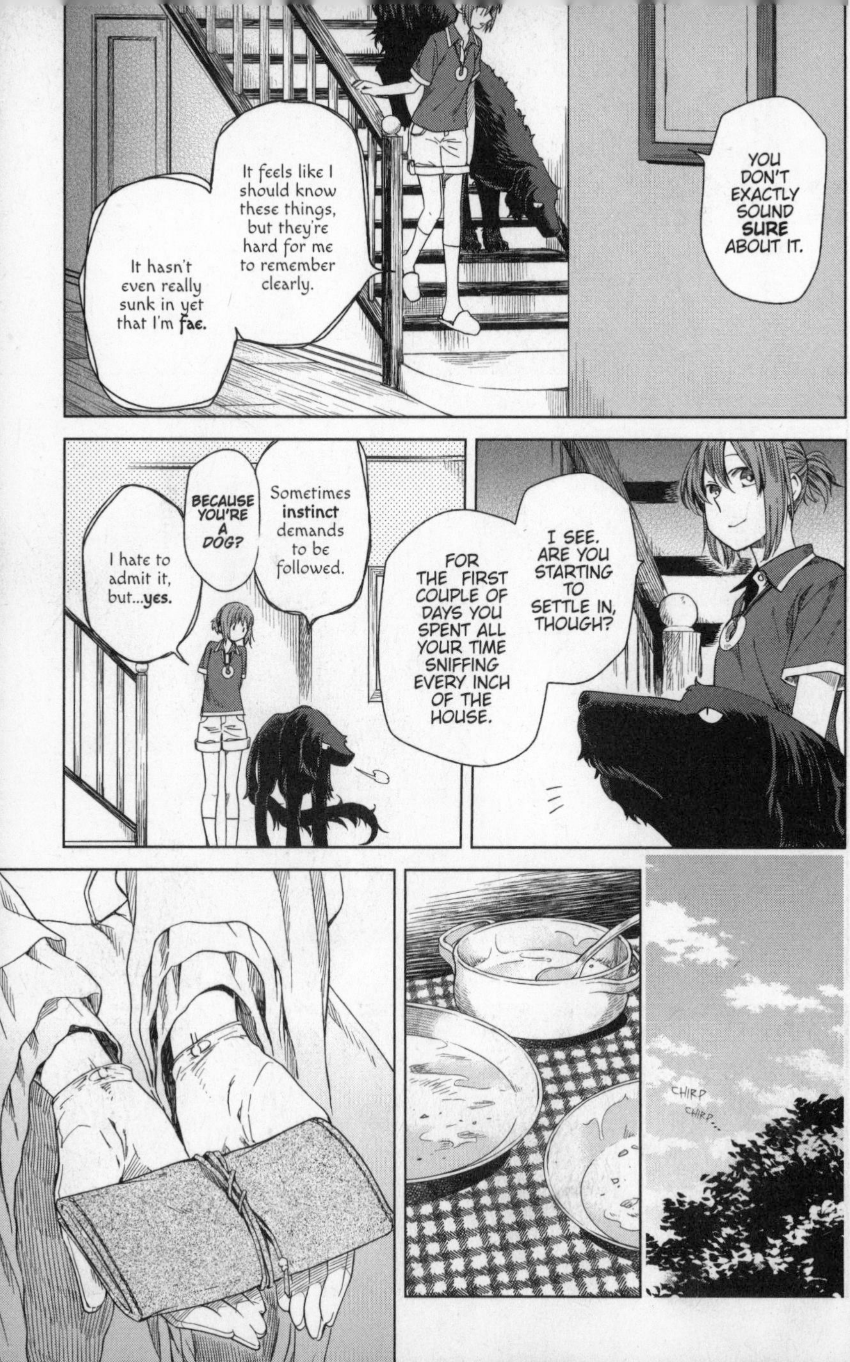
YOU DON'T EXACTLY SOUND SURE ABOUT IT.
It feels like I should know these things, but they're hard for me to remember clearly.
It hasn't even really sunk in yet that I'm fae.
I SEE. ARE YOU STARTING TO SETTLE IN, THOUGH?
FOR THE FIRST COUPLE OF DAYS YOU SPENT ALL YOUR TIME SNIFFING EVERY INCH OF THE HOUSE.
Sometimes instinct demands to be followed.
BECAUSE YOU'RE A DOG?
I hate to admit it, but...yes.
CHIRP
CHIRP...

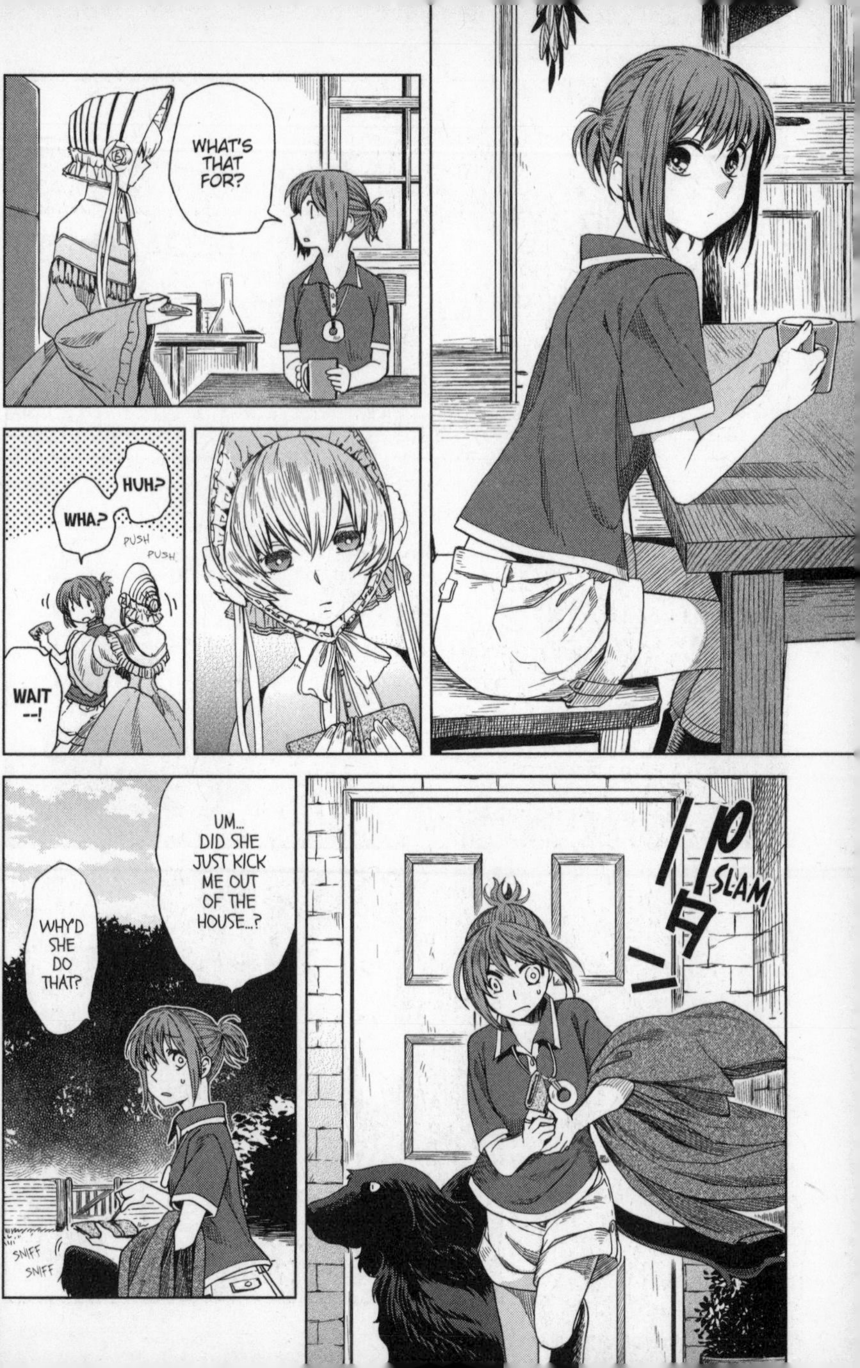
WHAT'S THAT FOR?
HUH?
WHA?
PUSH PUSH
WAIT --!
SLAM
UM... DID SHE JUST KICK ME OUT OF THE HOUSE...?
WHY'D SHE DO THAT?
SNIFF SNIFF

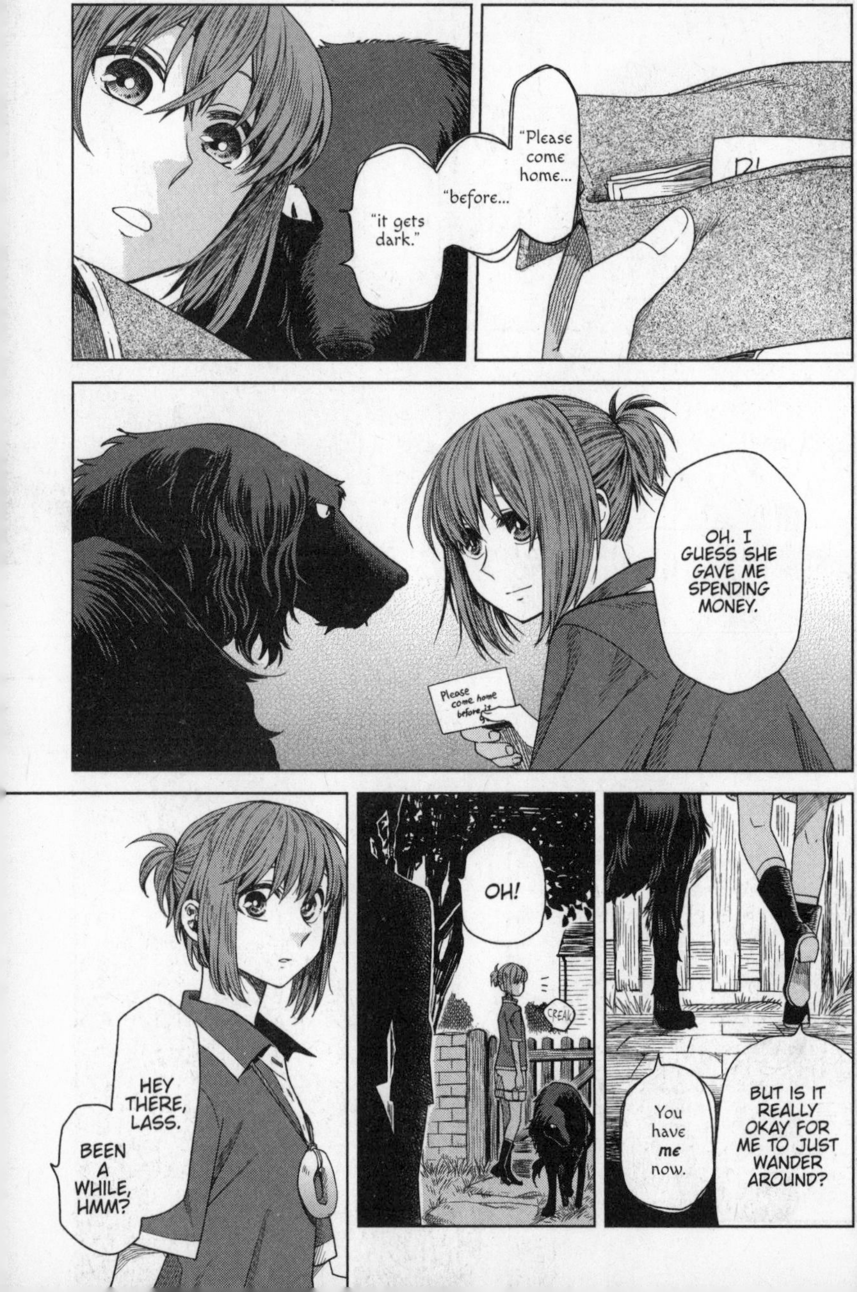
"Please come home...
"before...
"it gets dark."
OH. I GUESS SHE GAVE ME SPENDING MONEY.
Please come home before it
BUT IS IT REALLY OKAY FOR ME TO JUST WANDER AROUND?
You have me now.
OH!
CREAK
HEY THERE, LASS.
BEEN A WHILE, HMM?

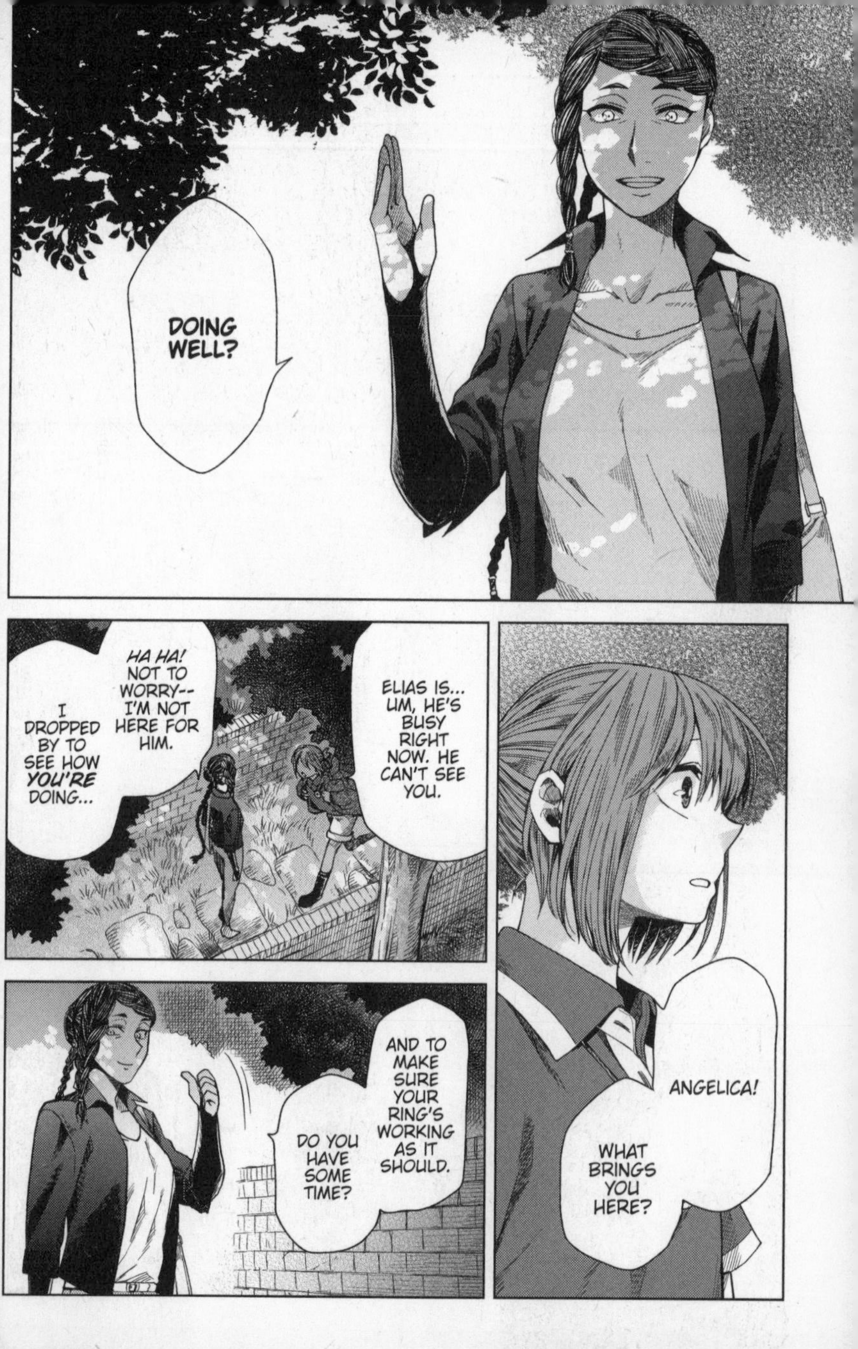
DOING WELL?
ANGELICA!
WHAT BRINGS YOU HERE?
ELIAS IS... UM, HE'S BUSY RIGHT NOW. HE CAN'T SEE YOU.
HA HA! NOT TO WORRY-- I'M NOT HERE FOR HIM.
I DROPPED BY TO SEE HOW *YOU'RE* DOING...
AND TO MAKE SURE YOUR RING'S WORKING AS IT SHOULD.
DO YOU HAVE SOME TIME?

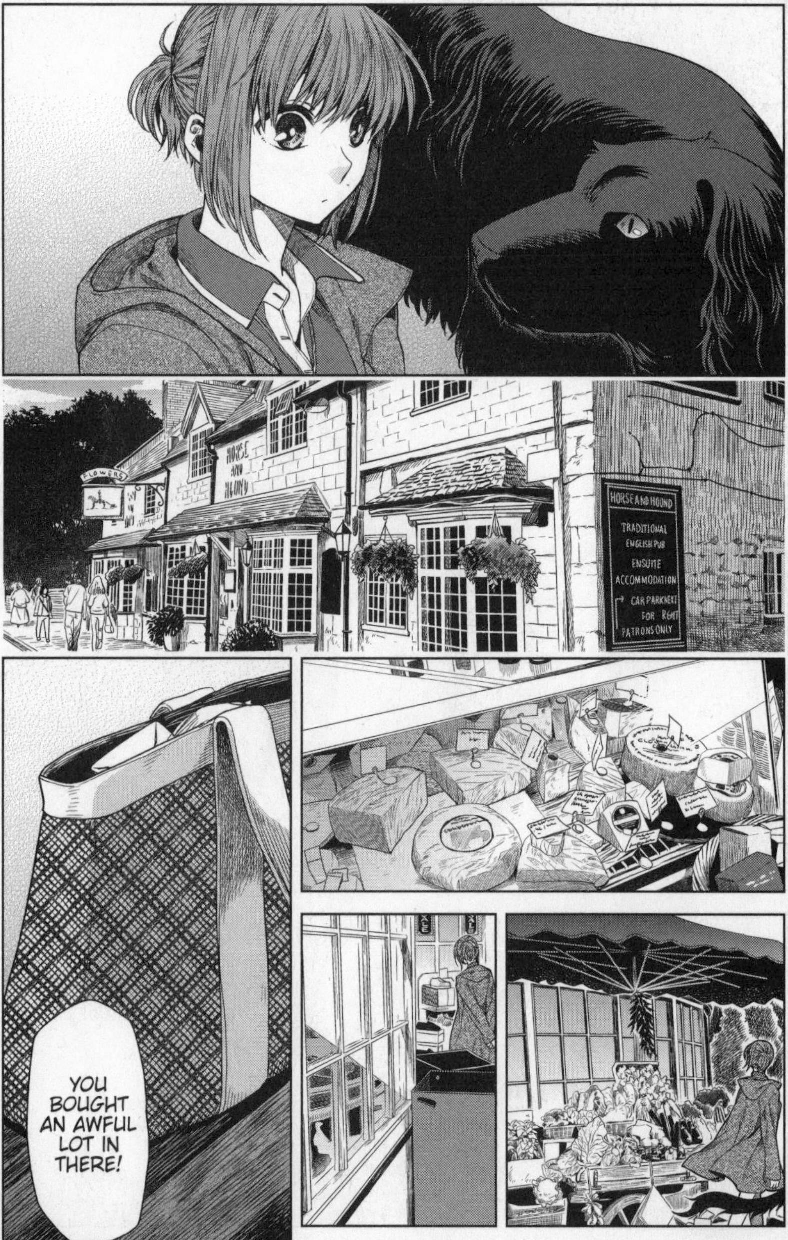
FLOWERS
HORSE AND HOUND
HORSE AND HOUND
TRADITIONAL ENGLISH PUB
ENSUITE ACCOMMODATION
CAR PARKNEXT FOR R6HT PATRONS ONLY
YOU BOUGHT AN AWFUL LOT IN THERE!

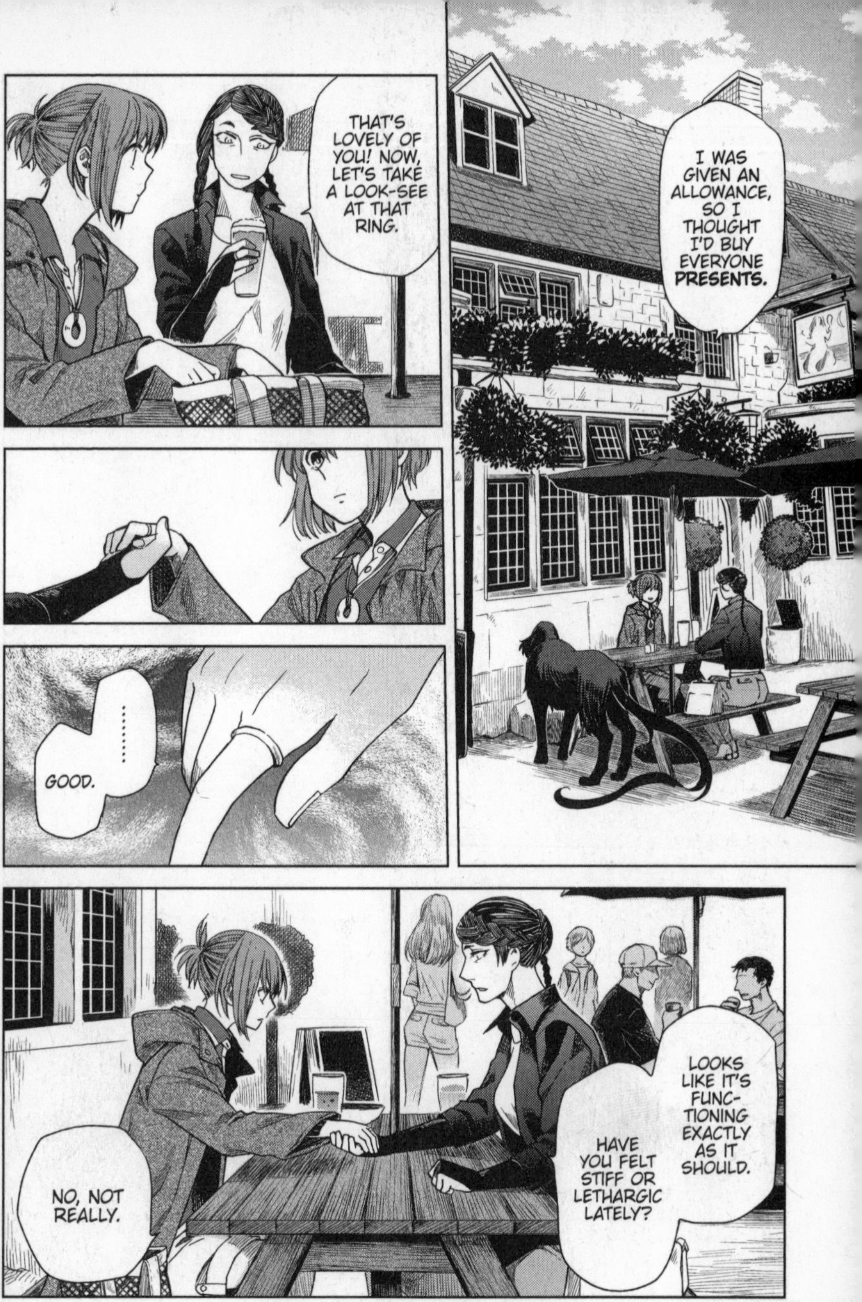
I WAS GIVEN AN ALLOWANCE, SO I THOUGHT I'D BUY EVERYONE PRESENTS.
THAT'S LOVELY OF YOU! NOW, LET'S TAKE A LOOK-SEE AT THAT RING.
......
GOOD.
LOOKS LIKE IT'S FUNC-TIONING EXACTLY AS IT SHOULD.
HAVE YOU FELT STIFF OR LETHARGIC LATELY?
NO, NOT REALLY.

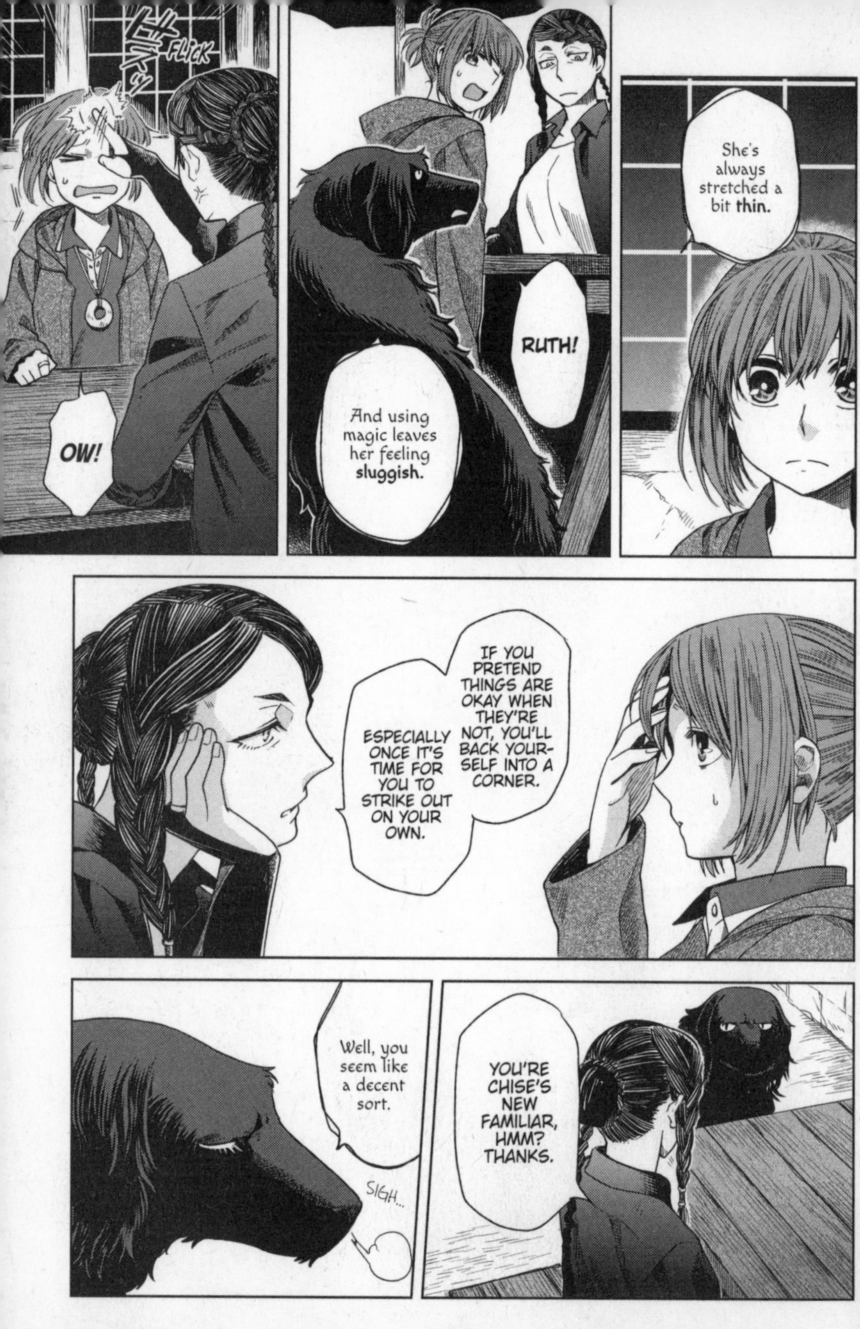
She's always stretched a bit thin.
And using magic leaves her feeling sluggish.
RUTH!
FLICK
OW!
IF YOU PRETEND THINGS ARE OKAY WHEN THEY'RE NOT, YOU'LL BACK YOURSELF INTO A CORNER.
ESPECIALLY ONCE IT'S TIME FOR YOU TO STRIKE OUT ON YOUR OWN.
YOU'RE CHISE'S NEW FAMILIAR, HMM? THANKS.
Well, you seem like a decent sort.
SIGH...

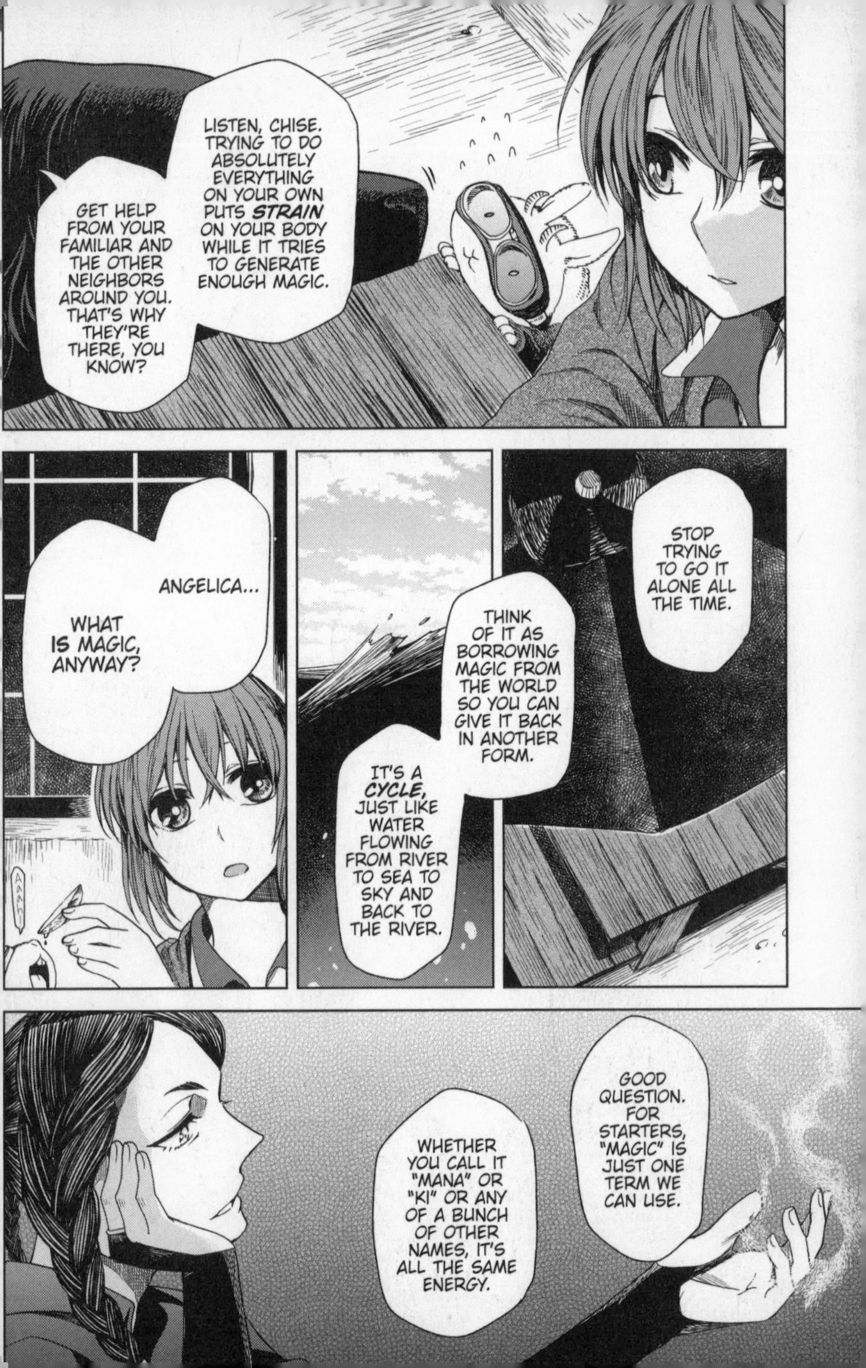
LISTEN, CHISE. TRYING TO DO ABSOLUTELY EVERYTHING ON YOUR OWN PUTS **STRAIN** ON YOUR BODY WHILE IT TRIES TO GENERATE ENOUGH MAGIC.
GET HELP FROM YOUR FAMILIAR AND THE OTHER NEIGHBORS AROUND YOU. THAT'S WHY THEY'RE THERE, YOU KNOW?
STOP TRYING TO GO IT ALONE ALL THE TIME.
THINK OF IT AS BORROWING MAGIC FROM THE WORLD SO YOU CAN GIVE IT BACK IN ANOTHER FORM.
IT'S A ***CYCLE***, JUST LIKE WATER FLOWING FROM RIVER TO SEA TO SKY AND BACK TO THE RIVER.
ANGELICA...
WHAT **IS** MAGIC, ANYWAY?
Aaah!
GOOD QUESTION. FOR STARTERS, "MAGIC" IS JUST ONE TERM WE CAN USE.
WHETHER YOU CALL IT "MANA" OR "KI" OR ANY OF A BUNCH OF OTHER NAMES, IT'S ALL THE SAME ENERGY.

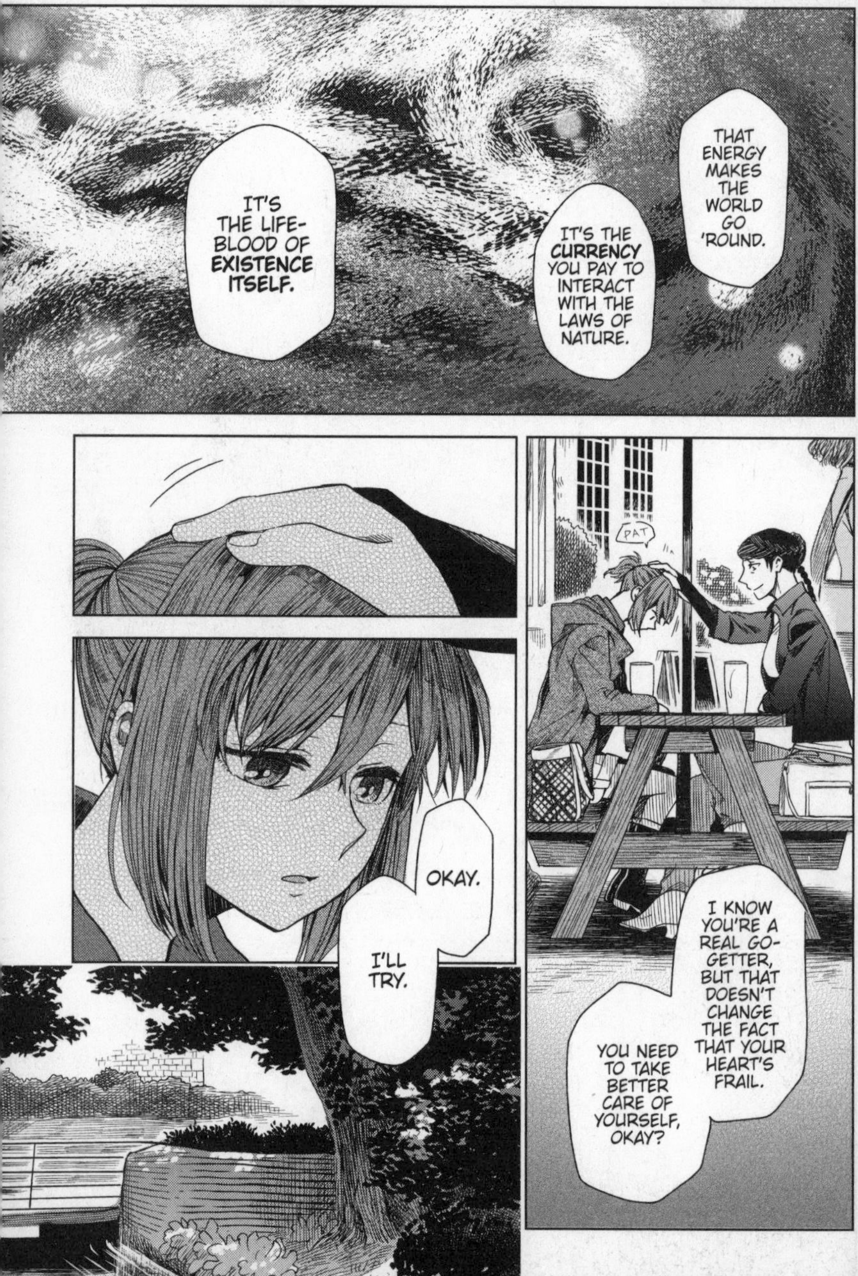
THAT ENERGY MAKES THE WORLD GO 'ROUND.
IT'S THE **CURRENCY** YOU PAY TO INTERACT WITH THE LAWS OF NATURE.
IT'S THE LIFE-BLOOD OF **EXISTENCE ITSELF.**
PAT
I KNOW YOU'RE A REAL GO-GETTER, BUT THAT DOESN'T CHANGE THE FACT THAT YOUR HEART'S FRAIL.
YOU NEED TO TAKE BETTER CARE OF YOURSELF, OKAY?
OKAY.
I'LL TRY.

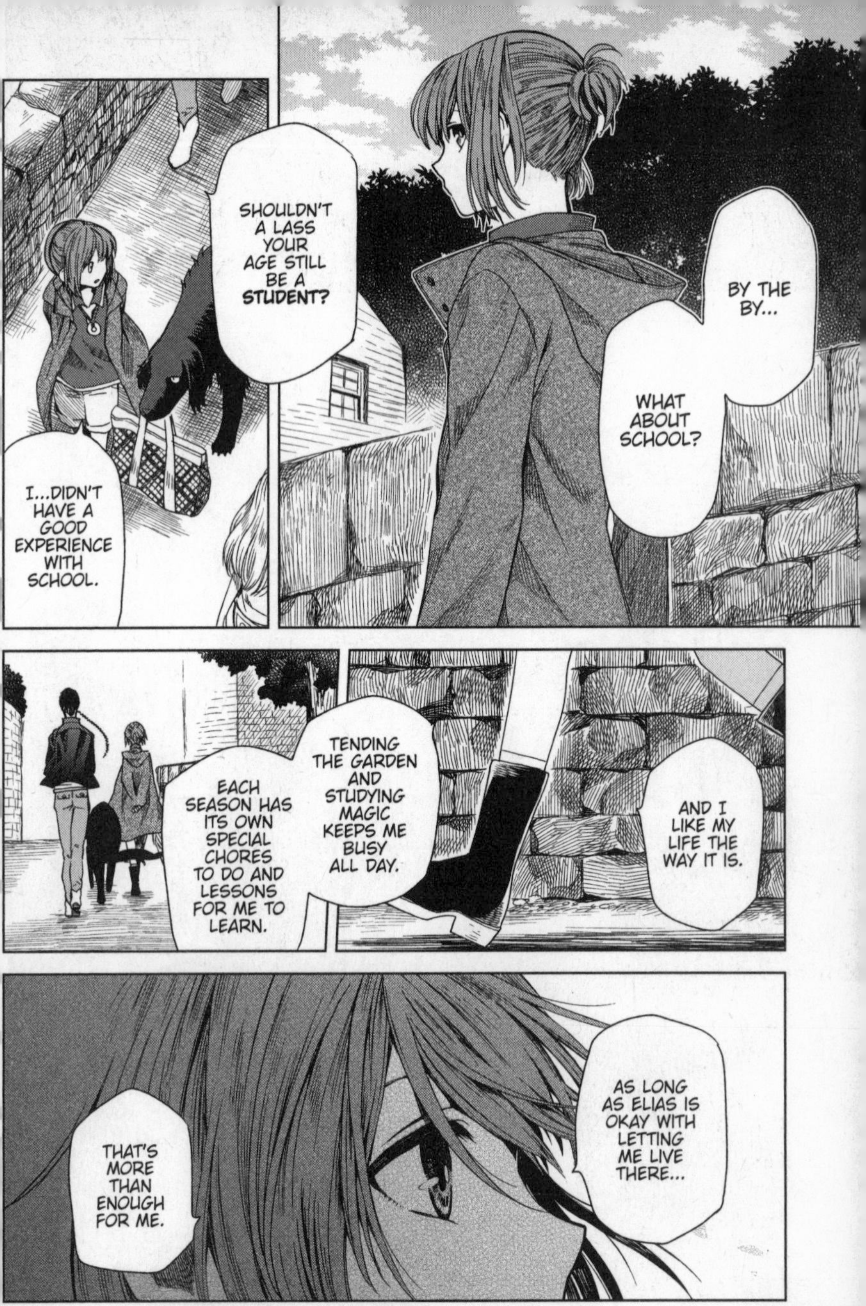
BY THE BY...
WHAT ABOUT SCHOOL?
SHOULDN'T A LASS YOUR AGE STILL BE A STUDENT?
I...DIDN'T HAVE A GOOD EXPERIENCE WITH SCHOOL.
AND I LIKE MY LIFE THE WAY IT IS.
TENDING THE GARDEN AND STUDYING MAGIC KEEPS ME BUSY ALL DAY.
EACH SEASON HAS ITS OWN SPECIAL CHORES TO DO AND LESSONS FOR ME TO LEARN.
AS LONG AS ELIAS IS OKAY WITH LETTING ME LIVE THERE...
THAT'S MORE THAN ENOUGH FOR ME.

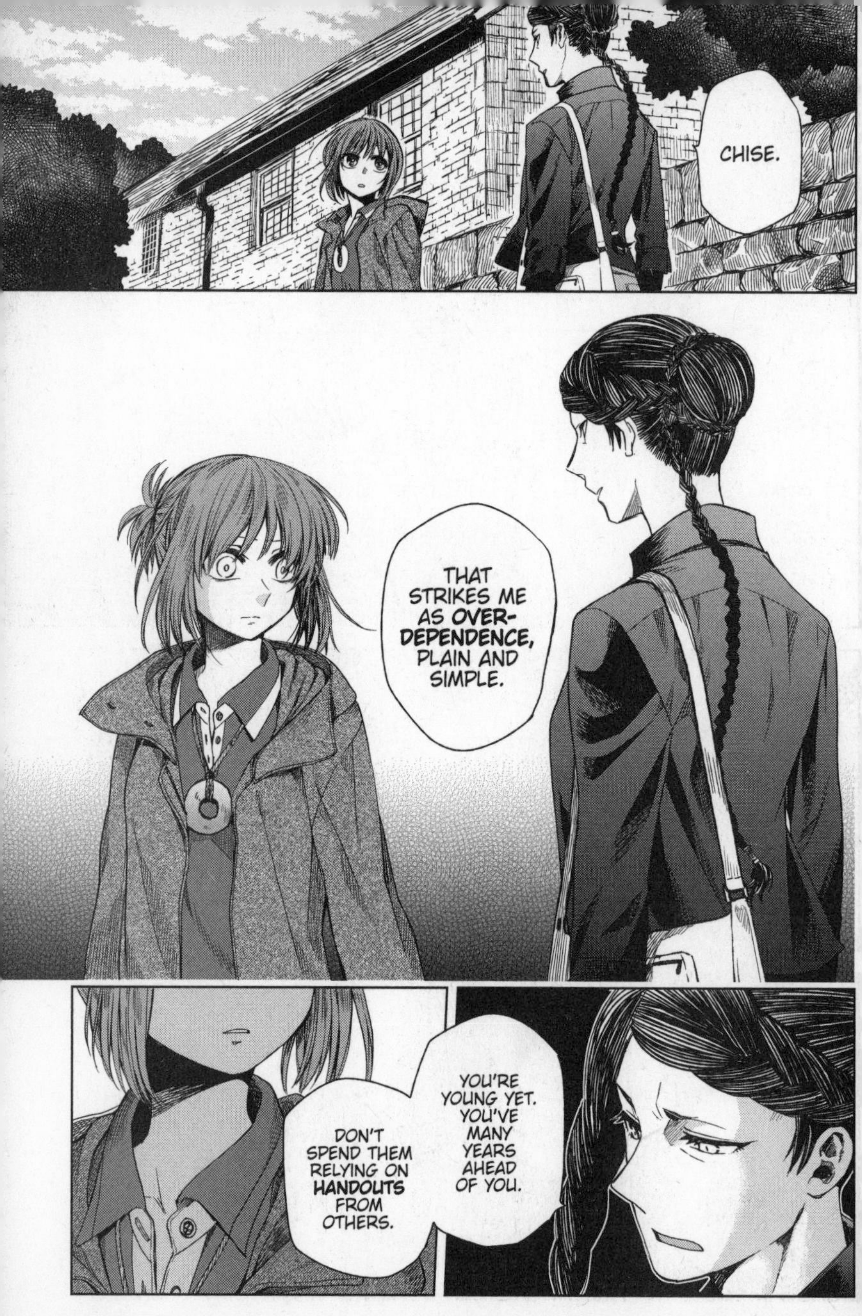
CHISE.
THAT STRIKES ME AS **OVER-DEPENDENCE**, PLAIN AND SIMPLE.
YOU'RE YOUNG YET. YOU'VE MANY YEARS AHEAD OF YOU.
DON'T SPEND THEM RELYING ON **HANDOUTS** FROM OTHERS.

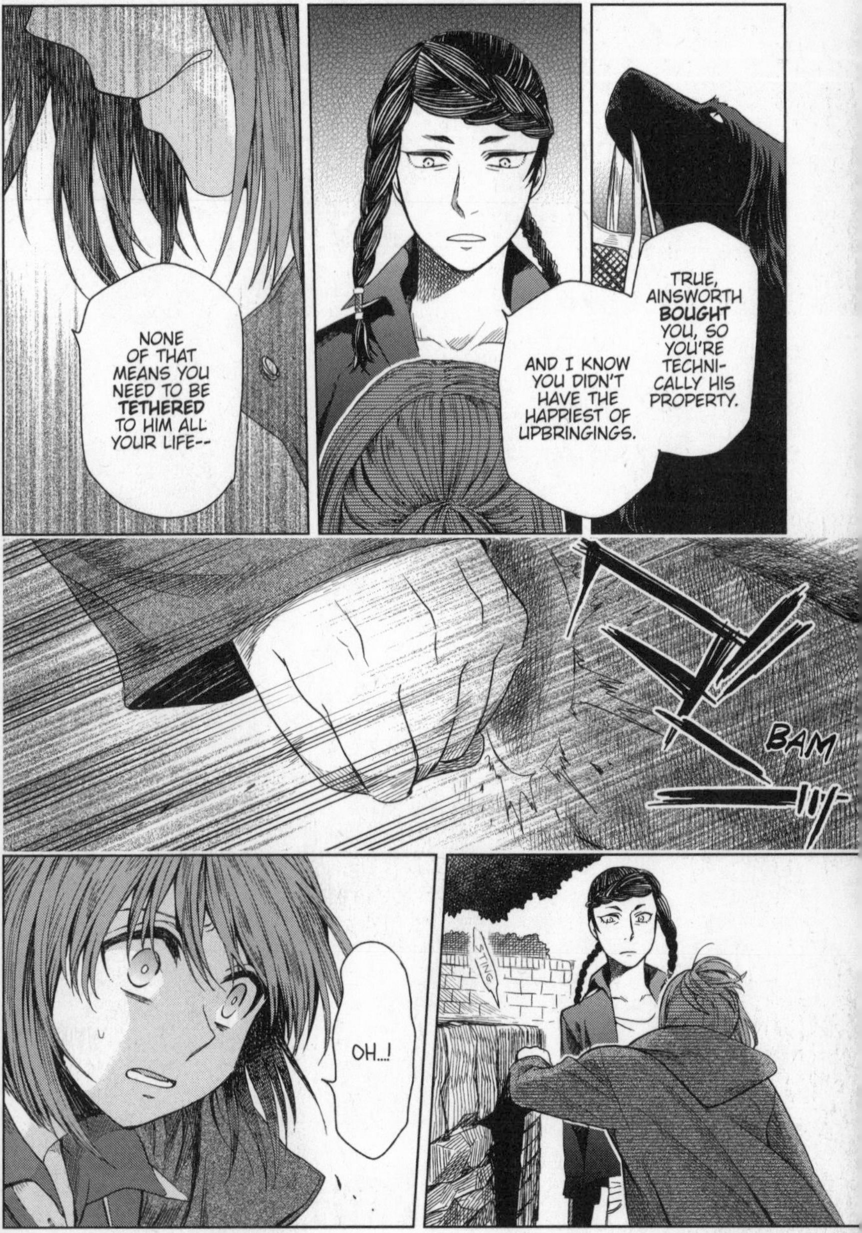
TRUE, AINSWORTH BOUGHT YOU, SO YOU'RE TECHNICALLY HIS PROPERTY.
AND I KNOW YOU DIDN'T HAVE THE HAPPIEST OF UPBRINGINGS.
NONE OF THAT MEANS YOU NEED TO BE TETHERED TO HIM ALL YOUR LIFE--
BAM
STING
OH...!

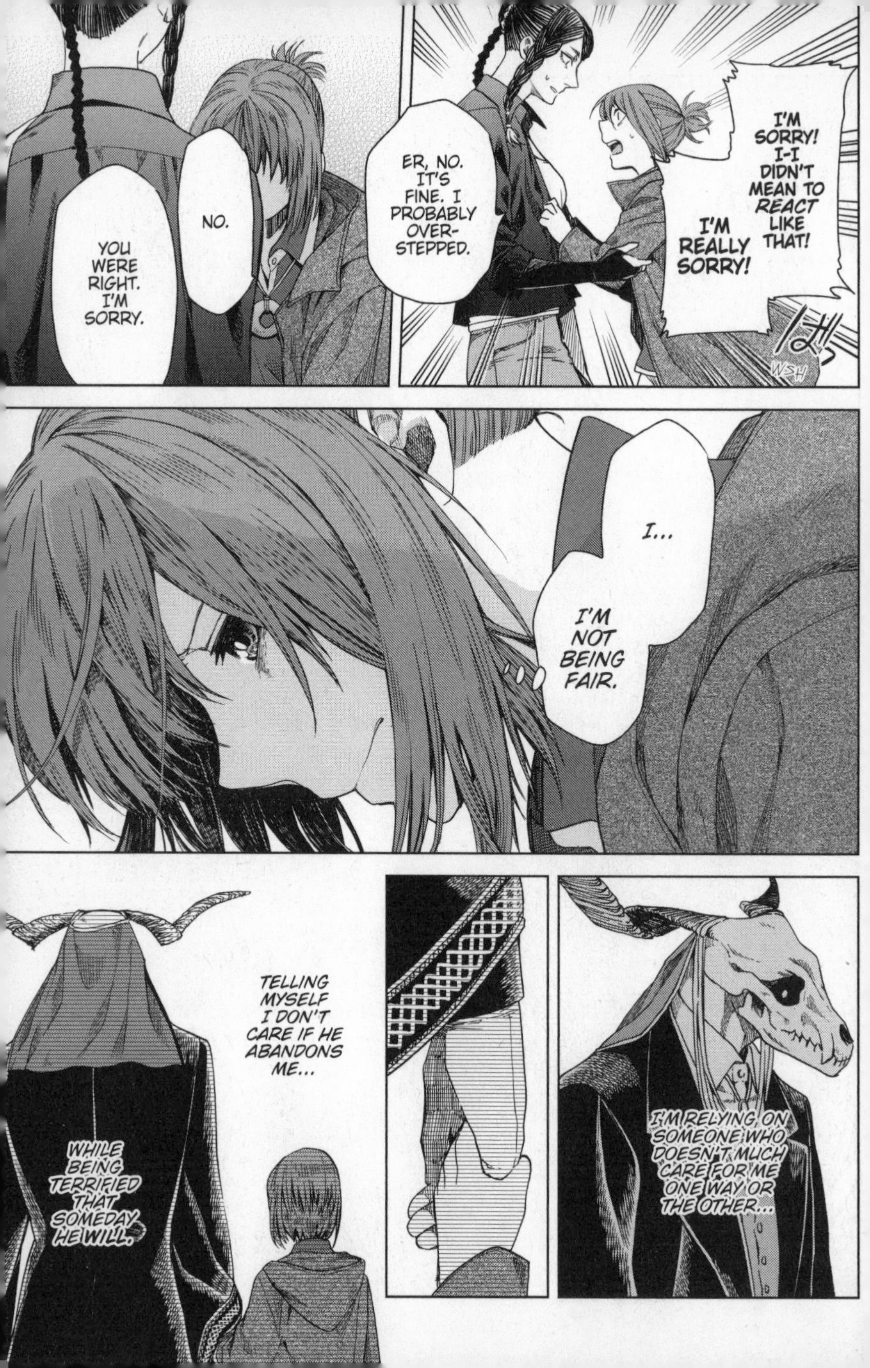
I'M SORRY! I-I DIDN'T MEAN TO REACT LIKE THAT!
I'M REALLY SORRY!
WSH
ER, NO. IT'S FINE. I PROBABLY OVER-STEPPED.
NO.
YOU WERE RIGHT. I'M SORRY.
I...
I'M NOT BEING FAIR.
I'M RELYING ON SOMEONE WHO DOESN'T MUCH CARE FOR ME ONE WAY OR THE OTHER...
TELLING MYSELF I DON'T CARE IF HE ABANDONS ME...
WHILE BEING TERRIFIED THAT SOMEDAY HE WILL.

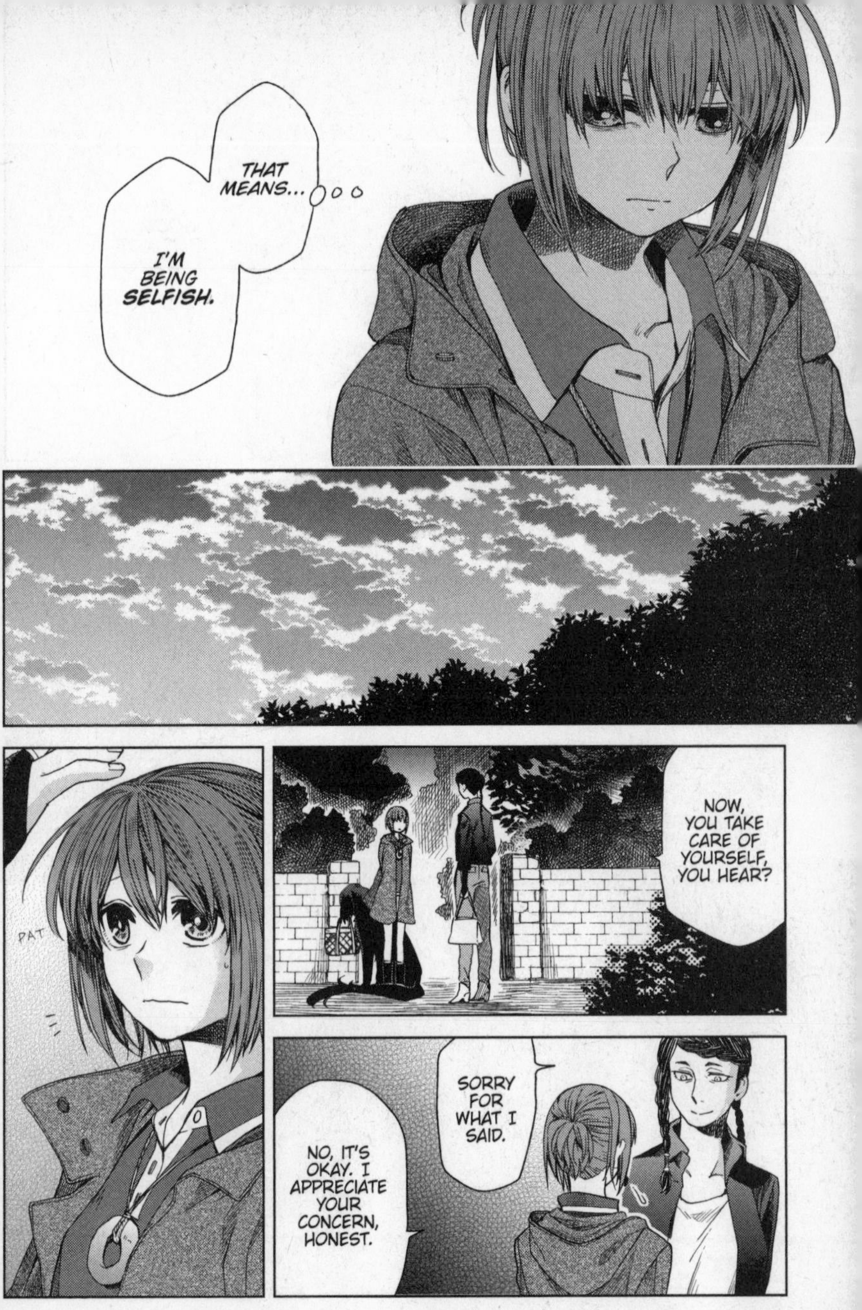
THAT MEANS...
I'M BEING SELFISH.
NOW, YOU TAKE CARE OF YOURSELF, YOU HEAR?
SORRY FOR WHAT I SAID.
NO, IT'S OKAY. I APPRECIATE YOUR CONCERN, HONEST.
PAT

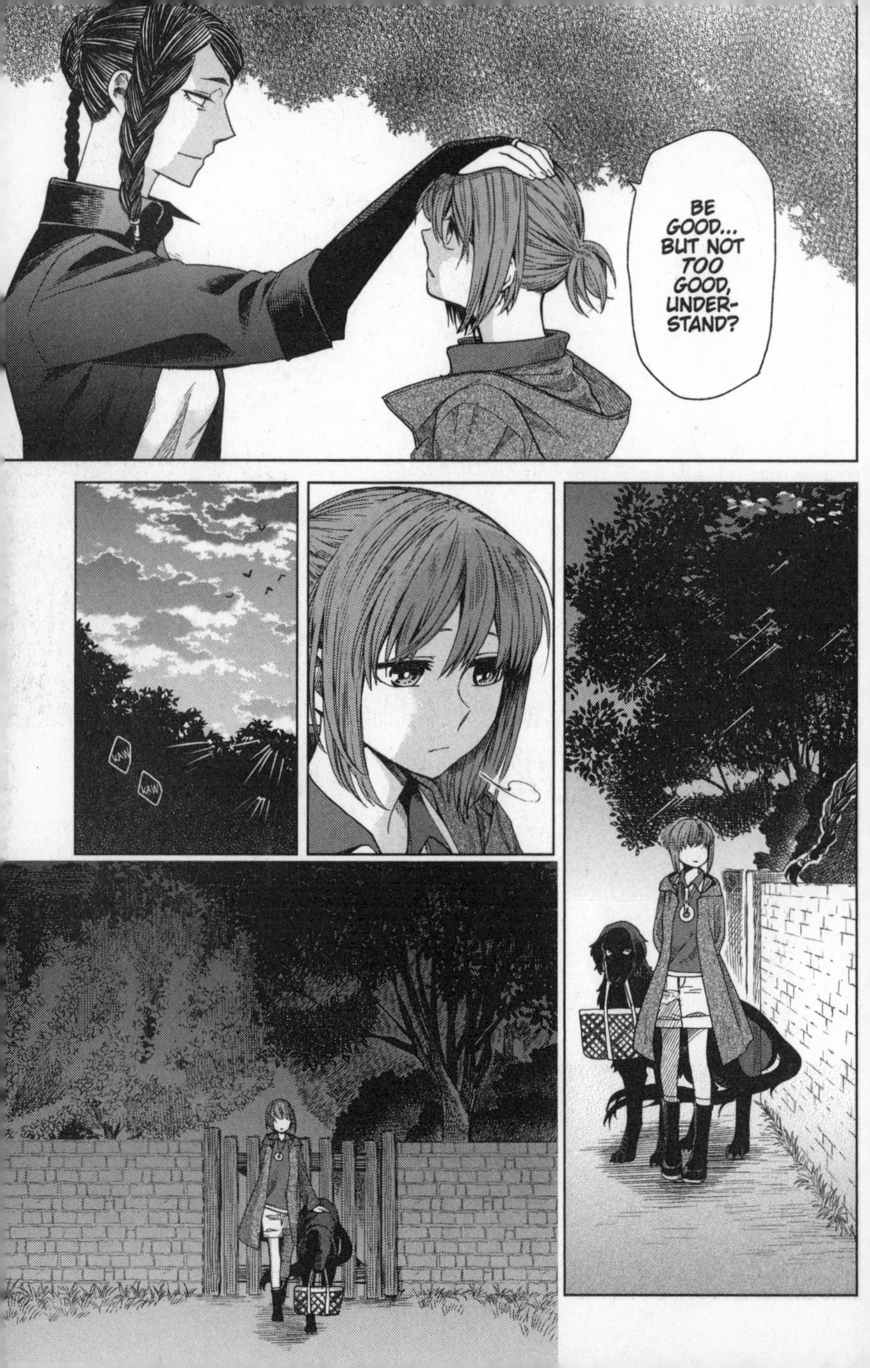
BE GOOD... BUT NOT *TOO* GOOD, UNDER-STAND?
KAW
KAW

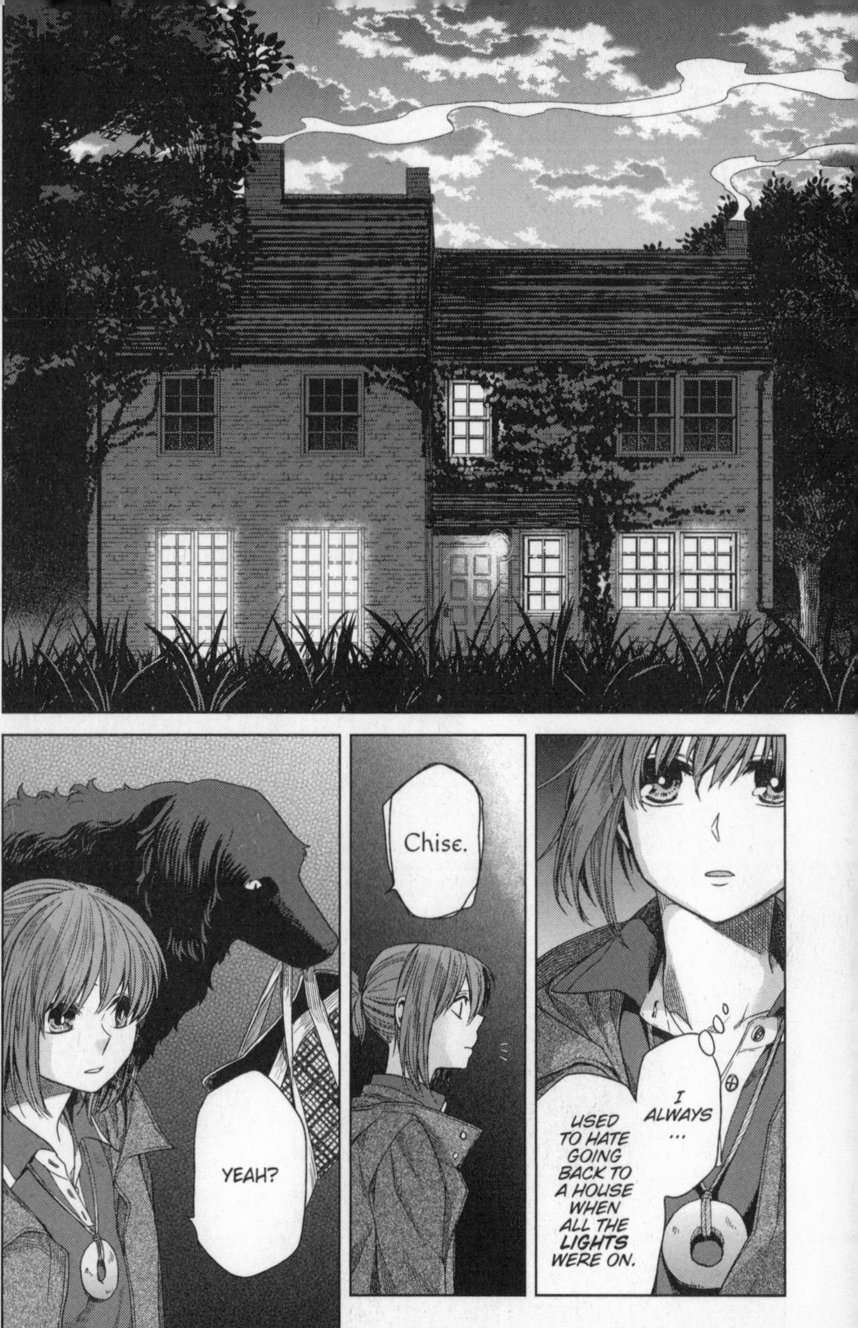
I ALWAYS ...
USED TO HATE GOING BACK TO A HOUSE WHEN ALL THE LIGHTS WERE ON.
Chise.
YEAH?

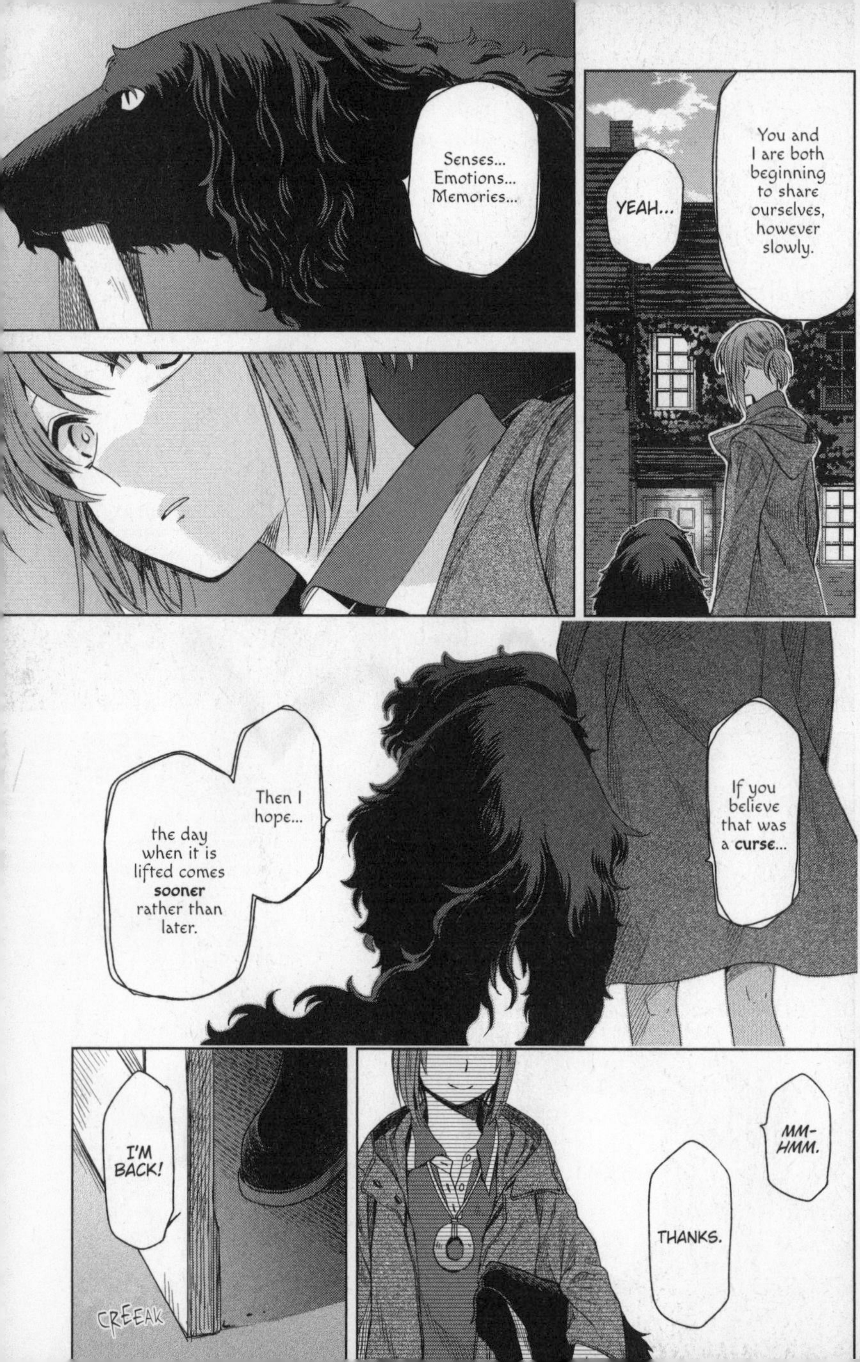
You and I are both beginning to share ourselves, however slowly.
YEAH...
Senses... Emotions... Memories...
If you believe that was a **curse**...
Then I hope...
the day when it is lifted comes **sooner** rather than later.
MM-HMM.
THANKS.
I'M BACK!
CREEAK

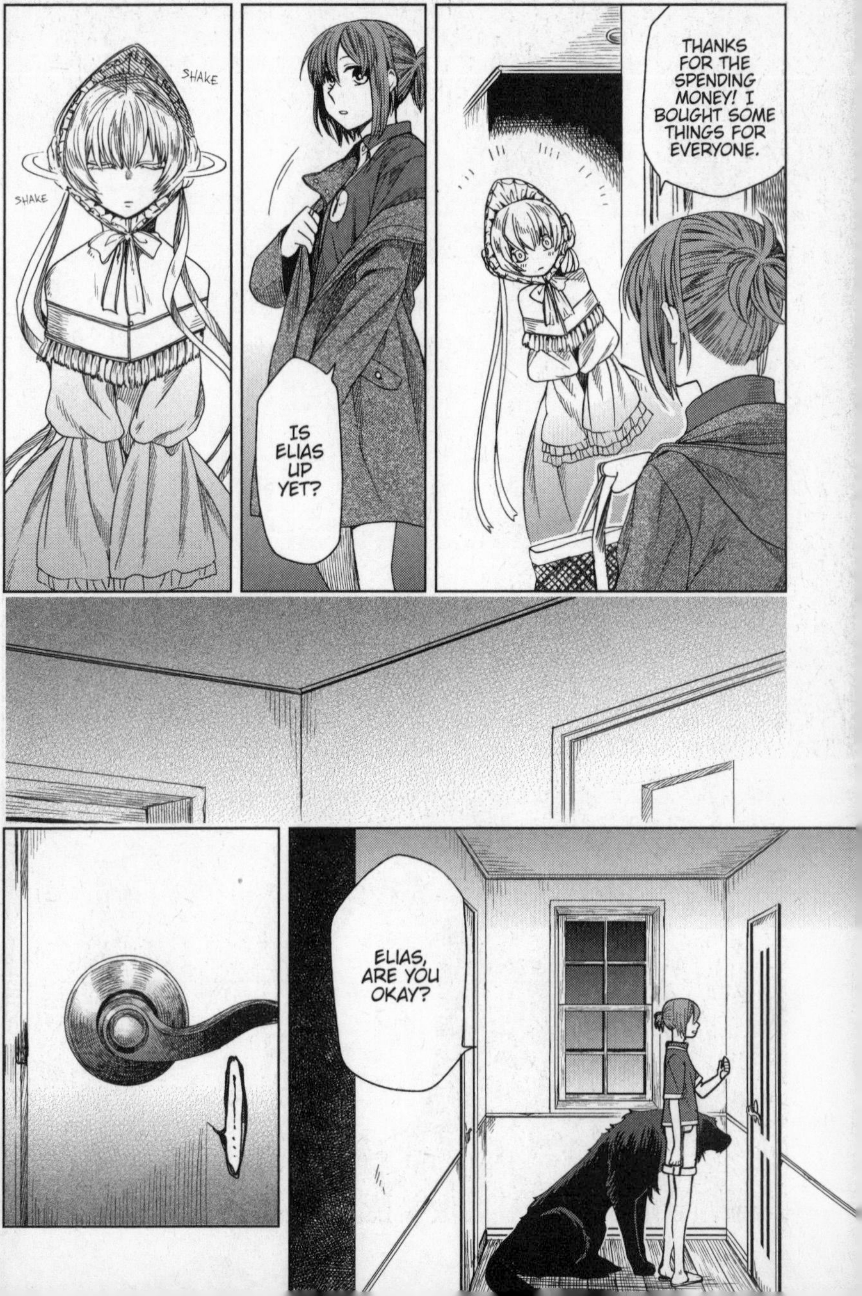
THANKS FOR THE SPENDING MONEY! I BOUGHT SOME THINGS FOR EVERYONE.
IS ELIAS UP YET?
SHAKE
SHAKE
ELIAS, ARE YOU OKAY?
......

......
KCHAK
カチャッ
CREAK
ELIAS?
ARE YOU IN HERE?
ELIA--
SLAM

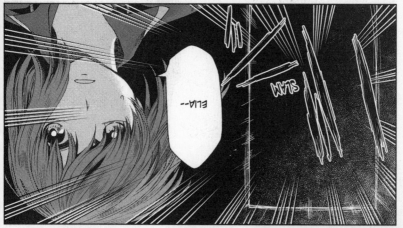

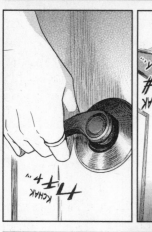

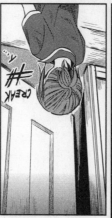

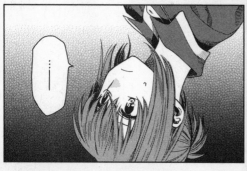

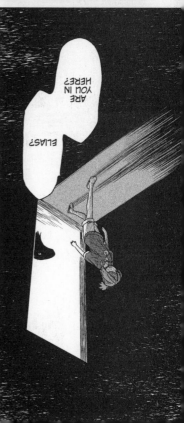

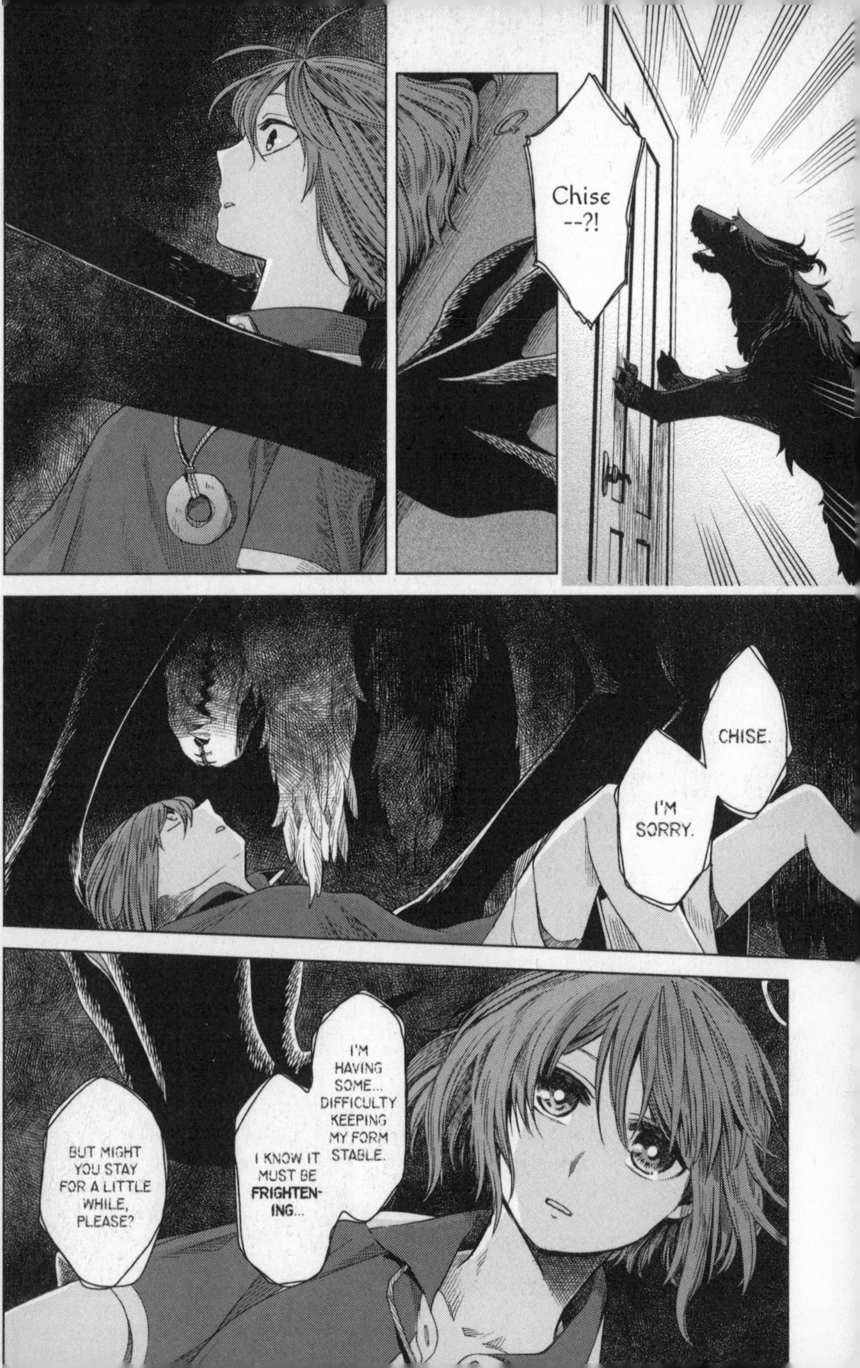
Chise --?!
CHISE.
I'M SORRY.
I'M HAVING SOME... DIFFICULTY KEEPING MY FORM STABLE.
I KNOW IT MUST BE FRIGHTENING...
BUT MIGHT YOU STAY FOR A LITTLE WHILE, PLEASE?

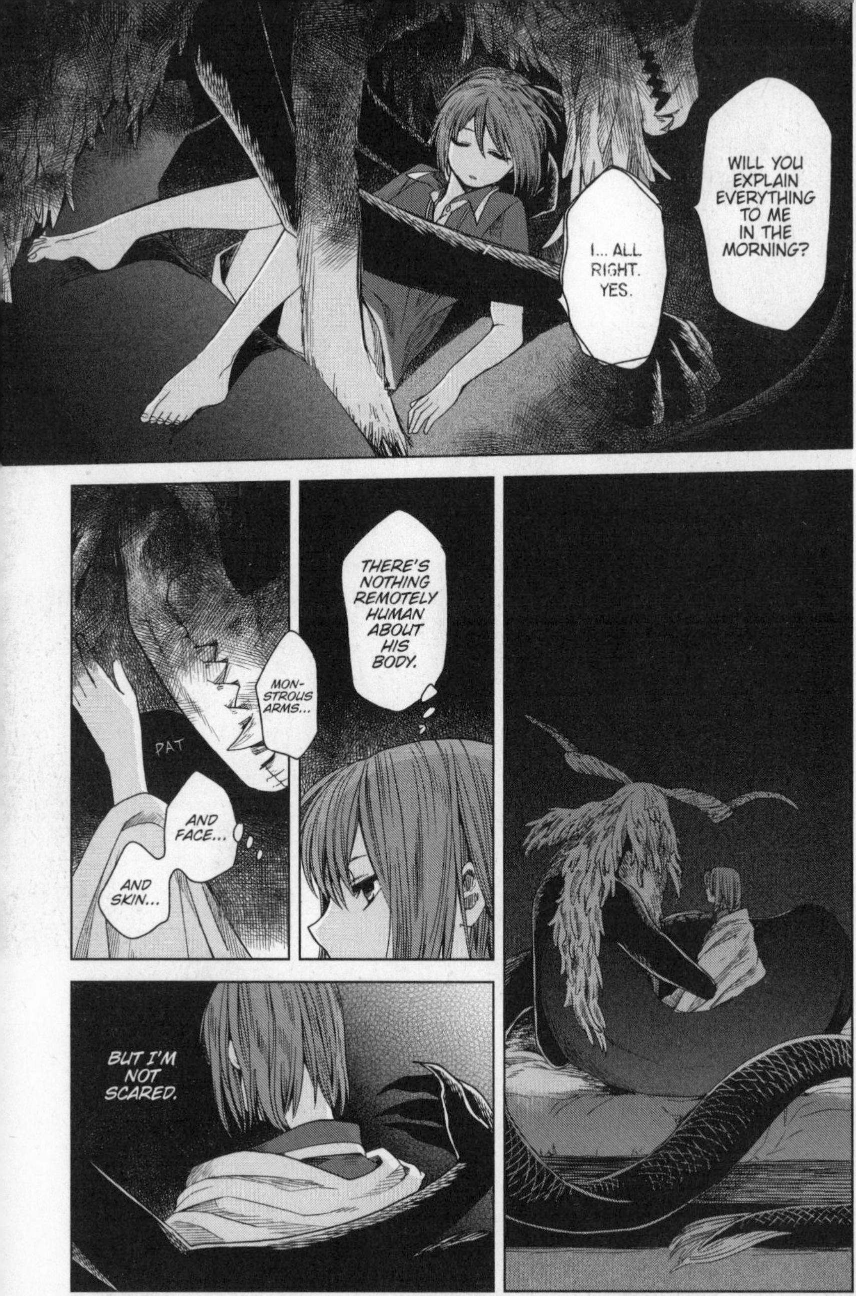
WILL YOU EXPLAIN EVERYTHING TO ME IN THE MORNING?
I... ALL RIGHT. YES.
THERE'S NOTHING REMOTELY HUMAN ABOUT HIS BODY.
MON-STROUS ARMS...
PAT
AND FACE...
AND SKIN...
BUT I'M NOT SCARED.

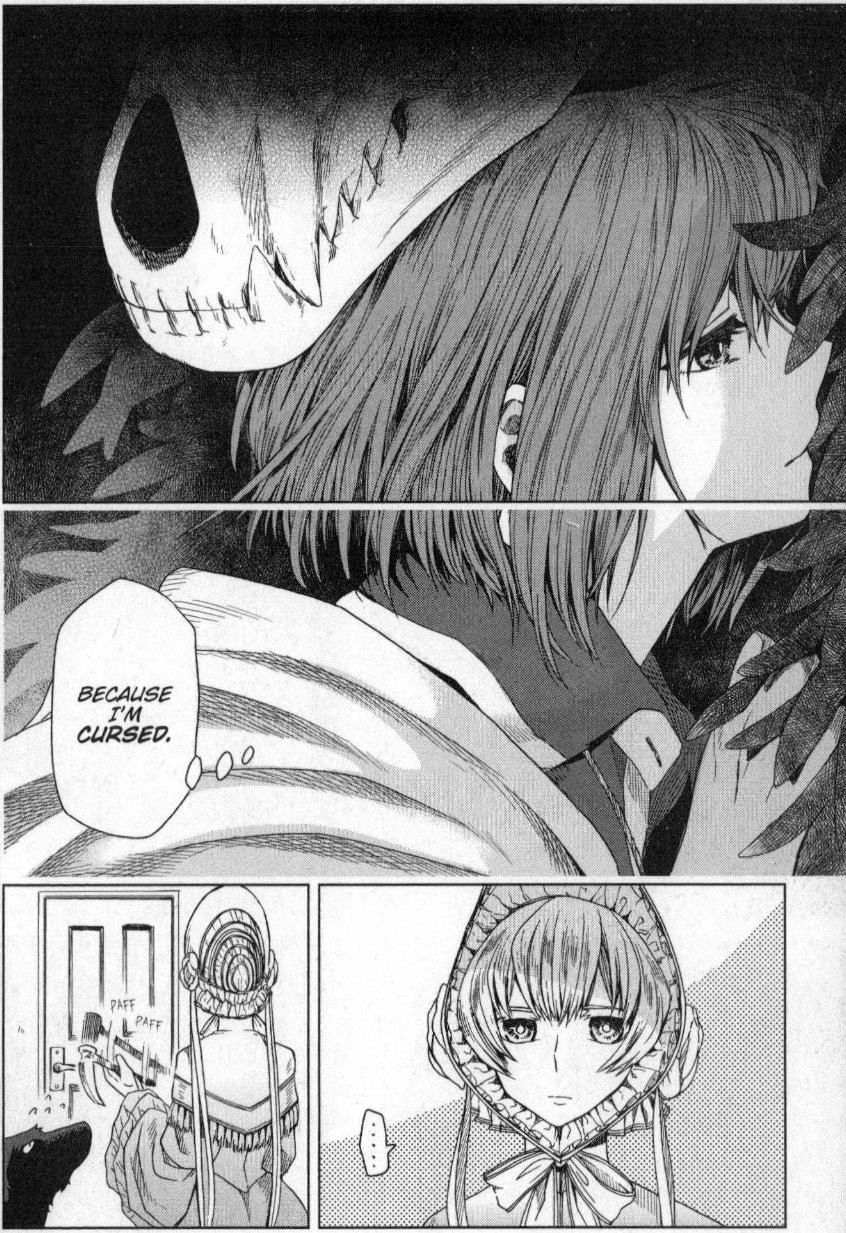
BECAUSE I'M CURSED.
.....
PAFF
PAFF

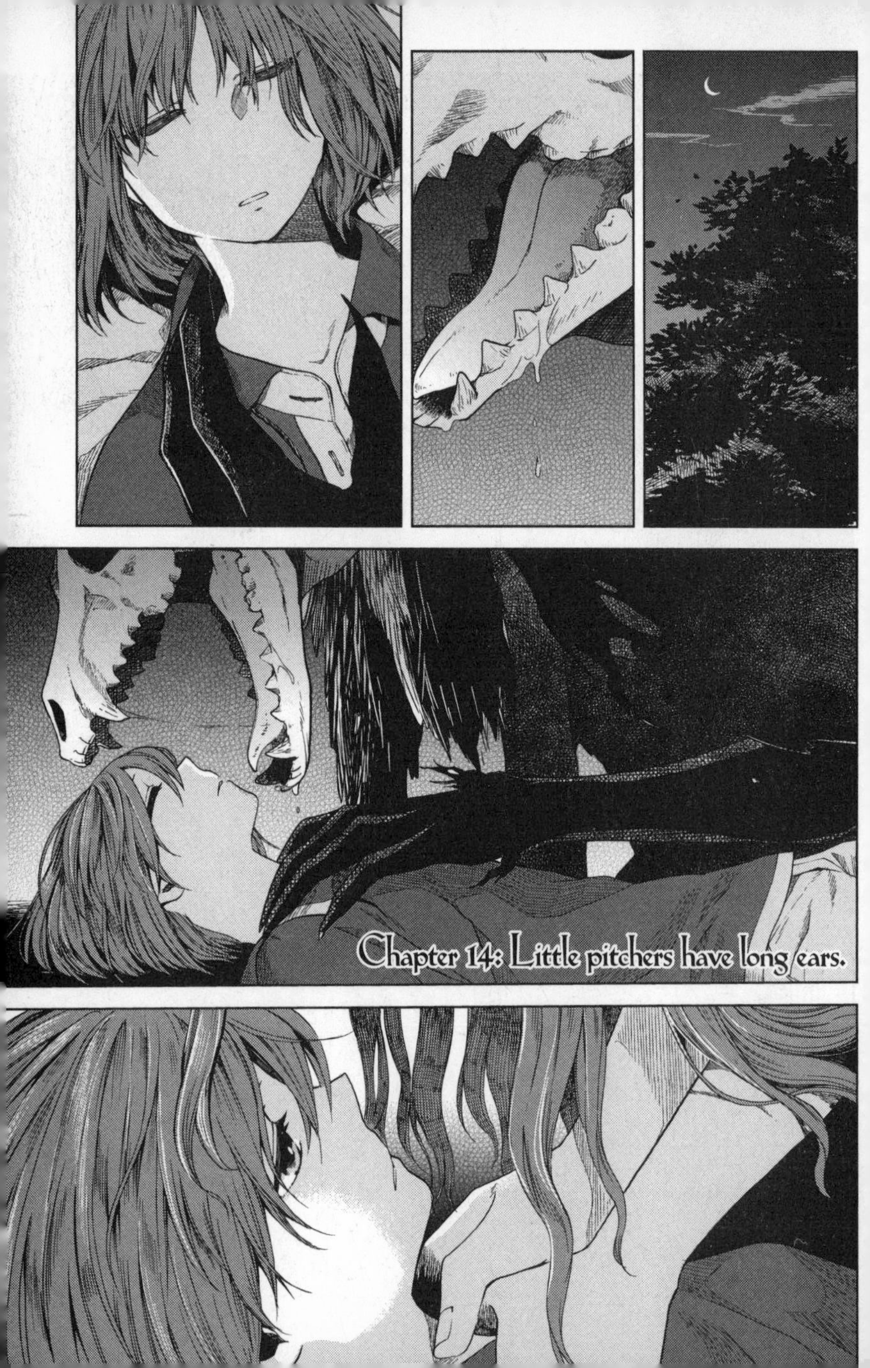
Chapter 14: Little pitchers have long ears.

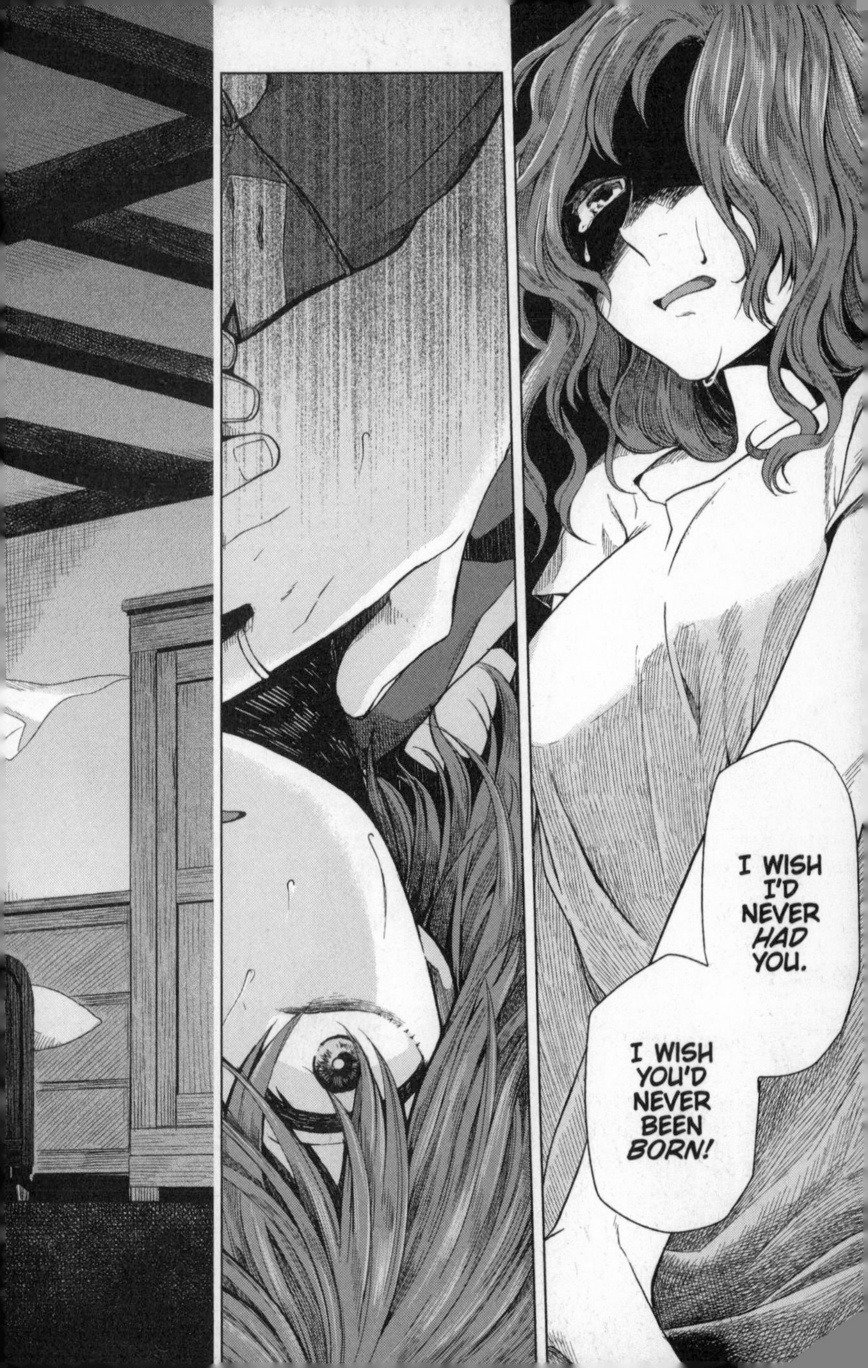
I WISH I'D NEVER *HAD* YOU.
I WISH YOU'D NEVER BEEN *BORN!*

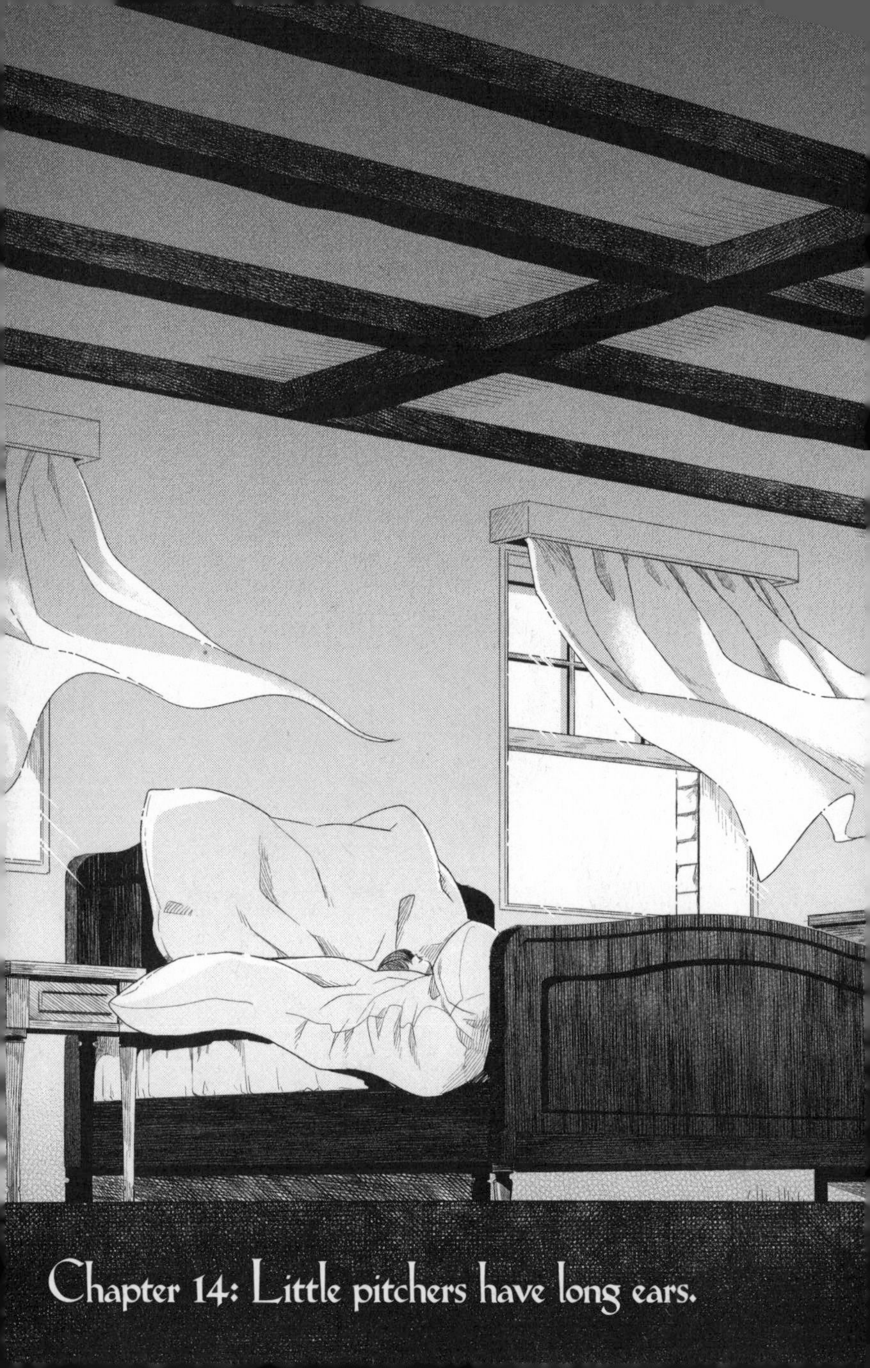
Chapter 14: Little pitchers have long ears.

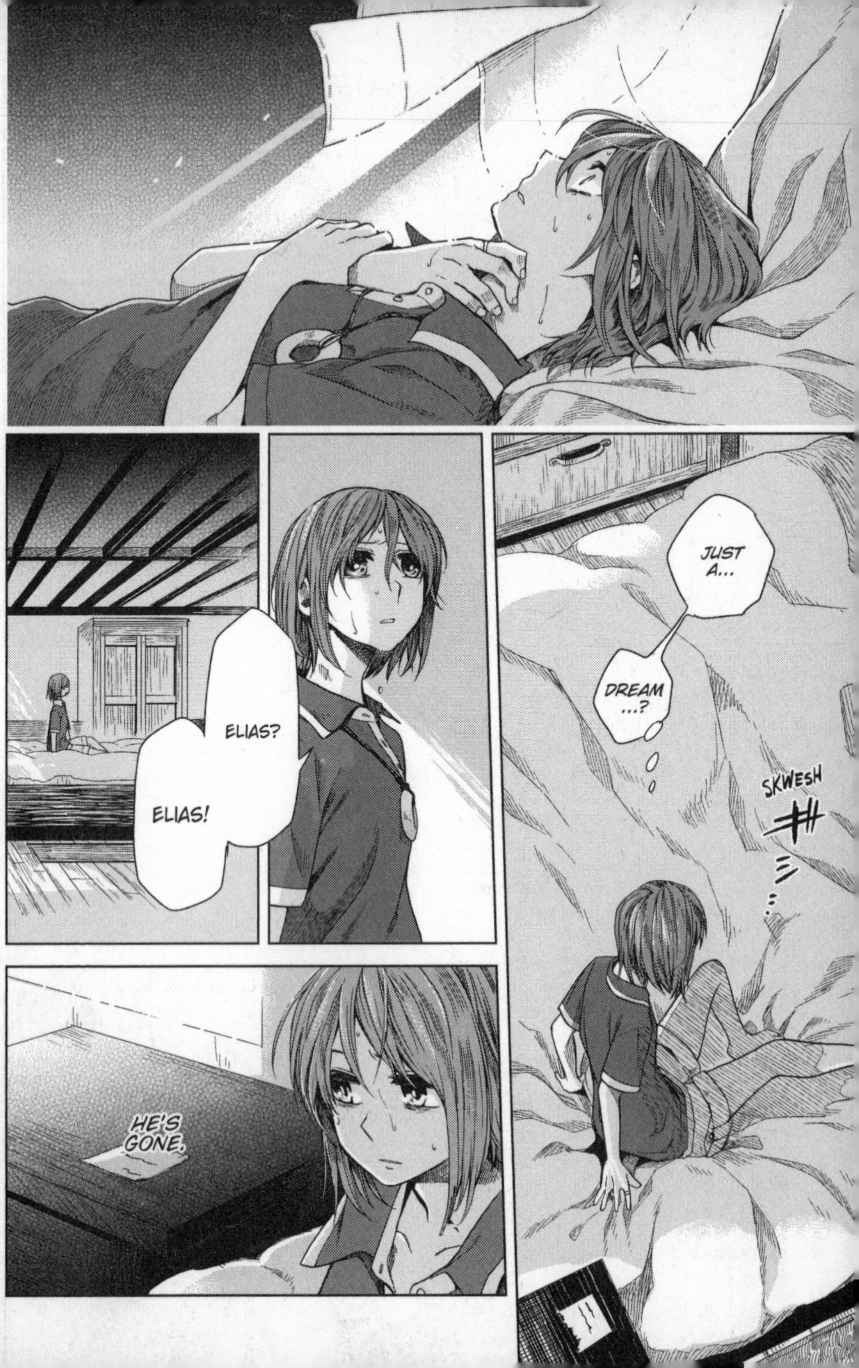
JUST A...
DREAM ...?
SKWESH
ELIAS?
ELIAS!
HE'S GONE.

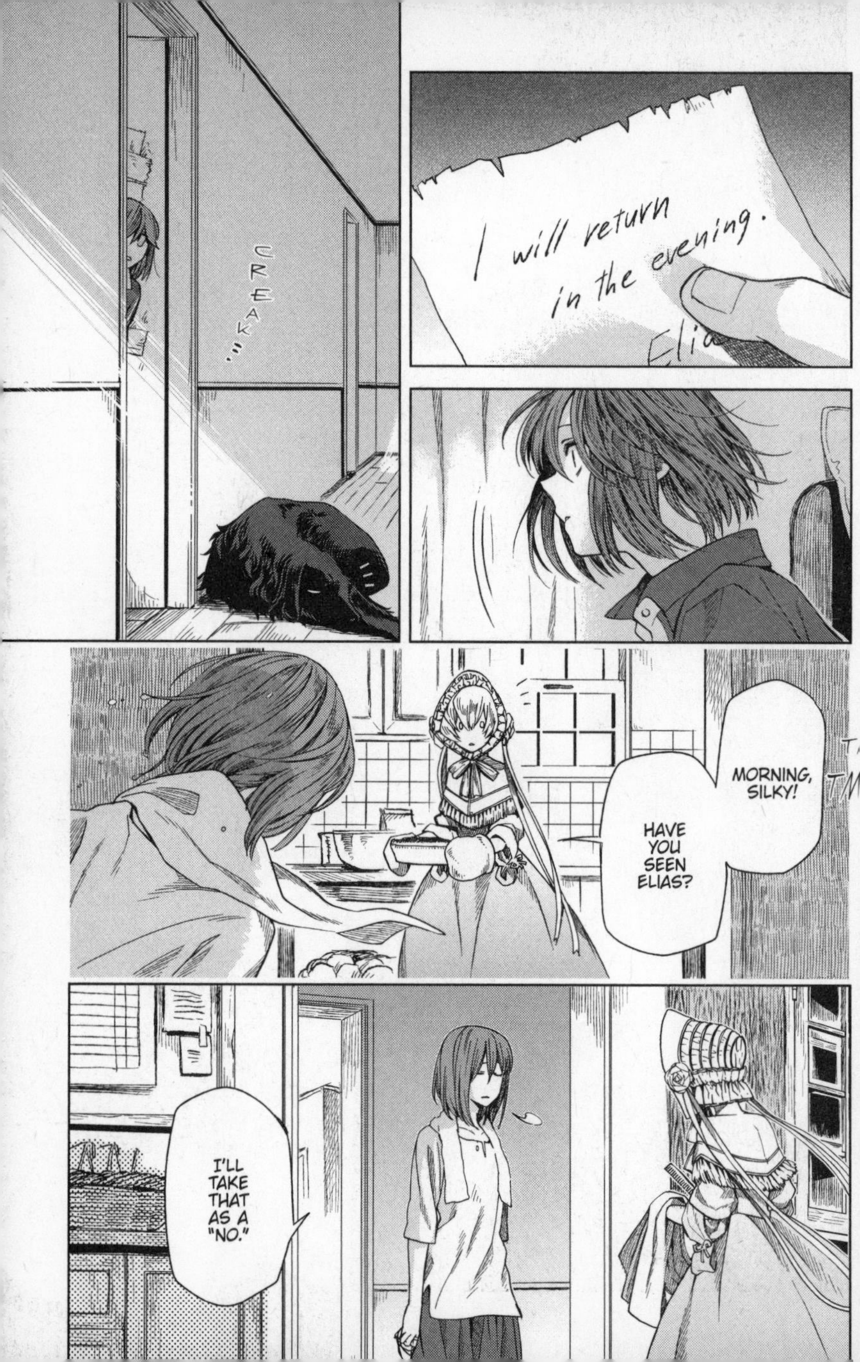
I will return in the evening.
CREAK...
MORNING, SILKY!
HAVE YOU SEEN ELIAS?
I'LL TAKE THAT AS A "NO."

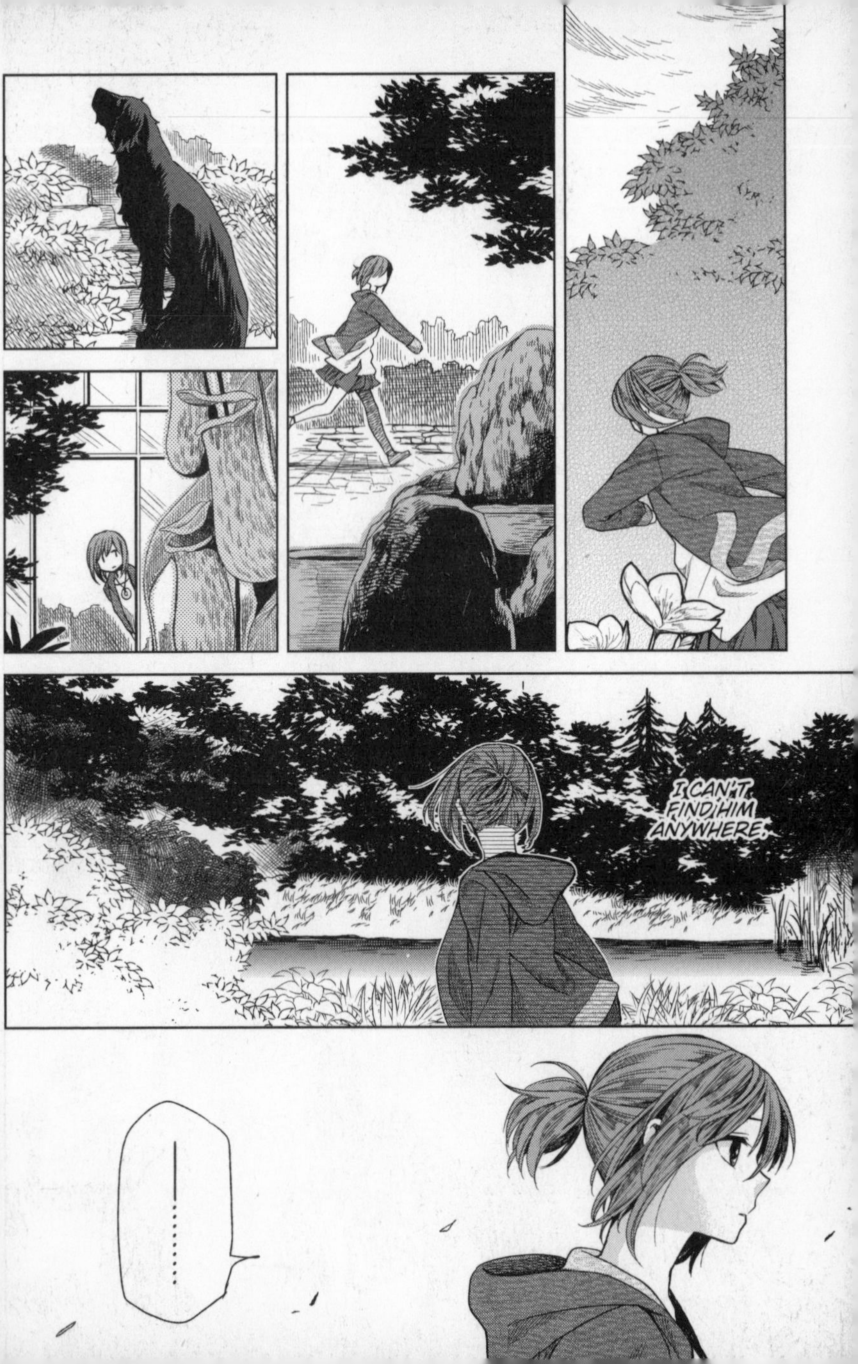
I CAN'T FIND HIM ANYWHERE.
—……

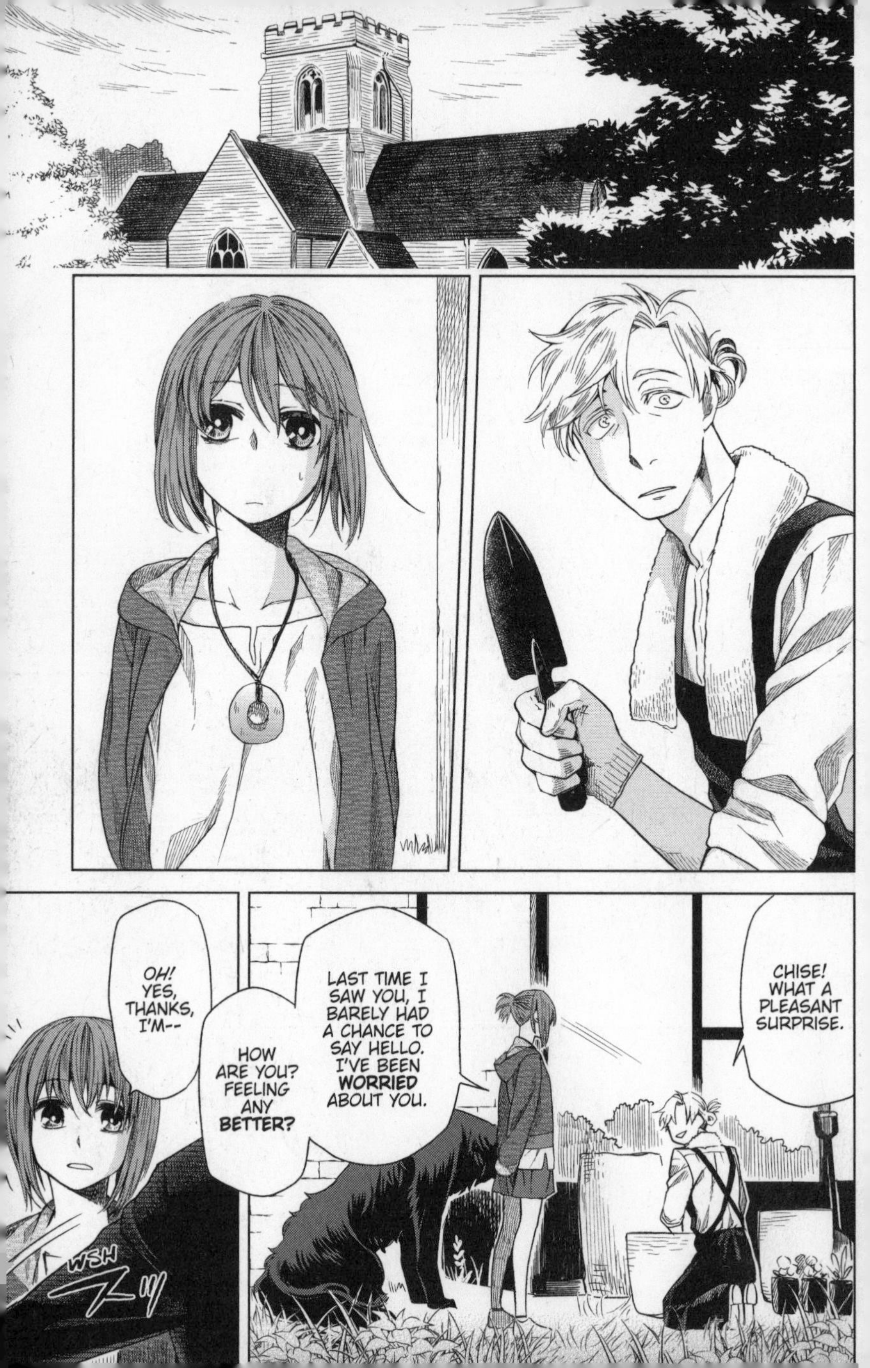
CHISE! WHAT A PLEASANT SURPRISE.
LAST TIME I SAW YOU, I BARELY HAD A CHANCE TO SAY HELLO. I'VE BEEN **WORRIED** ABOUT YOU.
HOW ARE YOU? FEELING ANY **BETTER?**
OH! YES, THANKS, I'M--
WSH

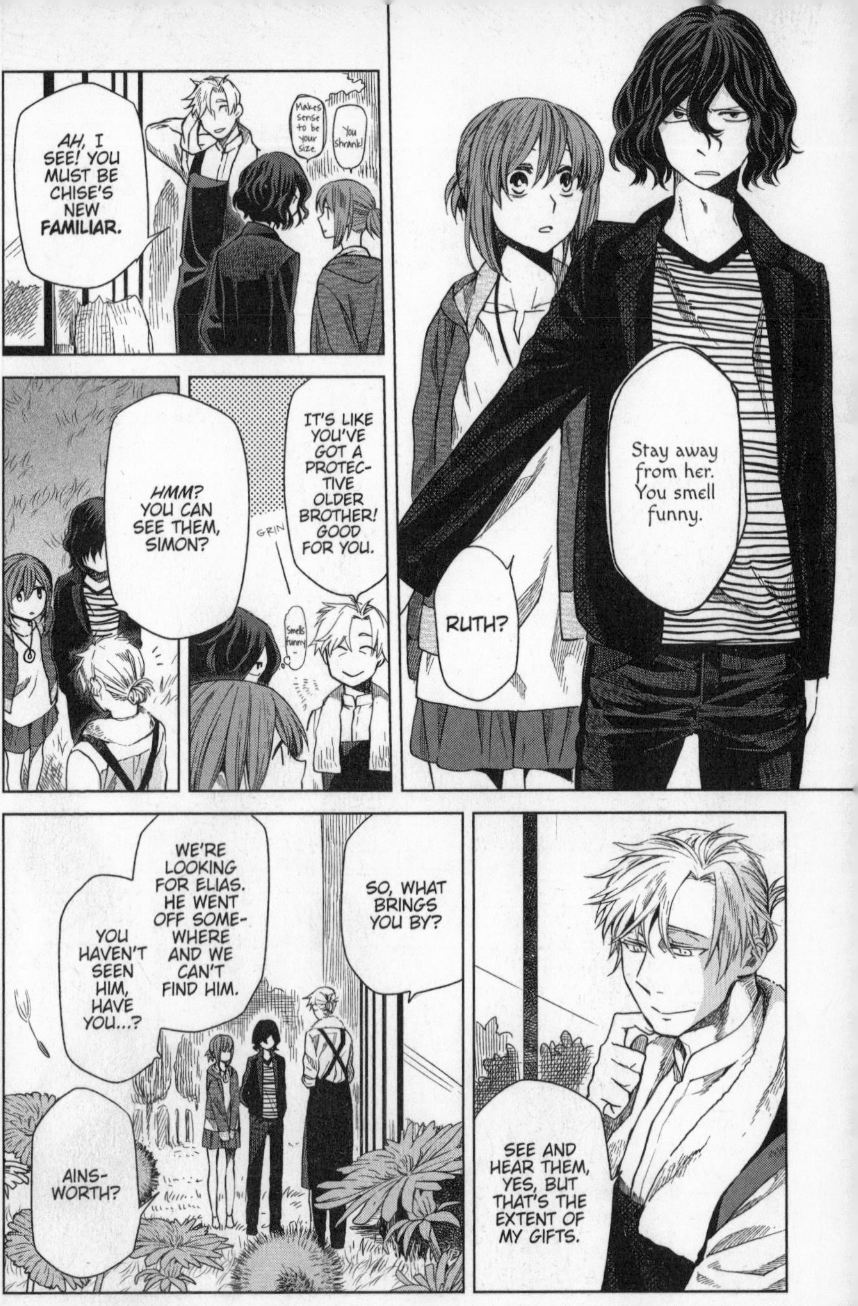
Stay away from her. You smell funny.
RUTH?
AH, I SEE! YOU MUST BE CHISE'S NEW FAMILIAR.
Makes sense to be your size.
You shrank!
IT'S LIKE YOU'VE GOT A PROTECTIVE OLDER BROTHER! GOOD FOR YOU.
GRIN
Smells funny
HMM? YOU CAN SEE THEM, SIMON?
SEE AND HEAR THEM, YES, BUT THAT'S THE EXTENT OF MY GIFTS.
SO, WHAT BRINGS YOU BY?
WE'RE LOOKING FOR ELIAS. HE WENT OFF SOMEWHERE AND WE CAN'T FIND HIM.
YOU HAVEN'T SEEN HIM, HAVE YOU...?
AINSWORTH?

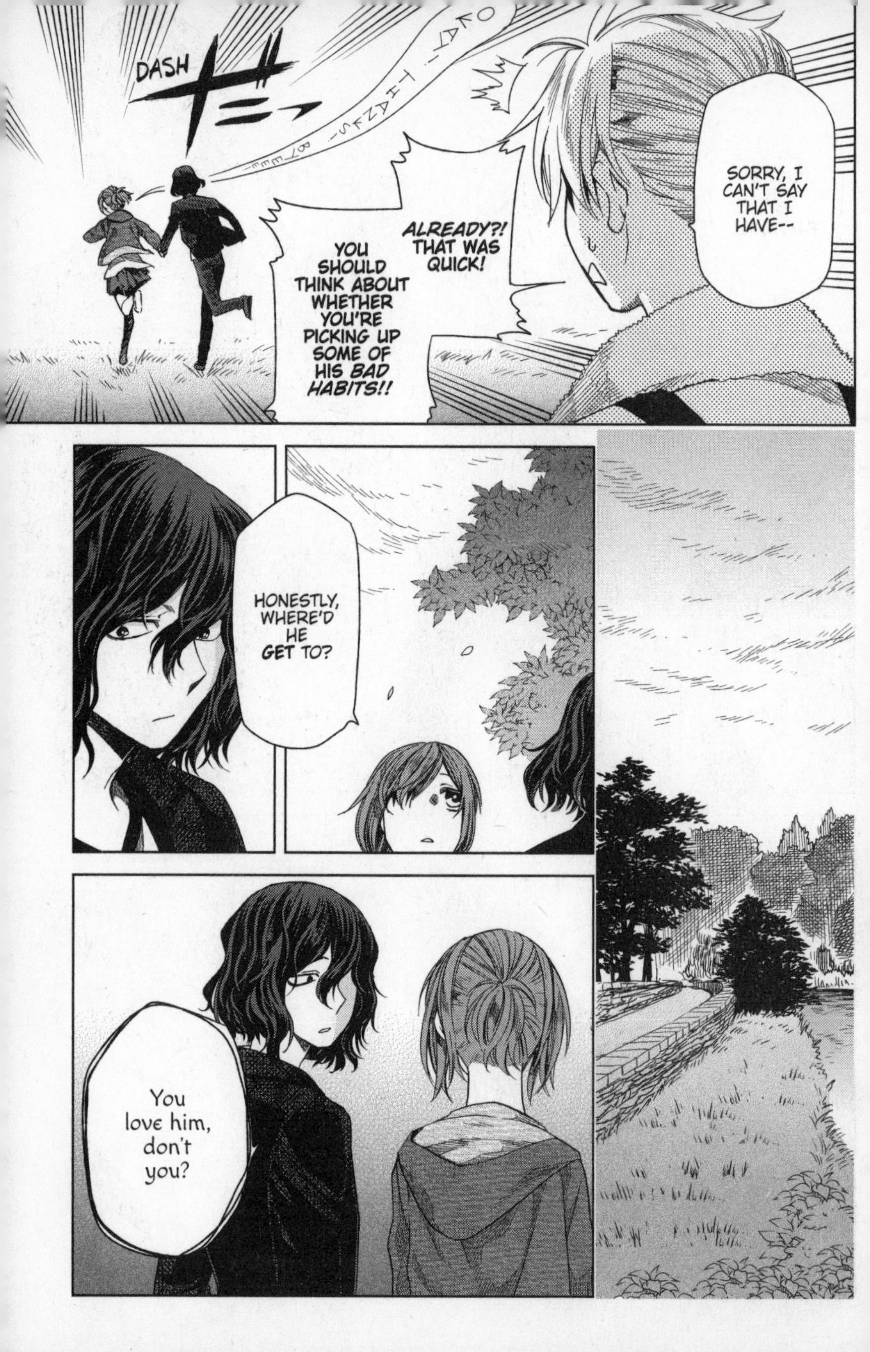
SORRY, I CAN'T SAY THAT I HAVE--
OKAY-- THANKS-- BYEEE--
DASH
ALREADY?! THAT WAS QUICK!
YOU SHOULD THINK ABOUT WHETHER YOU'RE PICKING UP SOME OF HIS BAD HABITS!!
HONESTLY, WHERE'D HE GET TO?
You love him, don't you?

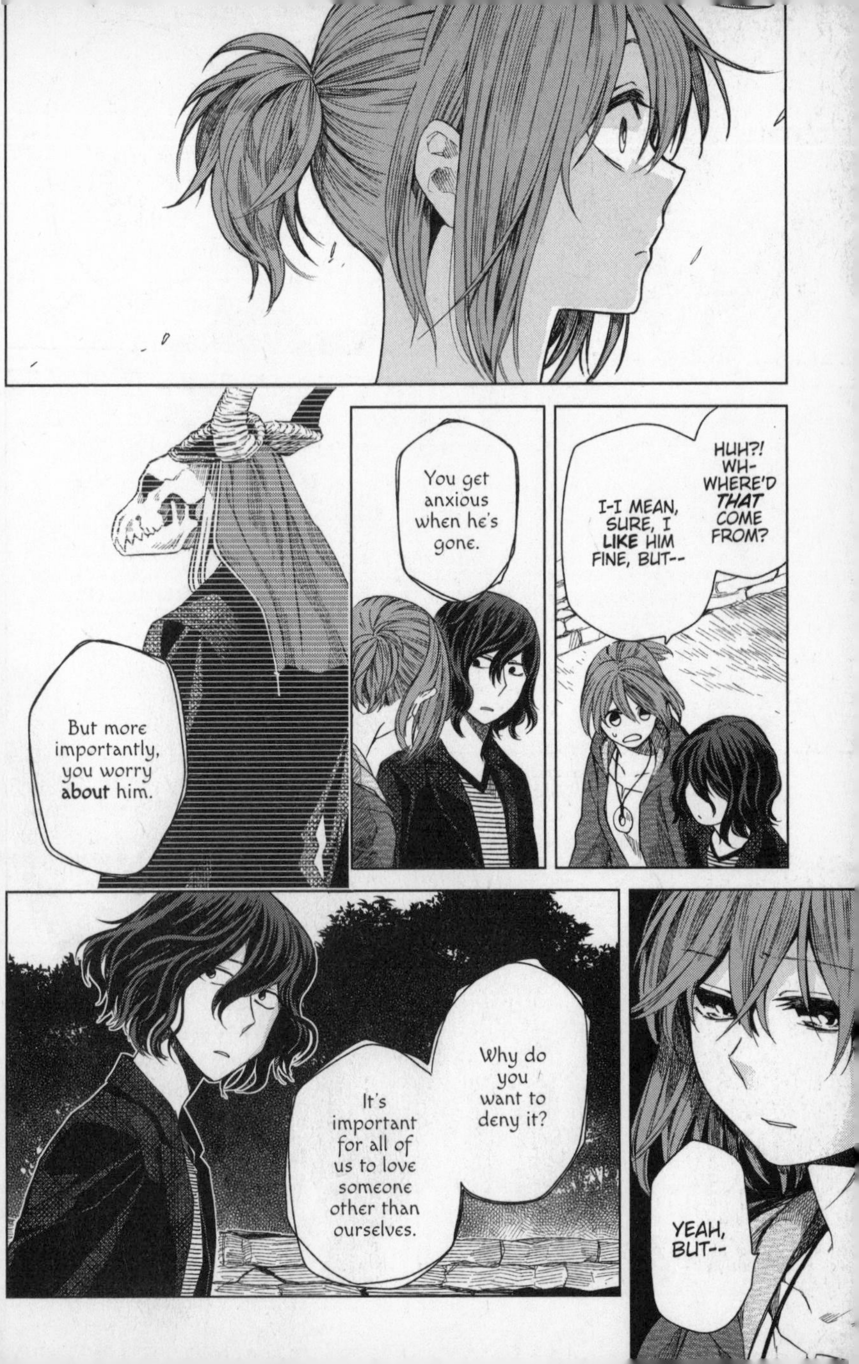
HUH?! WH- WHERE'D *THAT* COME FROM?
I-I MEAN, SURE, I **LIKE** HIM FINE, BUT--
You get anxious when he's gone.
But more importantly, you worry **about** him.
YEAH, BUT--
Why do you want to deny it?
It's important for all of us to love someone other than ourselves.

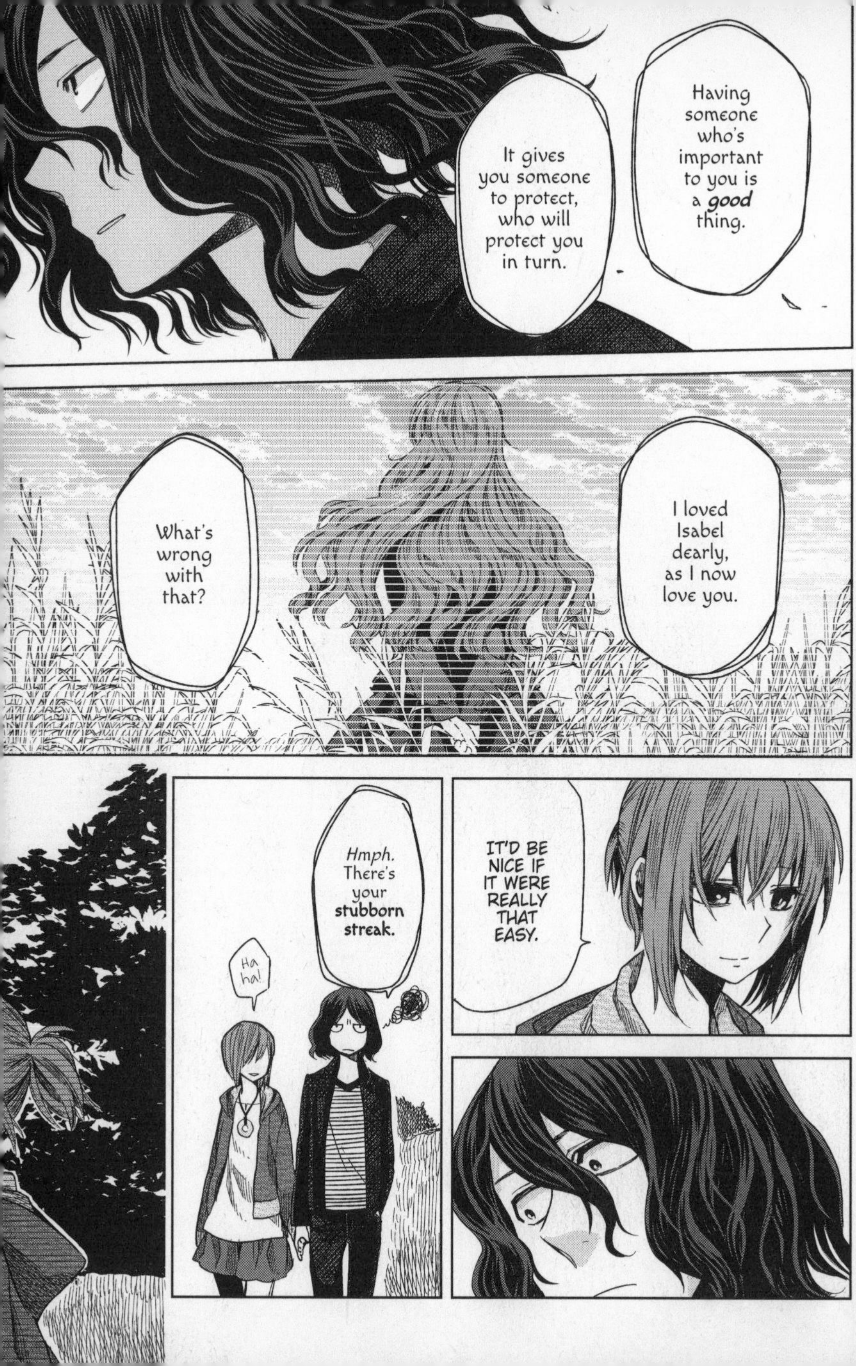
Having someone who's important to you is a ***good*** thing.
It gives you someone to protect, who will protect you in turn.
I loved Isabel dearly, as I now love you.
What's wrong with that?
IT'D BE NICE IF IT WERE REALLY THAT EASY.
Hmph. There's your **stubborn streak.**
Ha ha!

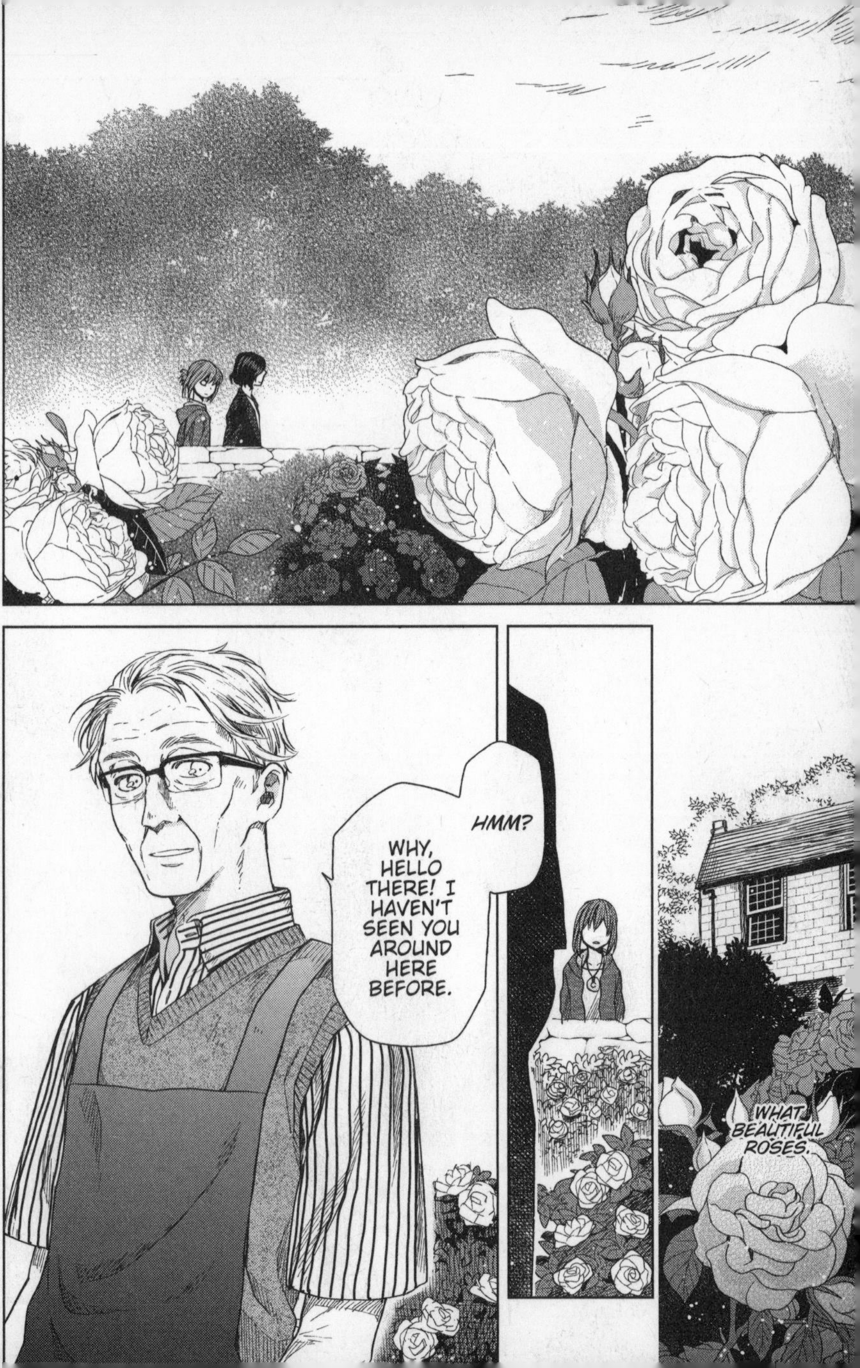
WHAT BEAUTIFUL ROSES.
HMM?
WHY, HELLO THERE! I HAVEN'T SEEN YOU AROUND HERE BEFORE.

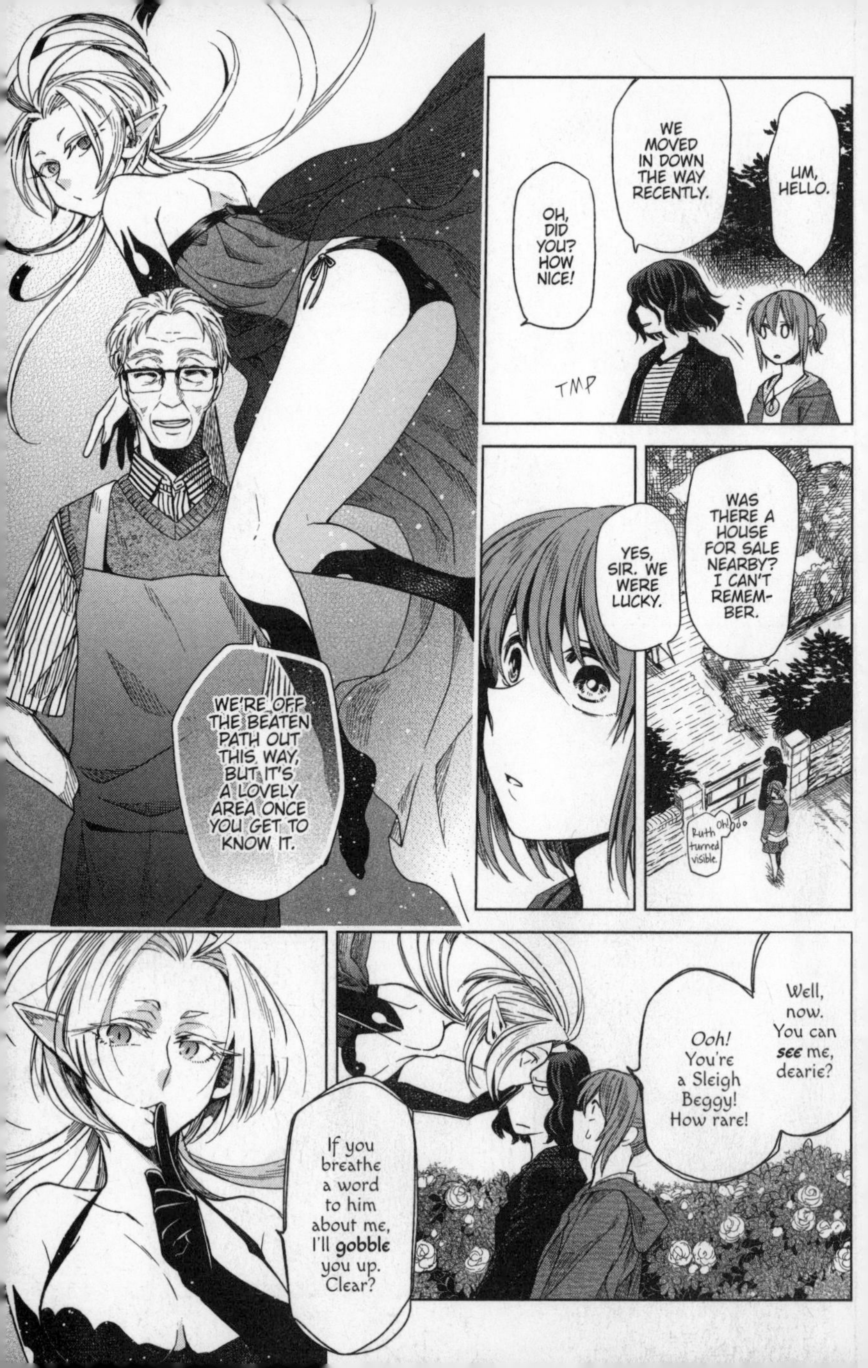
UM, HELLO.
WE MOVED IN DOWN THE WAY RECENTLY.
OH, DID YOU? HOW NICE!
TMP
WAS THERE A HOUSE FOR SALE NEARBY? I CAN'T REMEMBER.
Oh!
Ruth turned visible.
YES, SIR. WE WERE LUCKY.
WE'RE OFF THE BEATEN PATH OUT THIS WAY, BUT IT'S A LOVELY AREA ONCE YOU GET TO KNOW IT.
Well, now. You can **see** me, dearie?
Ooh! You're a Sleigh Beggy! How rare!
If you breathe a word to him about me, I'll **gobble** you up. Clear?

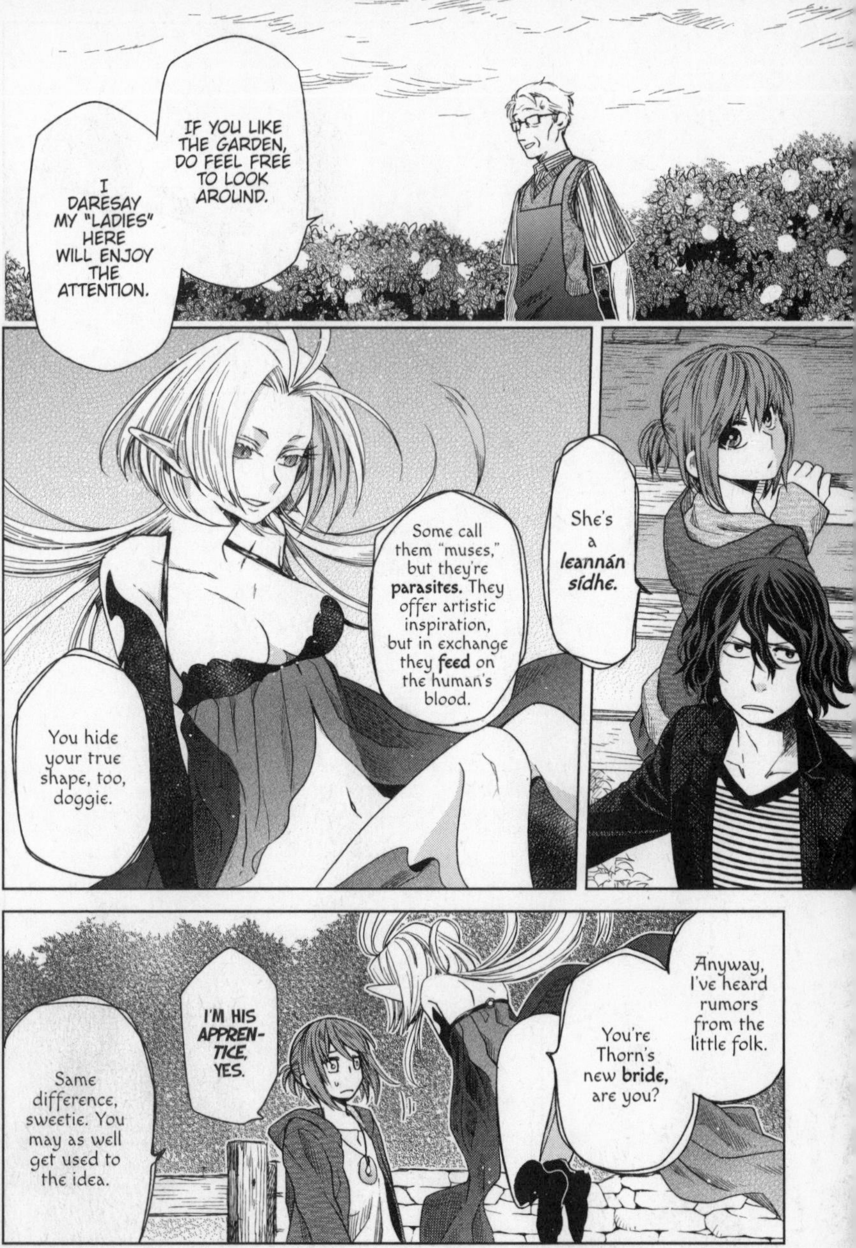
IF YOU LIKE THE GARDEN, DO FEEL FREE TO LOOK AROUND.
I DARESAY MY "LADIES" HERE WILL ENJOY THE ATTENTION.
She's a **leannán sídhe.**
Some call them "muses," but they're **parasites.** They offer artistic inspiration, but in exchange they **feed** on the human's blood.
You hide your true shape, too, doggie.
Anyway, I've heard rumors from the little folk.
You're Thorn's new **bride,** are you?
I'M HIS APPRENTICE, YES.
Same difference, sweetie. You may as well get used to the idea.

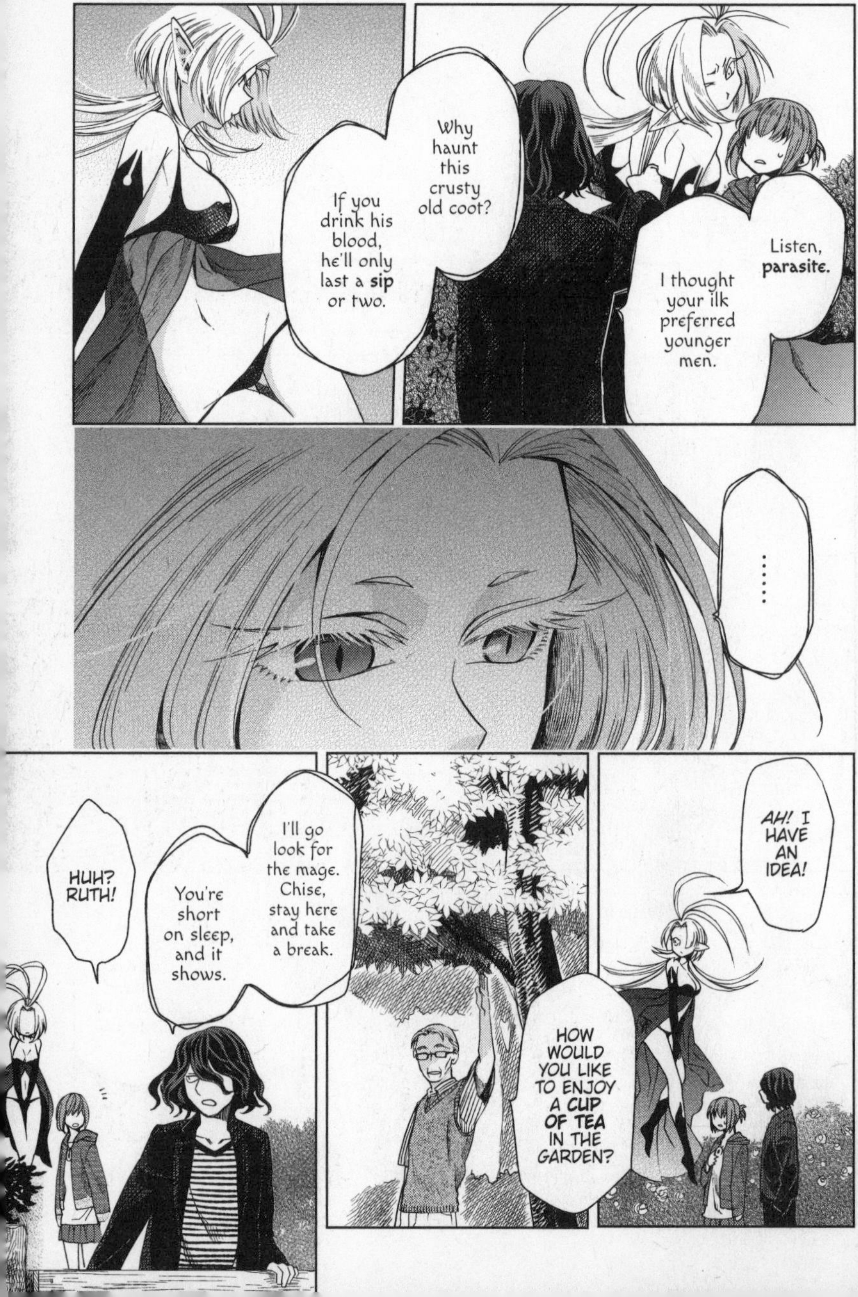
Listen, **parasite.**
I thought your ilk preferred younger men.
Why haunt this crusty old coot?
If you drink his blood, he'll only last a **sip** or two.
......
AH! I HAVE AN IDEA!
HOW WOULD YOU LIKE TO ENJOY A CUP OF TEA IN THE GARDEN?
I'll go look for the mage. Chise, stay here and take a break.
You're short on sleep, and it shows.
HUH? RUTH!

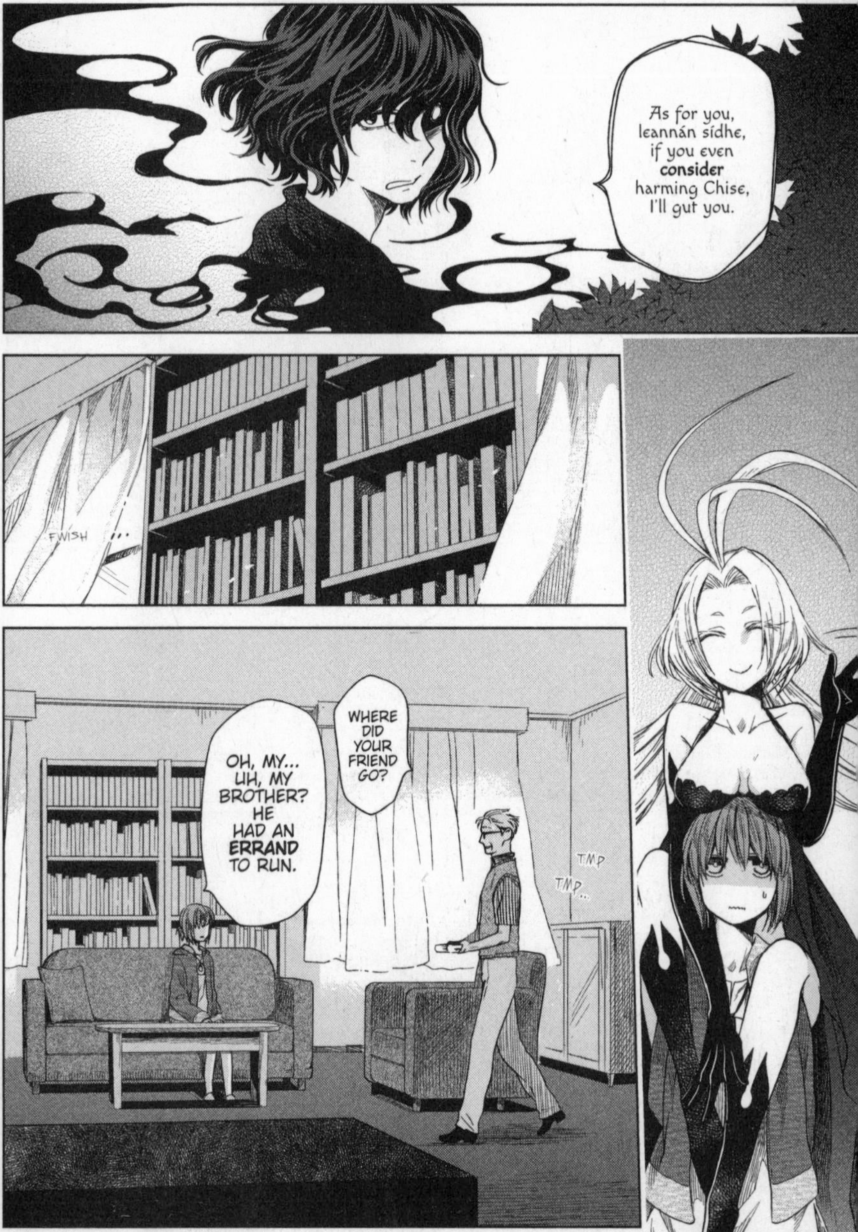
As for you, leannán sídhe, if you even **consider** harming Chise, I'll gut you.
FWISH
...
WHERE DID YOUR FRIEND GO?
OH, MY... UH, MY BROTHER? HE HAD AN **ERRAND** TO RUN.
TMP
TMP...

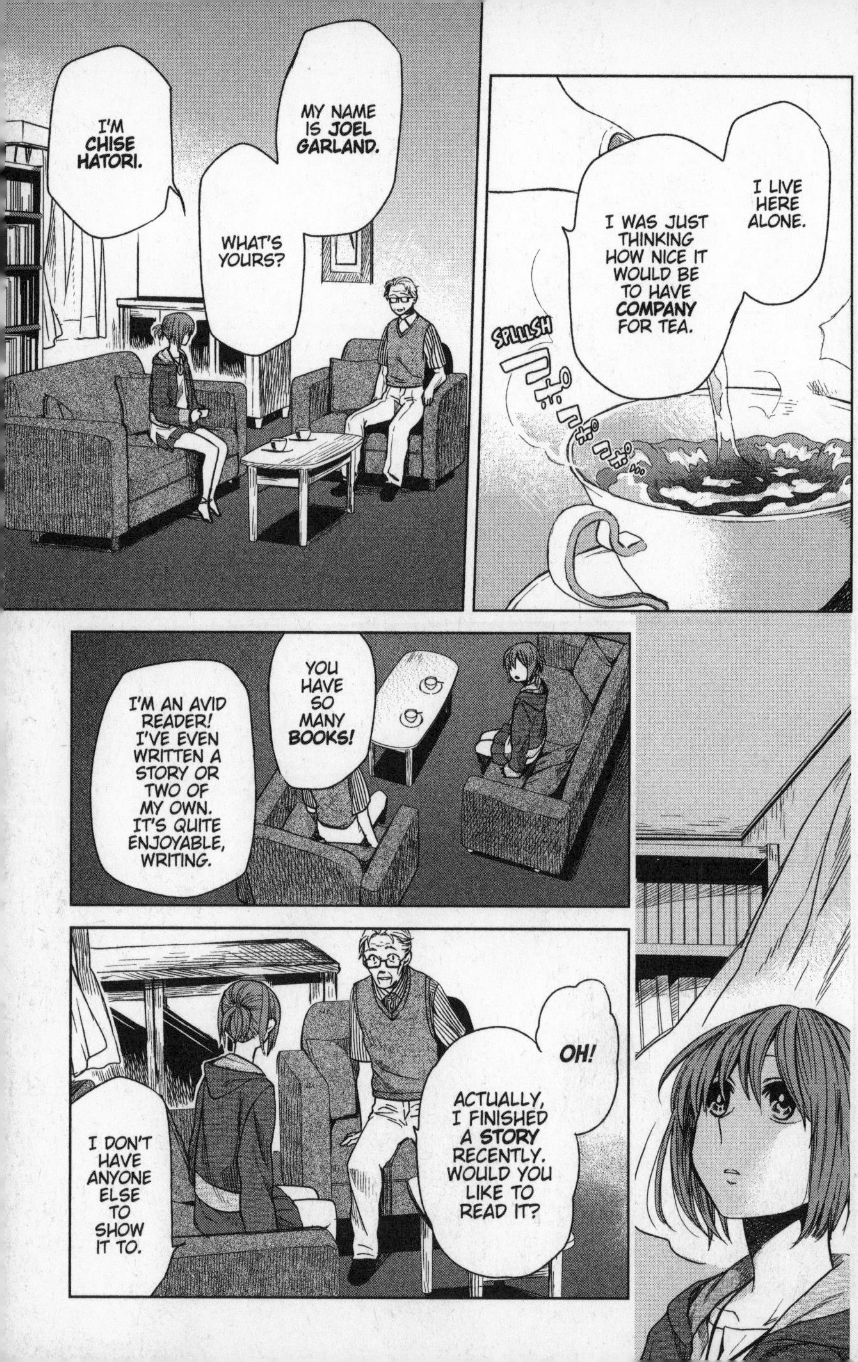
I LIVE HERE ALONE.
I WAS JUST THINKING HOW NICE IT WOULD BE TO HAVE COMPANY FOR TEA.
SPLLLSH
MY NAME IS JOEL GARLAND.
WHAT'S YOURS?
I'M CHISE HATORI.
YOU HAVE SO MANY BOOKS!
I'M AN AVID READER! I'VE EVEN WRITTEN A STORY OR TWO OF MY OWN. IT'S QUITE ENJOYABLE, WRITING.
OH!
ACTUALLY, I FINISHED A STORY RECENTLY. WOULD YOU LIKE TO READ IT?
I DON'T HAVE ANYONE ELSE TO SHOW IT TO.

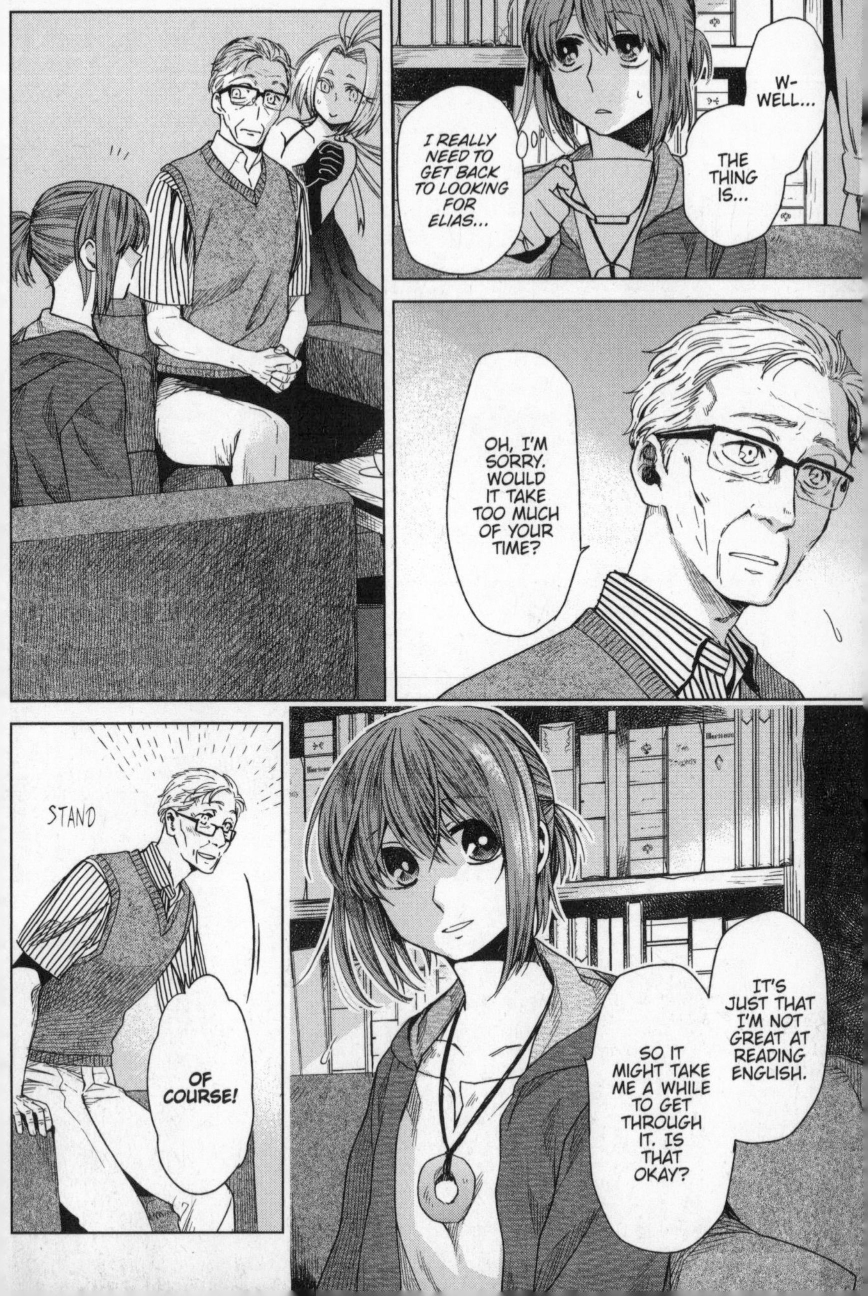
W-WELL...
THE THING IS...
I REALLY NEED TO GET BACK TO LOOKING FOR ELIAS...
OH, I'M SORRY. WOULD IT TAKE TOO MUCH OF YOUR TIME?
IT'S JUST THAT I'M NOT GREAT AT READING ENGLISH.
SO IT MIGHT TAKE ME A WHILE TO GET THROUGH IT. IS THAT OKAY?
STAND
OF COURSE!

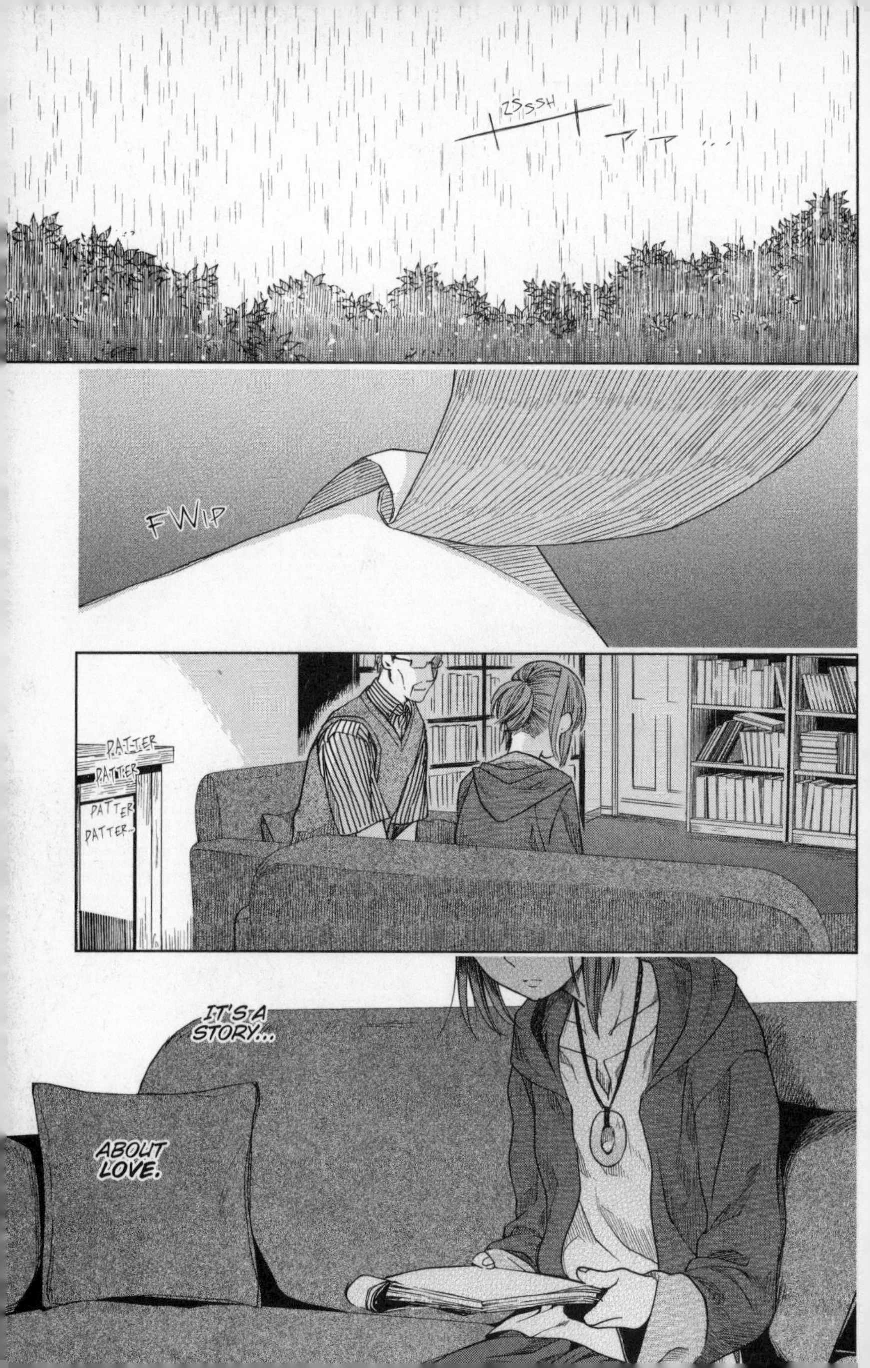
ZSSSH
FWIP
PATTER
PATTER
PATTER
PATTER...
IT'S A STORY...
ABOUT LOVE.

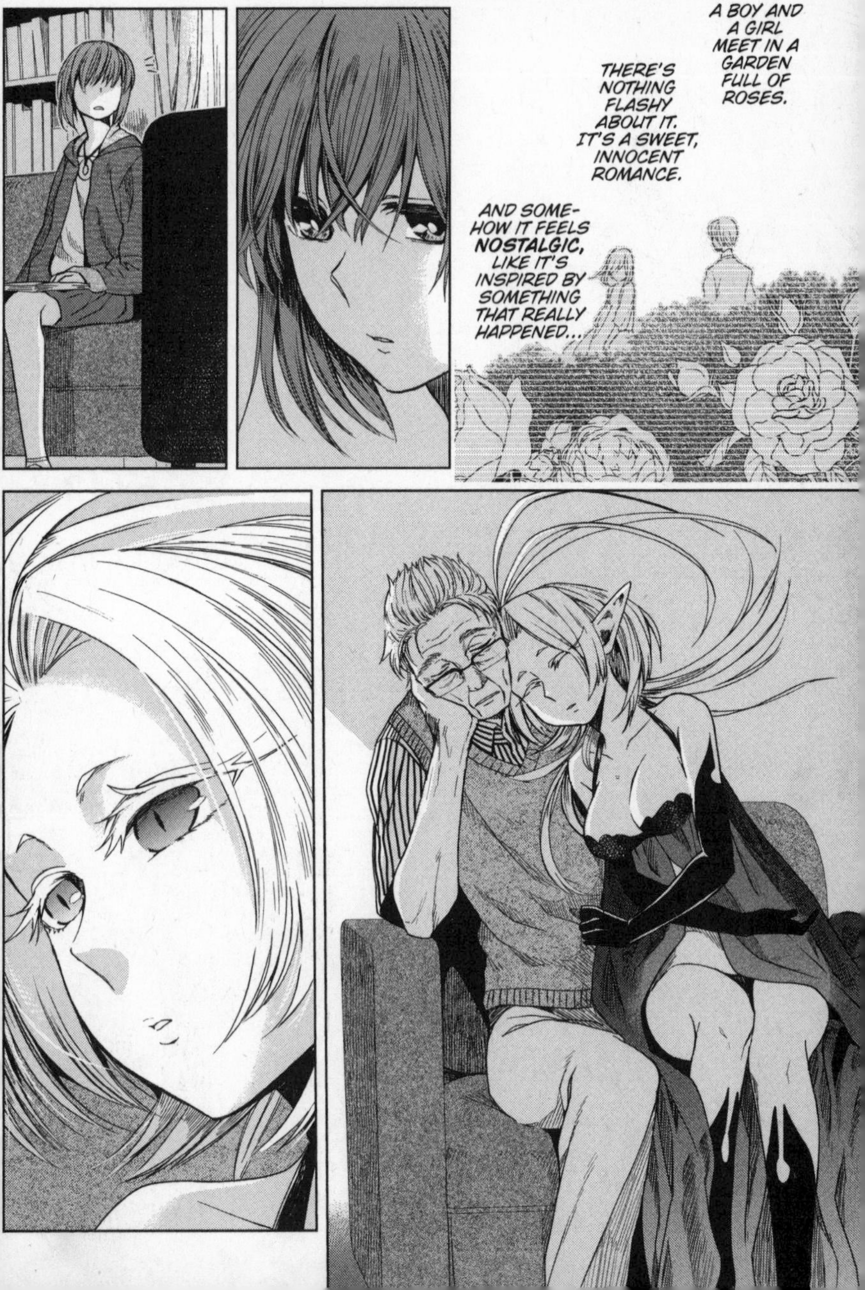
A BOY AND A GIRL MEET IN A GARDEN FULL OF ROSES.
THERE'S NOTHING FLASHY ABOUT IT. IT'S A SWEET, INNOCENT ROMANCE.
AND SOMEHOW IT FEELS NOSTALGIC, LIKE IT'S INSPIRED BY SOMETHING THAT REALLY HAPPENED...

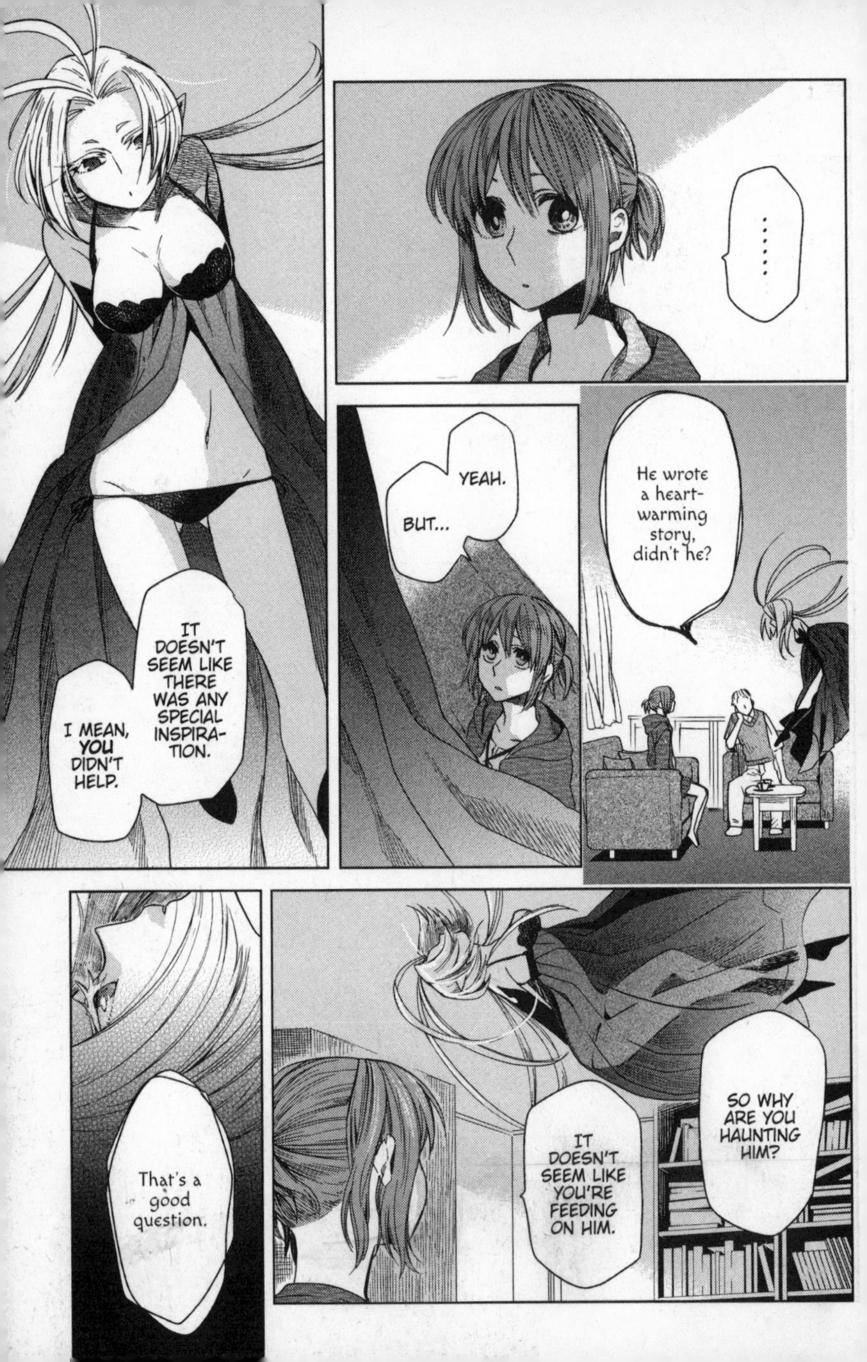
......
He wrote a heart-warming story, didn't he?
YEAH.
BUT...
IT DOESN'T SEEM LIKE THERE WAS ANY SPECIAL INSPIRA-TION.
I MEAN, YOU DIDN'T HELP.
SO WHY ARE YOU HAUNTING HIM?
IT DOESN'T SEEM LIKE YOU'RE FEEDING ON HIM.
That's a good question.

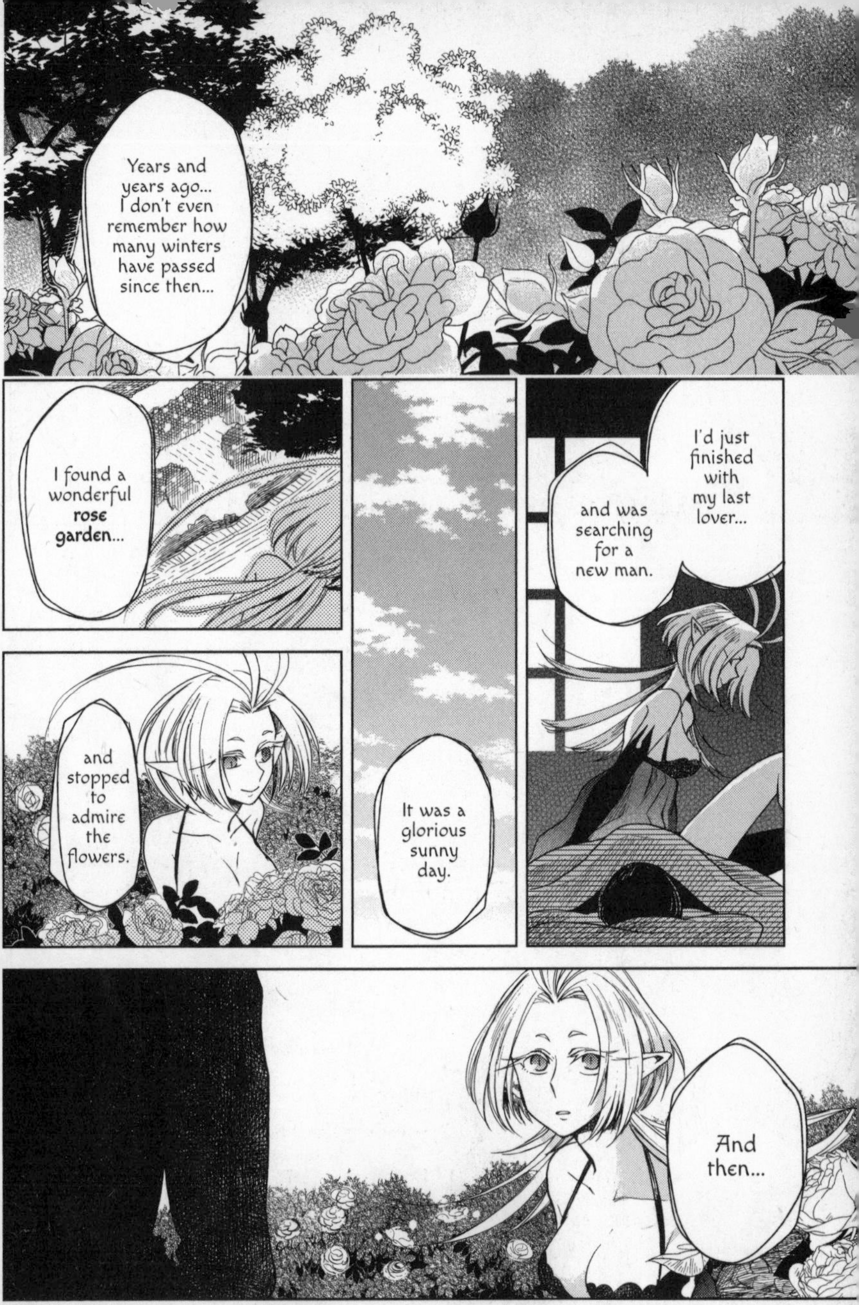
Years and years ago... I don't even remember how many winters have passed since then...
I'd just finished with my last lover...
and was searching for a new man.
It was a glorious sunny day.
I found a wonderful **rose garden**...
and stopped to admire the flowers.
And then...

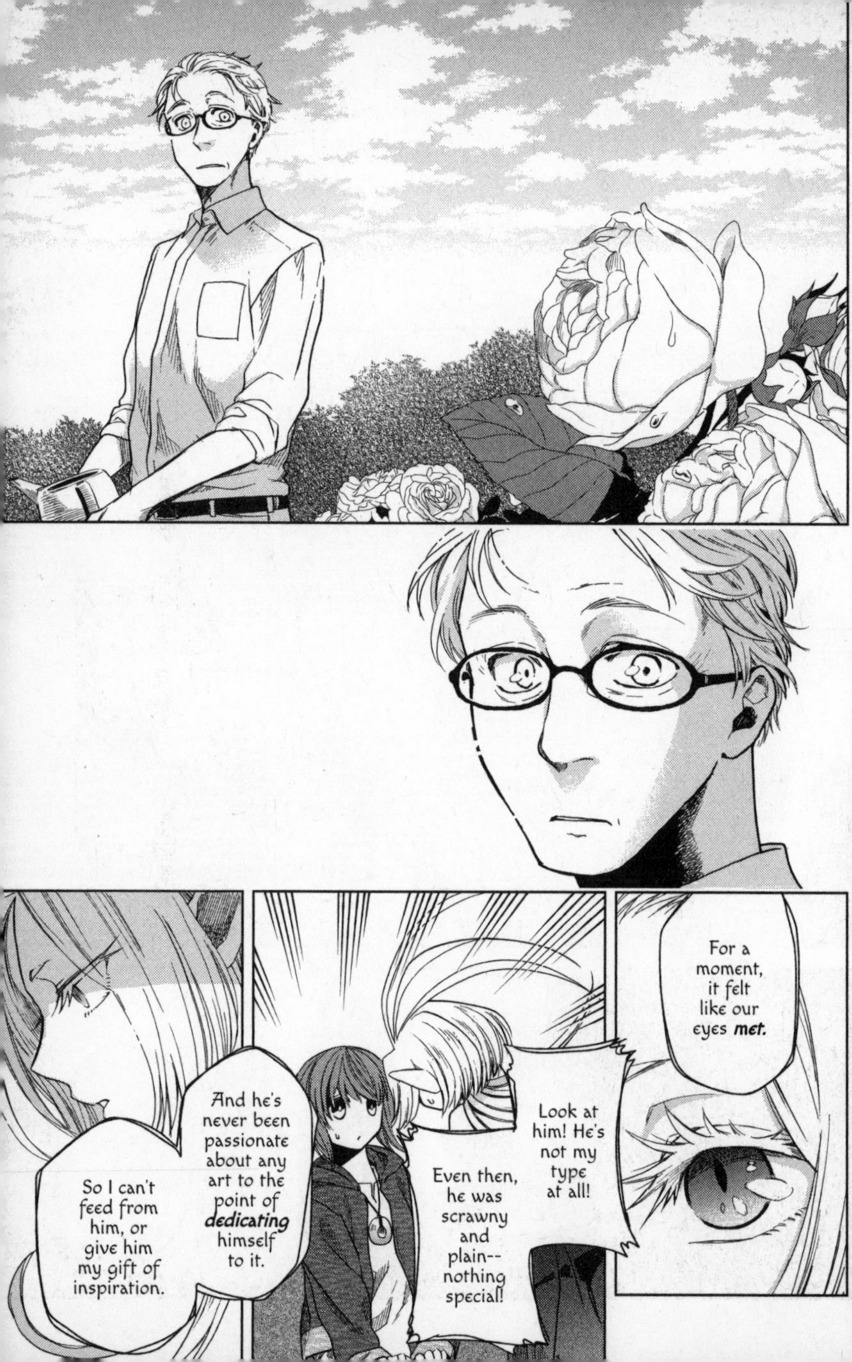
For a moment, it felt like our eyes ***met.***
Look at him! He's not my type at all!
Even then, he was scrawny and plain--nothing special!
And he's never been passionate about any art to the point of ***dedicating*** himself to it.
So I can't feed from him, or give him my gift of inspiration.

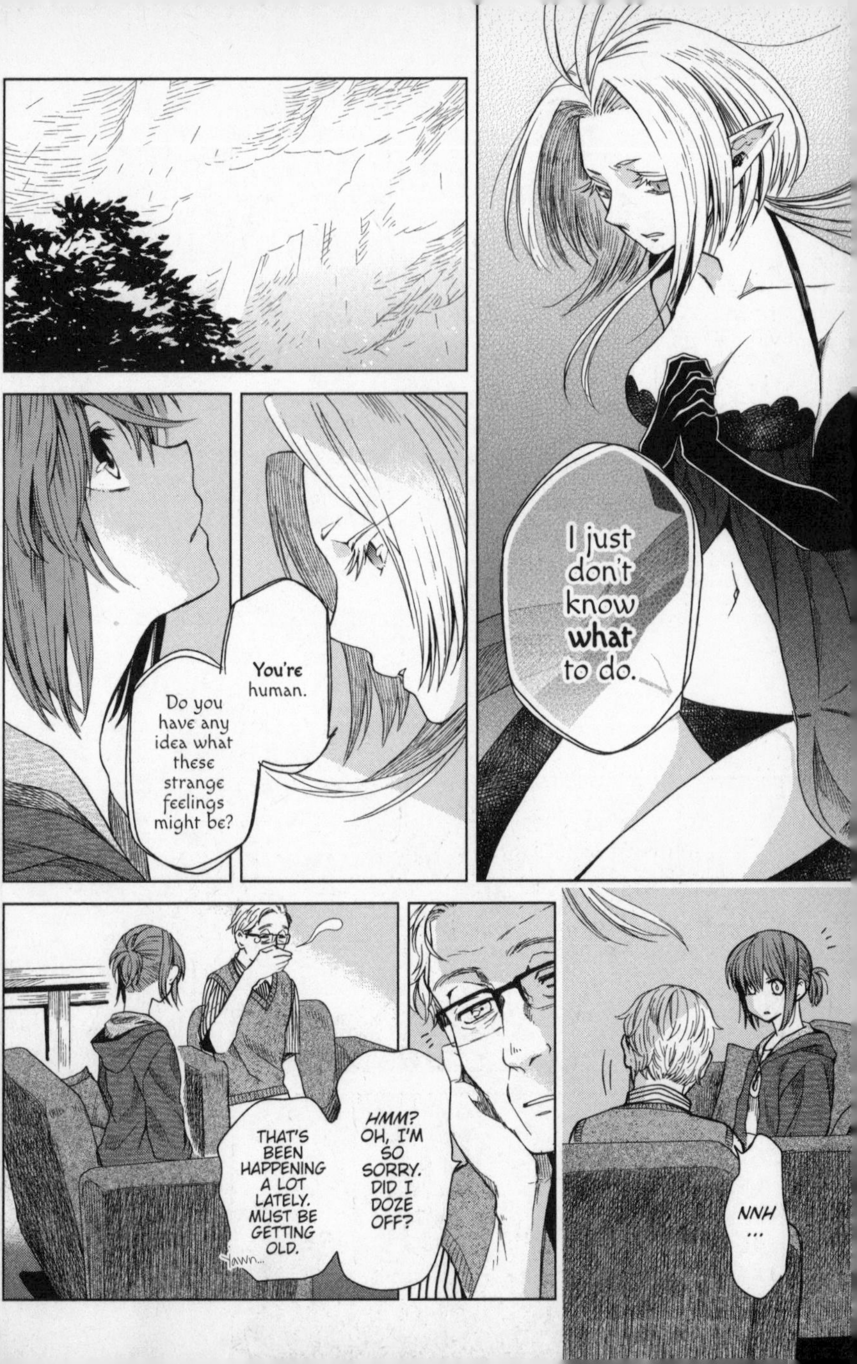
I just don't know **what** to do.
You're human.
Do you have any idea what these strange feelings might be?
NNH ...
HMM? OH, I'M SO SORRY. DID I DOZE OFF?
THAT'S BEEN HAPPENING A LOT LATELY. MUST BE GETTING OLD.
Yawn...

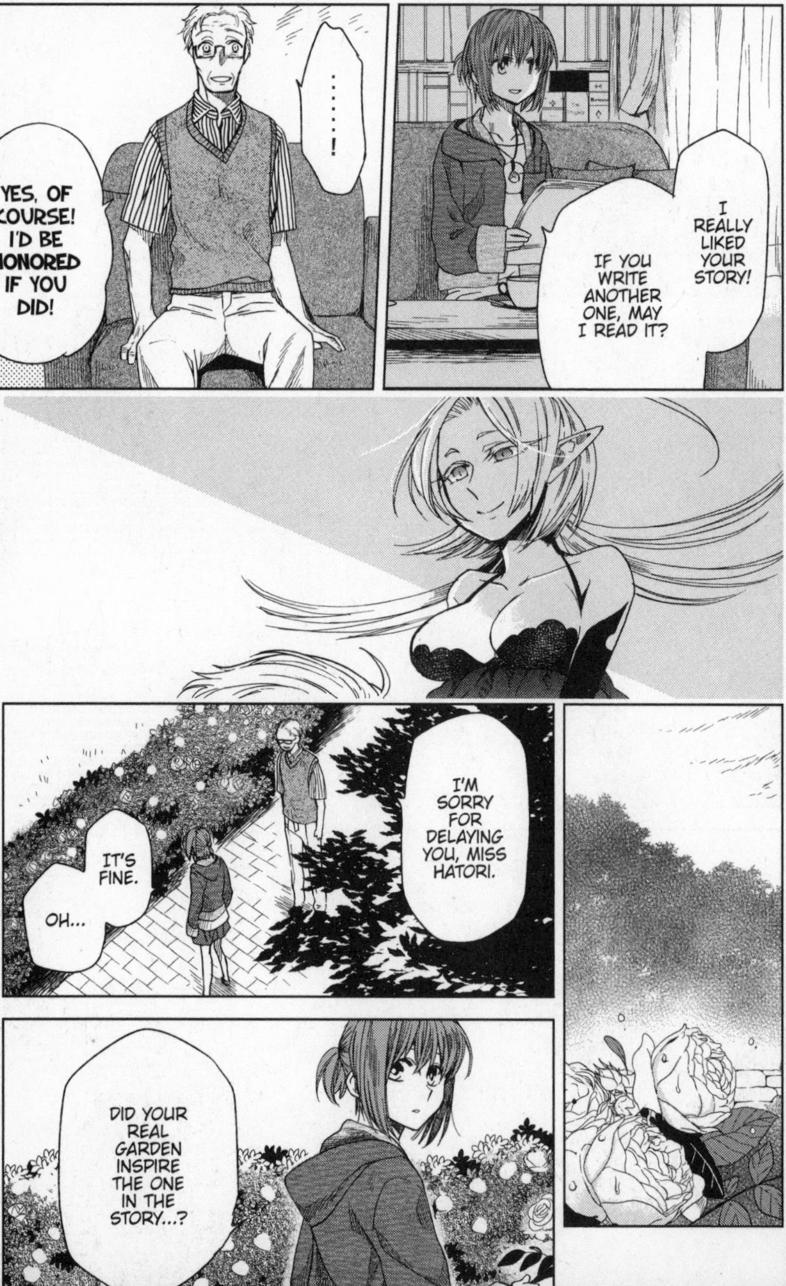
I REALLY LIKED YOUR STORY!
IF YOU WRITE ANOTHER ONE, MAY I READ IT?
......!
YES, OF COURSE! I'D BE HONORED IF YOU DID!
I'M SORRY FOR DELAYING YOU, MISS HATORI.
IT'S FINE.
OH...
DID YOUR REAL GARDEN INSPIRE THE ONE IN THE STORY...?

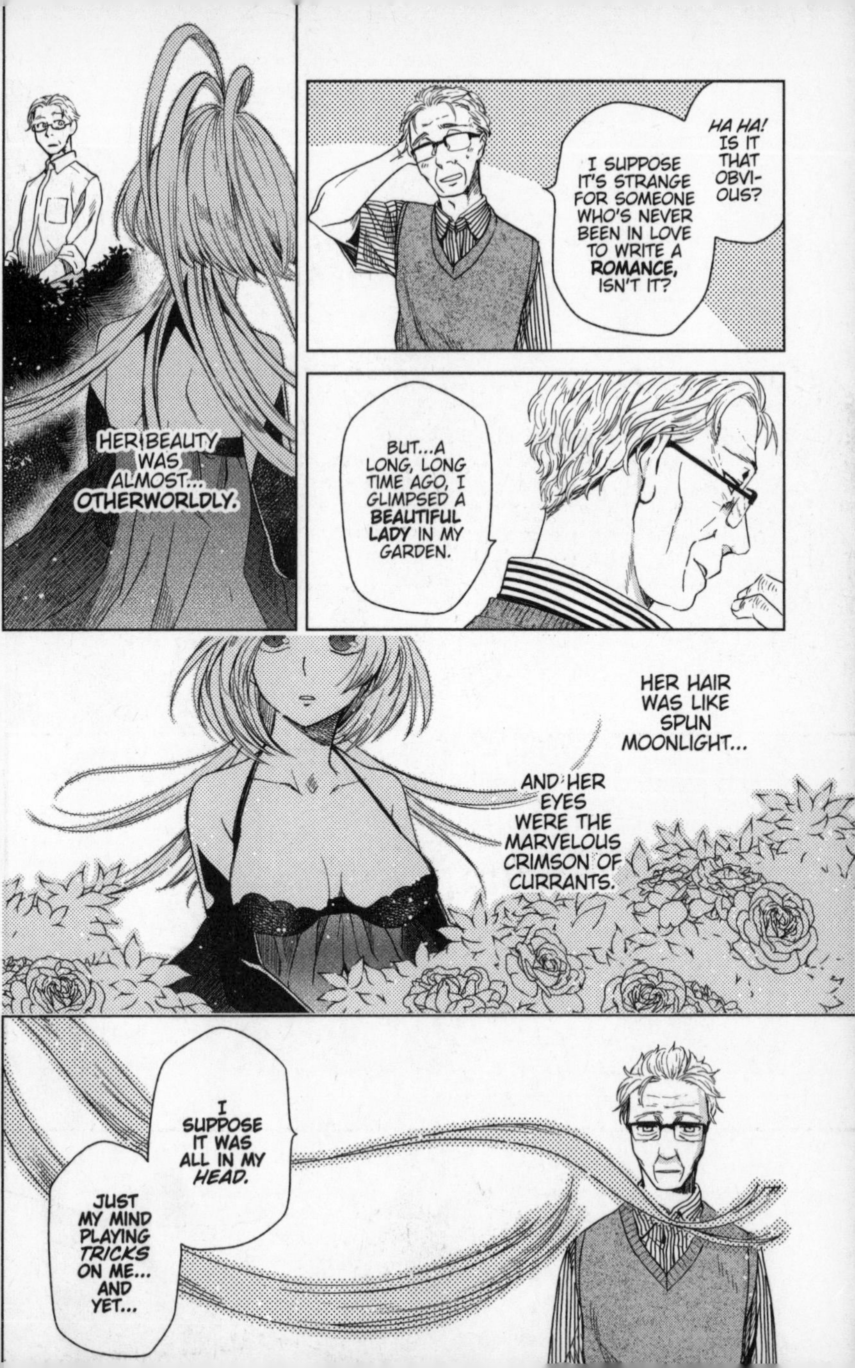
HA HA! IS IT THAT OBVI-OUS?
I SUPPOSE IT'S STRANGE FOR SOMEONE WHO'S NEVER BEEN IN LOVE TO WRITE A **ROMANCE,** ISN'T IT?
BUT...A LONG, LONG TIME AGO, I GLIMPSED A **BEAUTIFUL LADY** IN MY GARDEN.
HER BEAUTY WAS ALMOST... OTHERWORLDLY.
HER HAIR WAS LIKE SPUN MOONLIGHT...
AND HER EYES WERE THE MARVELOUS CRIMSON OF CURRANTS.
I SUPPOSE IT WAS ALL IN MY *HEAD.*
JUST MY MIND PLAYING *TRICKS* ON ME... AND YET...

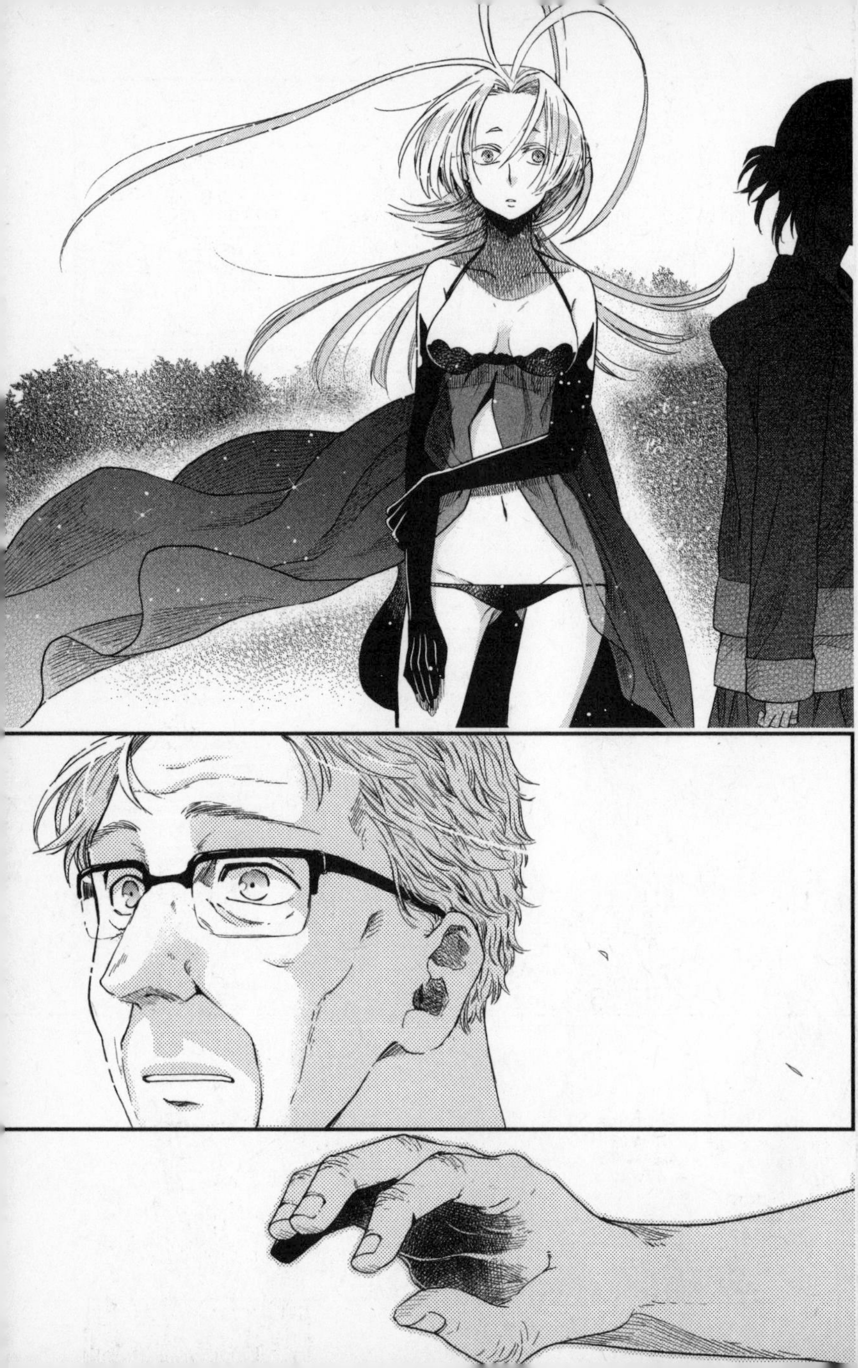

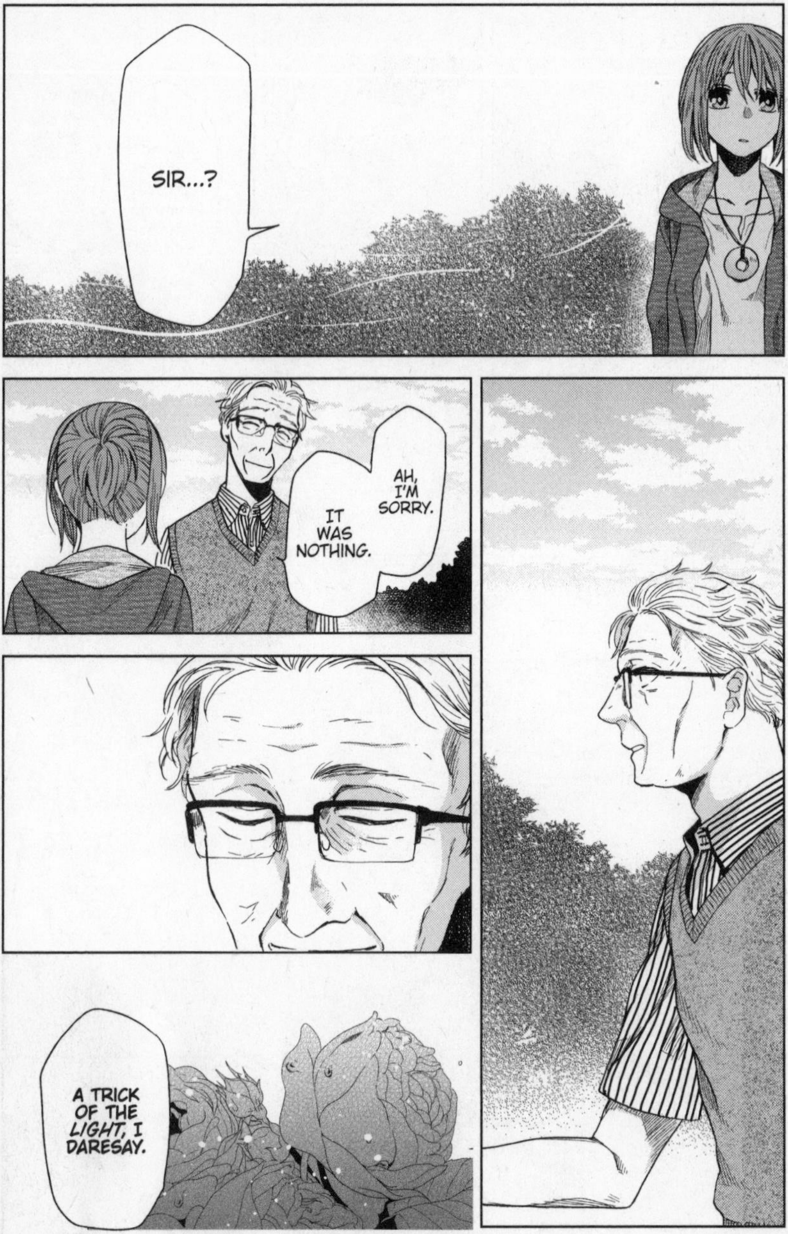
SIR...?
AH, I'M SORRY.
IT WAS NOTHING.
A TRICK OF THE *LIGHT*, I DARESAY.

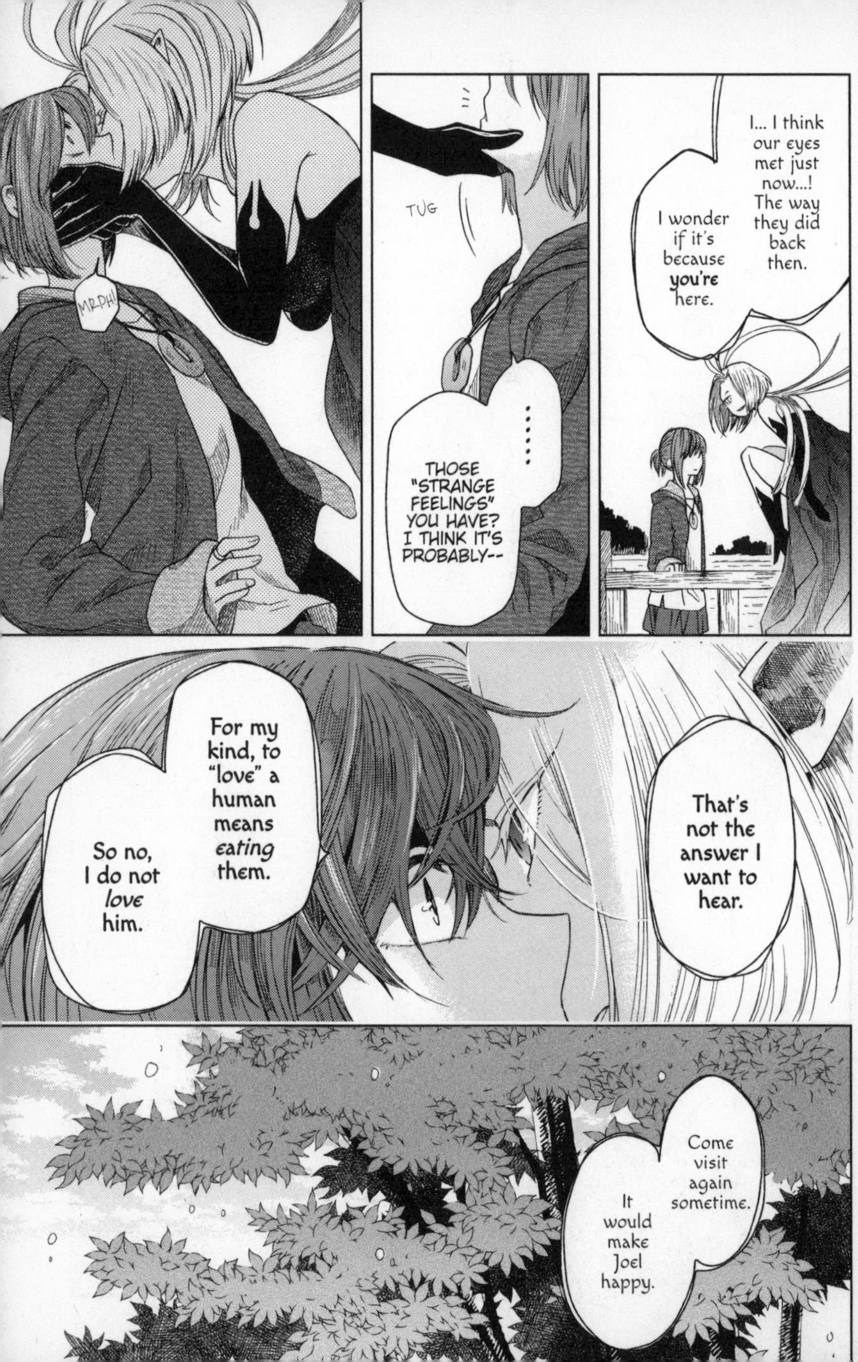
I... I think our eyes met just now...! The way they did back then.
I wonder if it's because **you're** here.
......
THOSE "STRANGE FEELINGS" YOU HAVE? I THINK IT'S PROBABLY--
TUG
MRPH!
That's not the answer I want to hear.
For my kind, to "love" a human means *eating* them.
So no, I do not *love* him.
Come visit again sometime.
It would make Joel happy.

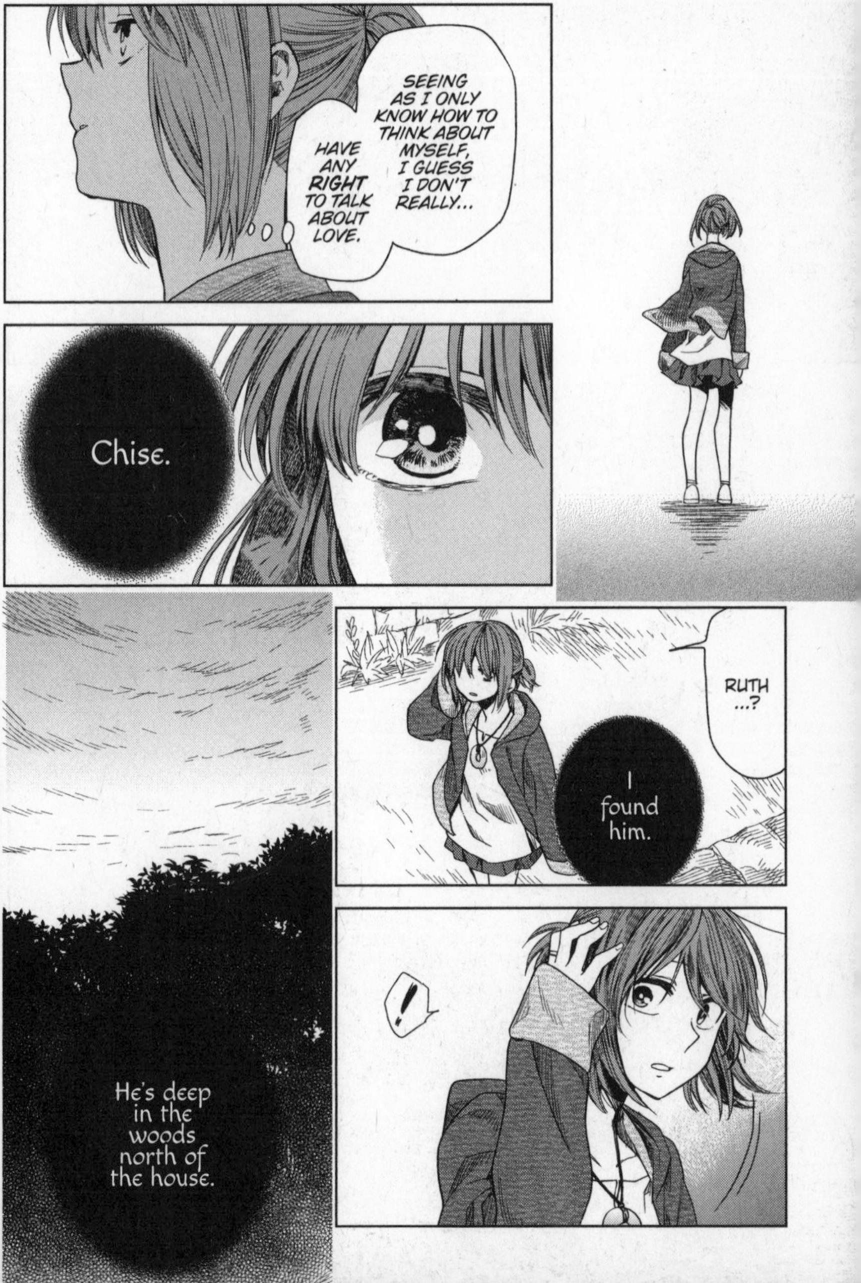
SEEING AS I ONLY KNOW HOW TO THINK ABOUT MYSELF, I GUESS I DON'T REALLY... HAVE ANY RIGHT TO TALK ABOUT LOVE.
Chise.
RUTH ...?
I found him.
!
He's deep in the woods north of the house.

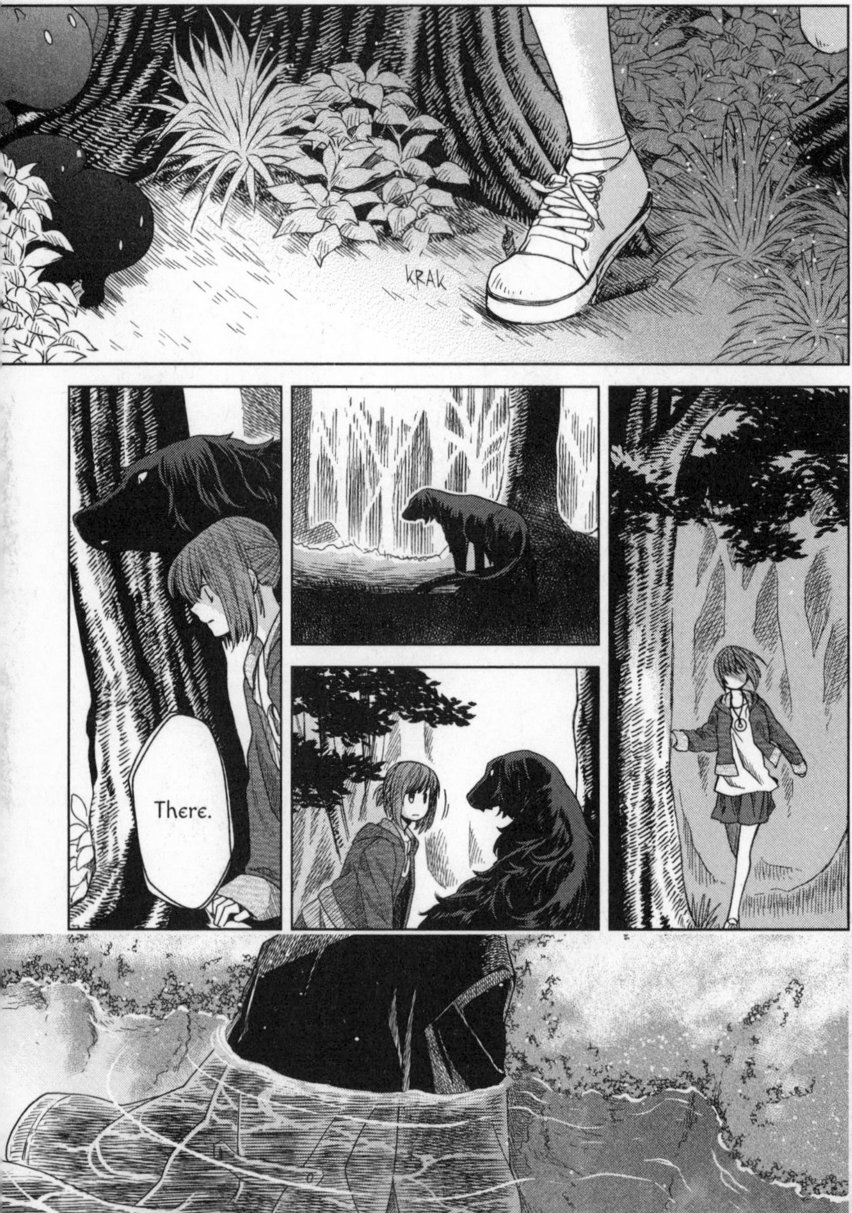
KRAK
There.

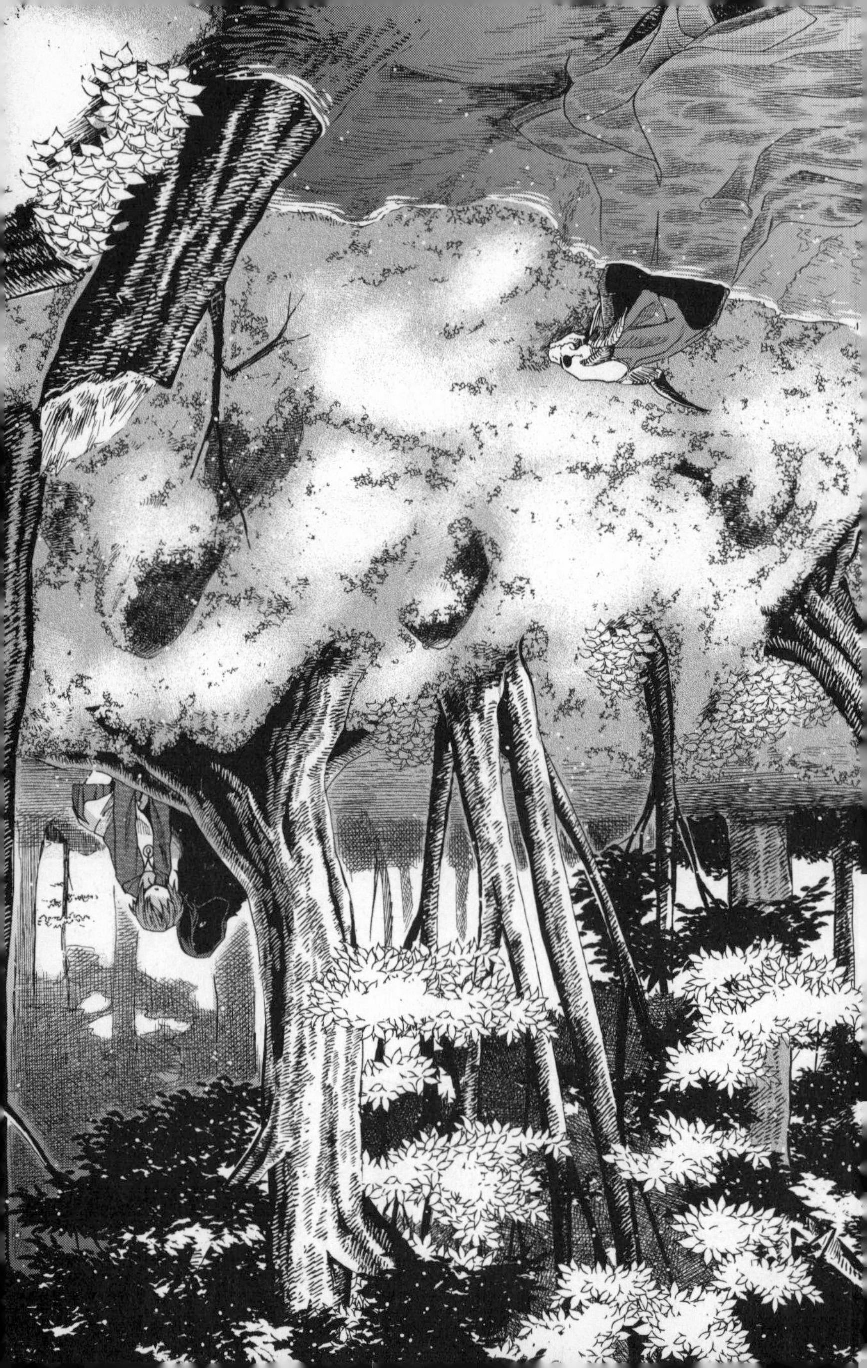

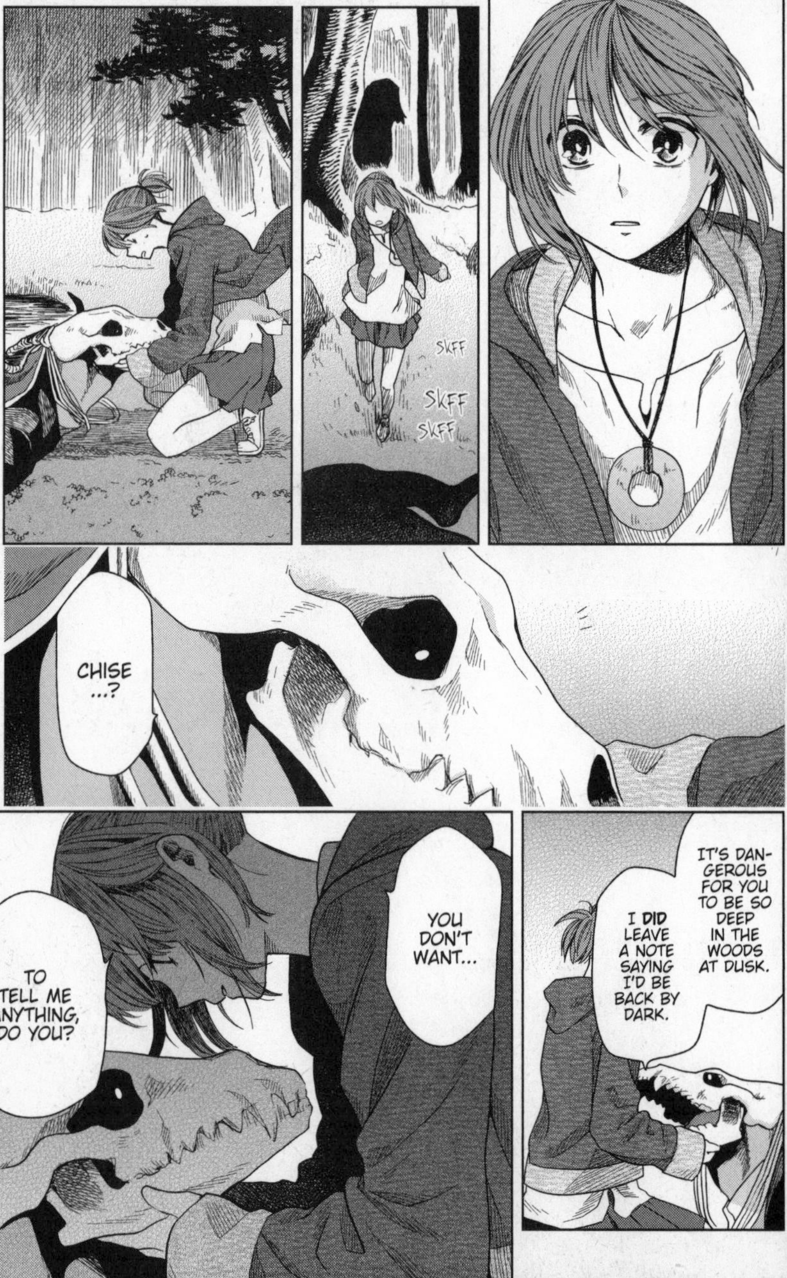
SKFF
SKFF
SKFF
CHISE ...?
IT'S DANGEROUS FOR YOU TO BE SO DEEP IN THE WOODS AT DUSK.
I DID LEAVE A NOTE SAYING I'D BE BACK BY DARK.
YOU DON'T WANT...
TO TELL ME ANYTHING, DO YOU?

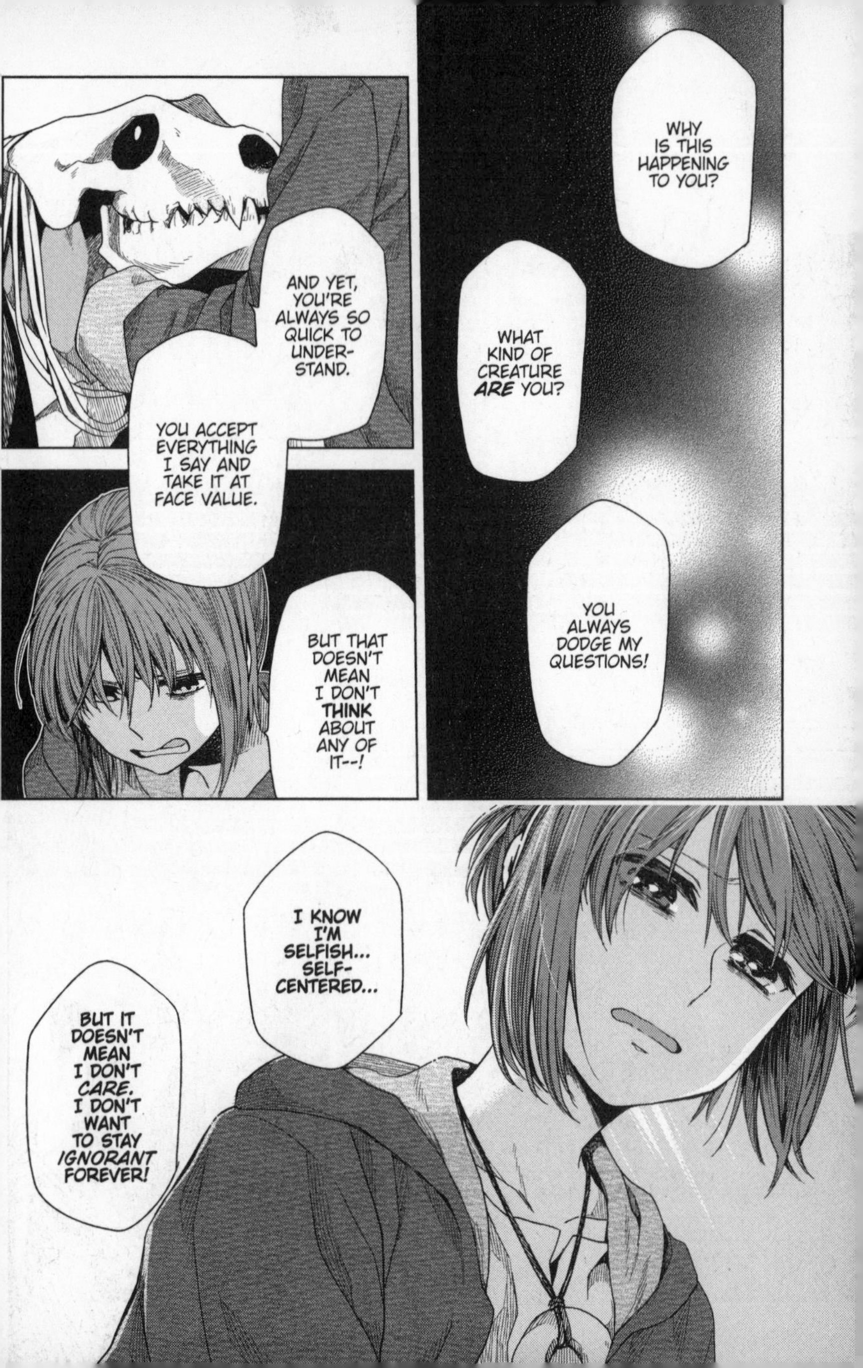
WHY IS THIS HAPPENING TO YOU?
WHAT KIND OF CREATURE *ARE* YOU?
YOU ALWAYS DODGE MY QUESTIONS!
AND YET, YOU'RE ALWAYS SO QUICK TO UNDER-STAND.
YOU ACCEPT EVERYTHING I SAY AND TAKE IT AT FACE VALUE.
BUT THAT DOESN'T MEAN I DON'T **THINK** ABOUT ANY OF IT--!
I KNOW I'M SELFISH... SELF-CENTERED...
BUT IT DOESN'T MEAN I DON'T *CARE*. I DON'T WANT TO STAY *IGNORANT* FOREVER!

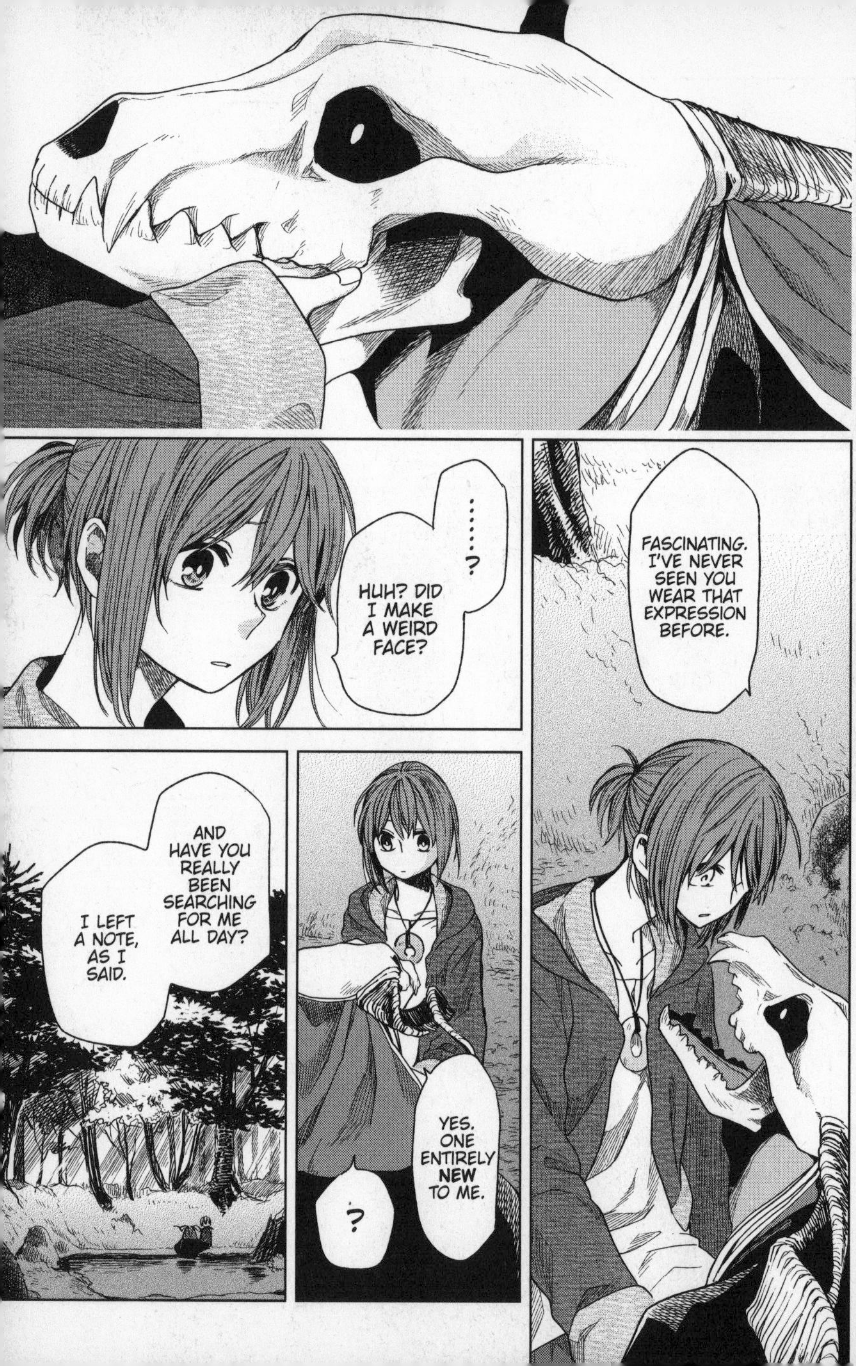
FASCINATING. I'VE NEVER SEEN YOU WEAR THAT EXPRESSION BEFORE.
......?
HUH? DID I MAKE A WEIRD FACE?
YES. ONE ENTIRELY **NEW** TO ME.
?
AND HAVE YOU REALLY BEEN SEARCHING FOR ME ALL DAY?
I LEFT A NOTE, AS I SAID.

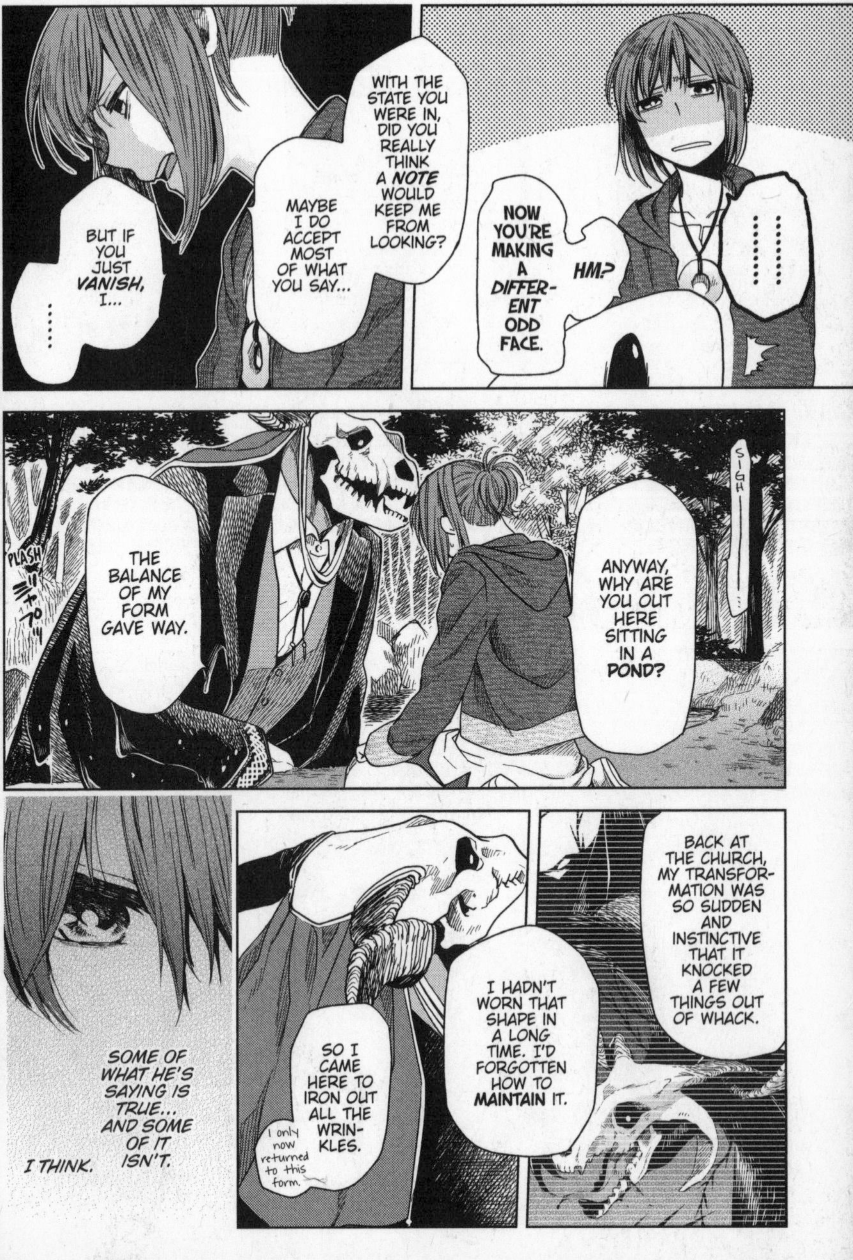
……
HM?
NOW YOU'RE MAKING A DIFFERENT ODD FACE.
WITH THE STATE YOU WERE IN, DID YOU REALLY THINK A NOTE WOULD KEEP ME FROM LOOKING?
MAYBE I DO ACCEPT MOST OF WHAT YOU SAY...
BUT IF YOU JUST VANISH, I...
……
SIGH
ANYWAY, WHY ARE YOU OUT HERE SITTING IN A POND?
PLASH
THE BALANCE OF MY FORM GAVE WAY.
BACK AT THE CHURCH, MY TRANSFORMATION WAS SO SUDDEN AND INSTINCTIVE THAT IT KNOCKED A FEW THINGS OUT OF WHACK.
I HADN'T WORN THAT SHAPE IN A LONG TIME. I'D FORGOTTEN HOW TO MAINTAIN IT.
SO I CAME HERE TO IRON OUT ALL THE WRINKLES.
I only now returned to this form.
SOME OF WHAT HE'S SAYING IS TRUE... AND SOME OF IT ISN'T.
I THINK.

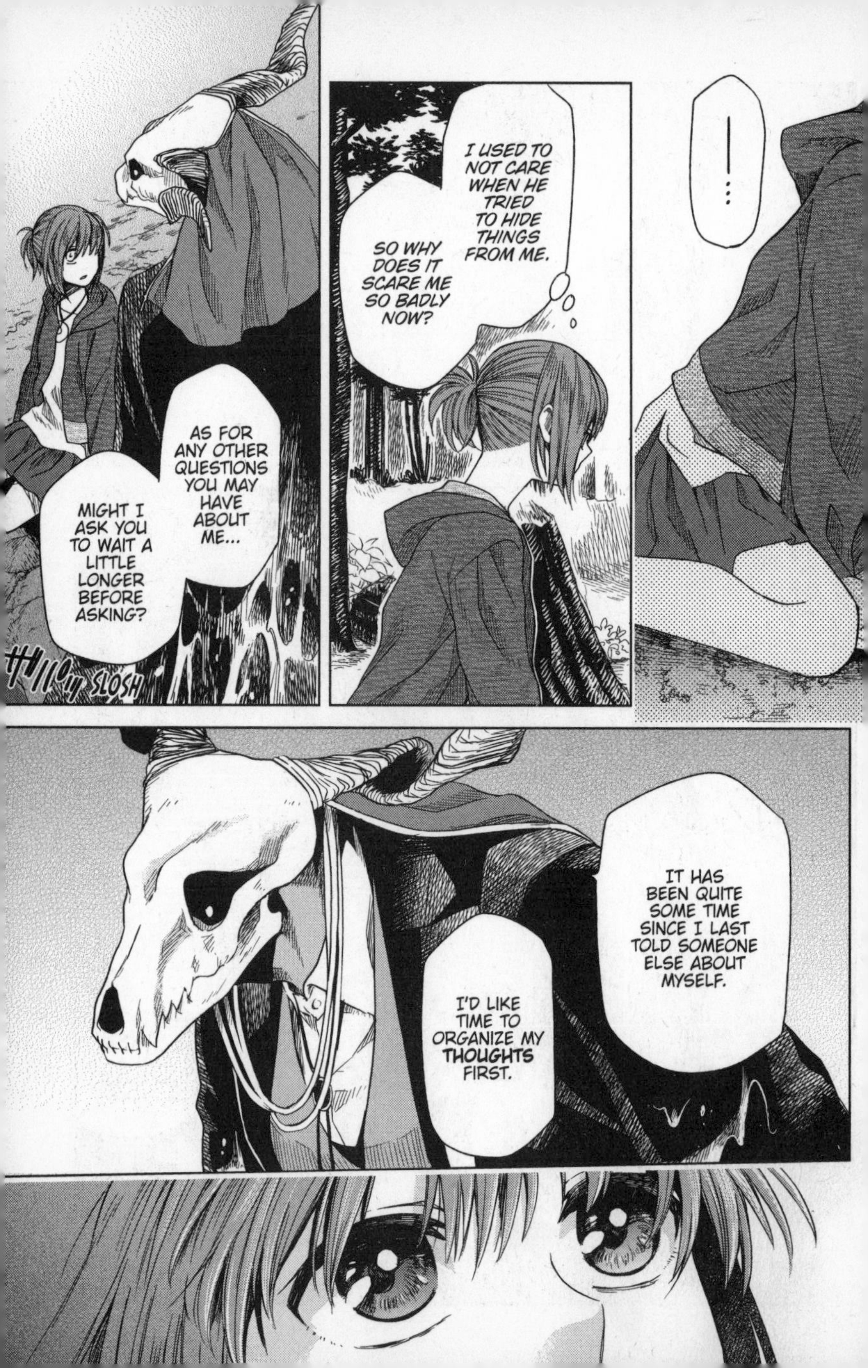
—...
I USED TO NOT CARE WHEN HE TRIED TO HIDE THINGS FROM ME.
SO WHY DOES IT SCARE ME SO BADLY NOW?
AS FOR ANY OTHER QUESTIONS YOU MAY HAVE ABOUT ME...
MIGHT I ASK YOU TO WAIT A LITTLE LONGER BEFORE ASKING?
SLOSH
IT HAS BEEN QUITE SOME TIME SINCE I LAST TOLD SOMEONE ELSE ABOUT MYSELF.
I'D LIKE TIME TO ORGANIZE MY THOUGHTS FIRST.

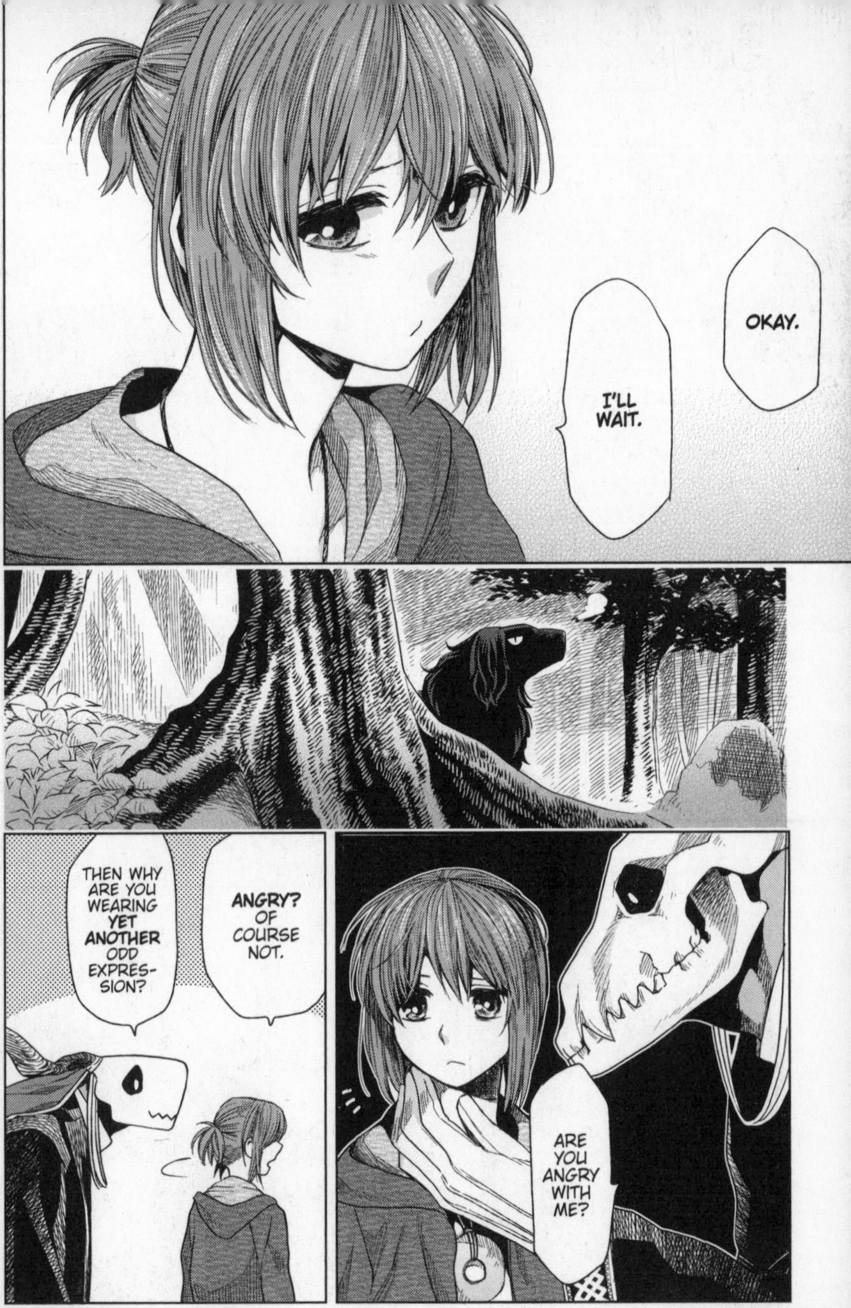
OKAY.
I'LL WAIT.
ARE YOU ANGRY WITH ME?
ANGRY? OF COURSE NOT.
THEN WHY ARE YOU WEARING YET ANOTHER ODD EXPRES-SION?

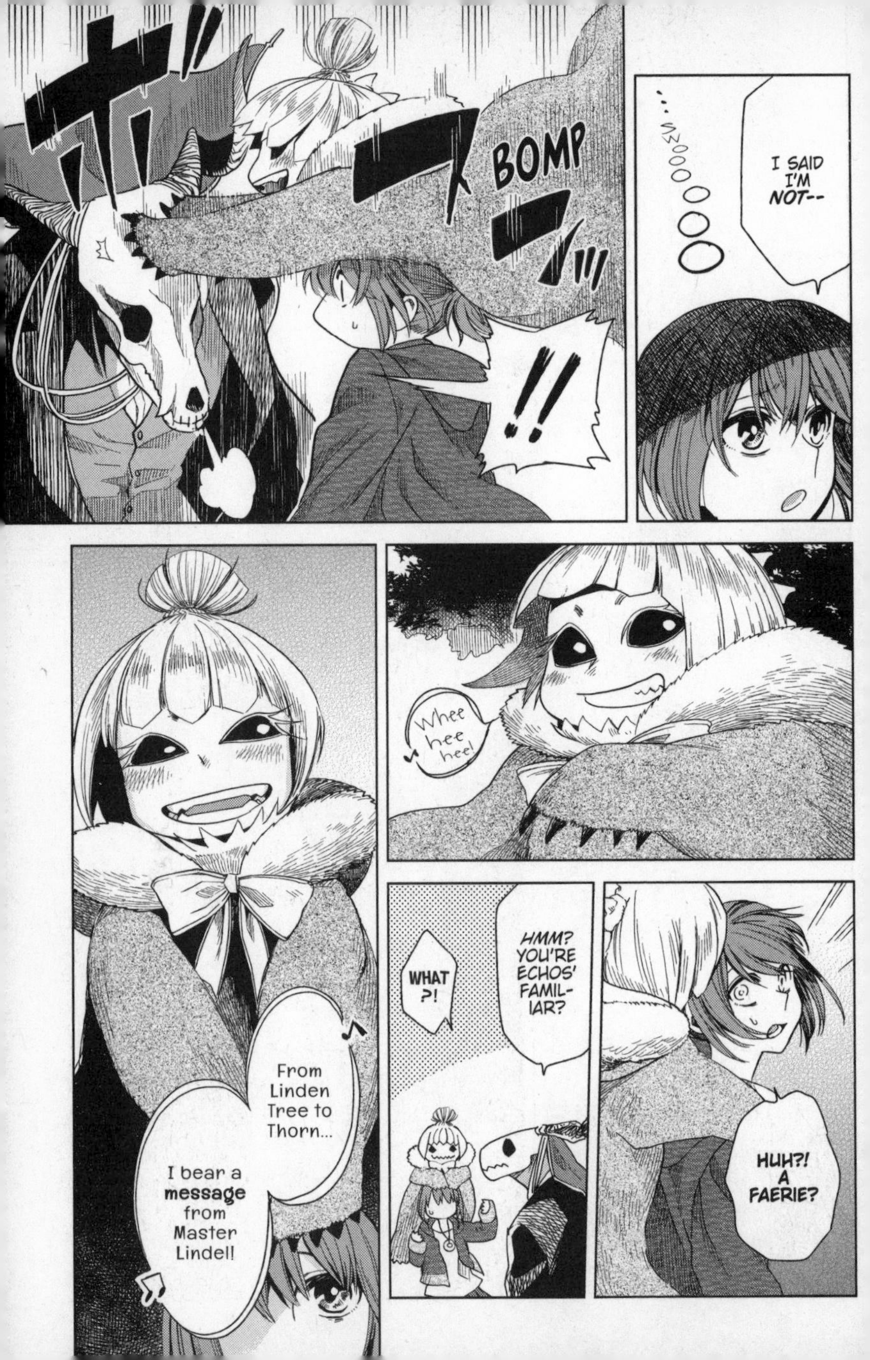
I SAID I'M NOT--
SWOOOOOO...
BOMP
!!
Whee hee hee!
HUH?! A FAERIE?
HMM? YOU'RE ECHOS' FAMIL-IAR?
WHAT ?!
From Linden Tree to Thorn...
I bear a message from Master Lindel!

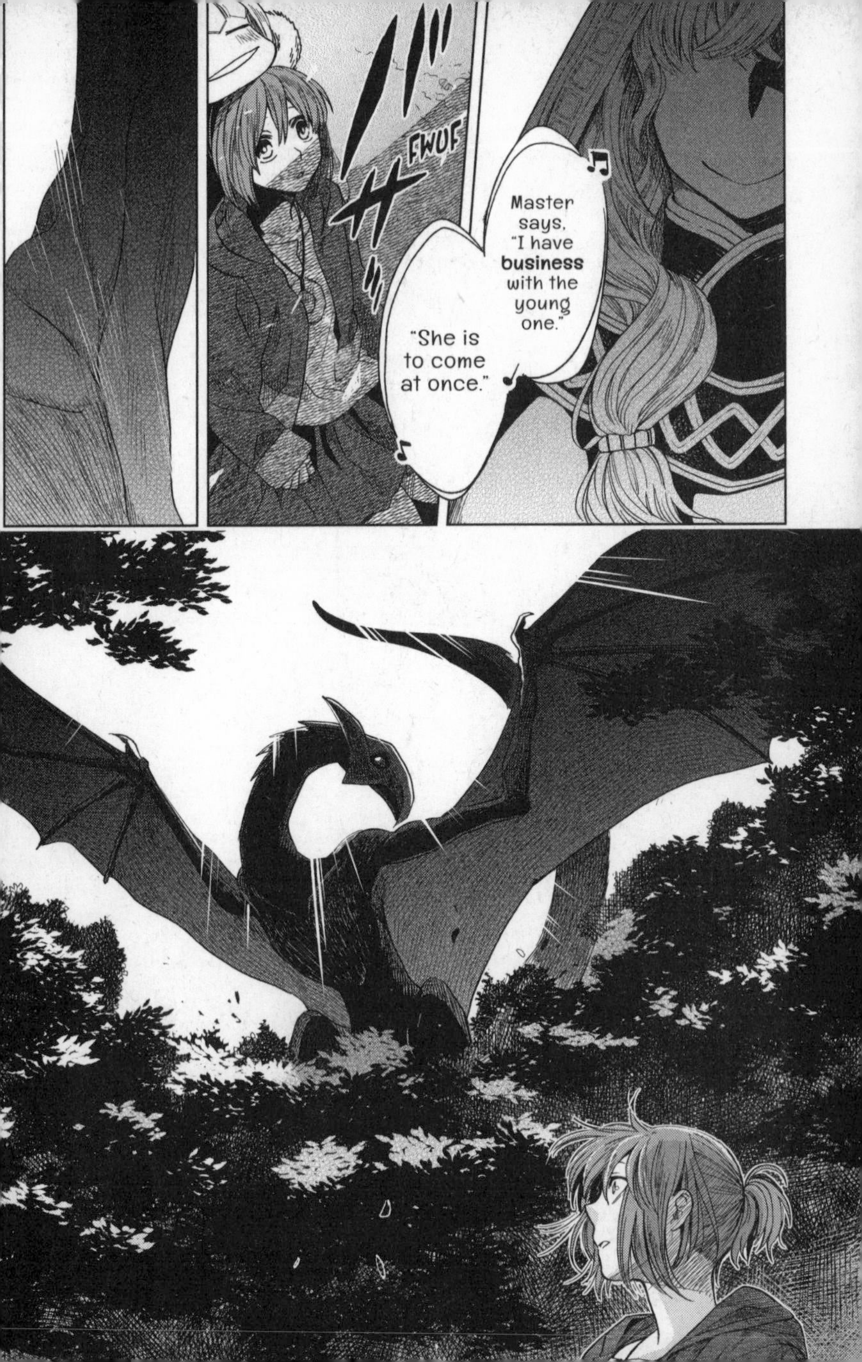
Master says, "I have **business** with the young one."
"She is to come at once."
FWUF

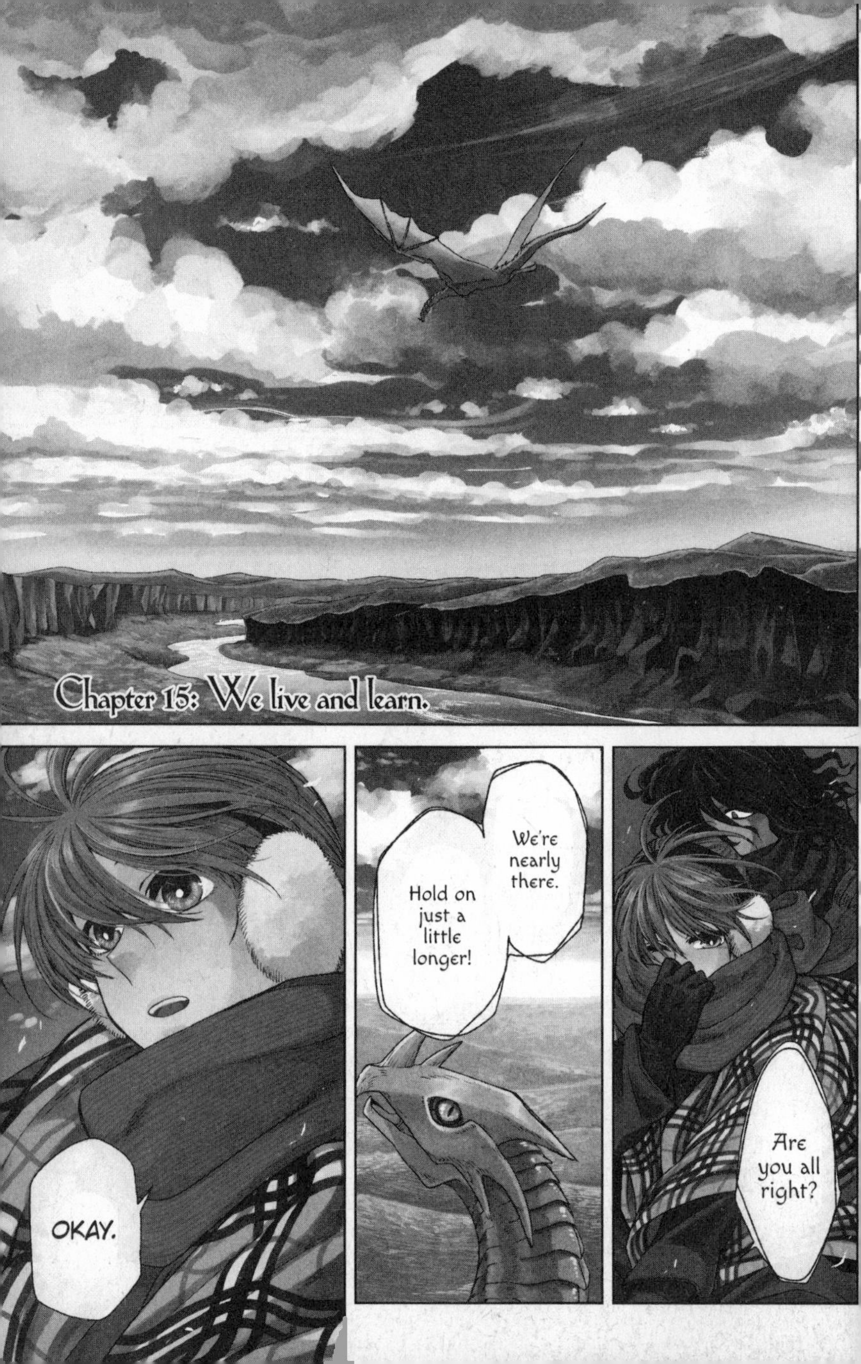
Chapter 15: We live and learn.
Are you all right?
Hold on just a little longer! We're nearly there.
OKAY.

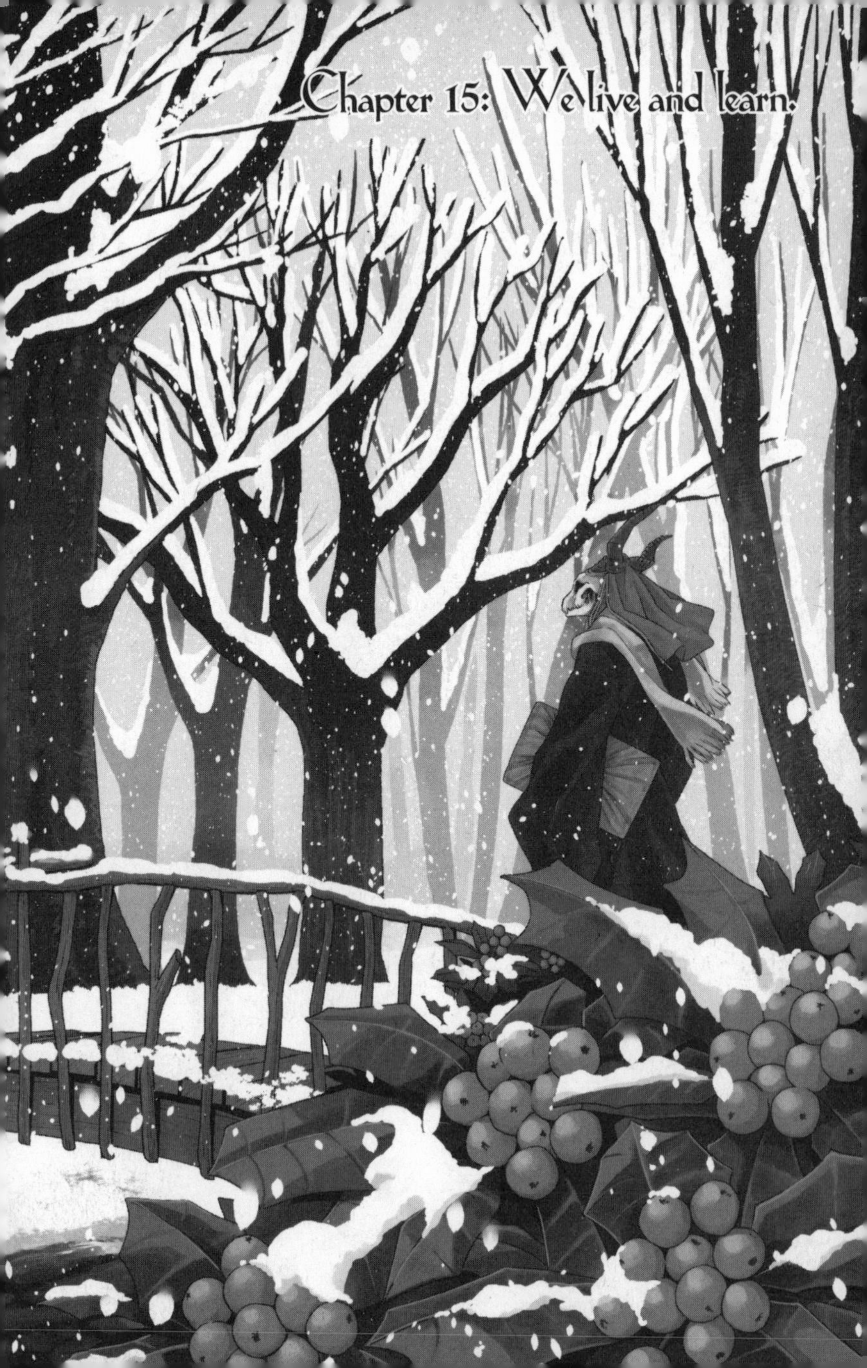
Chapter 15: We live and learn.

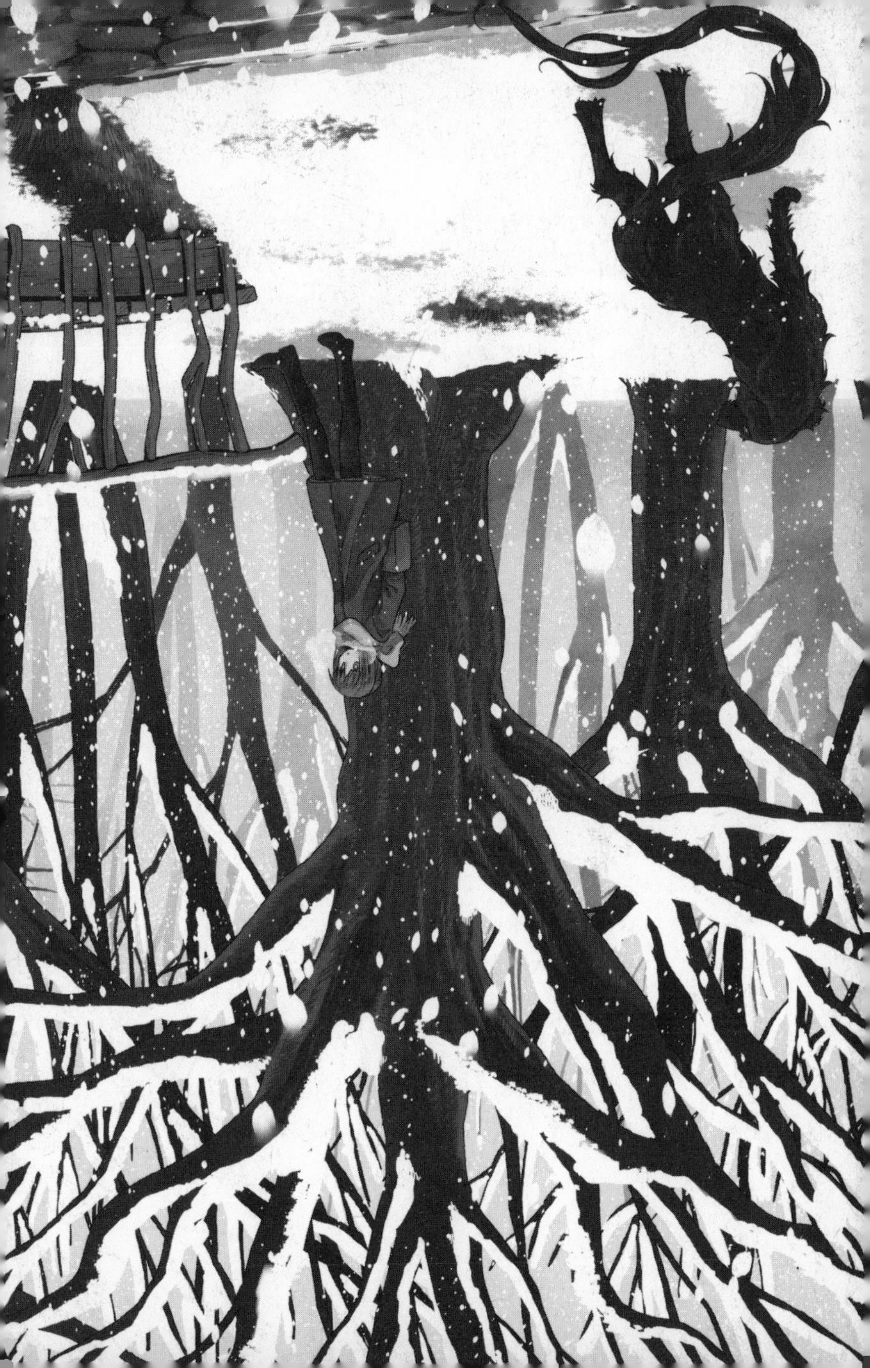

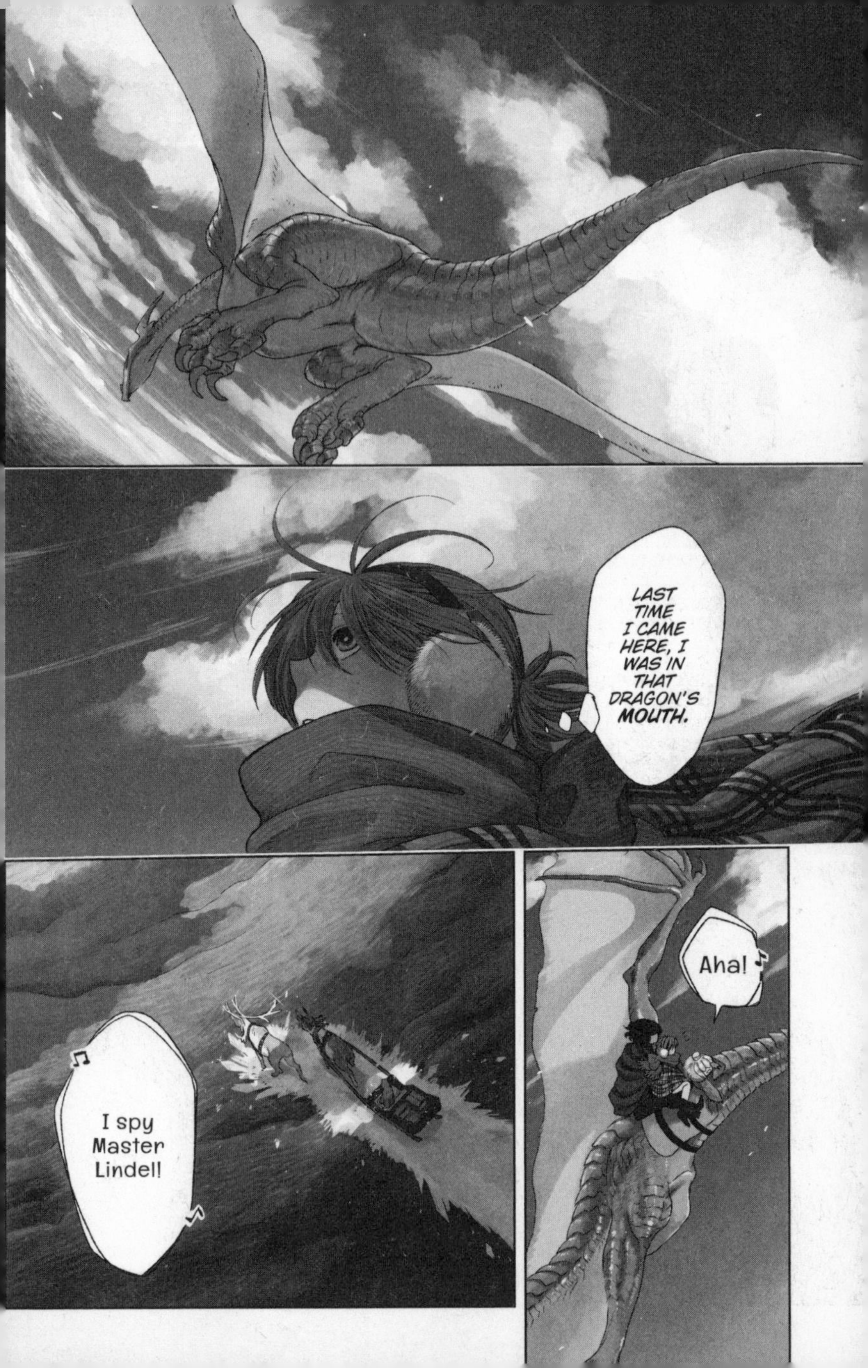
LAST TIME I CAME HERE, I WAS IN THAT DRAGON'S MOUTH.
Aha!
I spy Master Lindell!

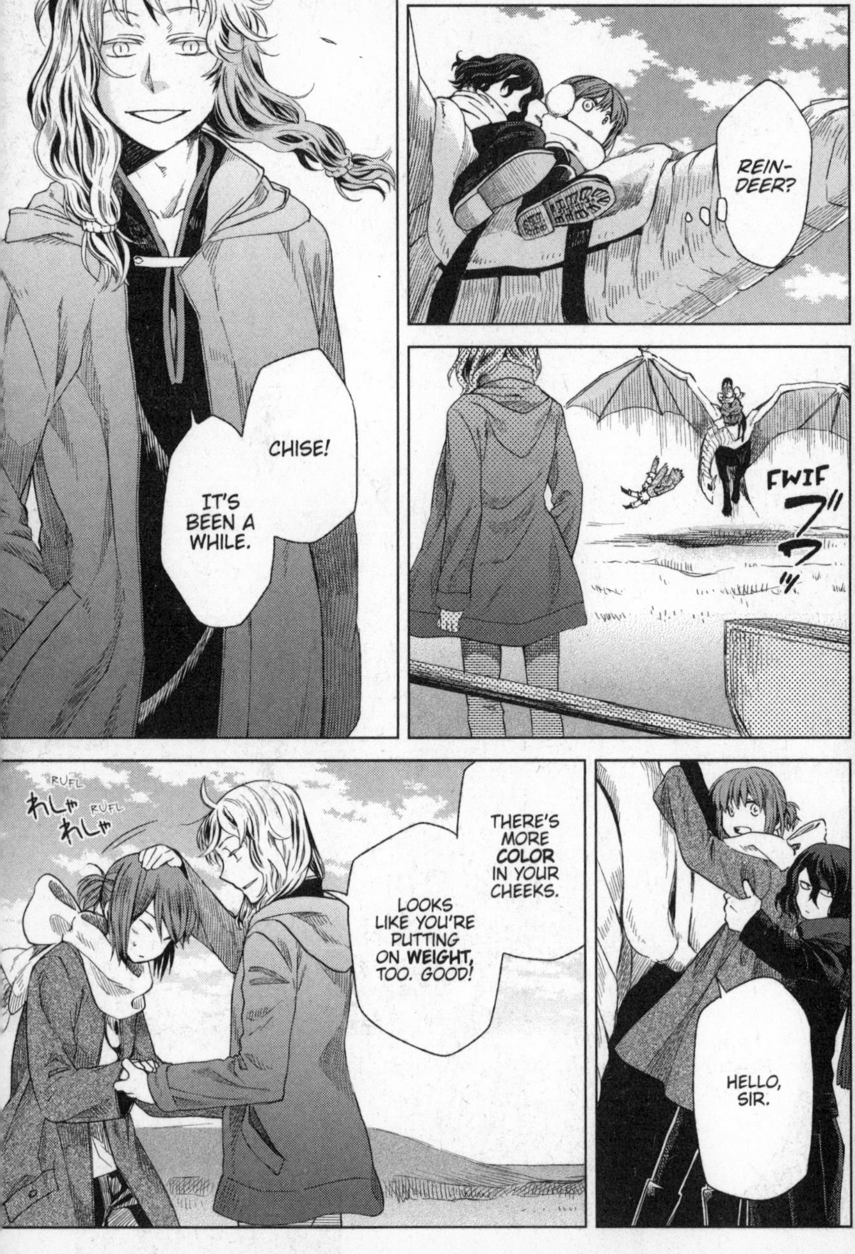
REIN-DEER?
FWIF
ブワッ
CHISE!
IT'S BEEN A WHILE.
HELLO, SIR.
THERE'S MORE COLOR IN YOUR CHEEKS.
LOOKS LIKE YOU'RE PUTTING ON WEIGHT, TOO. GOOD!
RUFL RUFL
わしゃ わしゃ

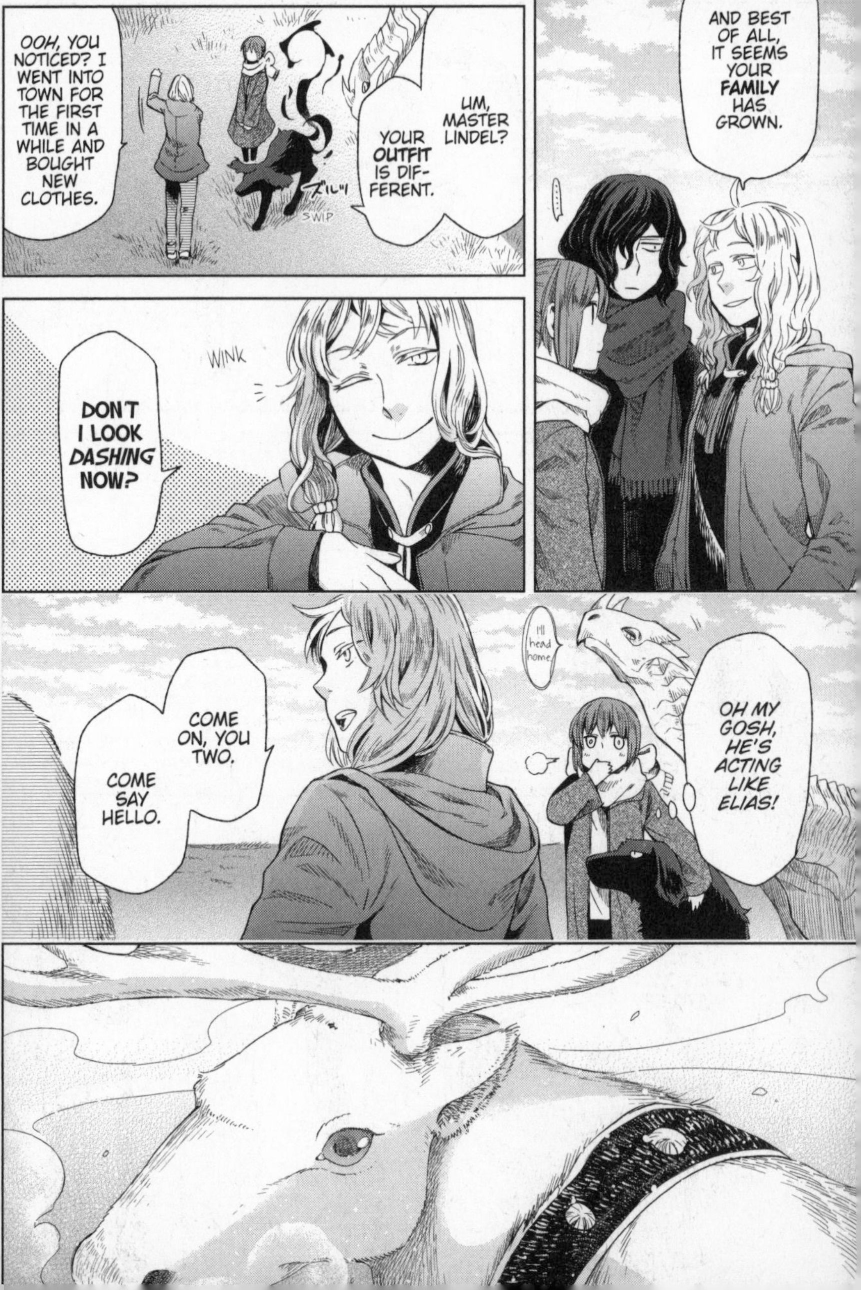
AND BEST OF ALL, IT SEEMS YOUR **FAMILY** HAS GROWN.
.....
UM, MASTER LINDEL?
YOUR **OUTFIT** IS DIF-FERENT.
SWIP
OOH, YOU NOTICED? I WENT INTO TOWN FOR THE FIRST TIME IN A WHILE AND BOUGHT NEW CLOTHES.
WINK
DON'T I LOOK *DASHING* NOW?
OH MY GOSH, HE'S ACTING LIKE ELIAS!
I'll head home.
COME ON, YOU TWO.
COME SAY HELLO.

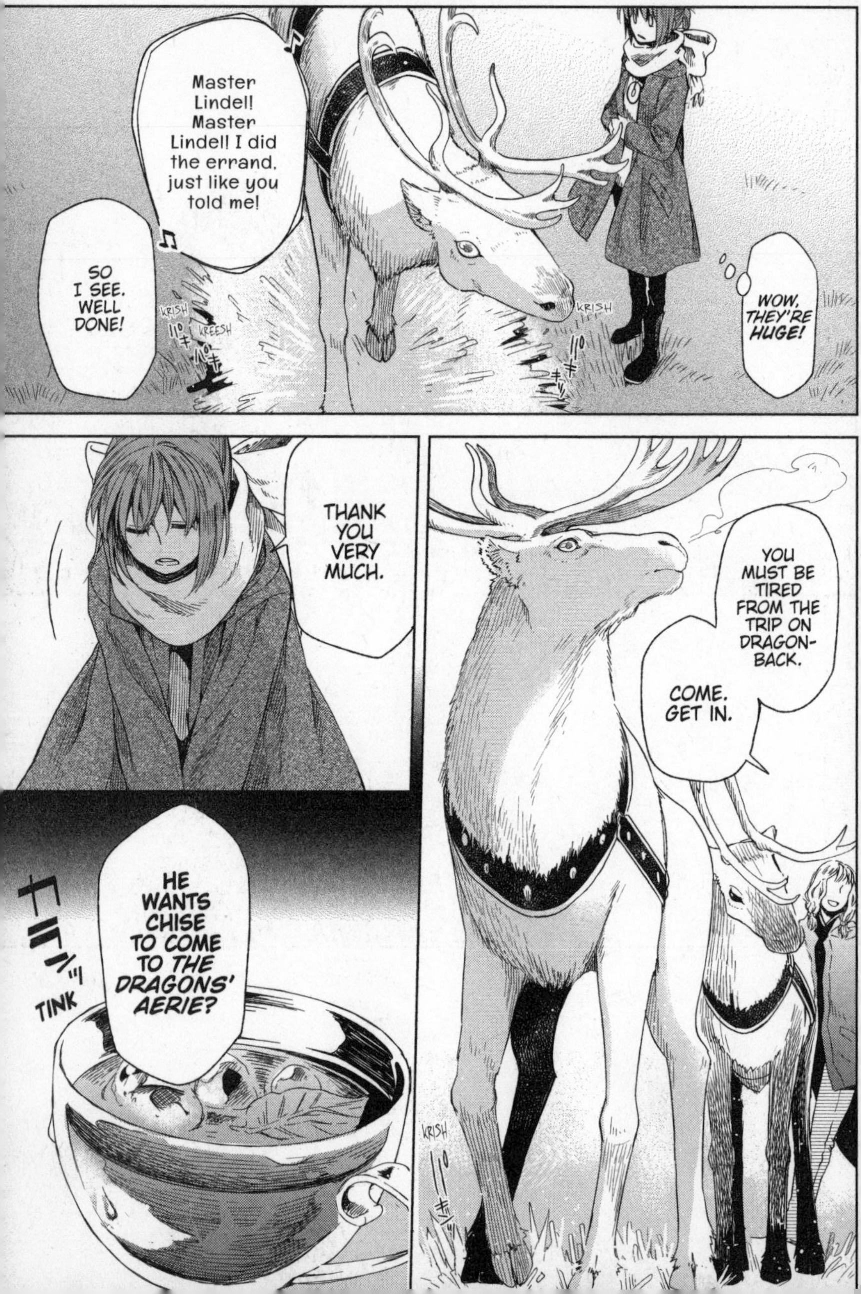
WOW, THEY'RE HUGE!
Master Lindel! Master Lindel! I did the errand, just like you told me!
KRISH
KRISH
KREESH
SO I SEE. WELL DONE!
YOU MUST BE TIRED FROM THE TRIP ON DRAGON-BACK.
COME. GET IN.
KRISH
THANK YOU VERY MUCH.
TINK
HE WANTS CHISE TO COME TO THE DRAGONS' AERIE?

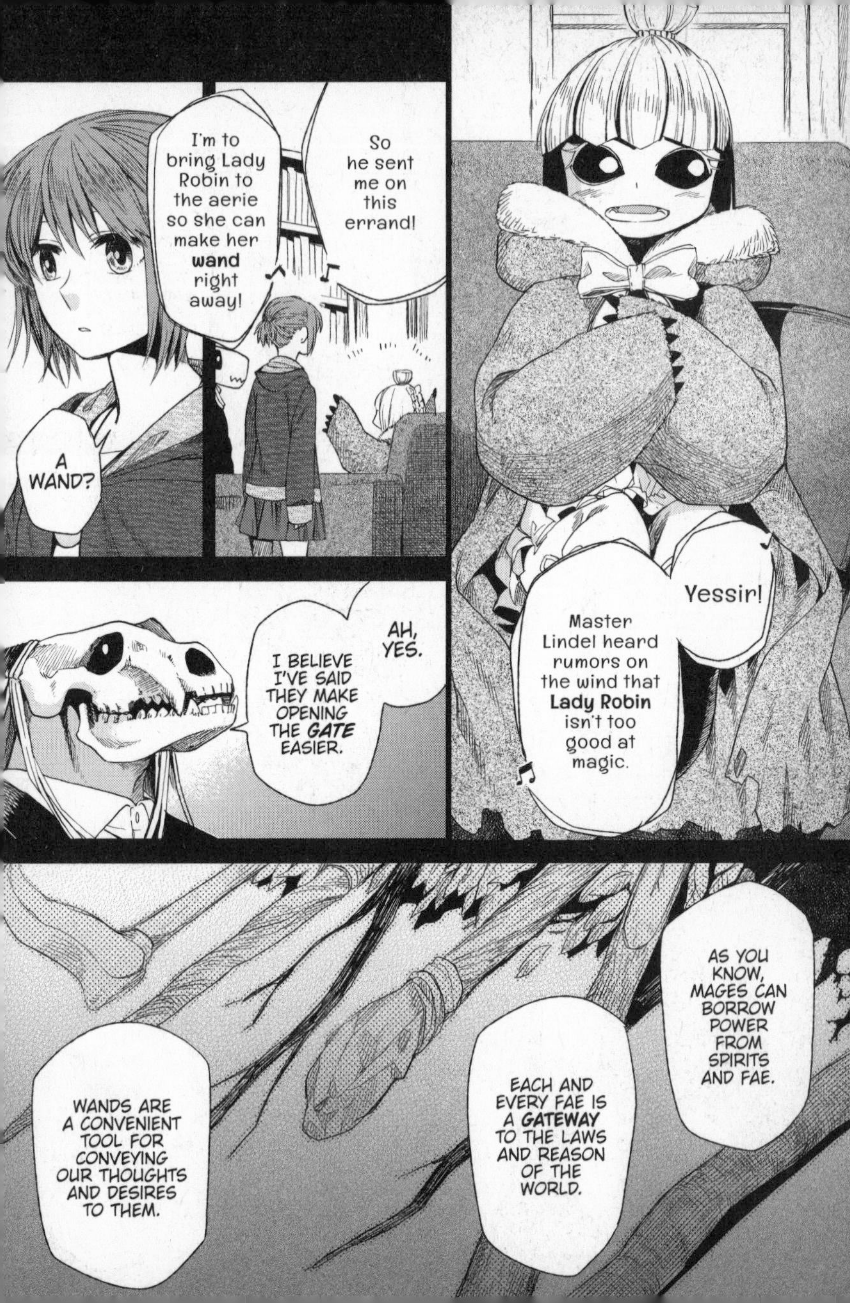
Yessir!
Master Lindel heard rumors on the wind that **Lady Robin** isn't too good at magic.
So he sent me on this errand!
I'm to bring Lady Robin to the aerie so she can make her **wand** right away!
A WAND?
AH, YES.
I BELIEVE I'VE SAID THEY MAKE OPENING THE ***GATE*** EASIER.
AS YOU KNOW, MAGES CAN BORROW POWER FROM SPIRITS AND FAE.
EACH AND EVERY FAE IS A **GATEWAY** TO THE LAWS AND REASON OF THE WORLD.
WANDS ARE A CONVENIENT TOOL FOR CONVEYING OUR THOUGHTS AND DESIRES TO THEM.

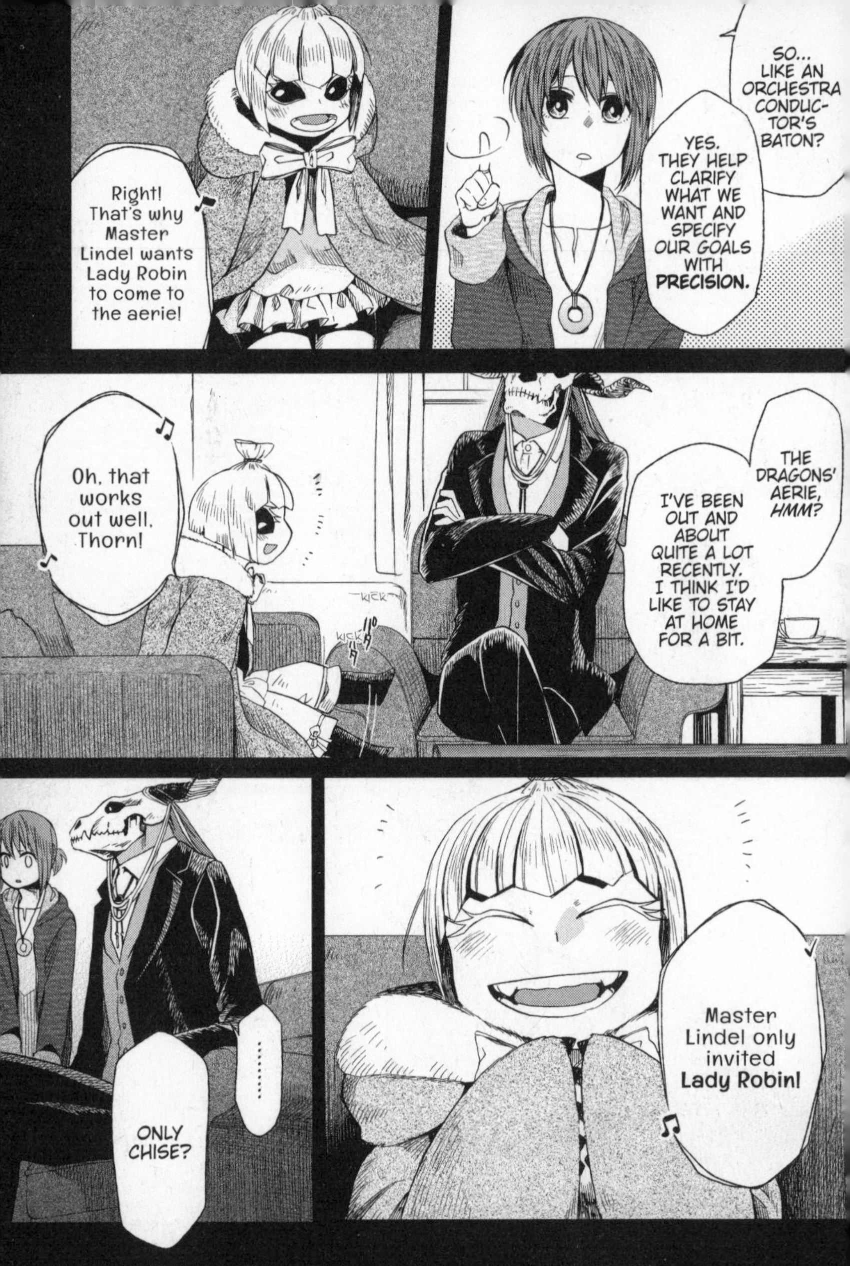
SO... LIKE AN ORCHESTRA CONDUC-TOR'S BATON?
YES. THEY HELP CLARIFY WHAT WE WANT AND SPECIFY OUR GOALS WITH **PRECISION.**
Right! That's why Master Lindel wants Lady Robin to come to the aerie!
THE DRAGONS' AERIE, *HMM?*
I'VE BEEN OUT AND ABOUT QUITE A LOT RECENTLY. I THINK I'D LIKE TO STAY AT HOME FOR A BIT.
Oh, that works out well, Thorn!
KICK
KICK
Master Lindel only invited **Lady Robin!**
......
ONLY CHISE?

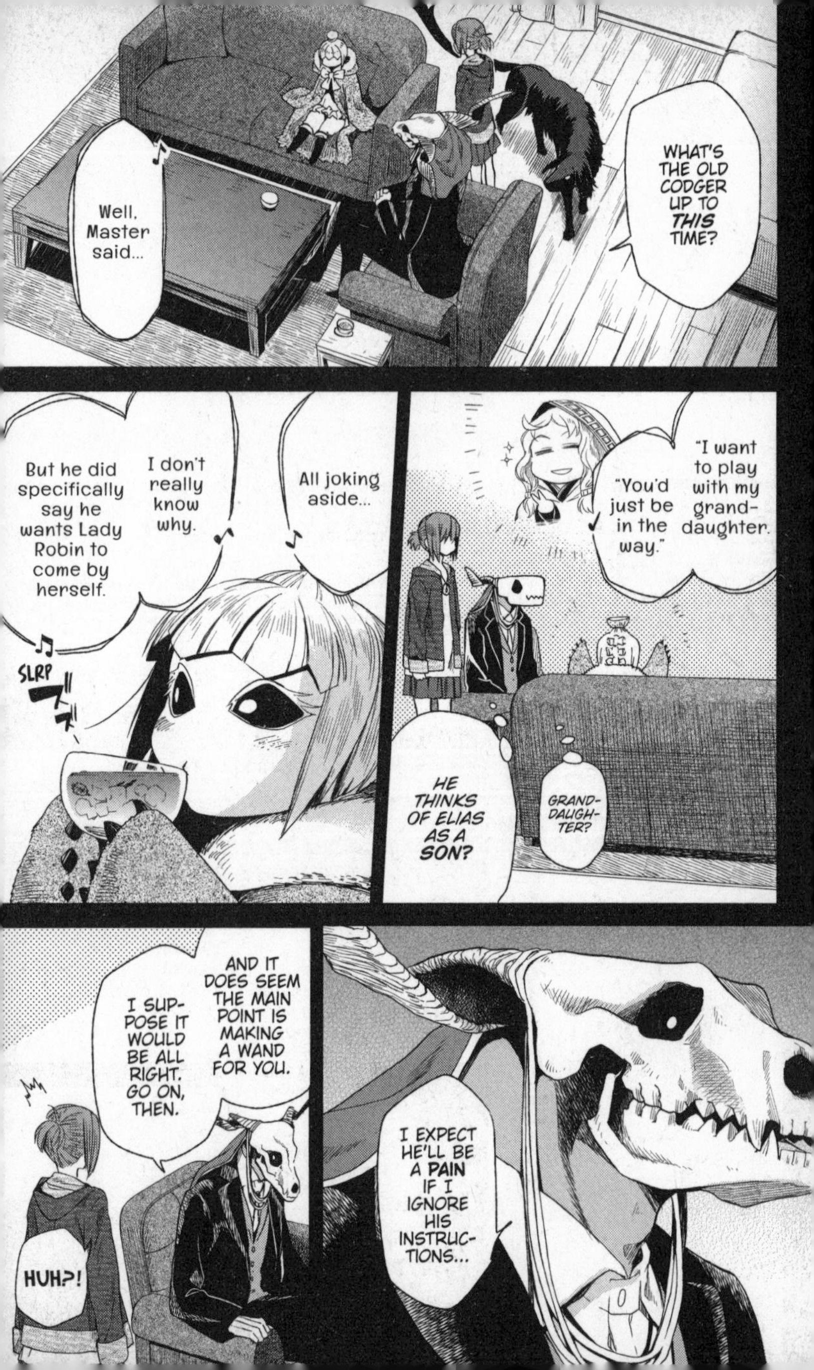
WHAT'S THE OLD CODGER UP TO THIS TIME?
Well, Master said...
"I want to play with my grand-daughter.
"You'd just be in the way."
HE THINKS OF ELIAS AS A SON?
GRAND-DAUGH-TER?
All joking aside...
I don't really know why.
But he did specifically say he wants Lady Robin to come by herself.
SLRP
I EXPECT HE'LL BE A PAIN IF I IGNORE HIS INSTRUC-TIONS...
AND IT DOES SEEM THE MAIN POINT IS MAKING A WAND FOR YOU.
I SUP-POSE IT WOULD BE ALL RIGHT. GO ON, THEN.
HUH?!

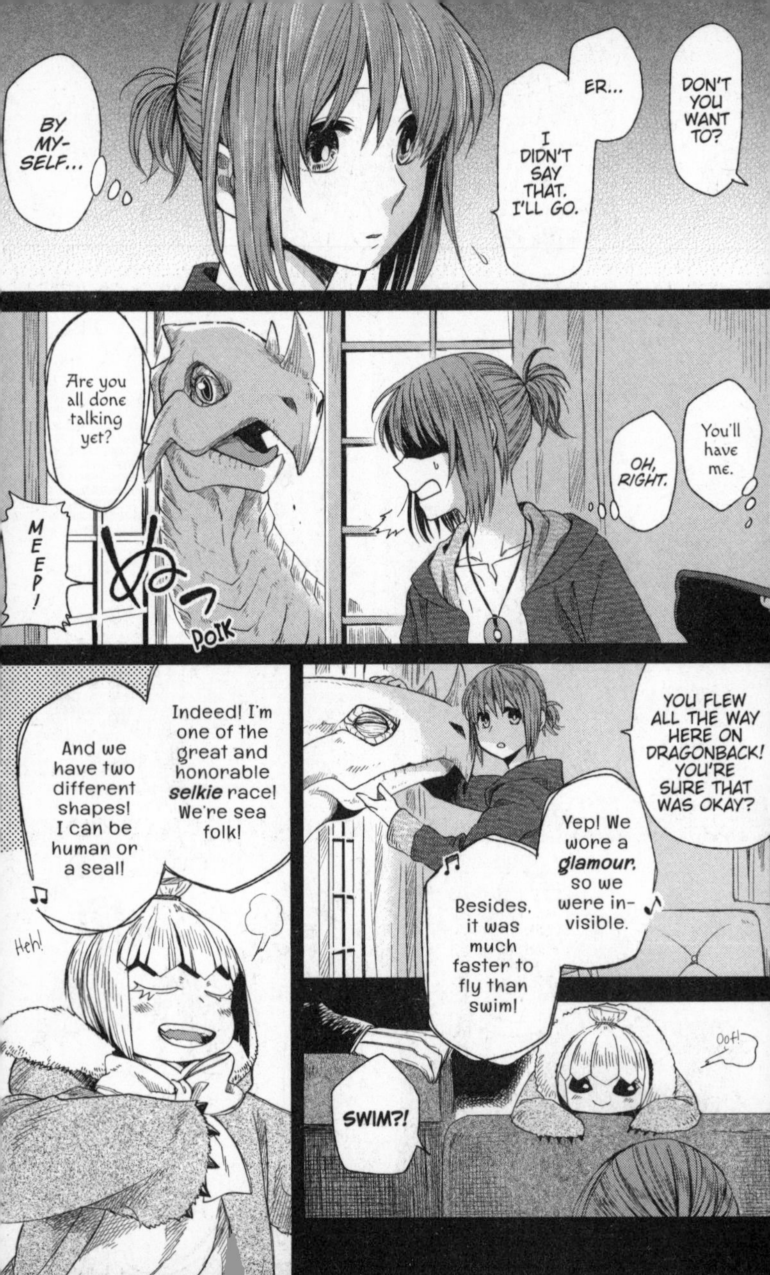
DON'T YOU WANT TO?
ER...
I DIDN'T SAY THAT. I'LL GO.
BY MY-SELF...
You'll have me.
OH, RIGHT.
Are you all done talking yet?
MEEP!
ぬっ
POIK
YOU FLEW ALL THE WAY HERE ON DRAGONBACK! YOU'RE SURE THAT WAS OKAY?
Yep! We wore a glamour, so we were in-visible.
Besides, it was much faster to fly than swim!
SWIM?!
Oof!
Indeed! I'm one of the great and honorable selkie race! We're sea folk!
And we have two different shapes! I can be human or a seal!
Heh!

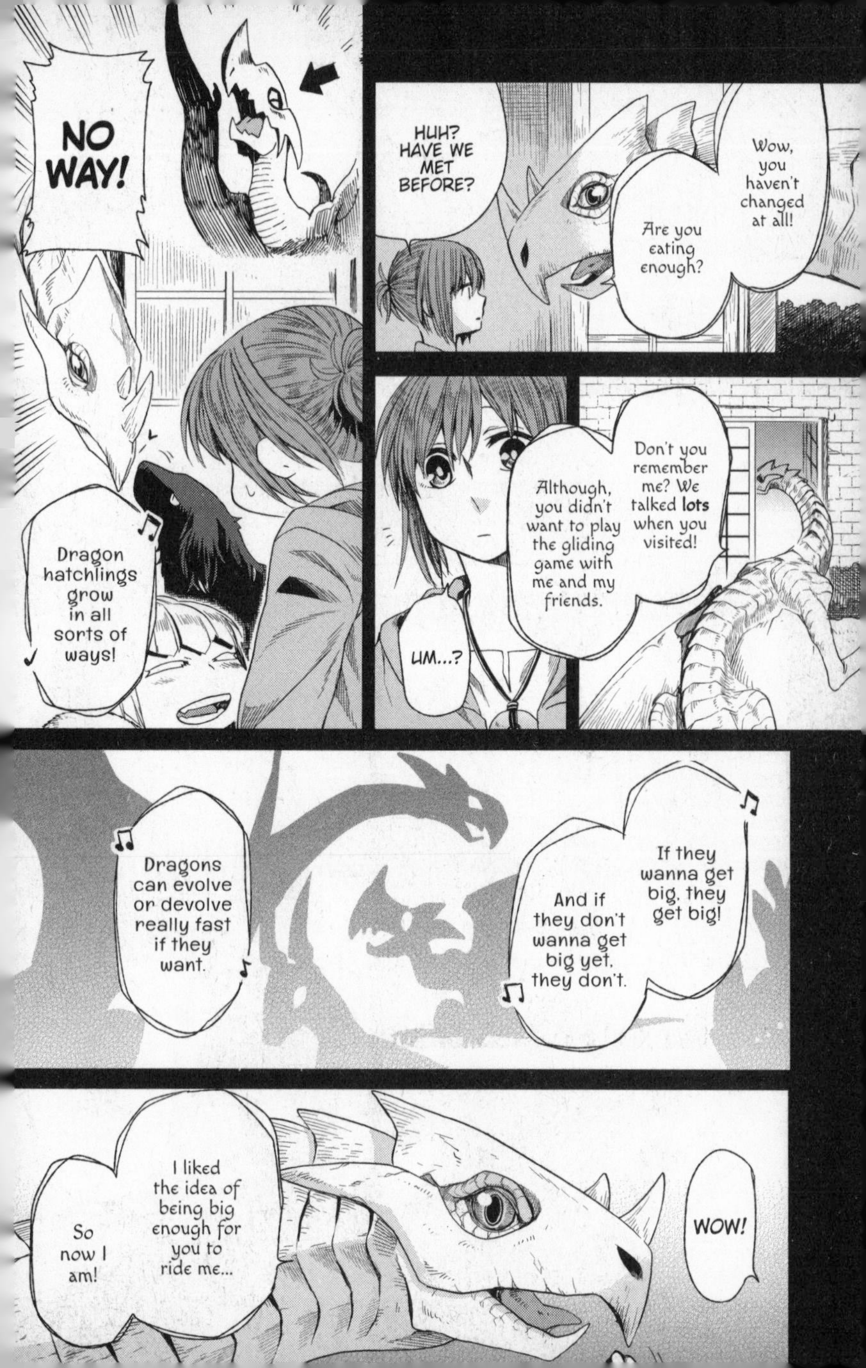
Wow, you haven't changed at all!
Are you eating enough?
HUH? HAVE WE MET BEFORE?
Don't you remember me? We talked **lots** when you visited!
Although, you didn't want to play the gliding game with me and my friends.
UM...?
NO WAY!
Dragon hatchlings grow in all sorts of ways!
If they wanna get big, they get big!
And if they don't wanna get big yet, they don't.
Dragons can evolve or devolve really fast if they want.
WOW!
I liked the idea of being big enough for you to ride me...
So now I am!

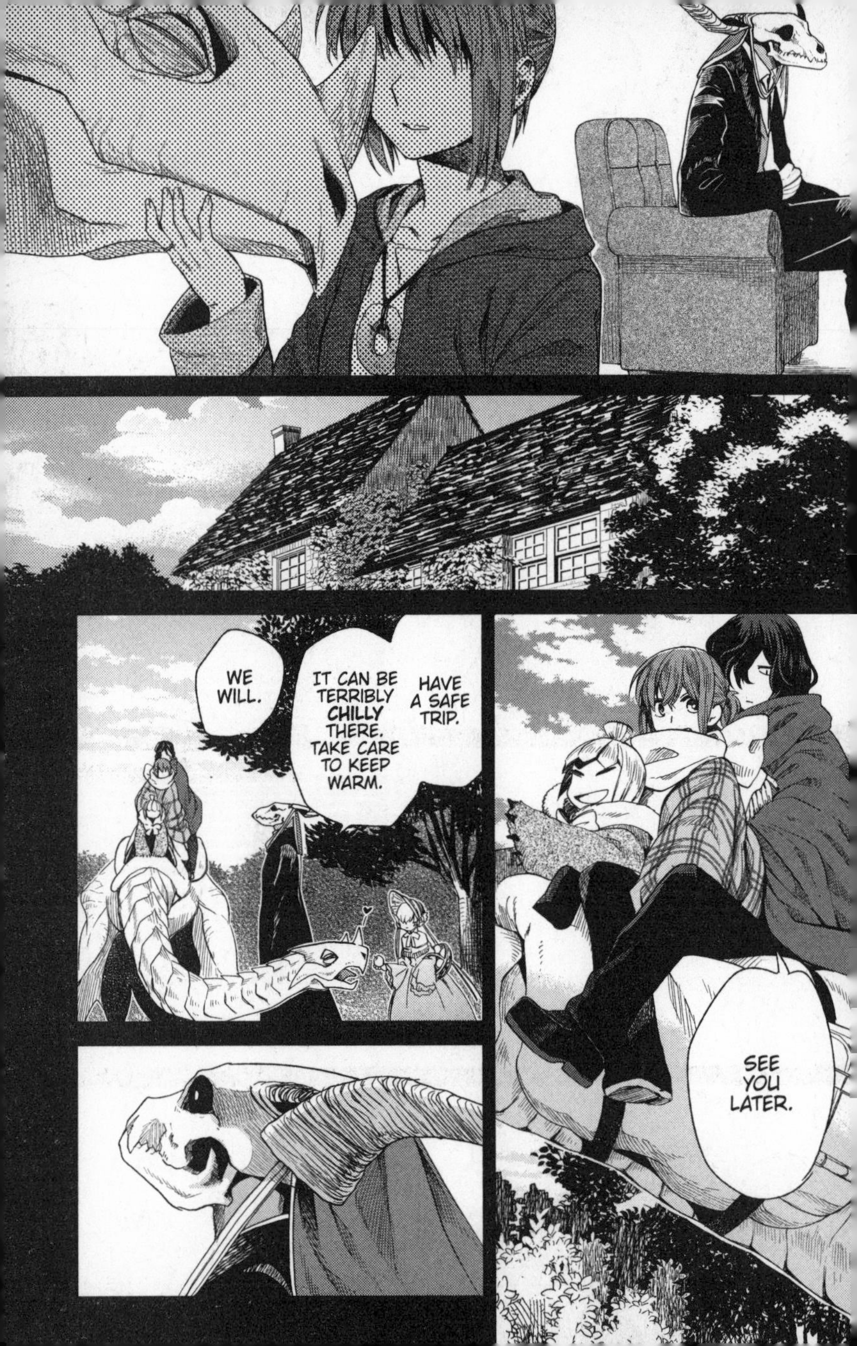
SEE YOU LATER.
HAVE A SAFE TRIP.
IT CAN BE TERRIBLY CHILLY THERE. TAKE CARE TO KEEP WARM.
WE WILL.

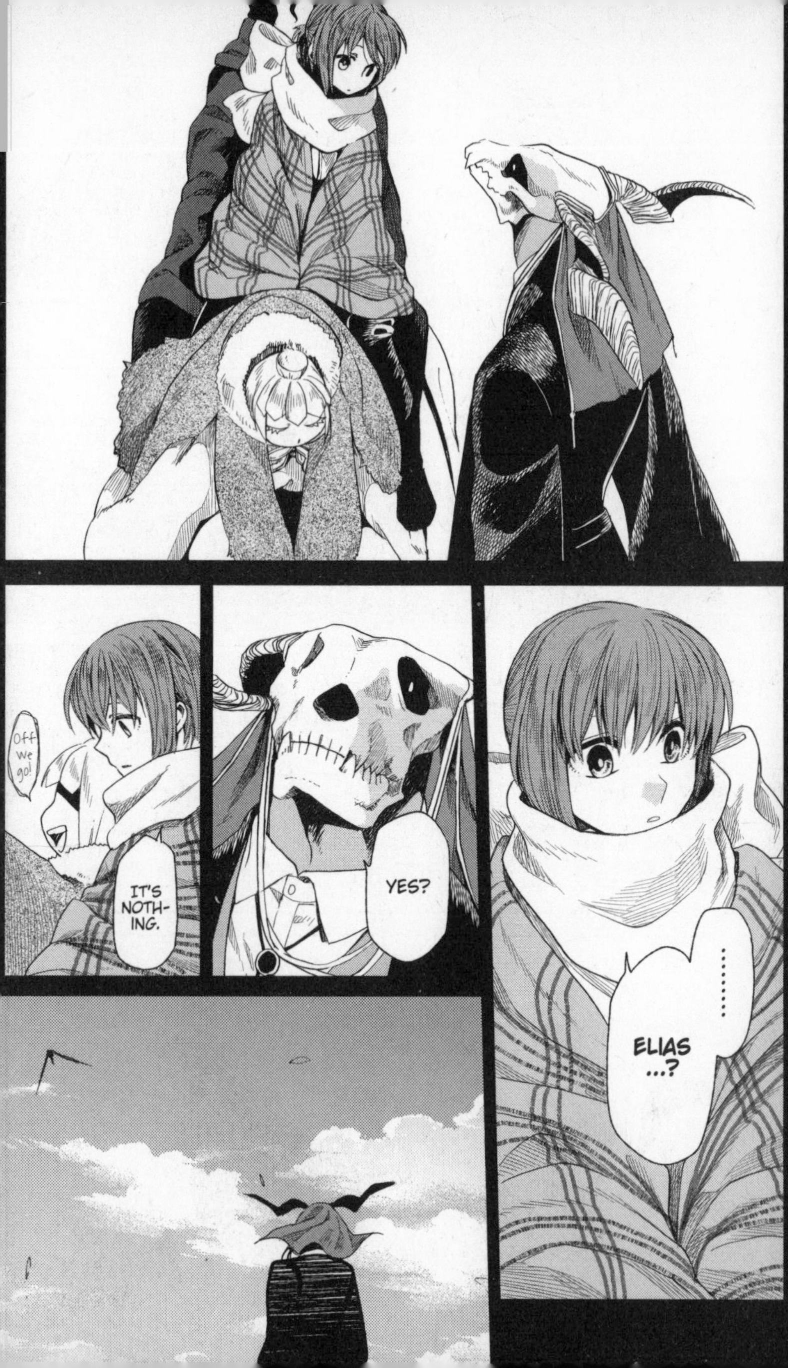
......
ELIAS ...?
YES?
IT'S NOTHING.
Off we go!

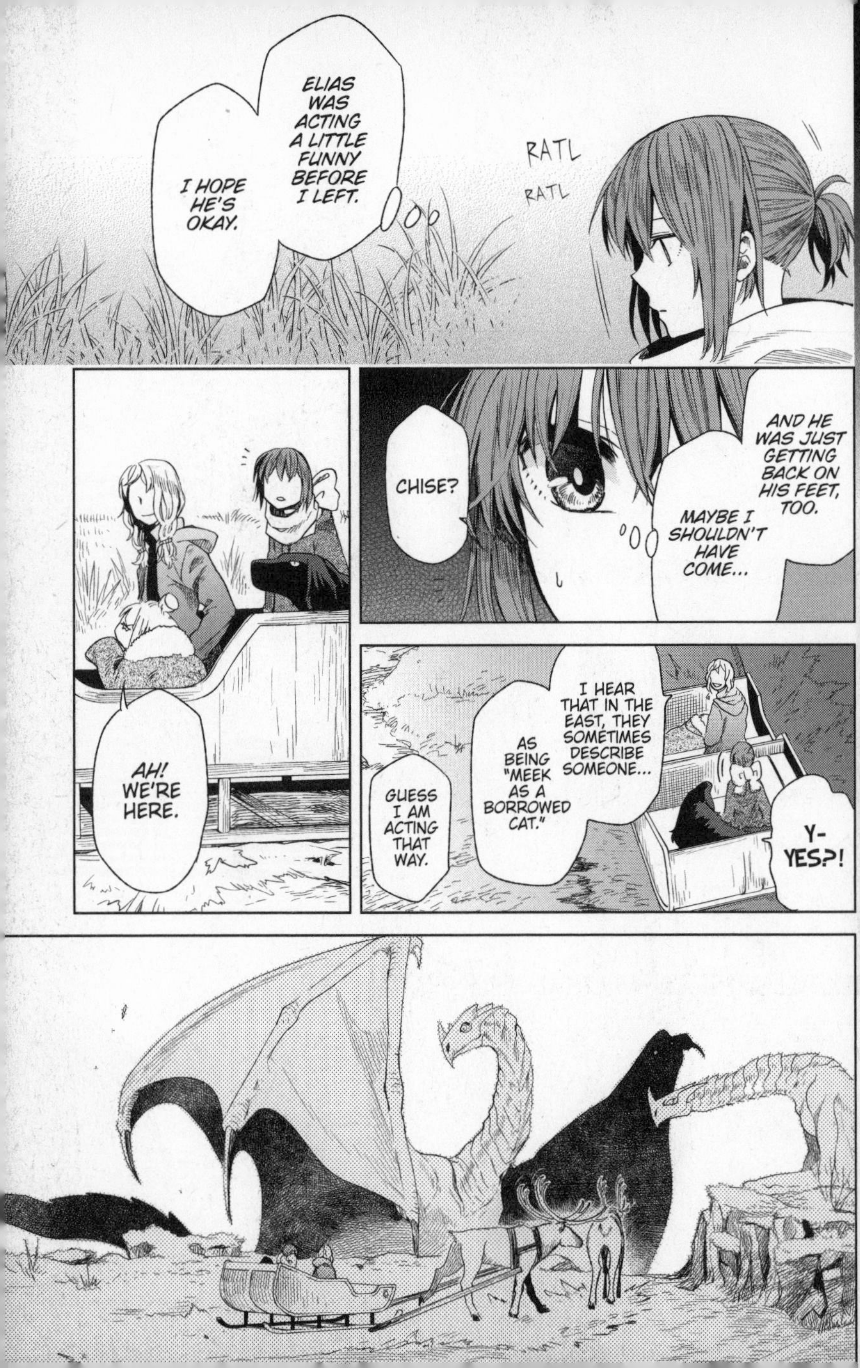
RATL
RATL
ELIAS WAS ACTING A LITTLE FUNNY BEFORE I LEFT.
I HOPE HE'S OKAY.
AND HE WAS JUST GETTING BACK ON HIS FEET, TOO.
MAYBE I SHOULDN'T HAVE COME...
CHISE?
Y- YES?!
I HEAR THAT IN THE EAST, THEY SOMETIMES DESCRIBE SOMEONE...
AS BEING "MEEK AS A BORROWED CAT."
GUESS I AM ACTING THAT WAY.
AH! WE'RE HERE.

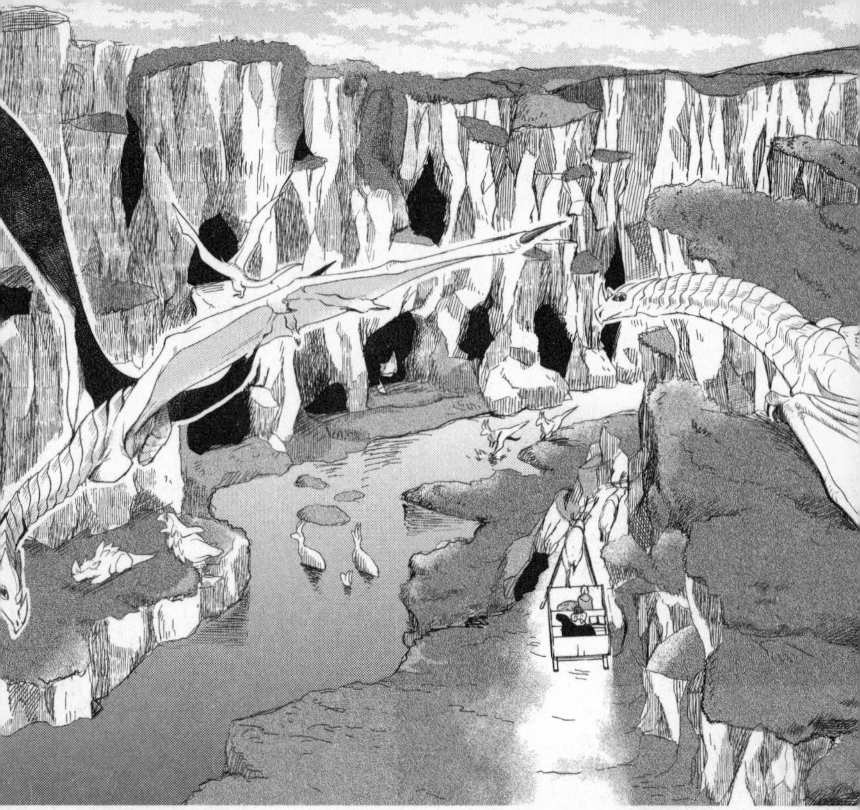

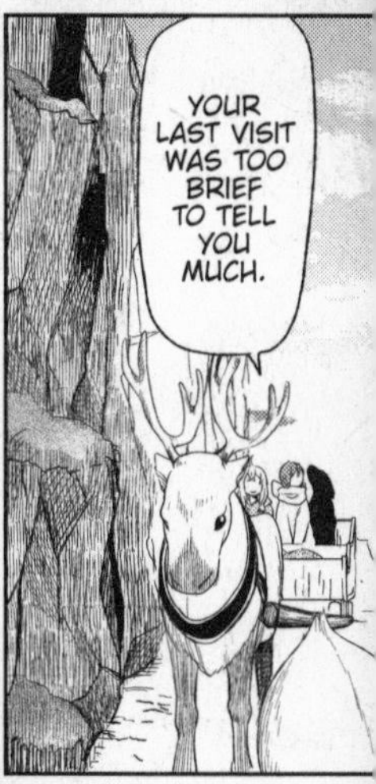
YOUR LAST VISIT WAS TOO BRIEF TO TELL YOU MUCH.

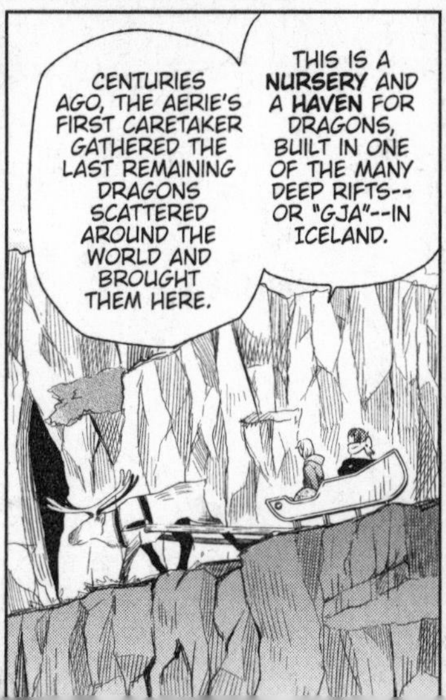
THIS IS A NURSERY AND A HAVEN FOR DRAGONS, BUILT IN ONE OF THE MANY DEEP RIFTS--OR "GJA"--IN ICELAND.
CENTURIES AGO, THE AERIE'S FIRST CARETAKER GATHERED THE LAST REMAINING DRAGONS SCATTERED AROUND THE WORLD AND BROUGHT THEM HERE.

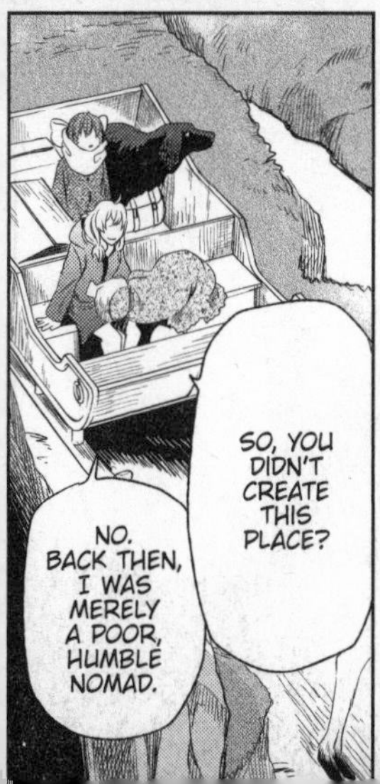
SO, YOU DIDN'T CREATE THIS PLACE?
NO. BACK THEN, I WAS MERELY A POOR, HUMBLE NOMAD.

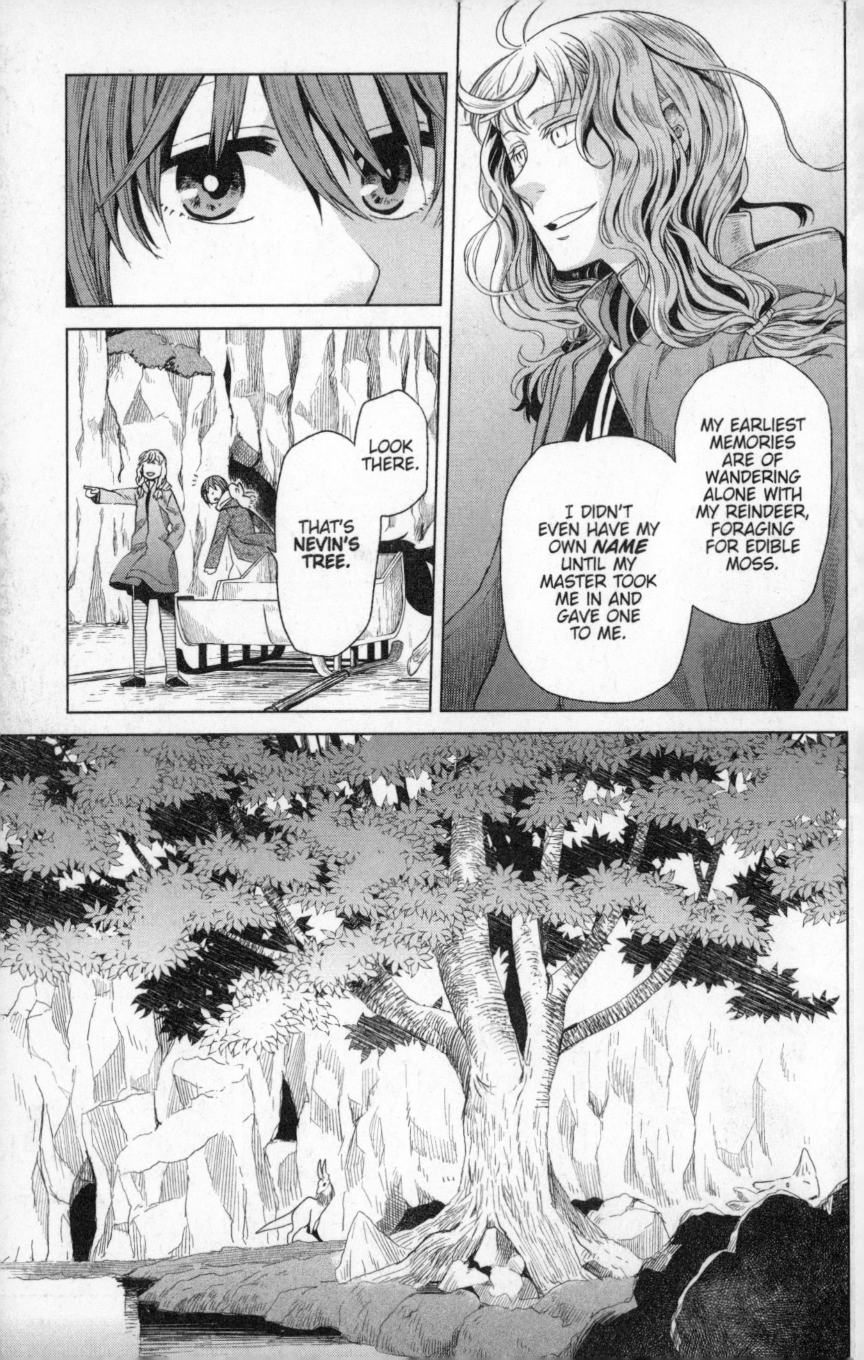
MY EARLIEST MEMORIES ARE OF WANDERING ALONE WITH MY REINDEER, FORAGING FOR EDIBLE MOSS.
I DIDN'T EVEN HAVE MY OWN ***NAME*** UNTIL MY MASTER TOOK ME IN AND GAVE ONE TO ME.
LOOK THERE.
THAT'S NEVIN'S TREE.

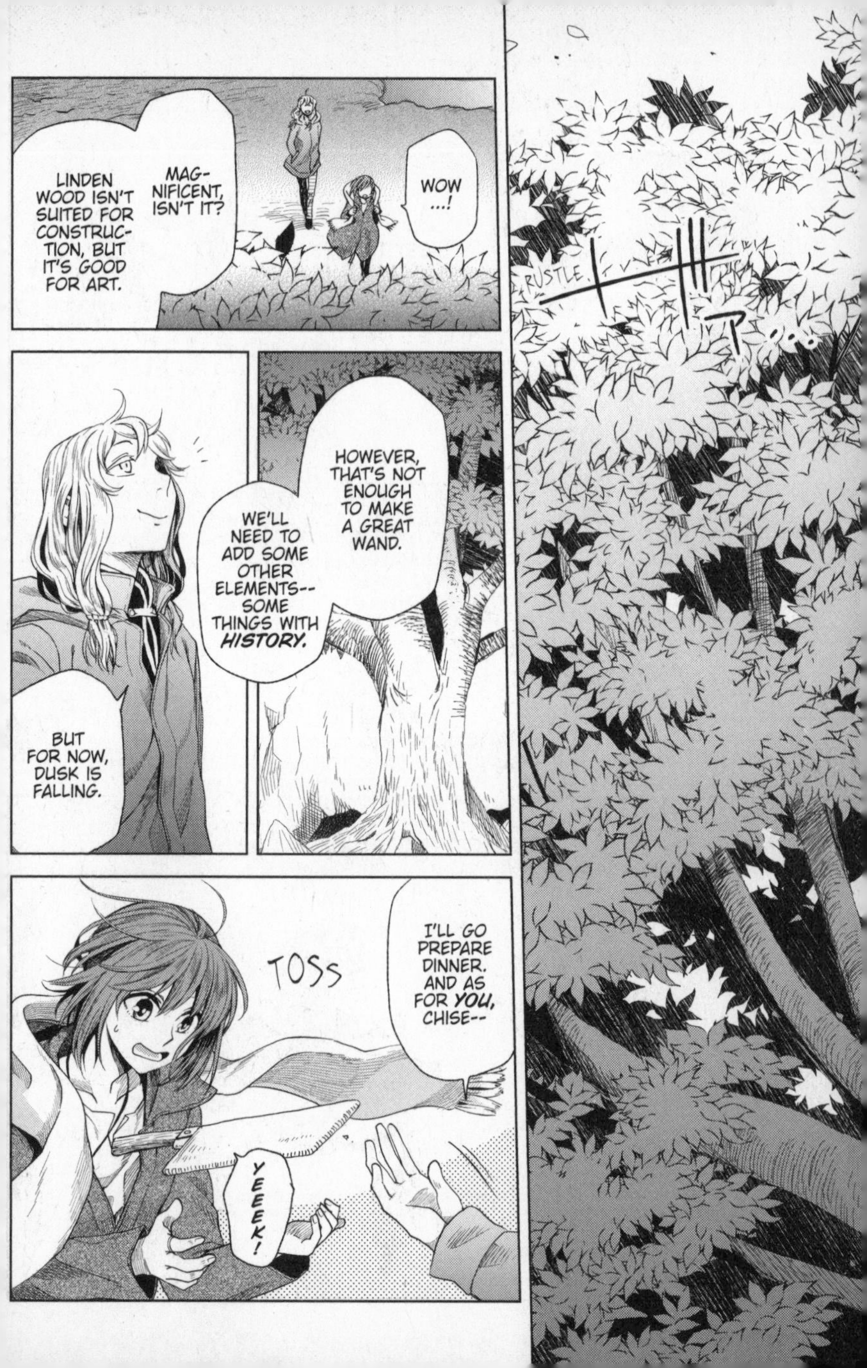
RUSTLE
WOW ...!
MAG-NIFICENT, ISN'T IT?
LINDEN WOOD ISN'T SUITED FOR CONSTRUC-TION, BUT IT'S GOOD FOR ART.
HOWEVER, THAT'S NOT ENOUGH TO MAKE A GREAT WAND.
WE'LL NEED TO ADD SOME OTHER ELEMENTS-- SOME THINGS WITH *HISTORY.*
BUT FOR NOW, DUSK IS FALLING.
I'LL GO PREPARE DINNER. AND AS FOR *YOU,* CHISE--
TOSS
YEEEK!

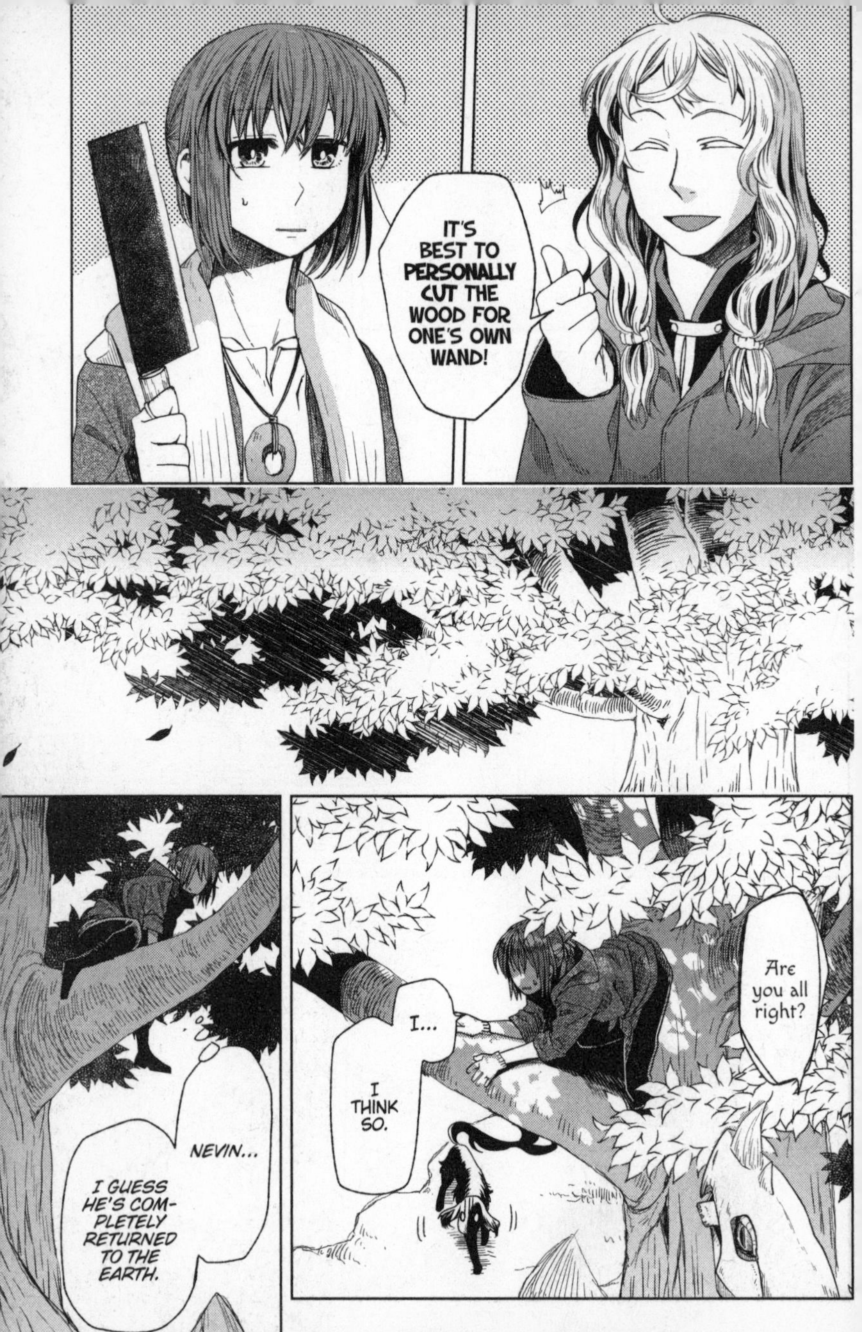
IT'S BEST TO PERSONALLY CUT THE WOOD FOR ONE'S OWN WAND!
Are you all right?
I...
I THINK SO.
NEVIN...
I GUESS HE'S COMPLETELY RETURNED TO THE EARTH.

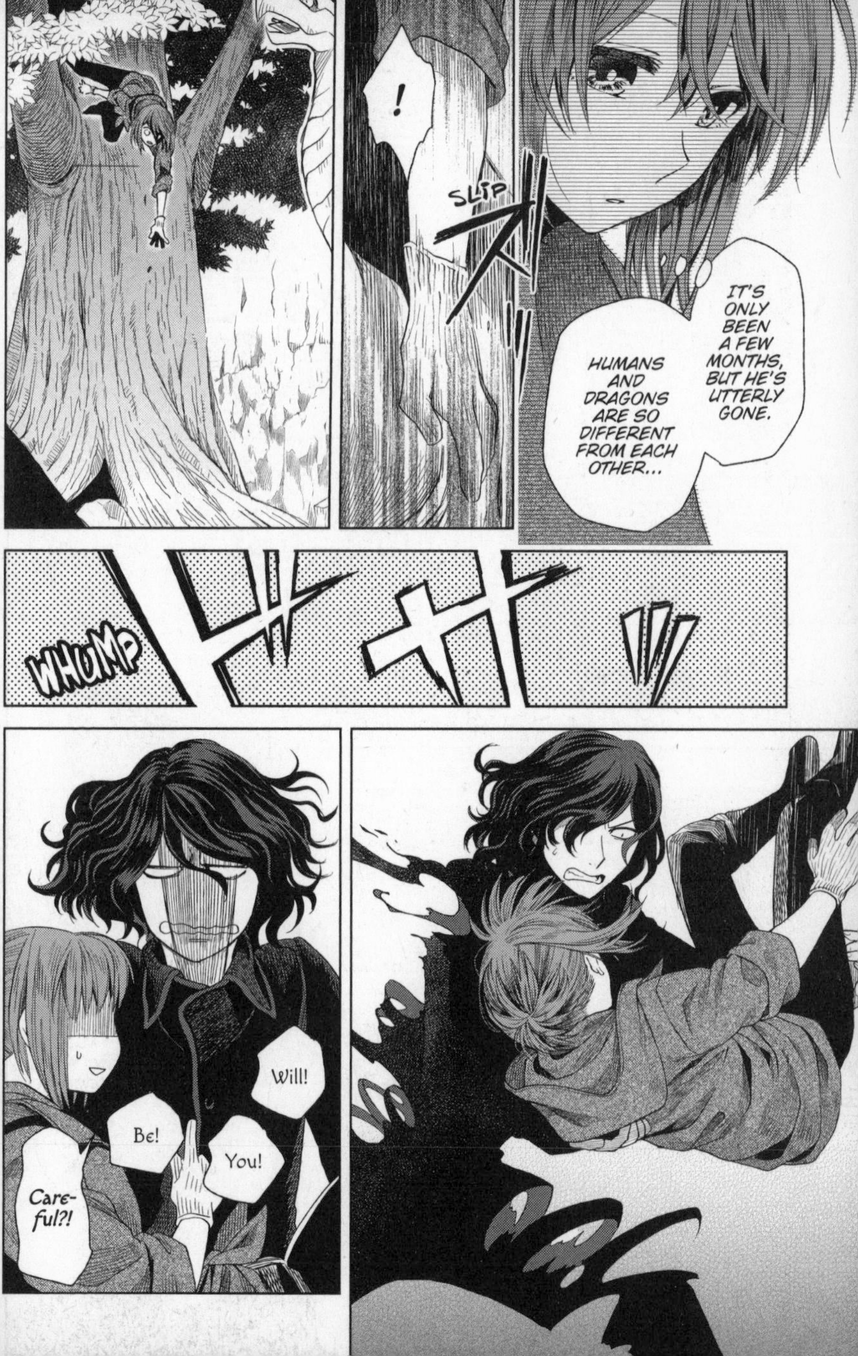
IT'S ONLY BEEN A FEW MONTHS, BUT HE'S UTTERLY GONE.
HUMANS AND DRAGONS ARE SO DIFFERENT FROM EACH OTHER...
SLIP
!
WHUMP
Will!
You!
Be!
Care-ful?!

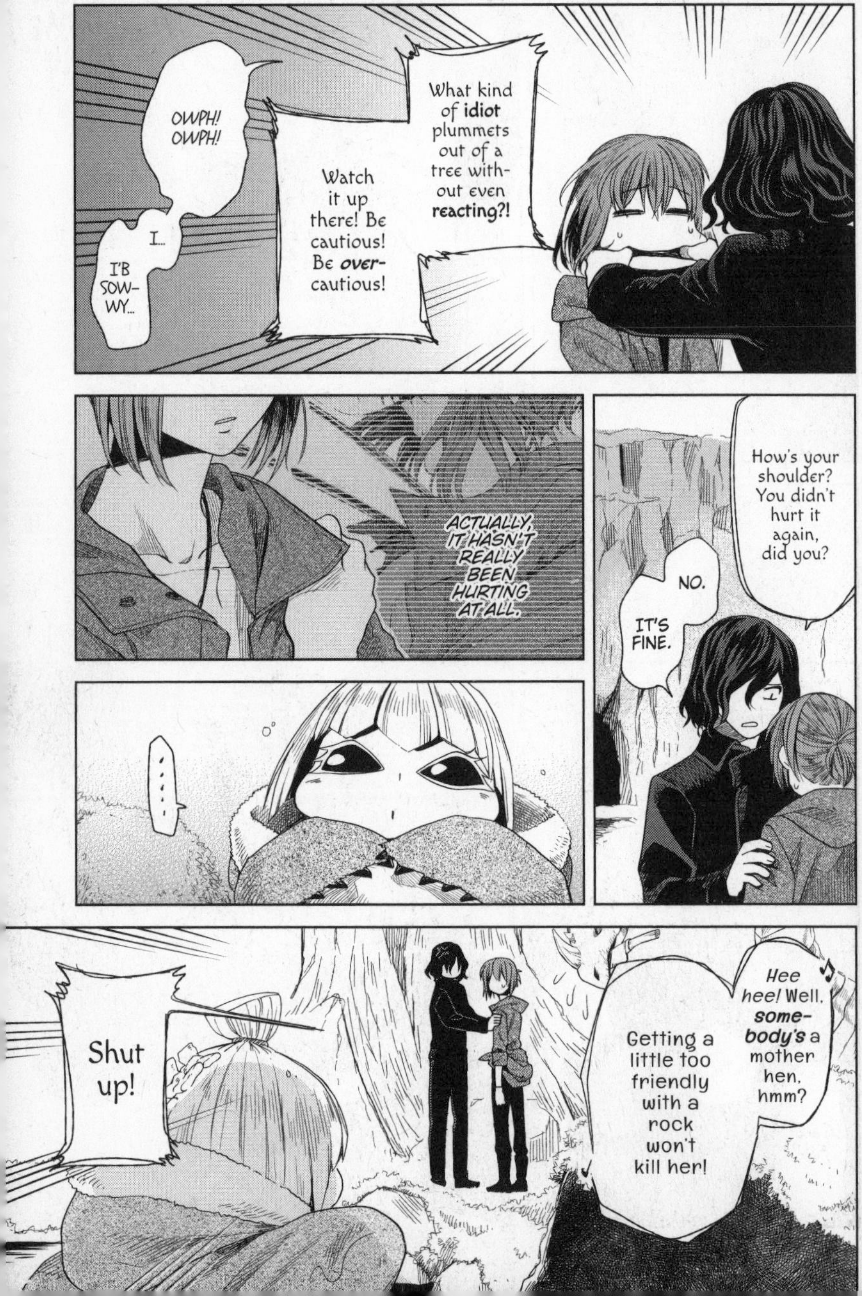
What kind of idiot plummets out of a tree without even reacting?!
Watch it up there! Be cautious! Be over-cautious!
OWPH! OWPH!
I...
I'B SOWWY...
How's your shoulder? You didn't hurt it again, did you?
NO.
IT'S FINE.
ACTUALLY, IT HASN'T REALLY BEEN HURTING AT ALL.
.....
Hee hee! Well, somebody's a mother hen, hmm?
Getting a little too friendly with a rock won't kill her!
Shut up!

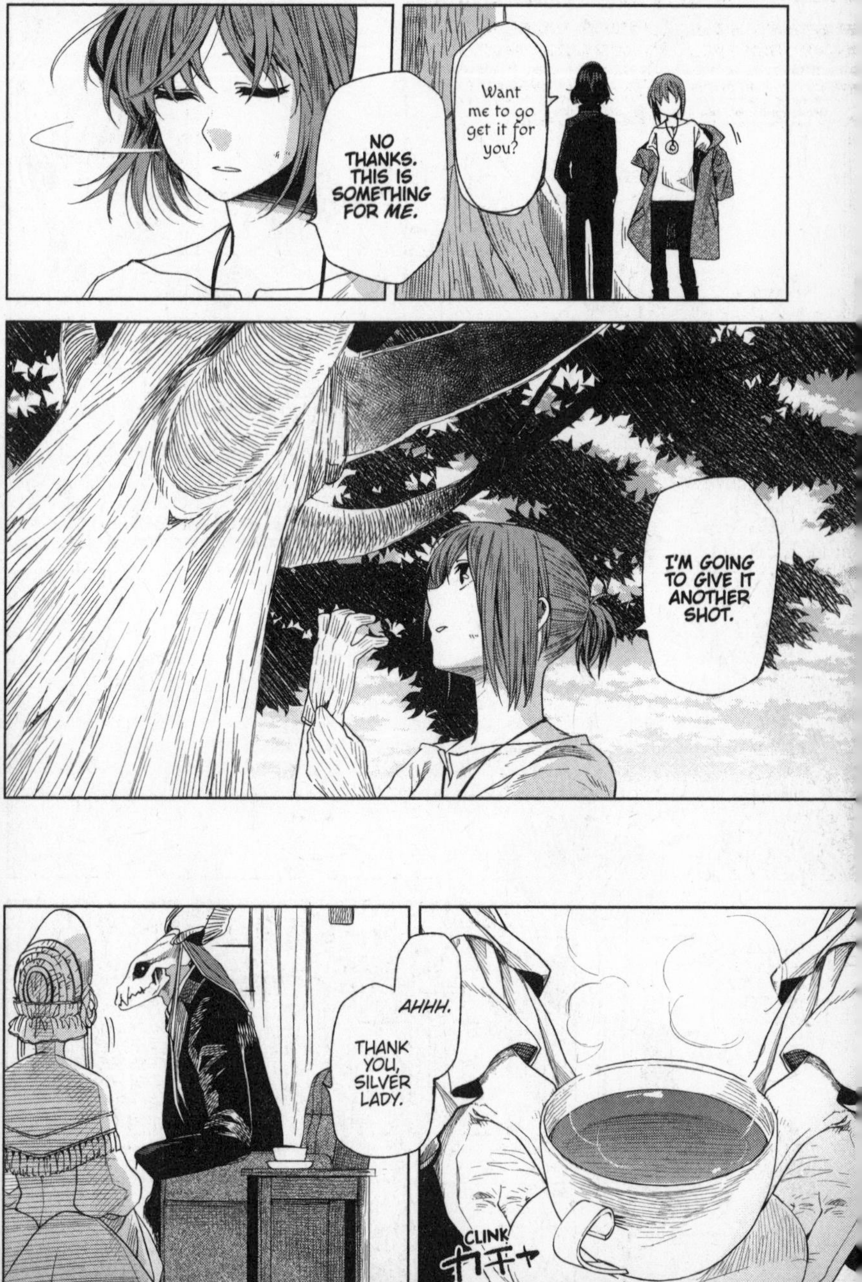
Want me to go get it for you?
NO THANKS. THIS IS SOMETHING FOR ME.
I'M GOING TO GIVE IT ANOTHER SHOT.
CLINK
カチャ
AHHH.
THANK YOU, SILVER LADY.

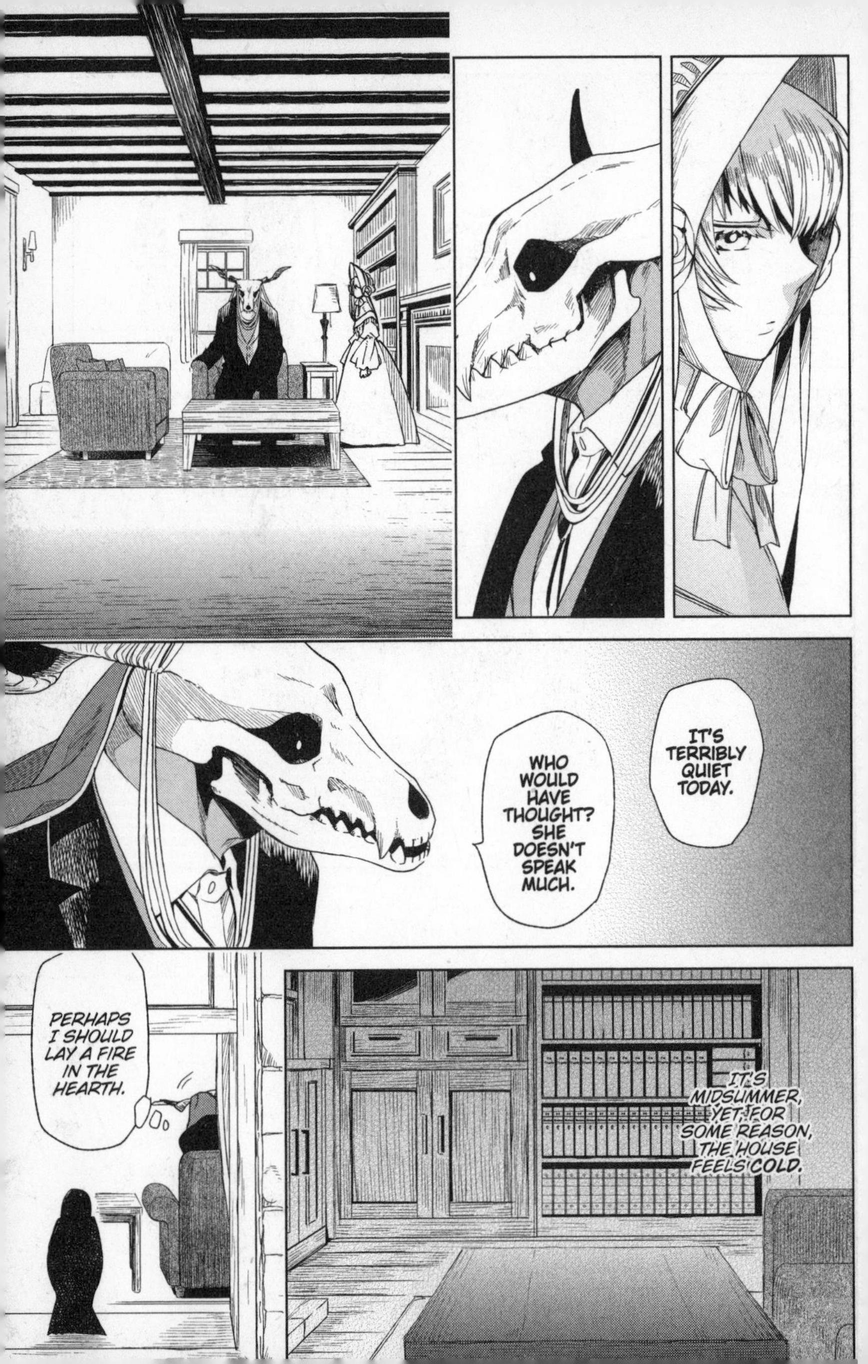
IT'S TERRIBLY QUIET TODAY.
WHO WOULD HAVE THOUGHT? SHE DOESN'T SPEAK MUCH.
IT'S MIDSUMMER, YET, FOR SOME REASON, THE HOUSE FEELS COLD.
PERHAPS I SHOULD LAY A FIRE IN THE HEARTH.

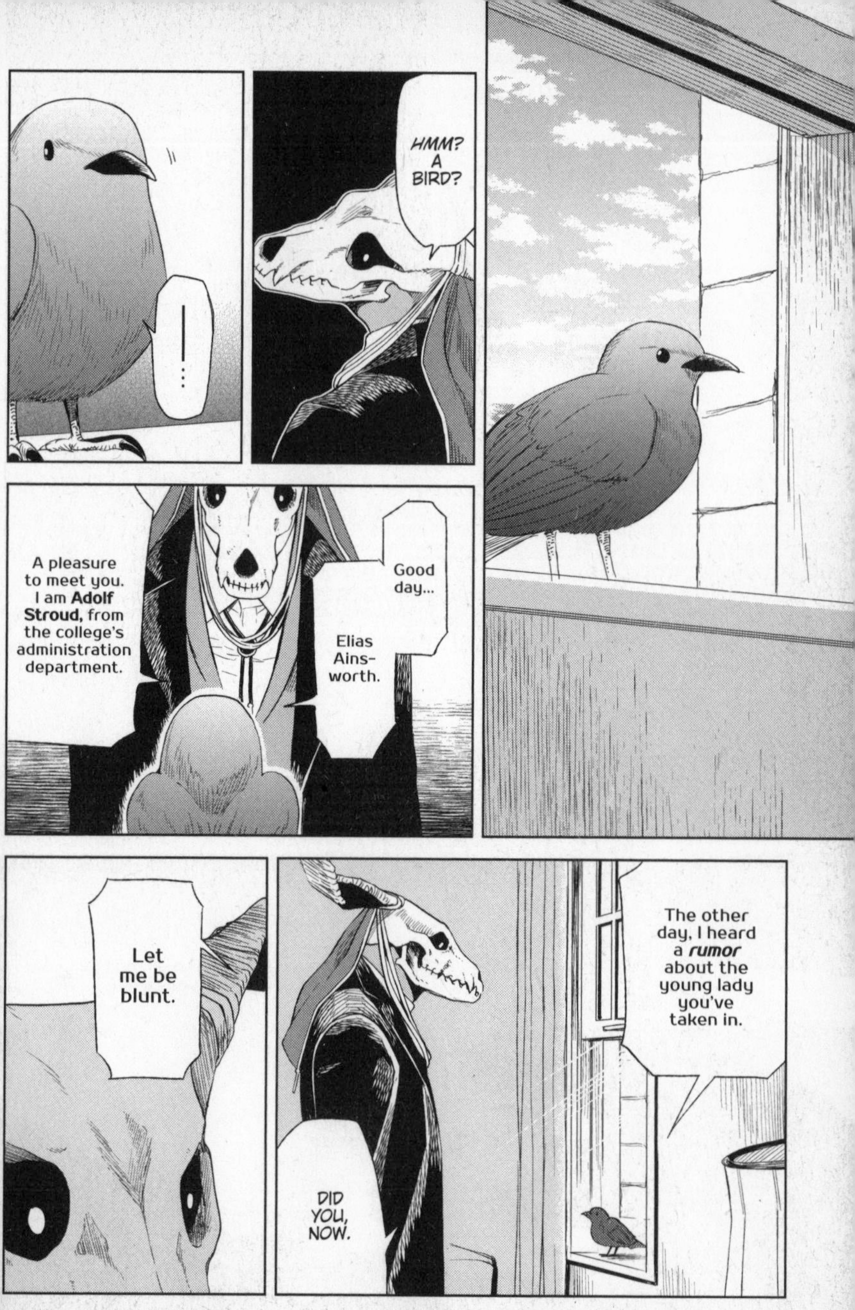
HMM? A BIRD?
—...
Good day...
Elias Ainsworth.
A pleasure to meet you. I am **Adolf Stroud,** from the college's administration department.
The other day, I heard a ***rumor*** about the young lady you've taken in.
DID YOU, NOW.
Let me be blunt.

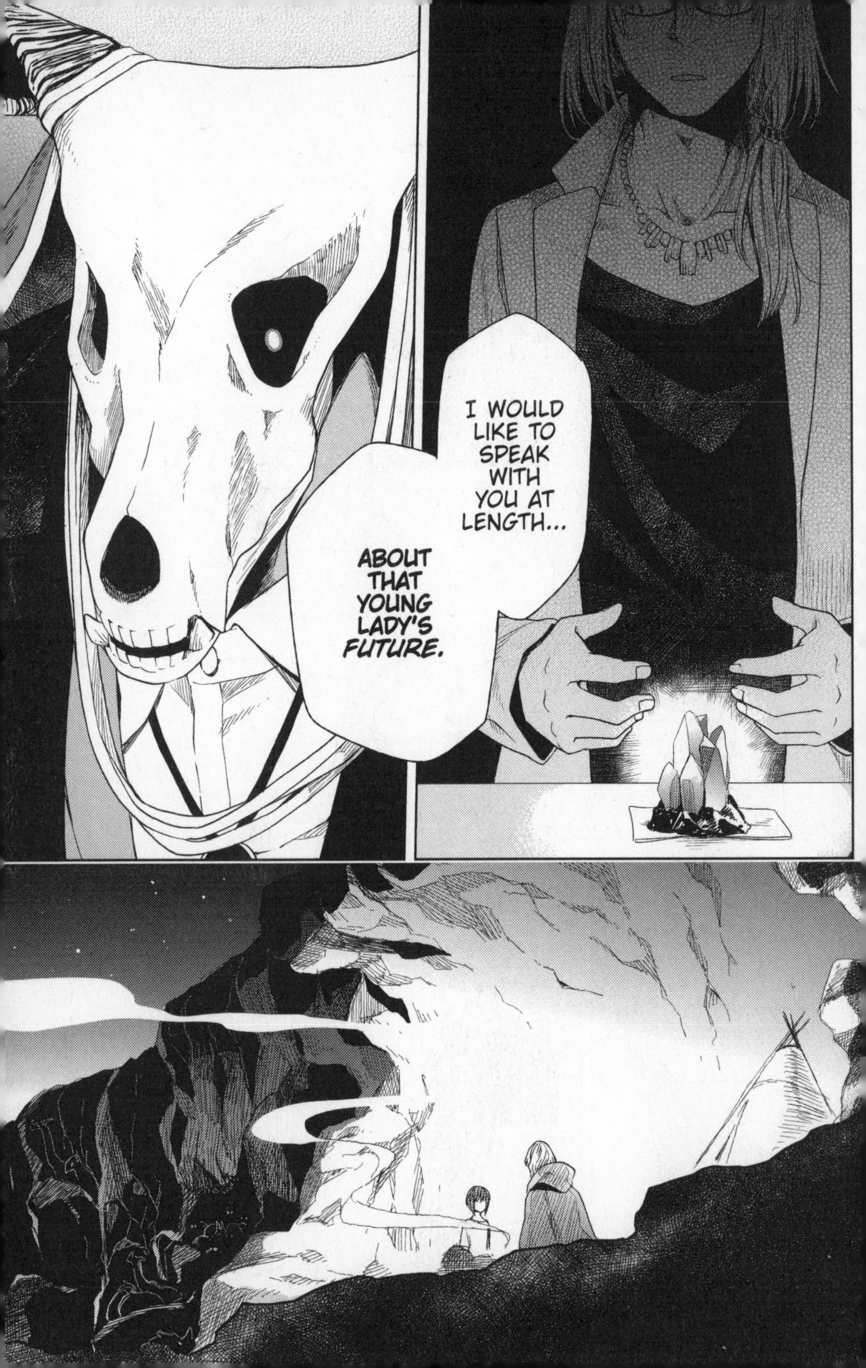
I WOULD LIKE TO SPEAK WITH YOU AT LENGTH...
ABOUT THAT YOUNG LADY'S FUTURE.

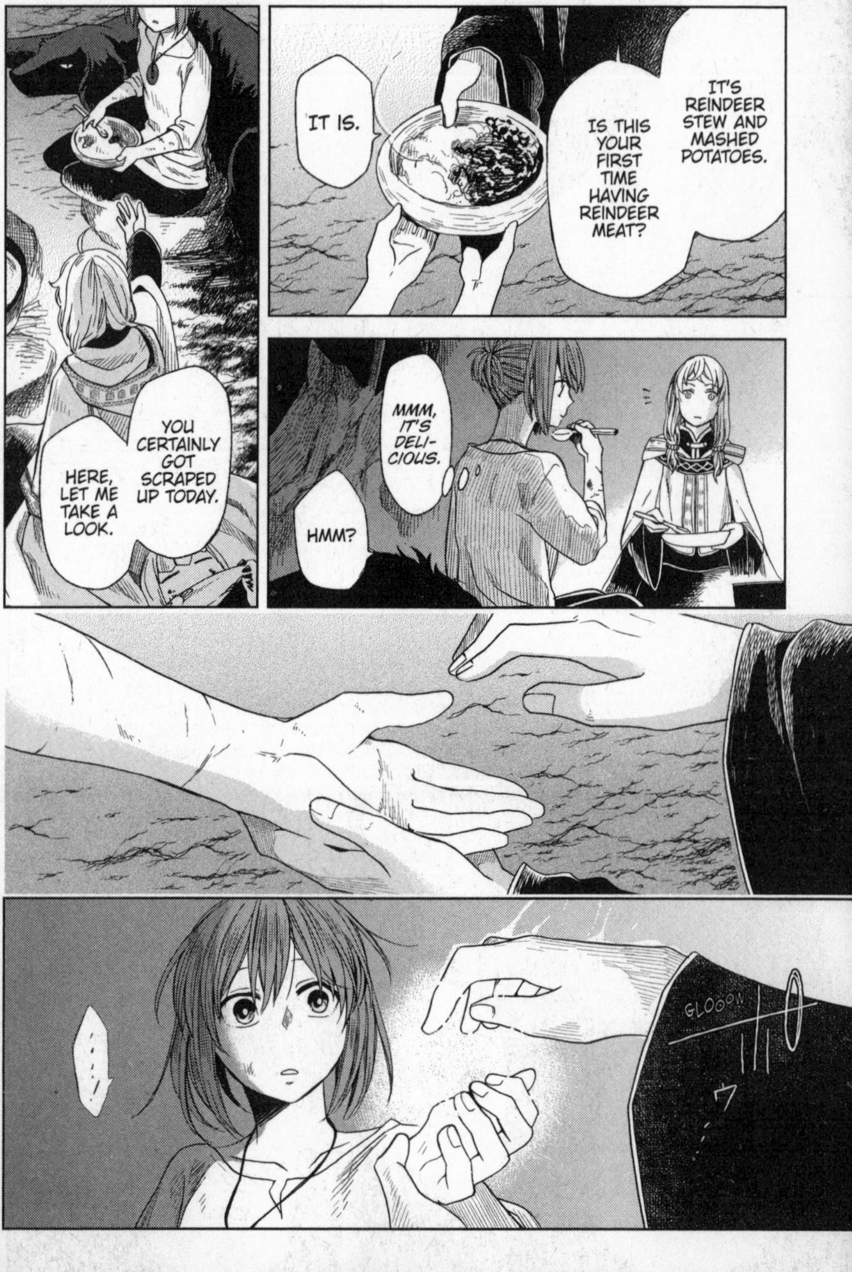
IT'S REINDEER STEW AND MASHED POTATOES.
IS THIS YOUR FIRST TIME HAVING REINDEER MEAT?
IT IS.
MMM, IT'S DELI-CIOUS.
HMM?
YOU CERTAINLY GOT SCRAPED UP TODAY.
HERE, LET ME TAKE A LOOK.
GLOOON
...!

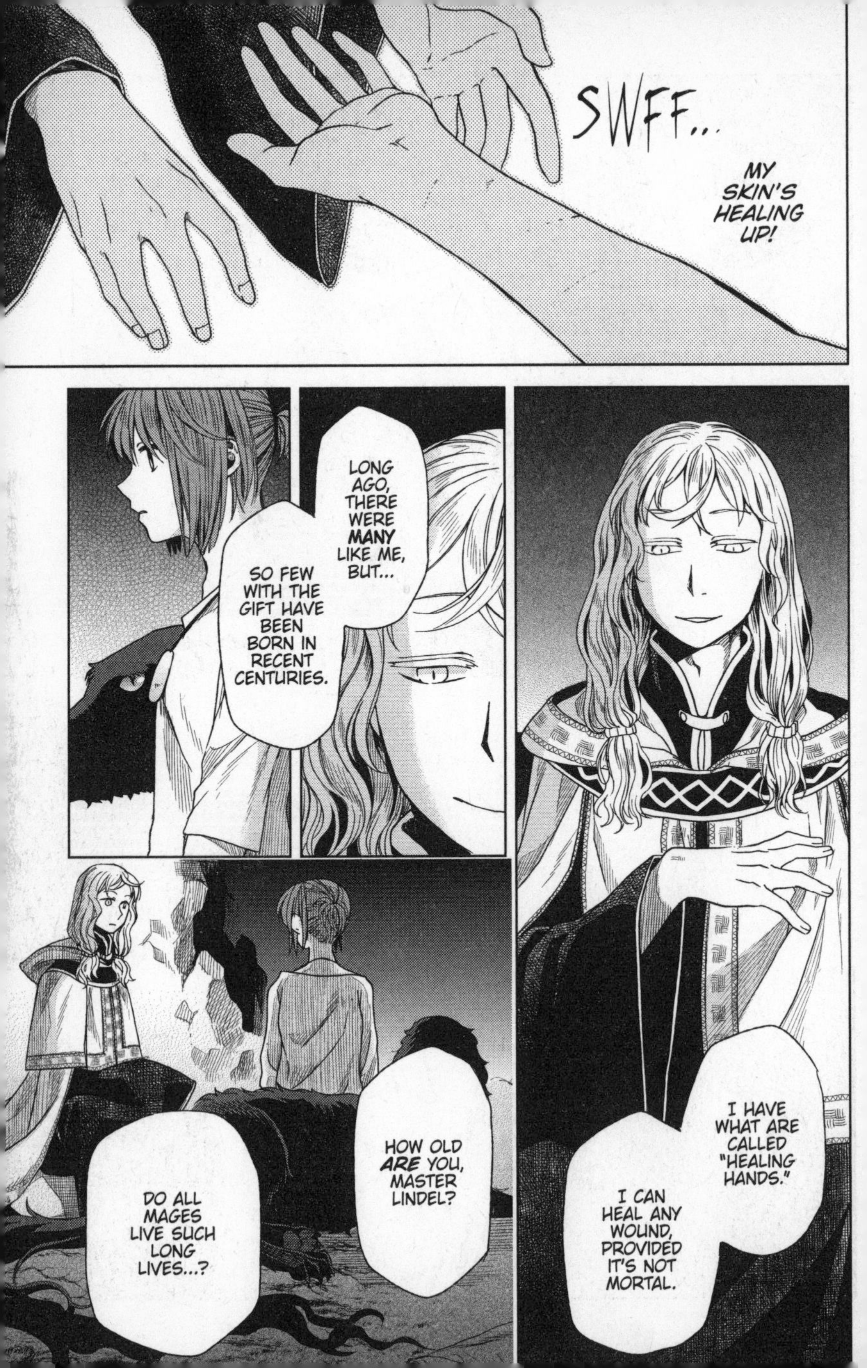
SWFF...
MY SKIN'S HEALING UP!
I HAVE WHAT ARE CALLED "HEALING HANDS."
I CAN HEAL ANY WOUND, PROVIDED IT'S NOT MORTAL.
LONG AGO, THERE WERE MANY LIKE ME, BUT...
SO FEW WITH THE GIFT HAVE BEEN BORN IN RECENT CENTURIES.
HOW OLD ARE YOU, MASTER LINDEL?
DO ALL MAGES LIVE SUCH LONG LIVES...?

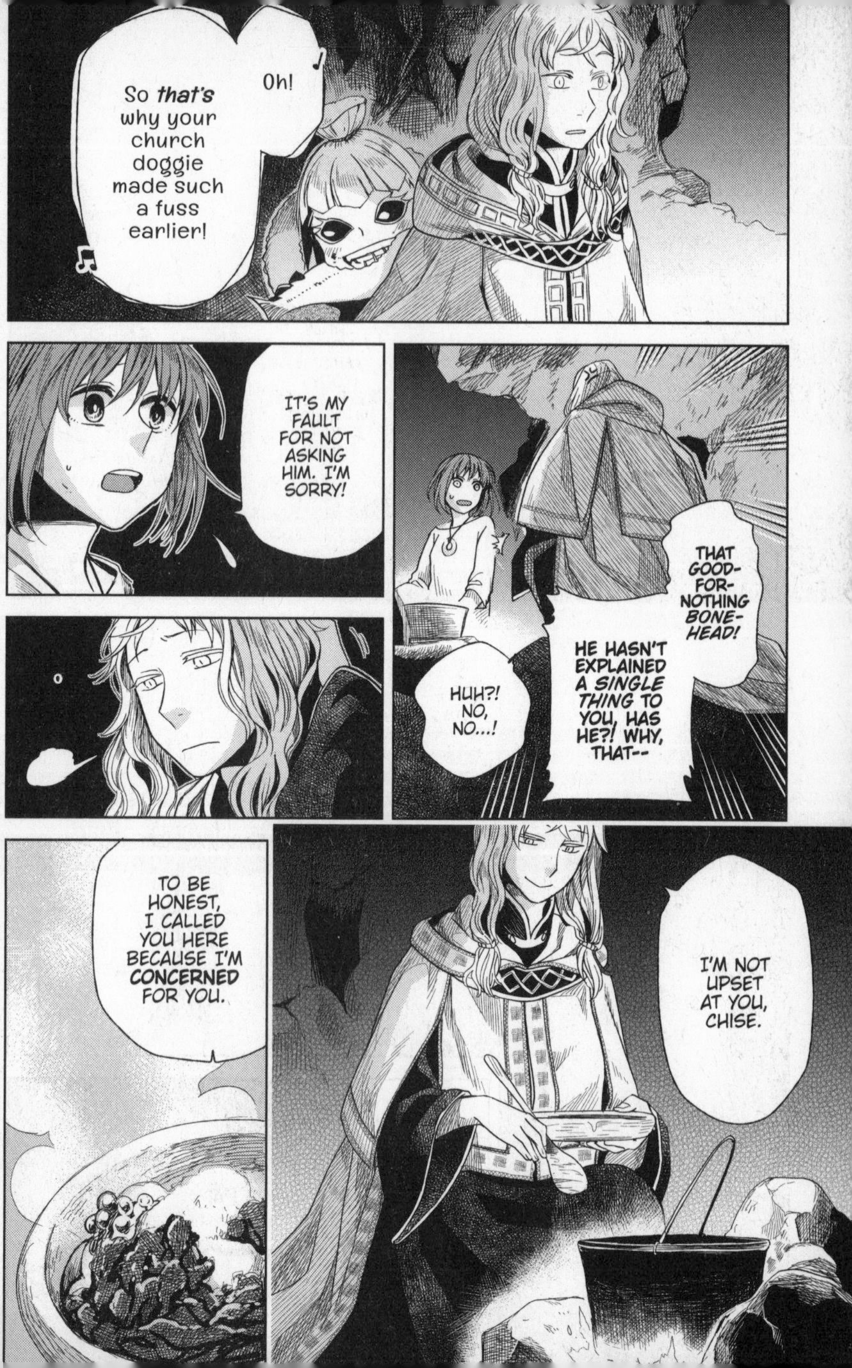
Oh!
So *that's* why your church doggie made such a fuss earlier!
THAT GOOD-FOR-NOTHING BONE-HEAD!
HE HASN'T EXPLAINED A *SINGLE THING* TO YOU, HAS HE?! WHY, THAT--
HUH?! NO, NO...!
IT'S MY FAULT FOR NOT ASKING HIM. I'M SORRY!
I'M NOT UPSET AT YOU, CHISE.
TO BE HONEST, I CALLED YOU HERE BECAUSE I'M **CONCERNED** FOR YOU.

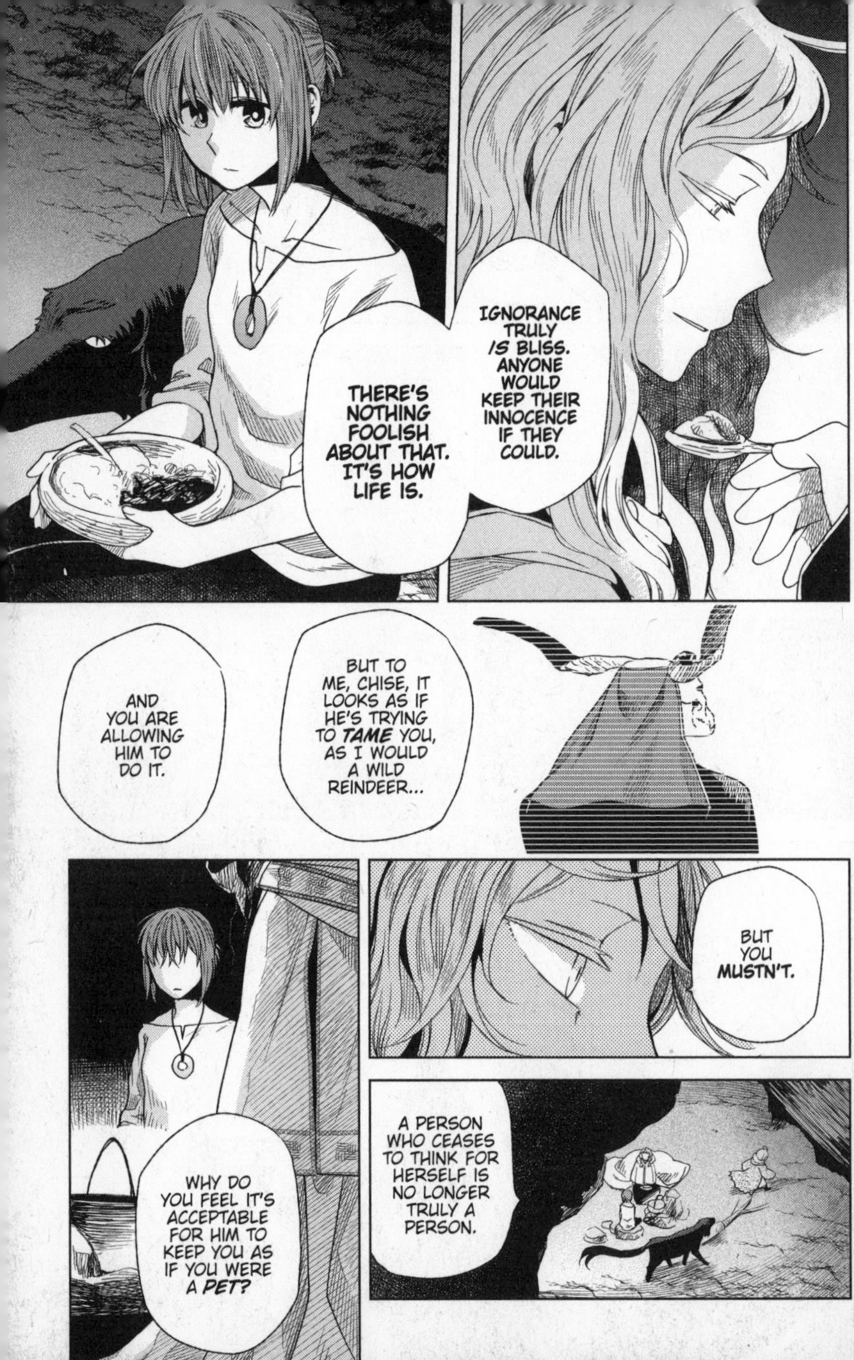
IGNORANCE TRULY *IS* BLISS. ANYONE WOULD KEEP THEIR INNOCENCE IF THEY COULD.
THERE'S NOTHING FOOLISH ABOUT THAT. IT'S HOW LIFE IS.
BUT TO ME, CHISE, IT LOOKS AS IF HE'S TRYING TO ***TAME*** YOU, AS I WOULD A WILD REINDEER...
AND YOU ARE ALLOWING HIM TO DO IT.
BUT YOU **MUSTN'T.**
A PERSON WHO CEASES TO THINK FOR HERSELF IS NO LONGER TRULY A PERSON.
WHY DO YOU FEEL IT'S ACCEPTABLE FOR HIM TO KEEP YOU AS IF YOU WERE A ***PET?***

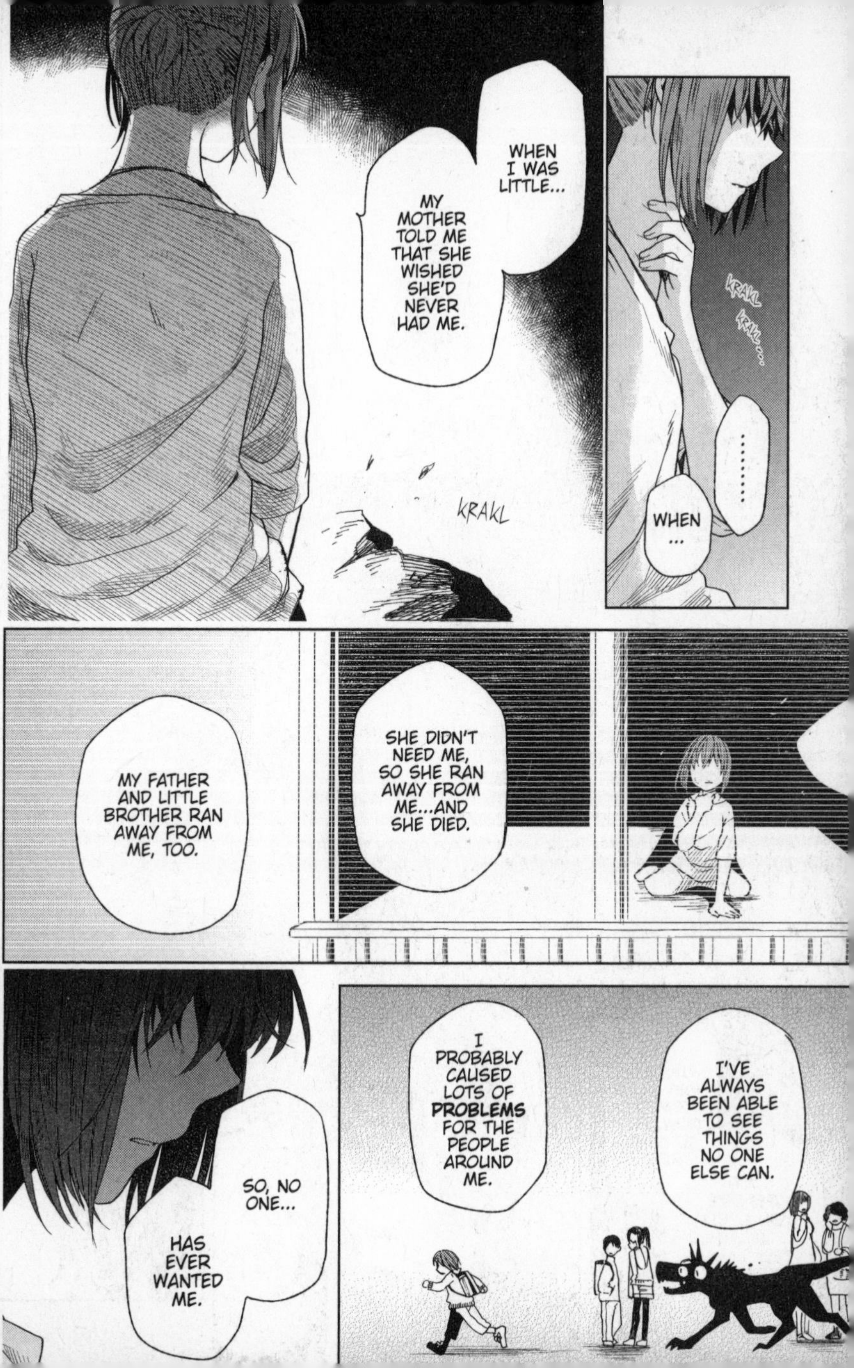
KRAKL
KRAKL...
......
WHEN...
WHEN I WAS LITTLE...
MY MOTHER TOLD ME THAT SHE WISHED SHE'D NEVER HAD ME.
KRAKL
SHE DIDN'T NEED ME, SO SHE RAN AWAY FROM ME...AND SHE DIED.
MY FATHER AND LITTLE BROTHER RAN AWAY FROM ME, TOO.
I'VE ALWAYS BEEN ABLE TO SEE THINGS NO ONE ELSE CAN.
I PROBABLY CAUSED LOTS OF **PROBLEMS** FOR THE PEOPLE AROUND ME.
SO, NO ONE...
HAS EVER WANTED ME.

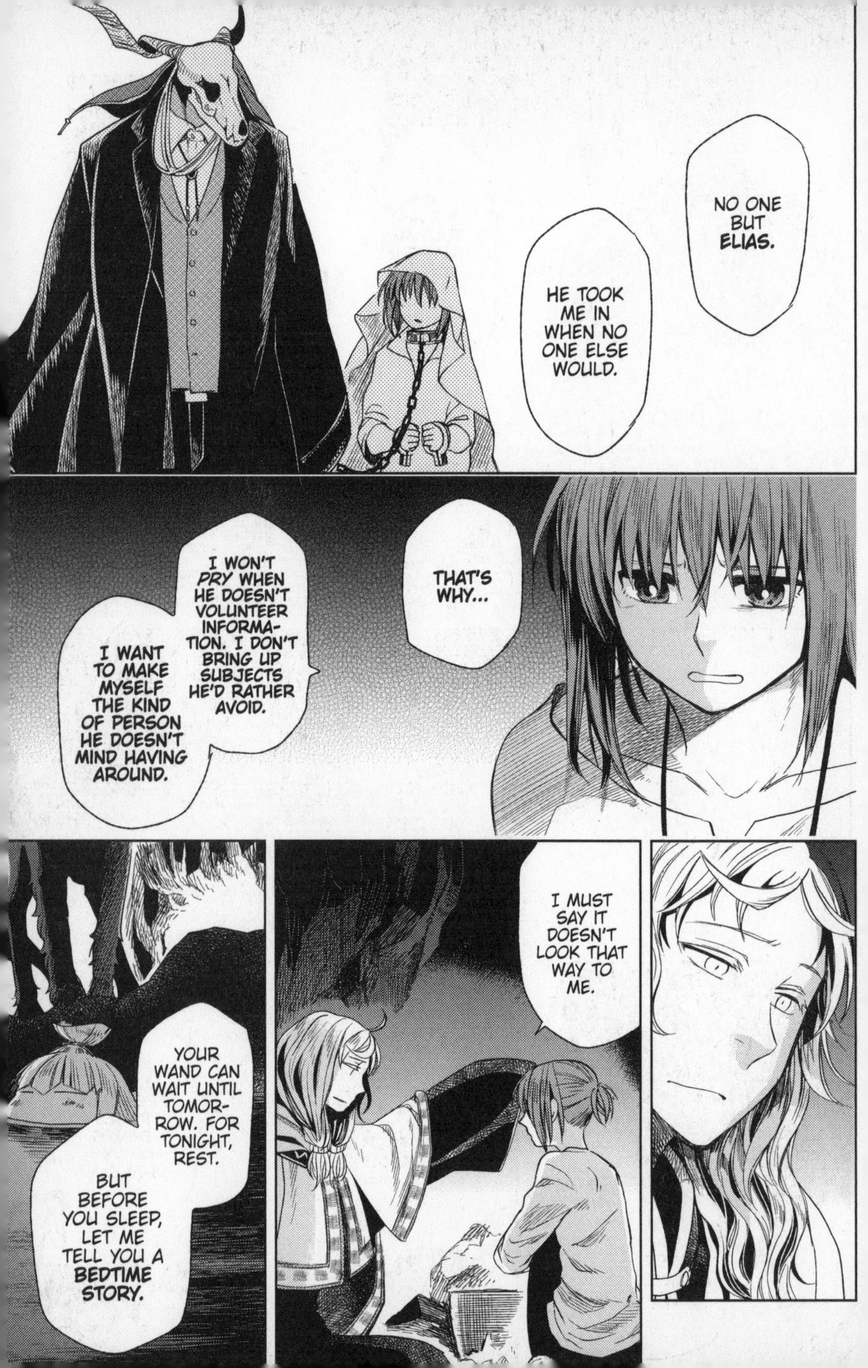
NO ONE BUT ELIAS.
HE TOOK ME IN WHEN NO ONE ELSE WOULD.
THAT'S WHY...
I WON'T PRY WHEN HE DOESN'T VOLUNTEER INFORMATION. I DON'T BRING UP SUBJECTS HE'D RATHER AVOID.
I WANT TO MAKE MYSELF THE KIND OF PERSON HE DOESN'T MIND HAVING AROUND.
I MUST SAY IT DOESN'T LOOK THAT WAY TO ME.
YOUR WAND CAN WAIT UNTIL TOMORROW. FOR TONIGHT, REST.
BUT BEFORE YOU SLEEP, LET ME TELL YOU A BEDTIME STORY.

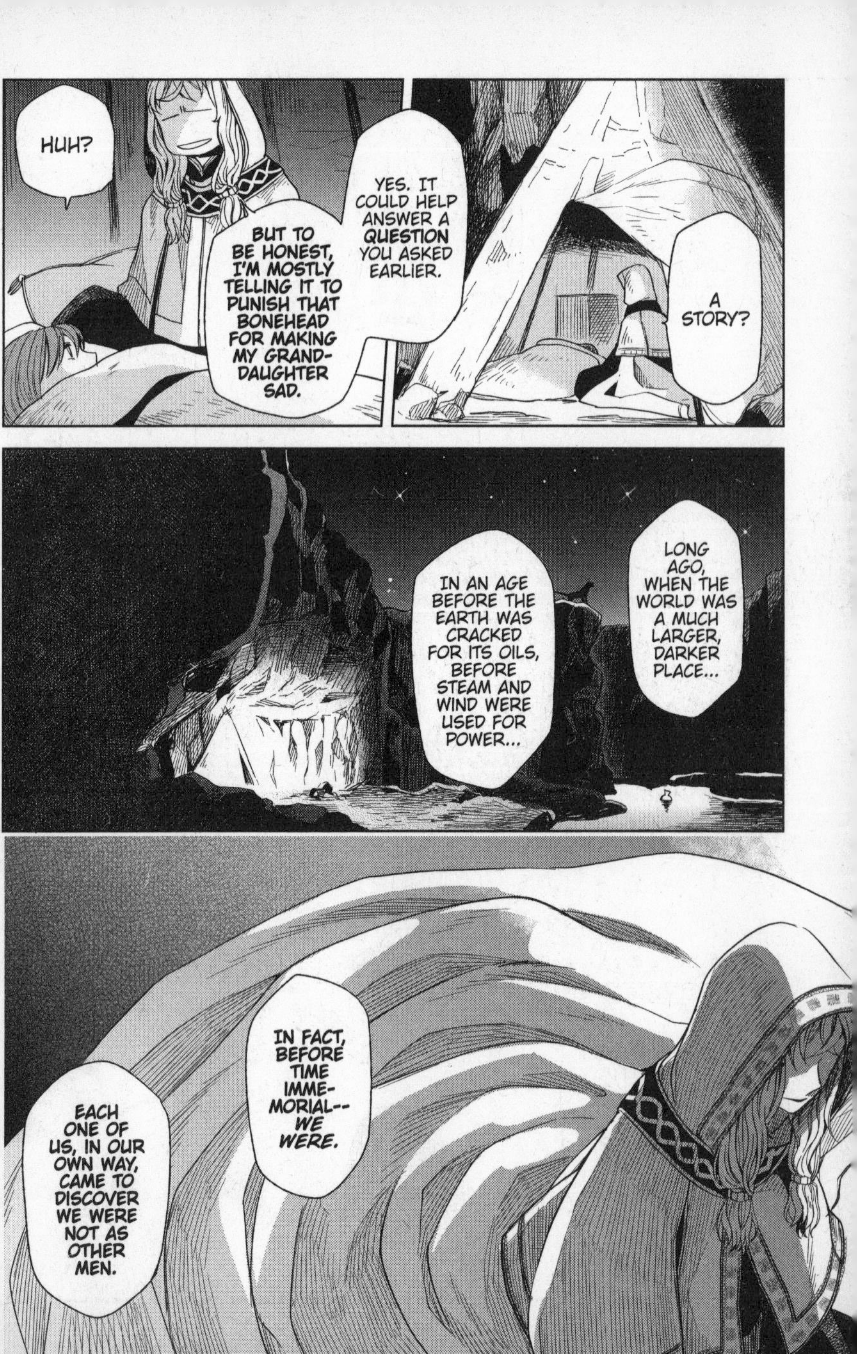
A STORY?
YES. IT COULD HELP ANSWER A QUESTION YOU ASKED EARLIER.
BUT TO BE HONEST, I'M MOSTLY TELLING IT TO PUNISH THAT BONEHEAD FOR MAKING MY GRAND-DAUGHTER SAD.
HUH?
LONG AGO, WHEN THE WORLD WAS A MUCH LARGER, DARKER PLACE...
IN AN AGE BEFORE THE EARTH WAS CRACKED FOR ITS OILS, BEFORE STEAM AND WIND WERE USED FOR POWER...
IN FACT, BEFORE TIME IMME-MORIAL-- *WE WERE.*
EACH ONE OF US, IN OUR OWN WAY, CAME TO DISCOVER WE WERE NOT AS OTHER MEN.

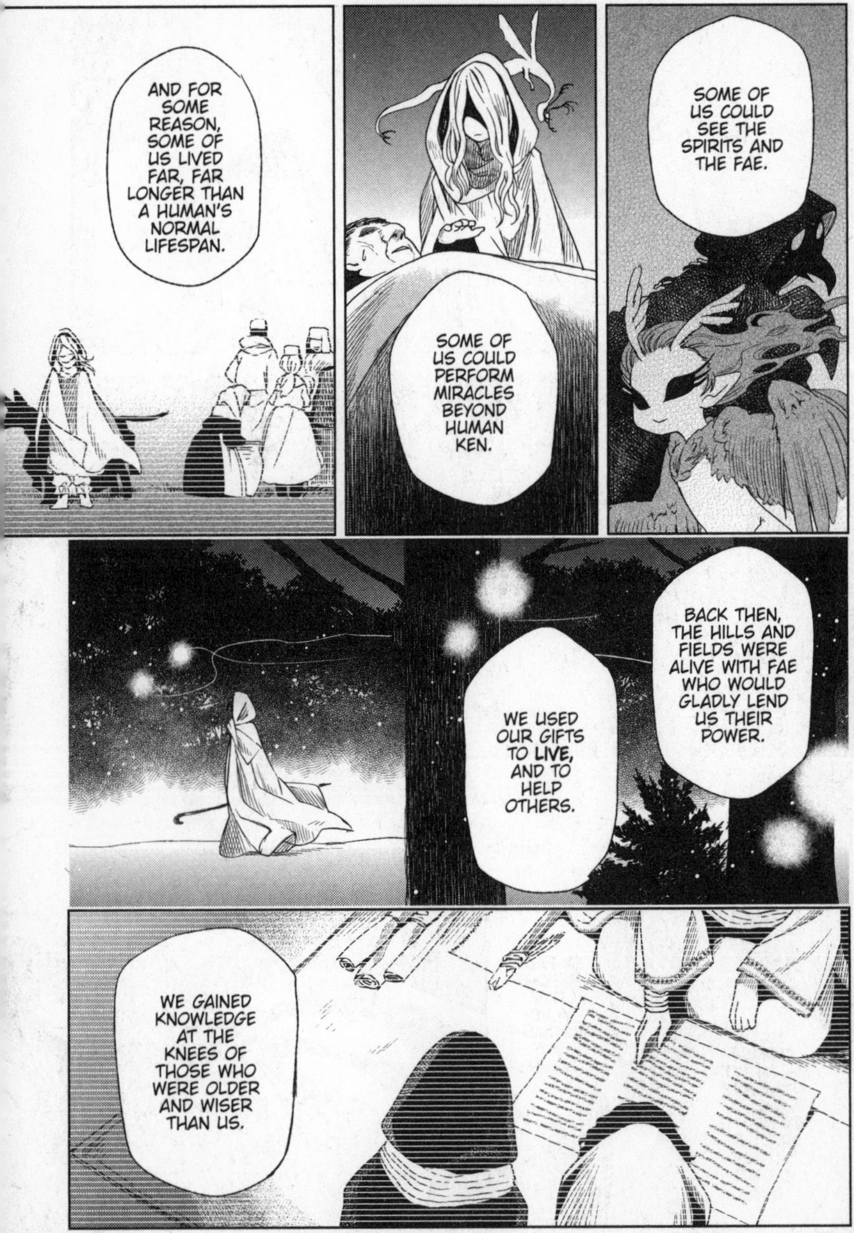
SOME OF US COULD SEE THE SPIRITS AND THE FAE.
SOME OF US COULD PERFORM MIRACLES BEYOND HUMAN KEN.
AND FOR SOME REASON, SOME OF US LIVED FAR, FAR LONGER THAN A HUMAN'S NORMAL LIFESPAN.
BACK THEN, THE HILLS AND FIELDS WERE ALIVE WITH FAE WHO WOULD GLADLY LEND US THEIR POWER.
WE USED OUR GIFTS TO LIVE, AND TO HELP OTHERS.
WE GAINED KNOWLEDGE AT THE KNEES OF THOSE WHO WERE OLDER AND WISER THAN US.

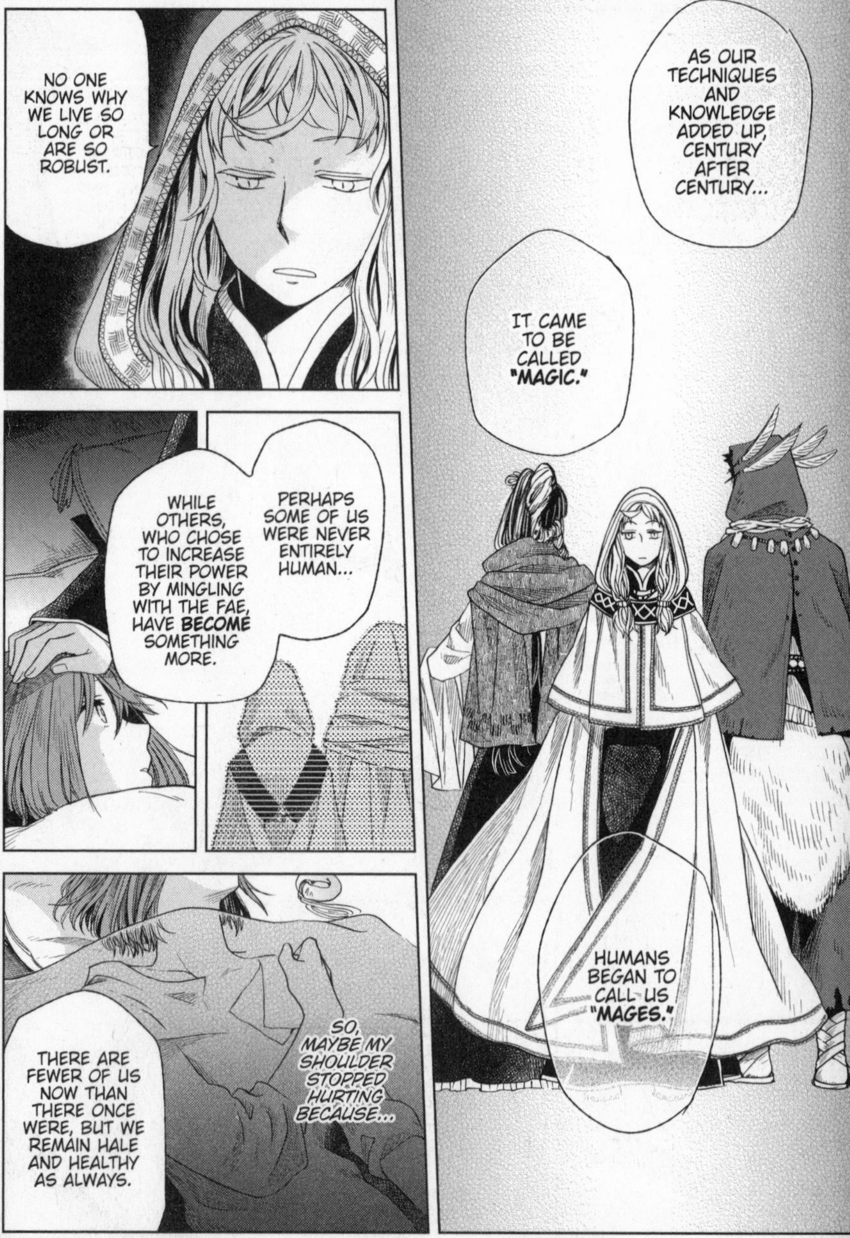
AS OUR TECHNIQUES AND KNOWLEDGE ADDED UP, CENTURY AFTER CENTURY...
IT CAME TO BE CALLED **"MAGIC."**
HUMANS BEGAN TO CALL US **"MAGES."**
NO ONE KNOWS WHY WE LIVE SO LONG OR ARE SO ROBUST.
PERHAPS SOME OF US WERE NEVER ENTIRELY HUMAN...
WHILE OTHERS, WHO CHOSE TO INCREASE THEIR POWER BY MINGLING WITH THE FAE, HAVE **BECOME** SOMETHING MORE.
THERE ARE FEWER OF US NOW THAN THERE ONCE WERE, BUT WE REMAIN HALE AND HEALTHY AS ALWAYS.
SO, MAYBE MY SHOULDER STOPPED HURTING BECAUSE...

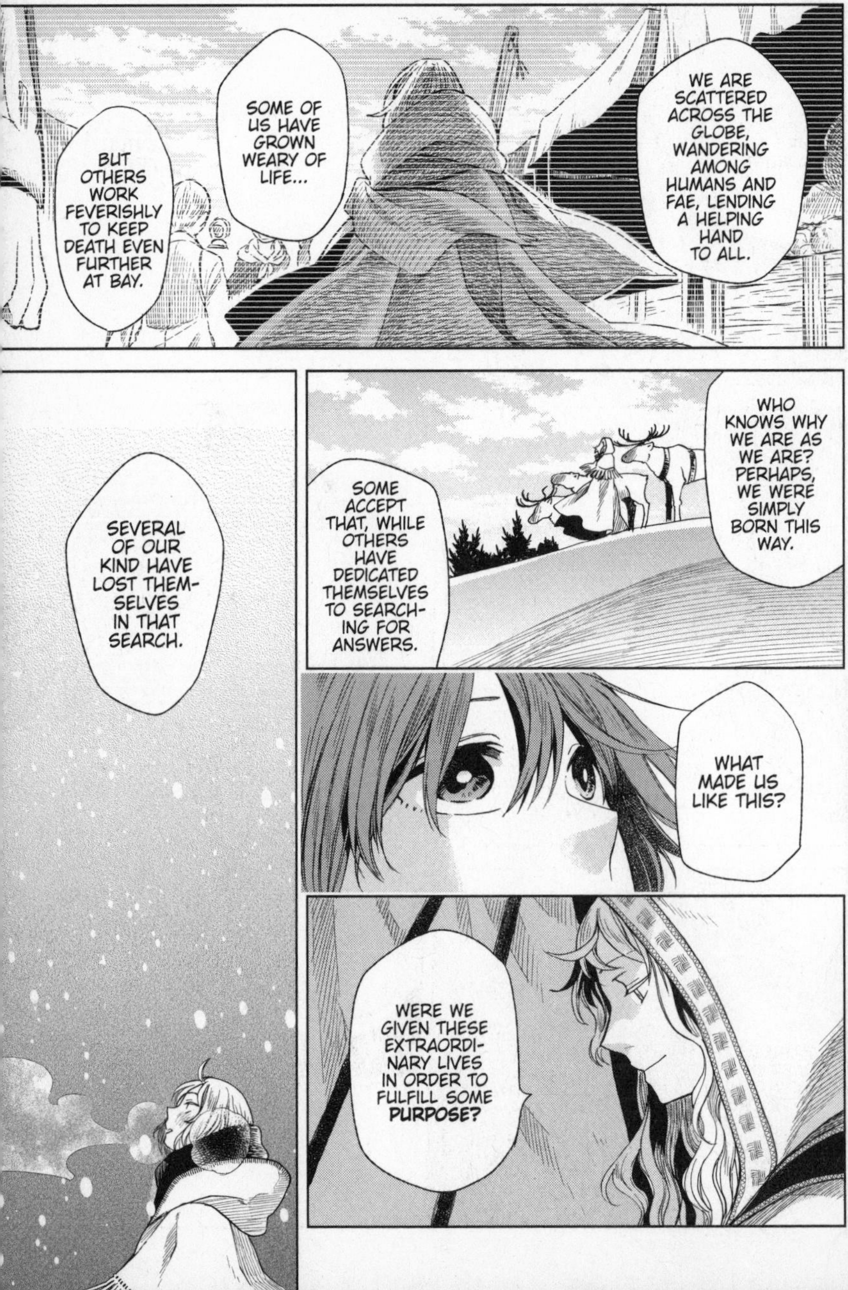
WE ARE SCATTERED ACROSS THE GLOBE, WANDERING AMONG HUMANS AND FAE, LENDING A HELPING HAND TO ALL.
SOME OF US HAVE GROWN WEARY OF LIFE...
BUT OTHERS WORK FEVERISHLY TO KEEP DEATH EVEN FURTHER AT BAY.
WHO KNOWS WHY WE ARE AS WE ARE? PERHAPS, WE WERE SIMPLY BORN THIS WAY.
SOME ACCEPT THAT, WHILE OTHERS HAVE DEDICATED THEMSELVES TO SEARCHING FOR ANSWERS.
WHAT MADE US LIKE THIS?
WERE WE GIVEN THESE EXTRAORDINARY LIVES IN ORDER TO FULFILL SOME PURPOSE?
SEVERAL OF OUR KIND HAVE LOST THEMSELVES IN THAT SEARCH.

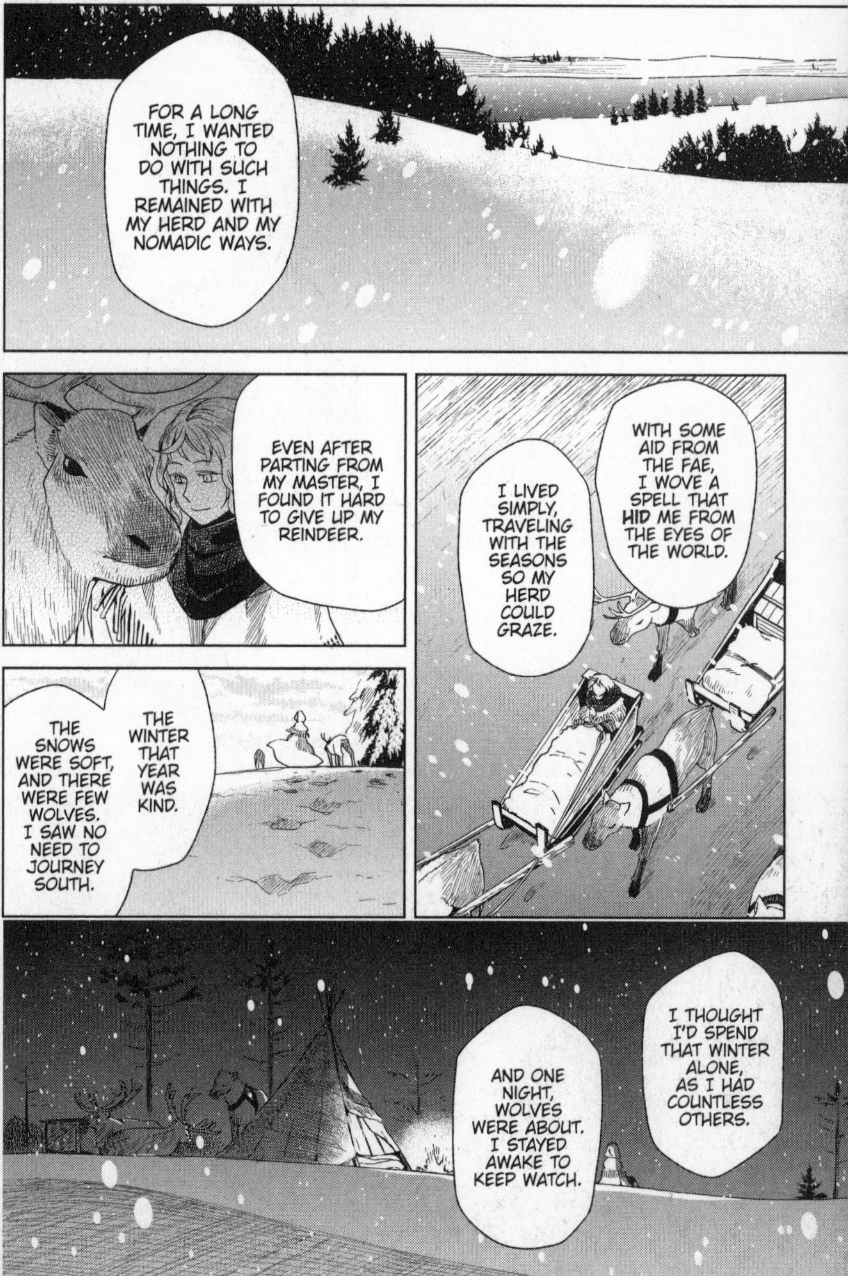
FOR A LONG TIME, I WANTED NOTHING TO DO WITH SUCH THINGS. I REMAINED WITH MY HERD AND MY NOMADIC WAYS.
WITH SOME AID FROM THE FAE, I WOVE A SPELL THAT **HID** ME FROM THE EYES OF THE WORLD.
I LIVED SIMPLY, TRAVELING WITH THE SEASONS SO MY HERD COULD GRAZE.
EVEN AFTER PARTING FROM MY MASTER, I FOUND IT HARD TO GIVE UP MY REINDEER.
THE WINTER THAT YEAR WAS KIND.
THE SNOWS WERE SOFT, AND THERE WERE FEW WOLVES. I SAW NO NEED TO JOURNEY SOUTH.
I THOUGHT I'D SPEND THAT WINTER ALONE, AS I HAD COUNTLESS OTHERS.
AND ONE NIGHT, WOLVES WERE ABOUT. I STAYED AWAKE TO KEEP WATCH.

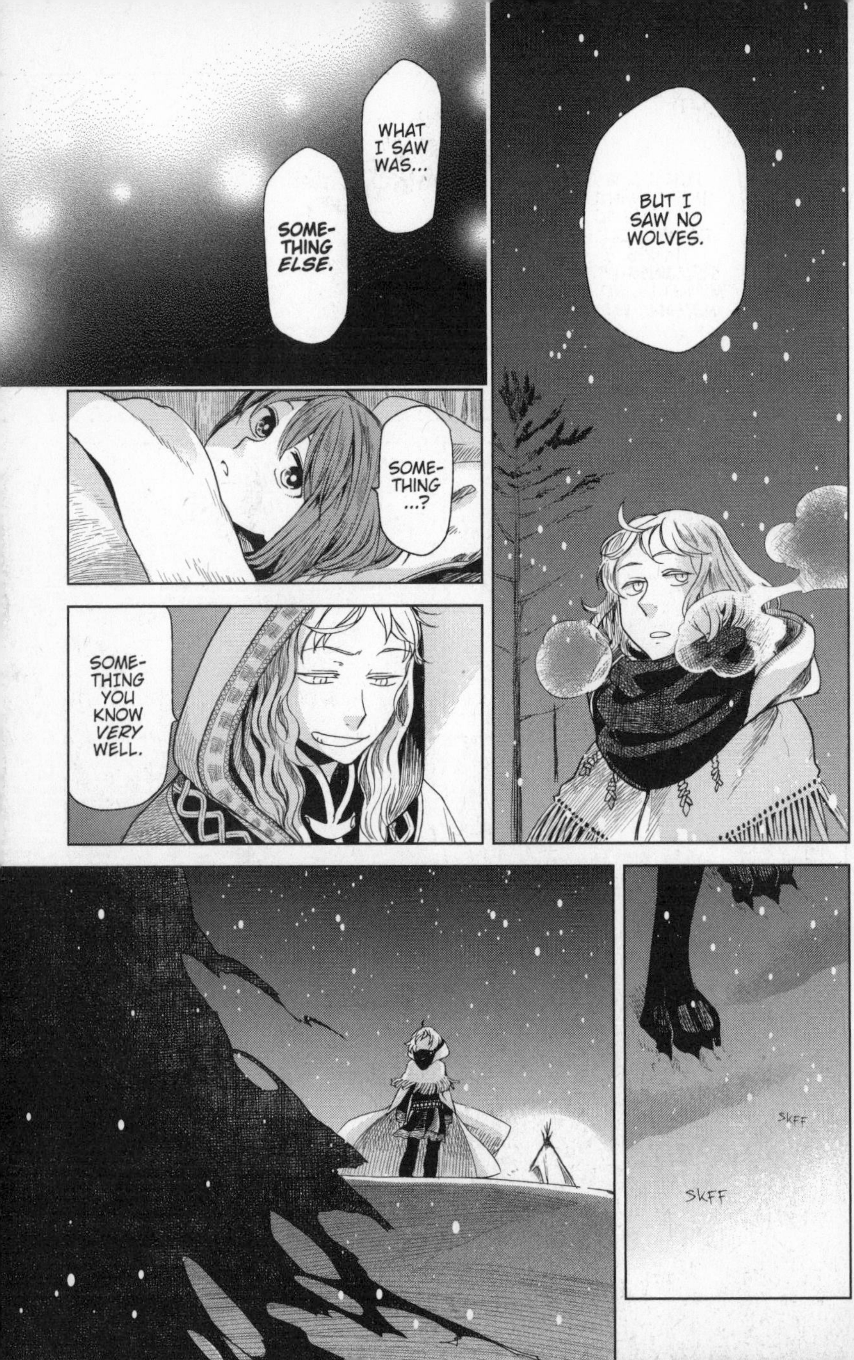
BUT I SAW NO WOLVES.
WHAT I SAW WAS...
SOME-THING ELSE.
SOME-THING ...?
SOME-THING YOU KNOW VERY WELL.
SKFF
SKFF

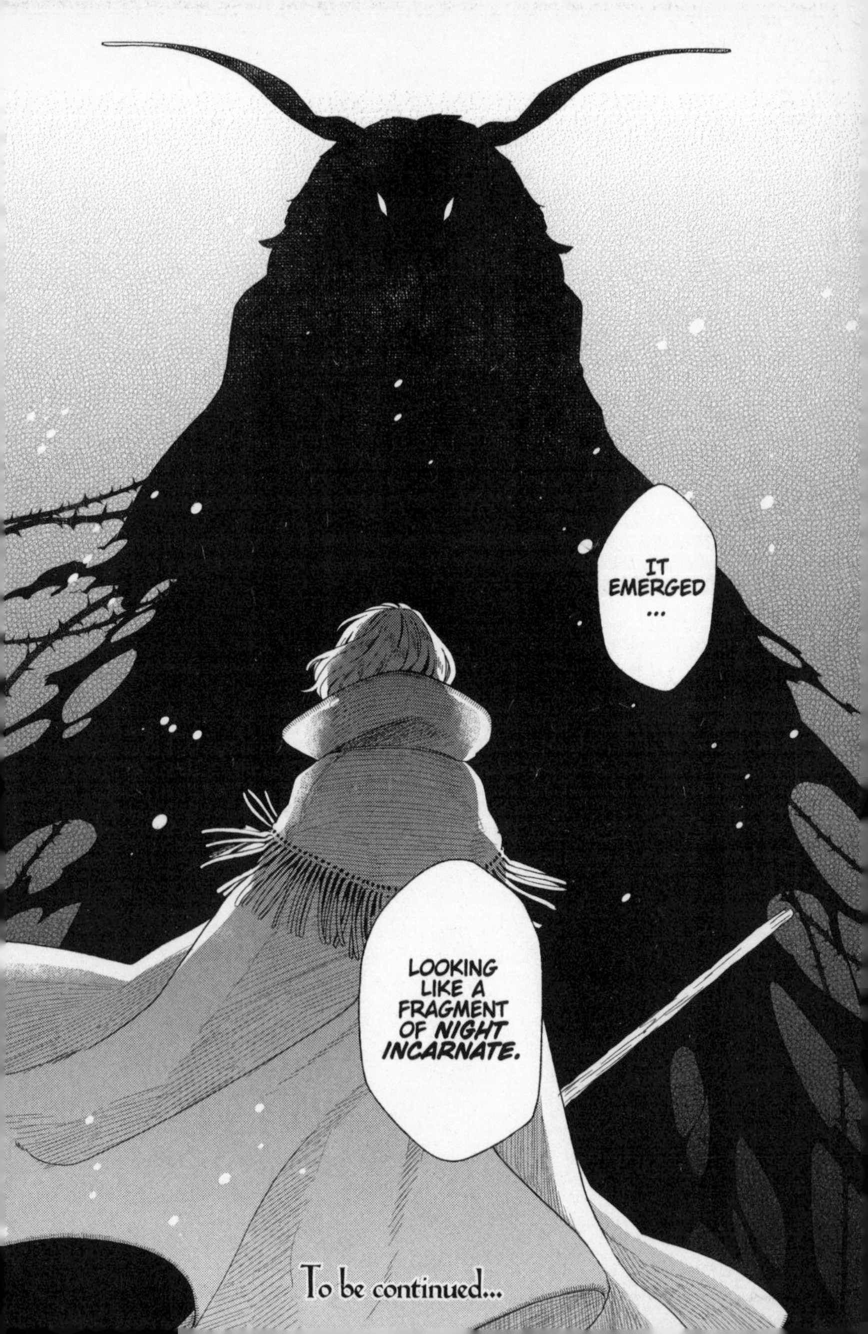
IT EMERGED ...
LOOKING LIKE A FRAGMENT OF NIGHT INCARNATE.
To be continued...

The Ancient Magus' Bride

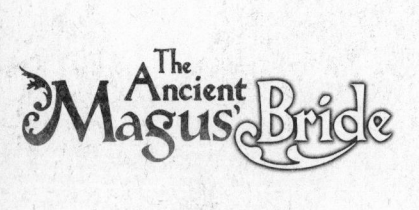

The Ancient Magus' Bride

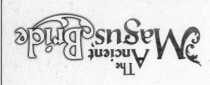

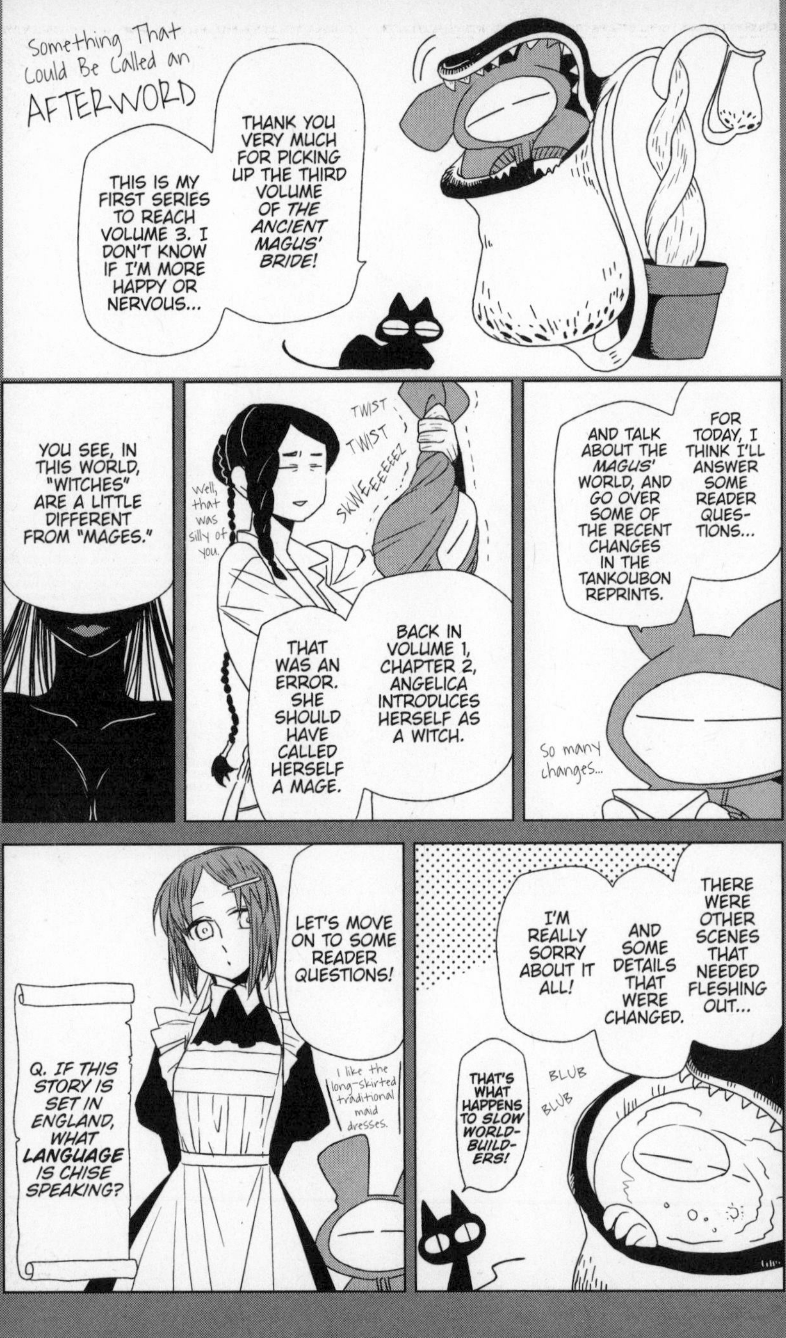
Something That Could Be Called an AFTERWORD
THANK YOU VERY MUCH FOR PICKING UP THE THIRD VOLUME OF THE ANCIENT MAGUS' BRIDE!
THIS IS MY FIRST SERIES TO REACH VOLUME 3. I DON'T KNOW IF I'M MORE HAPPY OR NERVOUS...
FOR TODAY, I THINK I'LL ANSWER SOME READER QUES-TIONS...
AND TALK ABOUT THE MAGUS' WORLD, AND GO OVER SOME OF THE RECENT CHANGES IN THE TANKOUBON REPRINTS.
So many changes...
BACK IN VOLUME 1, CHAPTER 2, ANGELICA INTRODUCES HERSELF AS A WITCH.
THAT WAS AN ERROR. SHE SHOULD HAVE CALLED HERSELF A MAGE.
TWIST
TWIST
SKWEEEEEEZ
Well, that was silly of you.
YOU SEE, IN THIS WORLD, "WITCHES" ARE A LITTLE DIFFERENT FROM "MAGES."
THERE WERE OTHER SCENES THAT NEEDED FLESHING OUT...
AND SOME DETAILS THAT WERE CHANGED.
I'M REALLY SORRY ABOUT IT ALL!
THAT'S WHAT HAPPENS TO SLOW WORLD-BUILD-ERS!
BLUB
BLUB
LET'S MOVE ON TO SOME READER QUESTIONS!
Q. IF THIS STORY IS SET IN ENGLAND, WHAT LANGUAGE IS CHISE SPEAKING?
I like the long-skirted traditional maid dresses.

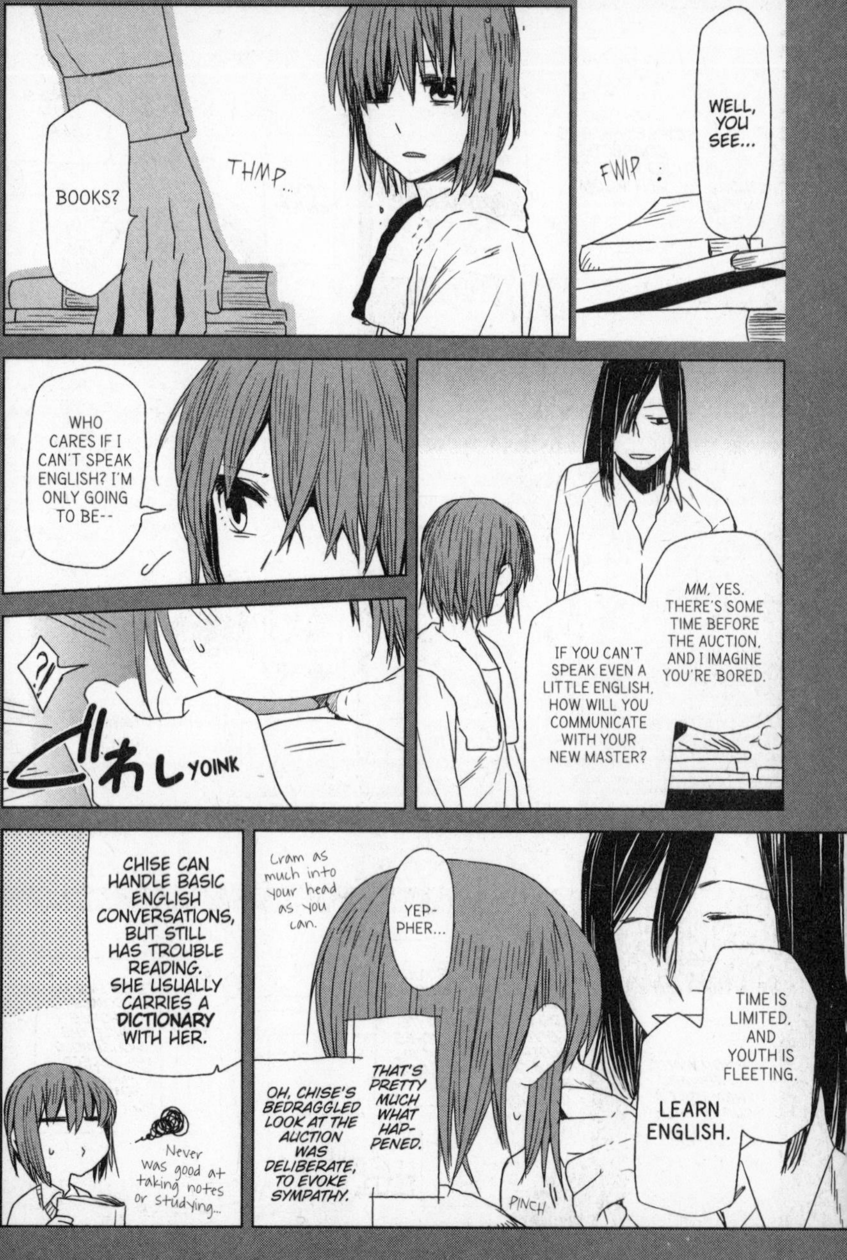
WELL, YOU SEE...
FWIP
THMP...
BOOKS?
MM, YES. THERE'S SOME TIME BEFORE THE AUCTION, AND I IMAGINE YOU'RE BORED.
IF YOU CAN'T SPEAK EVEN A LITTLE ENGLISH, HOW WILL YOU COMMUNICATE WITH YOUR NEW MASTER?
WHO CARES IF I CAN'T SPEAK ENGLISH? I'M ONLY GOING TO BE--
?!
YOINK
TIME IS LIMITED, AND YOUTH IS FLEETING.
LEARN ENGLISH.
YEP-PHER...
Cram as much into your head as you can.
THAT'S PRETTY MUCH WHAT HAP-PENED.
OH, CHISE'S BEDRAGGLED LOOK AT THE AUCTION WAS DELIBERATE, TO EVOKE SYMPATHY.
PINCH
CHISE CAN HANDLE BASIC ENGLISH CONVERSATIONS, BUT STILL HAS TROUBLE READING. SHE USUALLY CARRIES A DICTIONARY WITH HER.
Never was good at taking notes or studying...

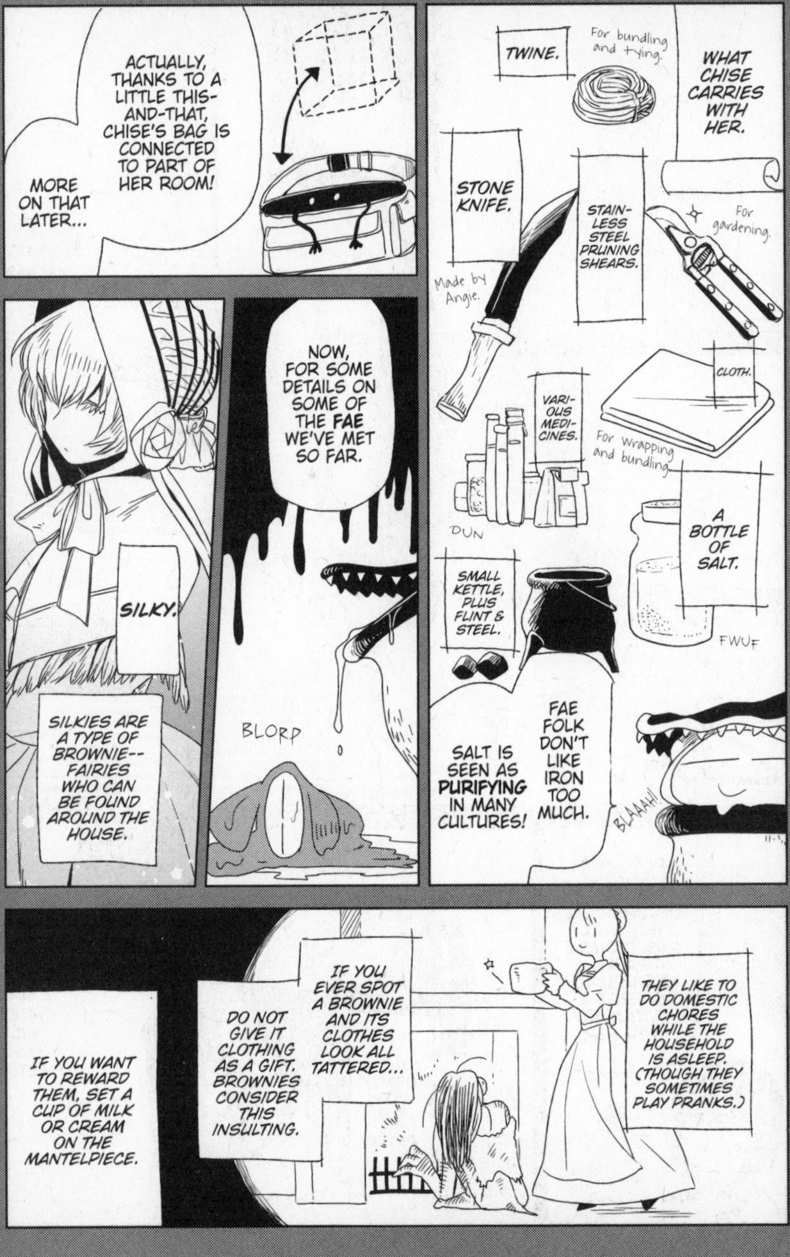
WHAT CHISE CARRIES WITH HER.
TWINE.
For bundling and tying.
STONE KNIFE.
Made by Angie.
STAINLESS STEEL PRUNING SHEARS.
For gardening.
CLOTH.
For wrapping and bundling.
VARIOUS MEDICINES.
DUN
A BOTTLE OF SALT.
FWUF
SMALL KETTLE, PLUS FLINT & STEEL.
FAE FOLK DON'T LIKE IRON TOO MUCH.
SALT IS SEEN AS PURIFYING IN MANY CULTURES!
BLAAAH!
ACTUALLY, THANKS TO A LITTLE THIS-AND-THAT, CHISE'S BAG IS CONNECTED TO PART OF HER ROOM!
MORE ON THAT LATER...
NOW, FOR SOME DETAILS ON SOME OF THE FAE WE'VE MET SO FAR.
BLORP
SILKY.
SILKIES ARE A TYPE OF BROWNIE--FAIRIES WHO CAN BE FOUND AROUND THE HOUSE.
THEY LIKE TO DO DOMESTIC CHORES WHILE THE HOUSEHOLD IS ASLEEP. (THOUGH THEY SOMETIMES PLAY PRANKS.)
IF YOU EVER SPOT A BROWNIE AND ITS CLOTHES LOOK ALL TATTERED...
DO NOT GIVE IT CLOTHING AS A GIFT. BROWNIES CONSIDER THIS INSULTING.
IF YOU WANT TO REWARD THEM, SET A CUP OF MILK OR CREAM ON THE MANTELPIECE.

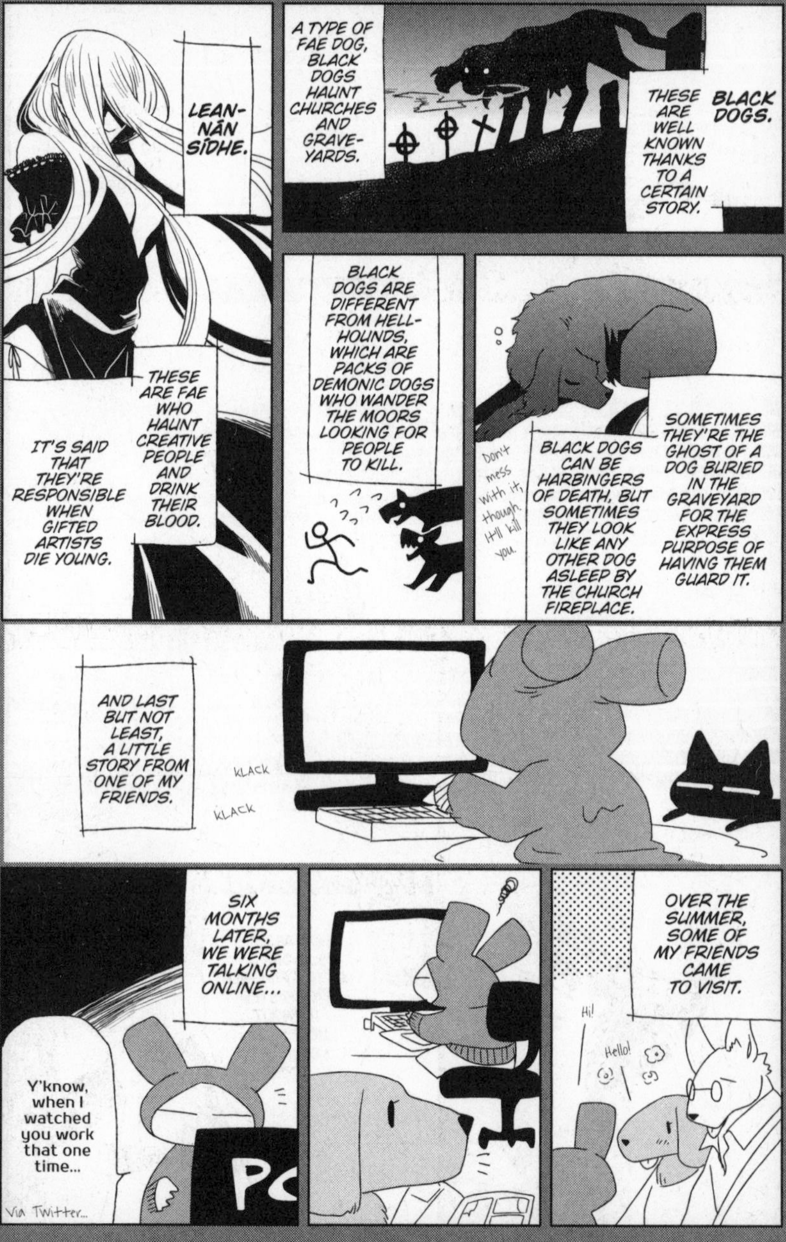
THESE ARE WELL KNOWN THANKS TO A CERTAIN STORY.
BLACK DOGS.
A TYPE OF FAE DOG, BLACK DOGS HAUNT CHURCHES AND GRAVE-YARDS.
SOMETIMES THEY'RE THE GHOST OF A DOG BURIED IN THE GRAVEYARD FOR THE EXPRESS PURPOSE OF HAVING THEM GUARD IT.
BLACK DOGS CAN BE HARBINGERS OF DEATH, BUT SOMETIMES THEY LOOK LIKE ANY OTHER DOG ASLEEP BY THE CHURCH FIREPLACE.
Don't mess with it, though. It'll kill you.
BLACK DOGS ARE DIFFERENT FROM HELL-HOUNDS, WHICH ARE PACKS OF DEMONIC DOGS WHO WANDER THE MOORS LOOKING FOR PEOPLE TO KILL.
LEAN-NĀN SÍDHE.
THESE ARE FAE WHO HAUNT CREATIVE PEOPLE AND DRINK THEIR BLOOD.
IT'S SAID THAT THEY'RE RESPONSIBLE WHEN GIFTED ARTISTS DIE YOUNG.
AND LAST BUT NOT LEAST, A LITTLE STORY FROM ONE OF MY FRIENDS.
KLACK
KLACK
OVER THE SUMMER, SOME OF MY FRIENDS CAME TO VISIT.
Hi!
Hello!
SIX MONTHS LATER, WE WERE TALKING ONLINE...
Y'know, when I watched you work that one time...
Via Twitter...
PC

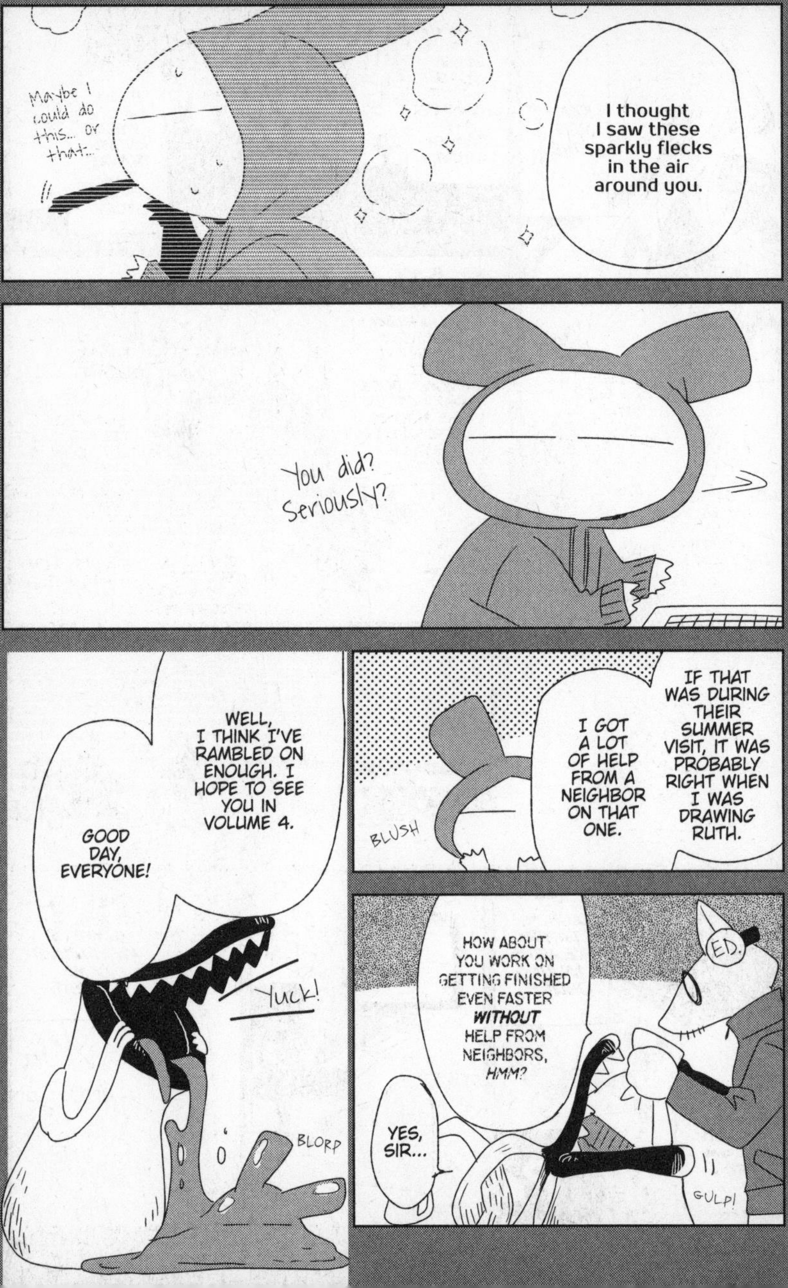
I thought I saw these sparkly flecks in the air around you.
Maybe I could do this... or that...
You did? Seriously?
IF THAT WAS DURING THEIR SUMMER VISIT, IT WAS PROBABLY RIGHT WHEN I WAS DRAWING RUTH.
I GOT A LOT OF HELP FROM A NEIGHBOR ON THAT ONE.
BLUSH
ED.
HOW ABOUT YOU WORK ON GETTING FINISHED EVEN FASTER WITHOUT HELP FROM NEIGHBORS, HMM?
GULP!
YES, SIR...
WELL, I THINK I'VE RAMBLED ON ENOUGH. I HOPE TO SEE YOU IN VOLUME 4.
GOOD DAY, EVERYONE!
Yuck!
BLORP

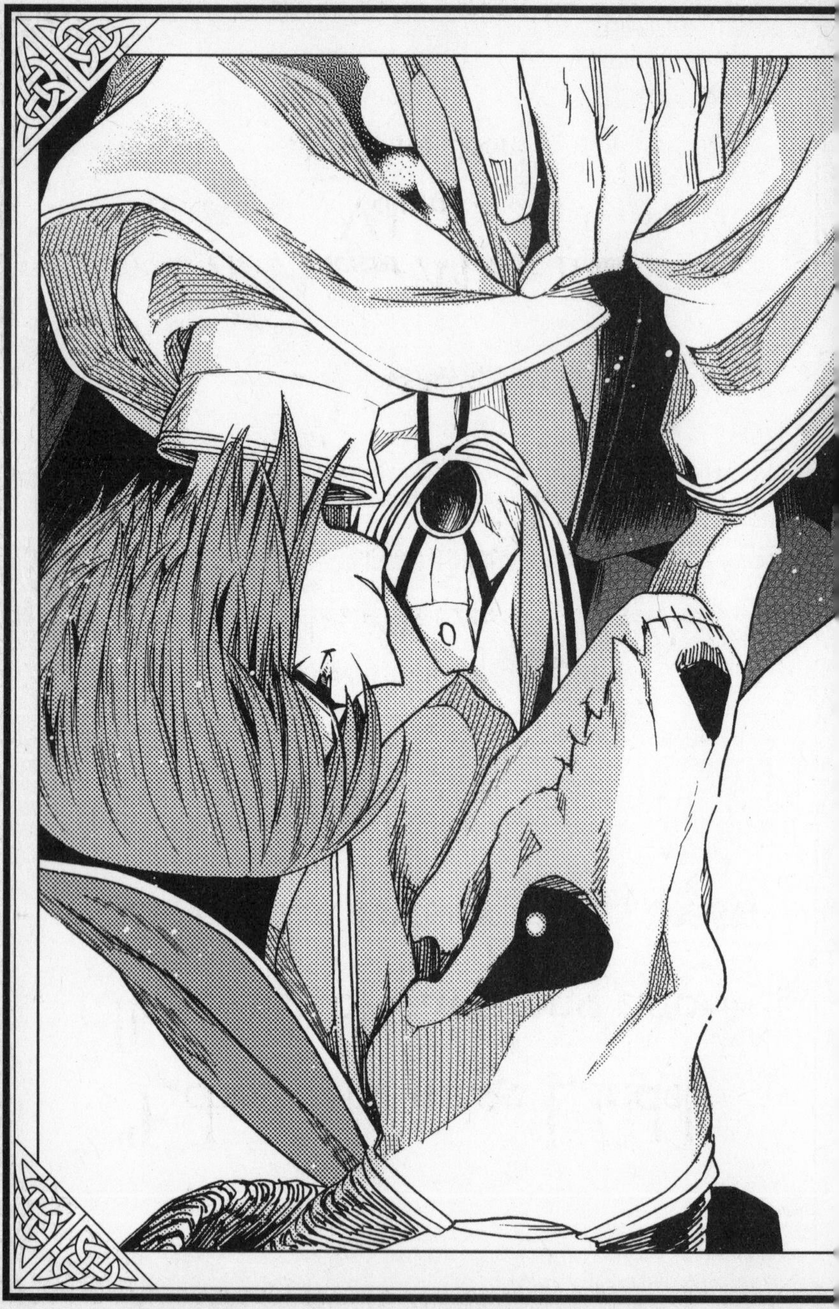